Pragmatic Existential Counseling and Psychotherapy

To Viktor Frankl who lit a new path for my life
And to Susan Bernadett-Shapiro who has walked with me down that winding road

⑤SAGE | 50 YEARS

Pragmatic Existential Counseling and Psychotherapy

Intimacy, Intuition, and the Search for Meaning

Jerrold Lee Shapiro
Santa Clara University

Los Angeles | London | New Delhi
Singapore | Washington DC

Los Angeles | London | New Delhi
Singapore | Washington DC

FOR INFORMATION:

SAGE Publications, Inc.
2455 Teller Road
Thousand Oaks, California 91320
E-mail: order@sagepub.com

SAGE Publications Ltd.
1 Oliver's Yard
55 City Road
London EC1Y 1SP
United Kingdom

SAGE Publications India Pvt. Ltd.
B 1/I 1 Mohan Cooperative Industrial Area
Mathura Road, New Delhi 110 044
India

SAGE Publications Asia-Pacific Pte. Ltd.
3 Church Street
#10-04 Samsung Hub
Singapore 049483

Acquisitions Editor: Kassie Graves
Editorial Assistant: Carrie Montoya
Production Editor: Bennie Clark Allen
Copy Editor: Michelle Ponce
Typesetter: C&M Digitals (P) Ltd.
Proofreader: Annie Lubinsky
Indexer: Karen Wiley
Cover Designer: Glenn Vogel
Marketing Manager: Shari Countryman
eLearning Editor: Lucy Berbeo

Printed in the United States of America

Library of Congress Cataloging-in-Publication Data

Shapiro, Jerrold Lee.

Pragmatic existential counseling and psychotherapy: intimacy, intuition and the search for meaning/Jerrold Lee Shapiro, Santa Clara University.

pages cm
Includes bibliographical references and index.

ISBN 978-1-4833-6899-3 (pbk.: alk. paper)

1. Counseling. 2. Existential psychology. 3. Psychotherapy. I. Title.

BF636.6.S53 2016
158.3—dc23   2015024099

This book is printed on acid-free paper.

SUSTAINABLE FORESTRY INITIATIVE

Certified Chain of Custody
Promoting Sustainable Forestry
www.sfiprogram.org
SFI-01268

SFI label applies to text stock

15 16 17 18 19 10 9 8 7 6 5 4 3 2 1

Brief Contents

Contents

Preface

Existential philosopher Martin Buber profoundly declared that "life is meeting" (between an *I* and a *thou*). *A Pragmatic Existential Approach to Counseling and Psychotherapy: Intimacy, Intuition, and the Search for Meaning* is potentially our sole such meeting.

The book is intended as an invitation for you to share with me both a personal journey and a still-evolving, professional memoir of my 5-decade career in the field of psychotherapy. I have been honored to be able to serve as a therapist, a mentor, a licensed clinical psychologist, and a professor in graduate programs training for practitioners since the late 1960s.

Practical application of esoteric existential philosophy seems on the surface to be enigmatic: at times counterintuitive, at times illogical, at times anxiety provoking, yet also the essence of human connection to self, others, and the world. Therein lies the curious and exciting conundrum. How may this one encounter of words on a page even begin to convey the levels of intimacy, intuition, and connection that mark the true *I-thou* meeting? My hope is that by sharing my personal experiences, those of my clients, and my intellectual understanding of those great minds from whom I have learned, I will convey some sense of the magic, wonder, and impact existential approaches bring to healing.

It may seem unusual to find the words *pragmatic* and *existential* in the same sentence. Yet from my experience, it is exactly that curious combination that makes the work effective. Existential therapy as a practice involves finding our clients where they are in their subjective worlds, joining them there and helping them develop courage and skills to face the inevitable anxieties of living.

There are some core principles here that center the work. These include the overriding importance of an individual's subjective experience, the manner in which meaning is created in our lives, and, most of all, the power of caring and emotional intimacy in healing and in living the best possible life.

I have long believed that intimacy is the antidote to our necessary human fears of mortality, meaninglessness, isolation, and freedom. This form of counseling and psychotherapy offers that possibility.

Jerrold Lee Shapiro
Los Altos, California, 2015

Acknowledgments

There are many influences and perspectives that are inevitably reflected in any book. Because this work represents an entire career as a psychotherapist and professor in graduate programs training clinicians, there is no way to comfortably pay proper respect to all of the mentors, clients, and students from whom I have learned about psychotherapy and life.

I have had the incredible professional good fortune to have been in the right places at the right times: Colby College, Hawaii State Hospital, and the University of Waterloo in the 1960s, the University of Hawaii and University of California at Santa Cruz in the 1970s, and the Santa Clara University Counseling Psychology program since 1982.

It is impossible to estimate all the powerful personal influences that have shaped my thinking. I have been blessed with many terrific colleagues, mentors, and students. Specifically, for this manuscript, several colleagues have read and made important recommendations for drafts of the manuscript. My colleague and editor for all of my writing is my wife of over 30 years, Dr. Susan Bernadett-Shapiro. She challenged my thinking and my writing and offered many valuable suggestions that appear in the book. In addition, my son, Gabriel Bernadett-Shapiro, provided artwork and editing. In alphabetical order, Nancy Andersen, MFT, Art Bohart, PhD, Dave Feldman, PhD, Susan Light, PhD, Jasmine Llamas, PhD, Lawrence Peltz, PhD, Kate Viret, MFT, and Jeffrey Zorn, PhD, generously provided valuable editing, insights, and recommendations.

I have had the great pleasure and honor of being able to disagree with and learn from colleagues whom I hold in high esteem. Among them are psychodynamically oriented clinicians Drs. Michael J. Diamond and Teri Quatman; Gestalt therapist Dr. Tom Glass; Humanistic therapists Art Bohart and Rene Tillich; the pragmatically oriented Drs. Dave Feldman and Larry Peltz; and my Jungian analyst, the late Dr. Louis Vuksinick. They have had a continuing influence on my life and work.

My graduate students over the years have helped shape my thinking by their thoughtful questions and avid discussions. In particular, the Santa Clara University students in my existential psychotherapy seminar during the past several years have, in many ways, made this possible.

As is evident in the text, several mentors have made a major difference in my thinking about existential psychotherapy and my practice. I mention many in the text, but the late Dr. Viktor Frankl, who both brought me to the field of psychology and introduced me to existential thinking, deserves special notice.

I want to especially thank Kassie Graves, my editor at SAGE Publications, for her faith in the project and for her gentle guidance through the process.

SAGE Publications also wishes to thank the following reviewers for their assistance:

Kirk Schneider, Saybrook University and Teachers College; Columbia University

Elaine Hatfield, University of Hawaii

Arthur C. Bohart, Professor Emeritus, California State University, Dominguez Hills; Saybrook University

About the Author

Jerrold Lee Shapiro, PhD, is professor in the graduate Department of Counseling Psychology at Santa Clara University, where he served three terms as department chair and a decade as director of the Center for Professional Development. He is managing partner of *Family Business Solutions* and was formerly president of *PsyJourn* Corporation, developers of self-help computer-assisted counseling software.

Dr. Shapiro has been a licensed clinical psychologist in Hawaii and California, held a Diplomate from the American Board of Medical Psychotherapists and a Certified Clinical Consultantship with the American Society of Clinical Hypnosis, and was a Certified Group Therapist. He is a fellow of the American Psychological Association.

He has authored and edited 13 books, several book chapters, and over 200 professional papers, presentations, and symposia. Three of his books have won literary awards.

Born and raised in Boston, he received an AB from Colby College, an MA from Northwestern University, and a PhD from the University of Waterloo in Ontario. From 1970 to 1982, he taught at the University of Hawaii, where he was awarded the *Regents Medal for Outstanding Teaching Among Senior Faculty.* A Professor at Santa Clara University since 1982, he received the *Award for Sustained Excellence in Scholarship* in 2006—the highest honor for scholarship awarded by Santa Clara University.

He lives with his wife, Susan, a clinical psychologist. They have two children and two grandchildren. He has been a singer and performer of folk music for several decades.

SOME BASIC CONVENTIONS IN THE BOOK

The terms *counseling* and *psychotherapy* are used somewhat interchangeably in this book. This is consistent with the varying manner in which the terms are used by authors in the field.

In case examples, sex of therapist and client is varied in an attempt to avoid stereotyping. Any inadvertent bias is purely coincidental.

In examples, the designation T stands for therapist. J is used when I am the therapist. The letter C stands for client in general, and all other initials are specific references to clients. All true identities are deliberately disguised.

In examples of therapy that occur throughout the text, parentheses are used to denote nonverbal action of therapist or client (e.g., T moved the box of tissues closer to client and also moved closer herself).

Parentheses with italics are used to indicate what the therapist is feeling or thinking (e.g., *following the history of her divorce is very compelling. I'd prefer now to stay in the moment and make a mental note to come back to that.*) T: What's it like for you to be telling me this?

A larger font size is used to denote higher levels of emotion (here the client is quite angry).

1

Context

The Author's Life as an Existential Experiment

Life is meeting.

Martin Buber

What is existential psychotherapy? There is no shortage of one-line characterizations of the essence of existential counseling and psychotherapy:

It's about meaning!

It's the *I-thou* relationship!

It's about adopting a particular philosophy of life!

It's phenomenology!

It's all about anxiety!

It's about facing the givens of human existence, especially mortality!

Like most clichés there is some truth to all of these, but reductionism of any sort is anathema to the philosophy and therapy in this book. Existential psychotherapists bring an intricate combination of personal experiences and professional capabilities to bear on their work with clients. We make maximum use of self in the unique context of interaction with another person.

1

We are guided by a philosophy of life that centers on meaning in life, and we consider anxiety about life's natural limits as the guiding engine of work.

Existential work is best done in an intimate relationship in which the therapist joins clients in their personal subjective worlds in the here-and-now. Desired changes for clients emerge from the context of the client's life and manner of being.

Successful existential work is both personal and professional.

The Personal: How I Became an Existential Therapist

In an attempt to be more congruent with the theory, I am beginning this first chapter by addressing my personal journey and evolution as an existential psychotherapist. My intent is to provide a parallel process between the book's contents and the relationship between author and reader and to provide a model that promotes a far more important phenomenological experience between therapist and client.

In my eighth decade of life, I am still working full time as a professor, clinician, author, and consultant. Getting to this comfortable, middle-class life in a quiet Bay Area neighborhood has not been a straight line or easy road. It is more a tribute to good luck, some choices that have worked out far better than I could have imagined, perseverance, genetics, and a lifelong curiosity about the meaning of life.

Early "Existential" Moments

The first "existential" moment I recall was as a grade schooler. One of my classmates was color-blind. As the teacher worked with him to identify cues with which to distinguish enough difference between hues to call one green and another red, I was struck with an amazing question about subjective experience: Being far too young to have ever even heard about protanopia, I had the rudimentary thought that Martin's perception was not any more unique than mine. Maybe, I wondered, Martin was also being true to his subjective experience, even though the teacher, my other classmates, and I all saw the colors similarly and "correctly." It was a somewhat disquieting notion that subjective reality was not always unanimous and that my friend was honestly describing his atypical perceptions. Although the question in my mind was quite undeveloped, it was my first budding question about epistemology.

As is my wont to this day, I verbalized the question in far less elegant language to my teacher and classmates, "How do I know if what I see and call green is the same as the green you see?" That first step into phenomenology got me a visit to the principal's office. This wasn't my first or last visit to those ominous environs, where corporal punishment for inquisitiveness was far too common. Arguably, this may have laid down the rudimentary notion that choices came with consequences.

That moment, when I thought the subjective experience more salient than the event itself, was likely my nascent experience as an existentialist. If so, I wasn't to hear the term until a decade later.

Once I discovered that Martin was diagnosed as "color-blind," I lost that inquisitive perspective for some time. There was obviously a "reality" of the visual color spectrum, and I accepted the "fact" that my friend had a disability, rather than an alternative perception.

During my school years, I was at least a decent student and was not one of those peers who was identified as an isolate or shunned. Typically, I had friends and engaged in sports, music, and other extracurricular activities. However, at Boston Latin School (BLS; Grades 7 through 12), my atypical subjective realities re-emerged. I became aware that the way I saw the world was at times noticeably different from many of my peers, my parents, and, most of all, my teachers. My subjective truths were viewed by others as clearly incorrect, and when I had the temerity to voice questions or objections to teachers, I was treated to an increasingly familiar path to the headmaster's and guidance counselor's offices. Was I somehow like Martin, blinded to some realities? Or, was I seeing things that subjectively were meaningful, even though others had differing perceptions?

At Latin School, the first public school in the United States, founded in 1635, alumni include many luminaries in American life, such as presidents John Adams and John Quincy Adams, George Santayana, Leonard Bernstein, and many others. Benjamin Franklin was a student but did not graduate. As I sat in the assembly hall for interminable speeches, addresses, and announcements, my eyes often drifted to the highest level of the walls. Just below the high ceiling was a ring of the names of many innovators, revolutionaries, and free thinkers. Yet the joke around the school was that the curriculum, books, and even teachers hadn't changed since that entering class the year before the founding of Harvard University.

My bewilderment (and upset) at the time was how a school that honored those who had broken away from the establishment could embody the very kind of restrictions that its most illustrious graduates transcended. From time to time, when I thought I had a receptive ear among the faculty, I would ask such questions—in a manner that seemed respectful to me as an adolescent.[1] It seemed that I was alone in my disquiet. I recall one day asking the guidance counselor why our academic curriculum for sophomore and junior year was four languages and math. His reply indicated that I was not to engage in such speculation but to trust my superiors who knew about how to "develop the mind." Besides, we did have a choice of German or Greek as our fourth language. In short, subjective explorations were inferior to the traditional rules.

There were two levels of disciplinary actions: misdemeanors (smaller offenses) and censure (larger breeches of decorum—Latin School "felonies"). With censure, one was exiled to a presumably lesser public high school. The speech our first day in the seventh grade was "look around you. If you are still here to graduate in 6 years, all of the boys who are adjacent to you will not be." The failure rate at BLS was around 75%! I managed to pay enough attention to the mandatory guidelines that I was able to stay (albeit uncomfortably) and learned to hold my tongue at least at most critical junctures.

Two adult men helped me manage the discrepancies and disquiet. I was fortunate to have a very understanding father and another far more unlikely source of support. In the 1950s, mandatory drill in uniform was part of the curriculum. Major Kelly was the drill instructor. He was generally feared by school boys, and most of my peers found him foreboding. By contrast, to me he was a kindred soul (probably because he also had a very different perspective from the hard-nosed academicians who taught the "real" subjects). Like me, he was at times an outsider. What was most important about my relationship to the Major (I only learned his given first name several years later when I read his obituary) was that he seemed genuinely interested in listening to my perceptual world. Although we disagreed on almost every topic, he was uniquely respectful and heard me out before letting me know what he considered the errors of my ways. He was never critical of my having these unacceptable ideas and questions, and I always considered him a rare member of the faculty who enjoyed conversing with me.

From this experience, I managed to develop a rudimentary sense of the power of relationship with an adult who was not related by blood and the value of listening to another perspective, especially with someone whose world view was so discrepant. One day in my senior English class, I asked the teacher why we were memorizing abridged versions of Shakespearian plays instead of the original. He became furious, called me "insolent" (today I would recognize it as a narcissistic injury), and vowed that he would keep me from going to college. The Major helped me work out both a strategy and tactics around this danger, as if it were a military operation.

Another important lesson came when the guidance counselor called my parents and me into a conference. After reporting that Latin School had a 100% college acceptance rate, he announced that based on my (checkered) record, I should only apply to local lower tier, "safety school" colleges. He offered to use his influence with one commuter school in Boston. His perspective did not sit well with a 17-year-old who was desperate for new adventures, far from my home community. It was clear to me that I was looking for a very different college experience, and I was determined to apply to an Ivy League School and other higher tier liberal arts colleges.

Thankfully, based on my subjective belief in myself and my expectation that college could not possibly be an extension of high school, I applied to three top tier schools, as well as the three schools he recommended. As it turned out, I was accepted at five of the six colleges, including an "Ivy" and two liberal arts colleges. Predictably, the one university that rejected me was the safety school he most recommended and for which he offered his "connections." I learned here that holding to my personal desires for freedom, without fully giving up my security (the three safety schools), far outweighed the alternative strategy of having authority figures limit my personal choices.

These were but a few of the subjective realities that I experienced during those years. It was important learning to begin to recognize that consensual reality or others' judgments were useful to hear, attend, understand, and hold, without losing my personal subjective perspective.

The confluence of "existential" moments that began for me during grade school and continued in high school came together dramatically in 1960. In the summer prior to freshman year, we were assigned several books to prepare for college life. Among these were Plato's *Republic*, Paul's *Epistles to the Corinthians*, and Viktor Frankl's *From Death Camp to Existentialism* (subsequently retitled *Man's Search for Meaning*). Early that semester, Dr. Frankl, the "Man of the Year" at Colby College, came to the school to give talks, discuss his work, and meet with students. The opportunity to hear him directly and meet him in person was a life-changing event for me. When he described existential phenomenological thinking and the notion of creating rather than decoding meaning, it seemed like he was speaking from within me as much as to me. He described the human condition as one in which many difficulties could occur and argued that the one unique human quality was our ability to choose how to respond.

Here was a genius whose perspective encompassed my personal thinking and feeling. During this first of three fortuitous meetings with Dr. Frankl, I was inspired sufficiently to change my major to psychology.

In my personal, often circuitous, route I actively pursued existential psychotherapy since. Recently at my 50th reunion at Colby, I was not surprised to discover that two fellow students also referred to Frankl's visit as "life-altering," and several who did not recall him at all; a tribute to the individualized subjective meaning that he would have been proud to hear.

Another existential reality moment came during those college years. I had always considered myself a decent baseball player and in what could most kindly be considered overconfidence, went to a major league try-out camp. They recommended that I go to college! In the summer following my sophomore year in college, I got to bat against a real major league pitcher. On the second pitch, I experienced my first major league curveball. I was lying face down in the dirt when the umpire declared, "Strike two!" I got up, dusted myself off, looked out at the pitcher, and realized (another existential limit) that I would be best served to pursue a career in psychology.

My idyllic college experience of inquiry and mental experimentation came to a surprising and abrupt end when I began graduate training (1964) in clinical psychology at Northwestern University. At Colby, questioning and heading down potentially fruitless intellectual paths were encouraged for their learning value. In the Humanities and Social Sciences, subjective and objective experiences were held in balance and regard. Cooperation superseded competition, and cross-disciplinary investigation was held in high regard. I expected that graduate school would be an expansion of that ambiance.

Instead, I was thrown back into my seventh-grade experience when during orientation new graduate students were informed that we were in competition. My class of 24 was told that they expected 12 to complete a PhD. Once again, it became clear that there was one "objective truth"—behaviorism in this case—and that any variance would be considered heresy. The apparent educational goal was to develop professorial clones, each working independently on his (there were no women with tenure lines at the time) own research. Competition was rife between faculty, and the relationship between students and faculty could best be described as "us versus them." A few of us formed lasting friendships and collaborated, but it was generally discouraged.

I was again a fish out of water. I had developed the questioning mode that colored my precollege years and had been rewarded for what I considered considerable personal growth at Colby. I was open and somewhat in touch with what my Freudian forebears would call primary process—those last six words of course were anathema to the behavioral perspective. Although my academic performance was acceptable, I was increasingly troubled by the initiation rites and demands for what seemed like fealty. My master's thesis, which was later described as "quite creative in concept and in use of technology," was fine until the oral defense. I was excoriated by an advisor who apparently saw his role as a modern-day Tomás de Torquemada, and his role in that oral exam emulated that Grand Inquisitor. In retrospect, I can see how an experimental investigation of the psychodynamic construct, perceptual defense, may have been a little heretical.

As I review my early graduate school experience, it seems quite evident that the fit was not good, that there was a significant price in that environment for choosing to stay with my subjective truth rather than agree and go along. When the aforementioned advisor, a person in authority, had asked me to be part of his research group, I was seduced into being part of a team and, because of some unfounded optimism, ignored my internal warning system that he was dangerous to me.

There were three valuable lessons here: I would be wise to pay attention to internal subjective warnings, my optimism needed to be kept in check, and the perseverance that got me through difficult situations earlier at Latin School could have painful as well as positive consequences.

I also learned an academic and existential lesson from that oral exam, although I was not able to articulate it for some time. Any body of work could be picked apart mercilessly simply by approaching it from an alternative theoretical position. The end result of such a successful attack was hardly beneficial as an educational experience. To the extent that surviving painful losses makes one stronger, that experience helped build my clinical and educational muscles. The lesson was the antithesis of the experience: Attending to and joining with the client's (student's) perspective created closeness, collaboration, and a far more heuristic outcome. It is a lesson that has had a significant impact on my personal, academic, and clinical endeavors.

During those 2 years, I was also doing clinical work (practica) at a couple of Veterans Administration facilities and taking a few classes from adjunct professors who were clinicians in the community. In these settings, once again, creativity and questioning were honored. The connection between the personal concerns of other human beings was held to be of equal importance to theory or technique.

A New Context

The third year was set aside for internship. We were told that we could go anywhere in the country. The faculty advisor informed us, "Although many people stayed in Chicago, some had gone as far away as Joliet, Illinois or Ann Arbor, Michigan." Partly to escape the wintry Lake Michigan weather and even more chilling emotional climate of the psychology program, and partly to explore new worlds and have novel experiences, I took an internship in Kaneohe, Hawaii. That choice was as life altering as the first meeting with Viktor Frankl.

When I landed at the Honolulu airport, something internal began to shift. I felt like this was in some very archaic and deep way, a true home for me. This was reinforced when a multiethnic group of hospital staff members picked me up at the airport and took me to an "Aloha," first Hawaiian style dinner, before driving me across the island to my quarters at the hospital.

Melting Pot (Integration) or Tossed Salad (Pluralism)?

From an existential perspective, Hawaii was for me a very unique place. One of the most powerful creators of the "aloha spirit" is that there is no majority group. Each cultural group maintains its unique identity and usually integrates with understanding and tolerance for others. The model, in Hawaii, primarily born of poly-cultural necessity, is of pluralism.

For the first time in my life, everyone was a member of a minority group, just like me. There were ubiquitous opportunities to learn about and explore other cultures, races, and ways of living. My peers, supervisors, and even patients were all seeking to understand and experience, without a penchant to convert anyone, but just to experience life in novel ways.

The intern training director had a favorite question in supervision, "Is there another way you could look at that?" Here was a request to allow me to tune into my natural manner of experiencing my world. For me, the ambiance at the state hospital, and in Hawaii in general, was to be open to new ways of feeling, thinking, and being and to try to be empathic with others as they live in their own subjective worlds. In Hawaii, behaviorism and contingencies of reinforcement were seen as one way, among many, to approach the world.

Apparently when my faculty nemesis at Northwestern learned of my plans, he contacted the internship director and provided what could only be described as an extraordinary denunciation and warning about me. As I was told about halfway through my internship, the mutual reaction of the intern training staff was "anyone who could so thoroughly piss off a professor must be really interesting." No wonder that it felt so much like home.

I was encouraged to be aware of my subjective experience and to put it in context of psychological theory and practice. At the same time, I was exposed to a new library of writers including Kelly, Sullivan, Rogers, Perls, and Frank. Each of these new perspectives both reinforced and altered my natural tendencies. My supervisors were open to discussing any of the new material and to listening to my own struggles to coalesce them: excellent models for both therapy and teaching.

I also got a deep immersion in group therapy and the psychology of group process. This was my first professional experience with therapy based on interpersonal interaction. It became a major change in my academic and clinical path.

That first year in Hawaii (many more were to follow) was sufficient to convince me that Northwestern and I were not copacetic. I was accepted at several new doctoral programs and chose the University of Waterloo in Ontario, Canada, because it offered a cultural experience in another country, because of the apparent openness of the program, and because of the generous fellowship they offered. It turned out to be an amazingly good choice. Canada was also guided by pluralism, from bilingualism to a respectful appreciation of differences, reflecting a tossed salad rather than melting pot metaphor.

Having completed all the required classes (and a master's degree) at Northwestern, I wasn't looking forward to redoing many of them. Rather than make it a problem or deal with it administratively, they problem solved with me. As the chair of the Clinical Psychology Department, the late Dr. Kenneth Bowers, told me, "Learn how we do things, and show us that you can master our approach, and we will allow you to be flexible." They were singing my song.

A Very Different Kind of Oral Exam

One example of existential attunement came when I was preparing for the oral defense of my dissertation. A few days before the exam, my advisor, Dr. Richard Steffy, heard well my neurotic anxiety, likely well-stoked by some posttraumatic stress disorder from the oral exam at Northwestern. He devised a strategy of having me anticipate even the most difficult critic. I am sure that we both knew that a statistical analysis of covariance of all my data was unnecessary, but it kept me busy for 3 days and confident that I could answer any questions from the committee. It also afforded me an opportunity to check in with him daily to go over findings.

He provided both a kindness and a model for experiencing anxiety from another's perspective, joining another in his distress and working together from that (the client's) perspective. In direct contrast to my earlier experience, his phone call to colleagues was to recommend me *for* positions as a new PhD. Two of them actually contacted me with offers, but I was bound back to my adopted homeland and the University of Hawaii.

Postgrad Existential Experiences: Renewed Contact With Dr. Frankl

Among other major developments in my becoming an existential therapist were two later meetings with Viktor Frankl. The first came in 1977 when he was teaching winter term at United States International University (U.S.I.U.) in San Diego. I was there working on my first book on group therapy and visiting a close friend. A series of events occurred that resulted in him asking me to share the stage at one point in his lectures[2] and to have dinner with him after several classes. My feelings for him as a person and impression of his genius only grew through those encounters and solidified my own sense of kinship with the centrality of a search for meaning. I have been very fortunate several times in life to meet those whose work I held in high regard. Most have been kind and gracious but few as much as Frankl.

My final contact was shortly before he died. He was given an honorary doctorate by Santa Clara University, where I have been teaching since 1982. The fact that he remembered me and our dinners was amazing to me. I wasn't alone in being impressed. At the degree ceremony, Fr. Leo Rock, a Jesuit, introduced Dr. Frankl with a speech that was incredibly moving for everyone in the university museum hall. Leo was the embodiment of the advice given to all speakers, "Never follow directly a clergyman on the dais!" Advice should also have been given to clergy, "Never follow Fr. Leo!"

Finding Meaning in a Chance Meeting in Guam

There was another powerful existential moment in 1977 that occurred quite by accident in Guam. Soon after my time in San Diego with Dr. Frankl, I was back on assignment in the Far East. Due to a series of administrative visa mishaps, I ended up in the Intransit Lounge in an airport for almost 24 hours, waiting for my flight to the Philippine Islands. There was little air traffic in or out and not much to distract my attention. During the evening hours, only one other person was in the lounge. Naturally, we started talking. He was from one of the Pacific islands and like me had a very long wait for a flight. When I inquired whether he travelled often, he replied, "No! This is only my second time."

After we talked about the current trip, I inquired, "What was the first trip? He said that he was a member of his country's Olympic team in 1956, in Melbourne. He told me that he was a runner. When I asked about his event and how he did, his face lit up with a gigantic smile, and he reported, "I ran dead last in my heat." I asked, "How was that for you?" and to my surprise and delight, he replied, "It was the most glorious day of my life. I was with all those great athletes, and I represented my nation. It was lovely."

His plane left before mine, and as I sat waiting, I appreciated that the meaning of the event for this man far outweighed the actual result. There was no sense of loss in his experience, just pleasure at the opportunity to fully experience the Olympics as a participant and to be with others whose skill he admired. For me, he exemplified what Frankl taught.

Another Strange Site for Insight

One final note of personal history involves the day I embraced the title of existential therapist. I had an affinity for many different approaches, although the more humanistic and interpersonal theories seemed to fit better in my work. I had long approached group therapy from an existential-humanistic perspective, although I wouldn't have claimed to be an existential psychotherapist per se.

I was teaching the theories of psychotherapy class at the graduate level, trying to advocate for whichever theory we were learning at the time. One day after class, I was seated in the bathroom, minding my own business. Three of my graduate students entered and started to argue about which theory I held personally. They agreed on existential. As I thought about it, I became aware that they were correct. That is where I have hung my theoretical hat from that day forward. It makes me chuckle that only an existential therapist would come to that kind of awareness in such a unique manner. I was kind enough to wait for them to depart before emerging from my stall but brought up in class the discussion of what theories each of the faculty held.

True Existential Moments

Like everyone else's, my life has been marked by many losses, many hellos, and many goodbyes. I have been touched by the passing of my parents and far too many friends and contemporaries. I have personally had several close calls. All of these heightened my awareness of the limits of human life and my personal mortality. Each brought with it a new resolve to live more fully in the time I do have, although follow-through is often tenuous, because of the questionable gift of denial (Becker, 1973).

None of the events so rocked through my personal denial of my mortality as much as two of the most joyous moments of my life: the births of my children. The miracles of birth were times of intense emotion and awareness at many levels. One of the most significant was a realization that welcoming new life to the world brings into much clearer focus life's inevitable ending. My personal replacements on this earth were now here. It is hard to imagine the complex array of emotions and thoughts, without an enhanced awareness of life's end.

For me, becoming a dad solidified my existential identity as nothing else could have. There was a lot of here-and-now to experience, feelings of vulnerability, and awareness of a greater range of subjective reality. Being a parent enhanced my understanding of others' truths and expanded experience of the world in which I lived. A considerably greater capacity for intimacy increasingly became available to me as man; as therapist; as professor; and as husband, father, and grandfather. It is these sensitivities and approaches to clients that I hope to bring to the remainder of this book.

The More Things Change . . .

As I write this, I have the opportunity to reflect on this journey. It's been over 60 years since my wonder about Martin's color vision. I consider myself to have been blessed with a wife, children, grandchildren, good long-term friends, and a lifestyle that seemed unimaginable when I was growing up in Dorchester, a working-class neighborhood in Boston. I have had many exciting adventures and a long career as a clinical psychologist and professor in graduate school training programs. I have been fortunate to have met and conversed with some of the innovative geniuses in my field and a lot of very good people. I was able to dabble with other (short) careers and had lots of pleasure as a ballplayer, entertainer, singer-musician, and part of a "Silicon Valley" start-up.

Yet with all that living, my early experiences of seeing the world through somewhat oblique, uncommon lenses have not changed all that much. Hopefully, I have matured and learned to choose somewhat more carefully where I divulge my less conventional, atypical perceptions and perspectives. I have learned to choose my battles and to listen before sharing my quick conclusions. I am proud to have held to my hard-earned learning about treating students and clients with respect and trying my best to join them in their unique worlds, rather than impose mine. I am also humbled by the role of perseverance in the face of adversity, luck, and of seeing all events, blissful and painful, as a path to new meaning in life.

The Professional Context

One of the essential aspects of existential counseling and psychotherapy is its intense focus on the individual and his or her subjective experience. The roots of psychology as a discipline are also defined as the pursuit of ideographic, more than nomothetic, inquiry.

When I was coming of age as a psychologist, each textbook proclaimed in the initial chapter that psychology is the science of individual differences; music to my existentially sensitized ears. The content of the ensuing chapters, however, focus primarily on what individuals have in common. To an existential therapist, this apparent contradiction between idiographic and nomothetic offers a remarkable opportunity.

Summarizing the extant literature on existential counseling and therapy, duPlock (1997) concluded that each individual therapist offers a unique form of therapy, based on who he or she is as a person. The nature of our theorizing and approach to therapy as existential therapists cannot be separated from who we are as people.

Van Deurzen and Adams (2010) concurred,

"To work existentially you have to be prepared to think deeply about life and human relations in ways that require you to make your own tracks rather than follow in the footsteps of the great gurus." (p. 341)

For this form of therapy, the goal is not to eliminate anxiety, adversity, confusion, emotional pain, or even symptoms but to recognize them as adaptations demonstrating strength and to use them to help the client become more courageous, tolerant, accepting, and willing to face personal fears of the unknown. For this type of journey, sometimes, an existentially informed companion and witness is far more salient than an expert with a full box of tools.

Existential counseling and psychotherapy are based on the individual experience of the client, the therapist and on the relationship between them (Bugental, 1987). To take duPlock's (1997) conclusion to another ideographic level, not only is each therapist unique, but each therapist-client relationship is also unique and in fact, so is each session with a client. Indeed, as will be explored in the ensuing chapters, shifts occur several times within sessions.

In addition, there are identifiable commonalities across all successful therapists including those with an existential orientation. Unlike those textbooks that informed the field decades ago, the current text is designed to integrate the interaction of the individual melody with the intricate harmonies across populations of therapists, clients, and phases of therapy.

The Reach of Existential Approaches to Counseling and Psychotherapy

Schneider (2008) described both the uniqueness and unappreciated role of existential psychotherapy. He commented on the irony of existential psychotherapy "being one of the most widely influential yet least officially embraced orientations on the professional scene" (p. 1).

Norcross (1987; 2014) agreed, noting that without explicit recognition, existential thinking frequently underlies clinical practice. Particularly relevant factors include the development of the attuned relationship between therapist and client and a focus on that relationship in the here-and-now during sessions.

As may seem evident from my personal journey, an important theory and therapy approach that is underrecognized, underappreciated, and unheralded has a strong personal resonance, especially when intimate relationship is at its core.

Subjective Realities

It has frequently been noted that in every marriage, there are three subjective relationships: his, hers, and theirs. All of them are accurate, yet none of them encompass an easy consensus. The goal of therapy isn't about correcting one of these to produce a homogenous truth that all can accept or even to discover the roots of why the perceptions are so different. The goal of existential therapy is to have them meet in a moment in which both partners feel understood, respected, and intimately connected.

To accomplish this, there are basic commonalities across the plethora of existential psychotherapies that are both identifiable and useful.

The Salience of Context

All experiences occur in a unique context of personal history, meaning we give to remembrance and scars from the past, psyche, external environment, current experience, and future expectations. We cannot understand what motivates a person or even how he or she thinks, feels, or acts without an understanding of the internal and external environment in which the person lives. In addition, behavior that is perfectly appropriate in one environment may be quite improper in another. For example, it is customary in most homes in Hawaii and Japan for visitors to remove their shoes on entering. If food is to be served, there may be a low table with futons (cushions) for sitting on the floor. The same behavior might be viewed differently in an apartment in New York.

Culture as Context

One of the most important aspects of individuals is the culture with which they identify. What does it mean if I experience myself as an American, a hyphenated American such as African-American, Chinese-American, Native-American, or Mexican-American? What generation of my family is living in this country? Am I *Isei* (first generation) with a mandate to keep alive my Japanese culture in a new land? Am I *Nisei* (second generation), serving as the bridge between the traditional Japanese culture of my parents and ancestors and probably speaking different languages with them than I do with my peers? Am I *Sansei* (third generation) where my acculturation is likely more American than Japanese?

What ethics, rules, and mores does my culture bring to my interactions? Am I from an individual-oriented, guilt-based culture such as many Northern European ethnicities or a collective, shame-oriented culture, common in many parts of East Asia and in many Latino countries of origin?

Gould (1993), a biographer of Frankl, demonstrates similarities and differences between Eastern and Western approaches to explaining life. The former is far more collective, viewing the individual as part of a larger organism that involves other people, living and ancestral, and to some extent, nature. They will often use terms like *destiny* or *Karma* to help understand the vagaries and vicissitudes of living. Western cultures tend more toward explanations of individualism and free will. These differences have major implications for therapeutic theorizing and interventions.

Existentialism and Cultural Context

Yalom (1980) noted a similarity between the existential approach and East Indian theology in which life is viewed as a mystery to be experienced, rather than the more Western notion that life is a problem to be solved. Indeed, this text is more aligned with a third option best described in this quotation often attributed to George Bernard Shaw, "*Life isn't about finding yourself. Life is about creating yourself.*"

Some areas of great concordance between existentialism and Eastern thought are that both focus on transcendence and choices within whatever environment an individual finds himself. As Vontress and Epp (2015) suggested, by virtue of a focus on individual responsibility, feelings of isolation, and fears of mortality and meaninglessness, existential therapy is able to overcome many blocks that may occasion problems in other more culturally bound approaches. Van Deurzen-Smith (1988) considers existential forms of counseling and therapy to be particularly relevant in cross-cultural settings.

In a sense, the entire notion of culture is an existential phenomenon. Specific metaphors and even ways of thinking may be quite divergent across cultures, but regardless of ethnic or racial identity, the most salient question is, "Who am I?" Although it may be entertained in many forms, with a host of personal, spiritual, and practical answers, that inquiry is transcultural. For present purposes, a process-centered therapy allows us the opportunity to explore all content in a personal bio-psycho-social-cultural context.

Gender as Context

It is clear that the first two things noticed when meeting new people are races/skin colors and gender. What is the impact of meeting a client from an apparently similar or quite different background? Do we assume that all people have similar dreams, goals, and methods of accomplishing these, or do we assume that each cultural and gender group is unique and has specific needs, desires, and methods?

Either assumption misses a lot of potential data. A female client will have some similarities to all females in the world and also differences from all others. We cannot have a single therapy for women as a group, because within each gender there is greater diversity than between genders.

The existential approach has both unique advantages and disadvantages when addressing culture and client-in-context. With an existential approach, we take all individuals as unique and try to join with them in a healing relationship. We try to understand the person from his or her subjective experience of the world. If I do not know what it's like to be a Pakistani woman, my authority is sitting across from me. She is the expert on what it's like to be her. Existential therapy is quite multicultural when I allow her to be my teacher.

Cultural Foundations of Existentialism

There are also underlying philosophical assumptions (derived primarily from the 19th and 20th European existential philosophers) that may make work with a particular client culturally insensitive. As Scharf (2004) indicates, one basic tenet of the approach is for women as well as men to live up to their potential to self-actualize and rise above cultural stereotypes. Women from some societies are expected to be subservient. For our Pakistani client, authenticity may look far different from a native-born American whose ancestors emigrated from Ireland in the late 1800s.

Therapist awareness and education may bridge that gap with the one female client, but the therapist must be aware that such a divergence may well exist, before making assumptions that may be unwarranted.

An Existential Orientation

Existential therapy involves the development of a certain form of intimate relationship that allows clients to develop courage in the face of anxiety and to gain a better sense of the meaning that they create in life. Bugental (1987) defines this intimacy in line with Buber's (1970) I-thou relationships:

a sharing of deep and immediate experiencing. It is not expressed in the content of what is said but in the depth of the client's inner awareness and the readiness to make that awareness open to the therapist and in the therapist's deep openness and resonance to the client's immediate inner living as it is expressed in any way. (p. 45)

Bugental calls this kind of therapy "life changing." He opens *The Art of the Psychotherapist* (1987) by distinguishing between objective and subjective dimensions of human experience. Objective approaches are consistent with therapeutic goals such as symptom reduction or adjustment problems. To engage in life-changing psychotherapy, a therapist must attend to his or her own subjective experiences as well as those of his or her client.

Without delving into the entire divisive issue of symptom substitution or the definition of the word *symptom* as a sign or manifestation of something else, the form of therapy described in the following pages views symptoms uniquely. To the existential therapist, as distressing as a symptom may be, it is considered an adaptation to anxiety. It may well serve to reduce the anxiety, but it may come at a high cost to the individual. All symptoms are seen as pulling toward the process of the status quo, maintaining functioning as it is. Often the symptom serves a valuable purpose described by the old aphorism "better the devil you know than the devil you don't."

It also points us to the important underlying anxiety—the fear of the unknown. Confronting this fear (ultimately mortality) can be daunting. The therapist's job is to open up the possibility for the client to become more aware of this existential fear and to try to embrace whatever parts of it are possible as a way to create meaning in life.

A unique manner of approaching and embracing client resistance[3] as a path to client strengths is offered. The starting focus on the positive value of anxiety and resistance to develop courage is quite contrary to approaches that begin with the weaknesses and help clients learn how to diminish or overcome them.

This form of existential work has some important components in common with positive psychology, humanistic therapies, relational-cultural therapy, and other strength-based therapies that are emerging in the literature.

Our Journey

We begin with a brief summary of the philosophical substrate of existential thinking and the manner in which it is adapted to psychotherapy practice. This is followed by identification and detailing of methods that distinguish existential work and by very specific methods of joining with clients in optimal ways. Ensuing chapters also highlight the scientific evidence for existential therapy, contextual matters such as gender and culture, life transitions, and applications of the method to group, family, and couples. Finally, the book concludes with a case study that demonstrates many of the constructs covered along the way.

Notes

1. Throughout my life, I seem to have had a special capacity to ask questions in a way that drew anger from authority figures. Although it was often somewhat inadvertent, my queries apparently had the quality reflected in Hans Christian Andersen's 1837 classic tale "The Emperor's New Clothes."

2. Although he was far more gracious, I saw my coteaching role as keeping my knees from knocking too loudly and to verbalize, "What he said!"

3. See Chapter 5.

2

How Philosophy Becomes Therapy

Logos is deeper than logic.

Viktor Frankl

It could legitimately be argued that philosophy is the mother tongue of all psychological therapies and theories. Determinism, pragmatism, epistemology, ontology, nativism, logic, phenomenology and many other philosophical perspectives underlie all modern psychological thinking. Psychodynamic, behavioral, and humanistic schools of therapy are informed by philosophers as divergent as Confucius, Descartes, Epictetus, James, Kierkegaard, Nietzsche, Pascal, and Socrates. The translation of philosophy into treatment is neither simple nor linear. Because all approaches to counseling and therapy require interpretation, practitioners may respond automatically to these "truths" without being fully aware of their philosophical underpinnings. Yet, cognizance of these roots is essential for existential work, because forms of treatment are closely tied to underlying philosophy.

Existential Philosophy

The following is a very brief description of some of the major figures and innovations in the existential movement. It is not meant as comprehensive or inclusive.[1] These are influences that relate directly to the development of

19

the therapy that I have practiced and are described in this book. Existential counseling and psychotherapy in Europe is far more closely tied to the philosophical foundations of existentialism. North American existential approaches, such as the current one, rely more narrowly on ontological, phenomenological, and pragmatic factors. I have limited the scope of inquiry to key innovators and influences from those realms in this chapter.

The existential movement in philosophy commonly refers to certain late 19th- and 20th-century philosophers who shared the belief that philosophical thinking begins with the living, acting, feeling, thinking human being. Philosophical understanding of the nature of man was still being influenced by dualism (separation of mind and body), the rational thinking of the 13th-century theologian Thomas Aquinas (God is perfectly rational and that He created the world in a rational manner to be discerned by the thinking capacity that He gave to humans), and Rene Descartes's 17th century establishment of existence by thinking about existence (*cogito ergo sum* "I think, therefore I am").

In the early and middle 19th century, traditional philosophies were dominated by abstract cognitive notions of being that give short shrift to more concrete affective spheres of experience. Philosophers who chose to focus on the nonrational have been controversial, even heretical since Socrates contested the Sophists' policy of elitism and certainty that all wisdom was already known, discoverable, and teachable. For Socrates, the journey through life was a path to wisdom that was to be constantly discovered. He argued that the path to knowing began with the concept that everything is unknown until explored by the individual.

Dual Trends

Existential thought developed somewhat independently in Christian-based philosophies and in the Jewish Mystical Tradition. In general, existential philosophers rebelled against the generally accepted dogma and "science" of the day, which embraced more than anything, objectivity and deductive methods of inquiry. Instead, their focus was on subjective, personal knowledge and inductive logic. For existential philosophers, there were dilemmas that are inherent in the human condition that were known affectively, illogically, and cognitively.

Christian Existentialists

Although there were precursors to existential thought in Christian theology before the Dark Ages and again during the reformation (i.e., Pascal, 1941), existentialism commonly dates its beginning to the 19th-century proposal of Søren Kierkegaard (1841, 1844) that each individual is solely responsible for giving meaning to life and for living it passionately and authentically. In the days in which Hegelian notions of absolute ultimate idealism held sway, this was heresy. For Kierkegaard, the individual, not the state, was the core of morality. He argued that the principle of subjective freedom represents a higher moral code. For him, it was essential to seek truth and live with fear, rather than act out of fear of some other entity, such as the state or religious dogma.

Nietzsche

Friedrich Nietzsche followed this train of thought when he promoted the notion that individuality transcends social mores in pursuit of personal standards. In his formulation, individuals are encouraged to face interacting core existential themes including freedom, responsibility, choice, and courage. Again, the center was the individual's subjective world.

Husserl

Edmund Husserl (2014) brought greater rigor to Nietzsche's principles. Living in a time when dualism and the deductive method that separated subject and object were common in scientific methodology, he preferred a far more subjective mode of exploration and awareness. To more fully understand the human condition, his phenomenological method favored description, experience, and clarification over explanation and analysis. In this way, Husserl's early 20th-century contribution to modern existential counseling and psychotherapy is evident. Like Nietzsche, he rejected the notion of objects being a constant reality, distinct from the perceiver. Instead, he proposed that objects were constituted by the observer—the essence of phenomenology. My grade school questioning about my friend Martin's color blindness might have been a naïve example of the role of the perceiver and phenomenology in determining reality.

Heidegger and Boss

Martin Heidegger expanded the phenomenological method to comprehend the meaning of being. His proposition was that deep philosophical inquiry and artistic expression could provide greater insight into what it means for humans to be-in-the-world and was preferable to derived scientific knowledge (Heidegger, 1962). For Heidegger, the human experience in the world included time, space, death, and human relatedness. He also promoted methods of knowing that began with the subjective experience over those which related a person's experience to a preestablished (deductive) theoretical framework.

Heidegger's student, Medard Boss, also found both Cartesian philosophy and Newtonian physics limiting and inaccurate in understanding what it meant to be human. Like many of Freud's early analysands, Boss (1963, 1979) broke with Freud in part over the deterministic underpinnings, hydraulic model, and deductive interpretation. He proposed an existential foundation for both psychology and medicine and a methodology he called *daseinanalysis.* The approach which combined existential and psychoanalytic methods was considered by many to be the first systematic application of existential philosophy to psychotherapy.

Tillich

The noted theologian Paul Tillich also had a significant influence on both existential philosophy and on existential therapy. Drawing on the works of Heidegger and to a lesser extent Kierkegaard, Tillich (1952) refers to the courage needed to face intrinsic anxiety, intensity, and depth of life. For Tillich, awareness of potential nonbeing is inherently anxiety provoking. He elucidates three basic fears of nonbeing: mortality, meaninglessness, and guilt (moral).

For Tillich (1952), courage is both source and outcome of dealing with these anxieties. Thus, courage involves facing the natural anxiety that emerges when confronted with nonbeing. In the process of confronting existential anxiety, an individual experiences an enhanced sense of courage. By contrast, failure to face the fears leads to despair. The distinction between existential anxiety (facing real aspects of the core human limits) and living with neurotic (avoidant) anxiety is a guidepost for existential psychotherapy.

Tillich, a Protestant theologian, found answers to the philosophical questions of anxiety in faith and in Christian symbolism. In his belief system, the Christ and crucifixion are intermediaries and a choice of faith both inspired and generated courage and love. Thus, the spiritual relationship precedes any I-thou encounter.[2] For Buber, and others in the Jewish Mystical tradition, the choice of love was a direct answer to meaninglessness. Philosophers in both traditions asserted that these crucial choices need to be made in the face of often considerable anxiety.

Tillich's influence in psychotherapy was both direct through his writing and indirect through his close association with Erich Fromm, Rollo May, Carl Rogers, and others (W. Rogers, 1985). His impact may be seen in midcentury psychoanalysis, self-psychology, object relations, Jungian psychology, and humanistic psychotherapy.

Sartre

Jean-Paul Sartre's influence on psychotherapy was decidedly indirect. He brought to the foreground of existential thought the significance of emotions, imagination, and the individual's interaction with his social and political world. Sartre's philosophy of existence was described in his own writing and in untold numbers of authors whom he inspired. One significant contribution was his focus on the dark side of human existence and despair based on life exigencies.

The Jewish Mystical Tradition

Often described as the province of Sephardic Judaism (Southwestern Europe, North Africa), mysticism is also found in Ashkenazi (France, Germany, Eastern Europe) traditions. Existential, relational thinking is prominent in many primary Jewish texts. There are subjective "Talmudic jokes" that have come down through the centuries:

"Put two Jews in a room for an hour and what will emerge are three different opinions."

There is also the story of the two men who were arguing vociferously two incompatible positions. They decide to take the conflict to the Rabbi for resolution. The Rabbi listens to the first complainant and agrees that he can see how his position is correct. Then he listens to the second man and agrees that his position is also correct. An observer approaches the Rabbi and queries, "How can they both be correct? They have opposite positions." In response, the Rabbi, reflecting the subjective, phenomenological aspects of existential theory, concludes, "You are correct also!"

Buber

The emergence of Jewish phenomenology and existential thought is nested directly in the realm of the relational world in Martin Buber's (1966) masterpiece, *I and thou (Ich und Du)*. He distinguishes between two modes of engagement in the world: *I-it* and *I-thou*.

I-it represents functional relating. The other (it) in a relationship is to be used in furtherance of goals. There is an inherent distance between the subject and the object. One does not participate in engaging the other's world; rather, he or she experiences it as an objective observer.

By contrast, the *I-thou* relationship is characterized as an "encounter" in which the I enters into the world of the thou. Instead of something to manipulate in space and time, the *thou* is experienced as if it were, at that moment, the entire universe. The relationship is intensely intimate, vulnerable, and loving. Buber viewed society of his day as alienating, because of its *I-it* focus. He attributes the absence of the *I-thou* encounter as generating fears of mortality, existential angst, feelings of isolation, and worries of meaninglessness.

For Buber, intimacy is the antidote. However, it is essential to note that the *I-thou* is always momentary and fleeting. It is not a state of being. Instead, each such encounter is transformational. The longer lasting value is the (process) openness to future intimacy. Buber concludes that a major component of this love is divine and is the answer to natural alienation.

What is particularly compelling in *"I and thou"* is the parallel process. It is a work that is itself best taken in as an encounter. Reading for intellectual comprehension pales beside the option of treating the book itself as a "thou." With Buber at least, to take in his philosophy, one has to also absorb the philosopher—the very core of his position.

The great late 19th- and early 20th-century physician Sir William Osler once remarked,

> *"The good physician treats the disease; the great physician treats the patient who has the disease."*

Mirroring this profound conviction, Buber separates healing from fixing. Analysis, behavior change, or symptom removal is viewed as potentially providing some relief or repair, but it falls short of the *"regeneration of a stunted personal center."* That requires the therapist enter the thou as a partner, in which he or she experiences both his or her own perceptions and those of the client.

Binswanger

Ludwig Binswanger[3] was influenced by both Freud and Jung but wrestled with both around the issue of phenomenology. He is considered the first to combine psychoanalysis, existentialism, and phenomenology. Heavily influenced by Buber's concepts of encounter and dialogue, he brought the concept of *intersubjectivity* to the fore as an essential component of therapy. He believed that one's existence could be observed only in context and through personal choices. For him, context involved one's surroundings (*umwelt*), relationships (*mitwelt*), the subjective (*eigenwelt*), and the spiritual (*uberwelt*).

Two overriding characteristics of Binswanger's work remain influential in modern existential counseling and psychotherapy: his systematic approach to discovering the unique personal meaning in a client's symptoms and the introduction of the term *love* into the healing equation. From his phenomenological perspective, true meaning and treatment direction is understood only in the deeply personal client-in-his-world. It cannot be deduced from theory or nomothetic understanding.

Frankl

Viktor Frankl provides a major bridge between the philosophy of Buber and treatment. For Frankl, the essence of human life involved the search for purpose and meaning—more accurately the *creation* of meaning. *Logotherapy*, a term he coined, involved a mutual, shared search for meaning.

Quoting Nietzsche freely, "He who has a why to live for can bear almost any how," Frankl believed that mental health was directly related to having a life goal, purpose, calling, or dedication, which is outside of and greater than the self.

Frankl's suffering and personal losses in the Nazi death camps allowed him to experience and to describe in exquisite detail the salience of love; the highest aspirational goal for human beings. Like Buber, he considered love (I-thou) to be essential to living fully and the path to salvation. Frankl discovered that even in those horrific experiences, a spiritual freedom and independence could be mentally created. His work leaned heavily on the existential notion that the human always has choices, even if it's only about the way we die.

Table 2.1	A Brief Summary of What Therapists Can Take From Existential/Phenomenological Philosophy
1. Anti-reductionist: Understanding requires experiencing the whole person, not just the symptoms	
2. Technique is secondary to relating	
3. The importance of subjectivity and subjective experience	
4. Addressing feelings as well as thoughts	
5. Choice-making and responsibility	
6. Freedom and security as poles of an inherent tension	
7. The centrality in anxiety about the limitations of human life	

(Continued)

Table 2.1   (Continued)
8. The interactive roles of courage and anxiety
9. Differences between existential anxiety and neurotic anxiety
10. Addressing the human need to find/create meaning in life
11. The salience of intimacy and relationship
12. Context: Understanding the client-in-his-or-her world

Philosophy Becomes Therapy

Existential counseling and psychotherapy drew directly from the philosophies that focused on understanding and defining human existence and essence. The two primarily germane philosophical movements were phenomenology and existential philosophy.

As early as the first decade in the 20th century, existential philosophy was becoming integrated into nascent psychoanalytic thinking. Boeree (1998) considered Otto Rank (1936) to be the first psychoanalyst who broke away from Freud's inner circle to directly apply these constructs. Like Freud, he introduced the notions of contrasting life and death instincts. However, his were more psychosocial than drive oriented. For Rank, the life instinct was a pull toward individuation (freedom) and the death instinct was a pull toward connection (security) (Boeree, 1998). These contrasting presses were held in tension and balance through life. When there was too great an emphasis on individuation, it produced the fear of abandonment. Excessive leaning toward security and connection resulted in overdependency, stagnation, and loss of self.

Rank (2004) saw birth (separation) trauma as the generator of the ongoing struggle between the necessary desires for reunion and autonomy. Existential anxiety emerges from those opposing fears of abandonment and suffocation. Rank's belief in the tension between freedom and security needs continues to be a core of existential counseling and psychotherapy today.

Binswanger (1963) may have an equally legitimate claim as the pioneer who brought existentialism and phenomenology to the practice of psychotherapy.[4]

In addition to working with Bleuler, Freud, and Jung, he was also deeply influenced by Buber, Heidegger, and Husserl. Binswanger had more of a phenomenological perspective than Rank, introducing subjective meaning and emotional intimacy into the work.

Divergent Existential Therapies

Given a primary existential tenet of subjective, narrative truth and distaste for categorization and "school" labels, there are a host of approaches covered under the existential umbrella. There are similarities and considerable variations across perspectives and emphasis. Norcross (1987) concluded that each exponent of existential psychotherapy and counseling describes a fairly unique personal perspective.

Despite the lack of a universal consensual definition, therapeutic approaches may be grouped as a way of delineating common differences and similarities. Recently, Vos, Craig, and Cooper (2014) revised Cooper's (2003) earlier categorization into four major existential "schools"[5] that vary from the more cognitive and philosophical to the more humanistic and from intrapsychic to relational perspectives:

(1) The *British School of existential therapy*, including the work of Laing; also called *existential analysis* (Spinelli, 2007; van Deurzen, 2012). This approach is a more descriptive and phenomenological approach, designed to help clients focus on their lived experiences by joining them in their *being-in-the-world*.

(2) *Logotherapy.* This meaning-centered approach, including existential analytical (Frankl, 1959a), is primarily aimed at assisting clients to create meaning in their lives.

(3) *Daseinanalysis* (Binswanger, 1963; Boss, 1963). This primarily continental approach employs a permissive relationship to encourage patients to express themselves freely and develop greater openness toward their subjective worlds.

(4) *American existential-humanistic.* This approach (Bugental, 1987; May, 1977; Schneider, 2008; Schneider & Krug, 2010; Yalom, 1980) has a primary focus on the centrality of anxiety and how it arises from facing the givens of life: mortality, freedom (and responsibility), isolation, and meaninglessness. Practitioners vary on the intrapsychic-interpersonal dimension.

Short-term approaches such as existential family therapy (Lantz, 1993; Lantz & Walsh, 2007), brief approaches, and group therapy approaches (Classen et al., 2001; Shapiro, Peltz and Bernadett-Shapiro, 1997; Yalom, 2005) are often categorized more for their client population than for theoretical differences. The most notable existential family therapist pioneer was Whitaker (1988; Neill & Kniskern, 1982).

Although all have roots in existential philosophy, some approaches are also deeply influenced by psychoanalysis or humanistic psychology, and those lines are not always clear-cut. For example, Binswanger, Boss, May, and Frankl had psychoanalytic training before creating their more existential stances. Tillich, Rogers, and May had interesting influences on each other, and Bugental's and Yalom's work have a host of mixed influences.

Despite the interwoven fabric that informs most existential therapists, we turn first to the "old world" schools, before exploring similarities and differences between existential and humanistic models.

European Schools

Modern European approaches appear to be more directly connected to the philosophical roots of existentialism. There is a popular saying in Germany that to Americans, "a long history is 100 years and a short distance is 100 miles!" It is the opposite in European sensibilities. As with most things, there are unique existential approaches that correspond to countries in which they are practiced. A comprehensive review of all of the schools is beyond the scope of this text. Excellent reviews can be found in Cooper (2003), Correia, Cooper & Berdondini (2014), and van Deurzen (2010).

British Existential Therapy

The British School and Existential Analysis have a deep abiding connection to the phenomenological writings of Husserl and Heidegger. Spinelli (2005) encouraged a strong concentration on the data of personal experience. In his approach, each subjective moment of a client's experience has significance, and the method of therapy is to help the client describe (rather than analyze) their experience as fully as possible.

A prolific writer from the same school, Emmy van Deurzen was more influenced by the writings of R. D. Laing (particularly his conclusion that there is no such thing as mental illness) and Sartre. She draws more directly on existential philosophy and less phenomenology than Spinelli, although she concurs with his underscoring client description (versus explanation) of experience and shares his aversion to technique-driven treatment.

Van Deurzen viewed problems-in-living as the essence of the therapeutic challenge. Acceptance of "what is" and courage to face these challenges are core in her approach. Following Binswanger's (1958) earlier conceptualization, she explores with clients their unique experience of physical, social, psychological, and spiritual dimensions of their lives. For van Deurzen, disturbance and health coexist in each aspect of life challenges. She noted that individuals are stretched between the positive pull of aspiration and the negative pull of fearfulness on each of the four dimensions. Successful therapy allows clients to be open to, and make peace with, the experience of both positive and negative reality.

Logotherapy (Meaning-Oriented Therapies)

Although Frankl's work is highlighted in the American influences, he is a bridge to European practices as well. Logotherapy is designed to help clients reflect on the process of finding (or creating) meaning in their lives, regardless of external circumstances. A less purely present-oriented or phenomenological approach, Logotherapy encourages clients to draw connections between past, present, and future time frames to explore meaning in life.

Längle's (2001) existential-analytic therapy reintroduces a wider range of primary human motivations into the meaning-generating processes. Drawing from Frankl, Längle's "anthropological approach" is directed toward four primary motivations: the need to be able to accept the basic conditions and building blocks of life, the need to have values and relationships, the quest to become one's own person, and the need to achieve something meaningful in the world.

Practitioners of logotherapy and its derivatives all place primary import on creating value-syntonic meaning as an antidote to the existential vacuum; feelings of meaninglessness and emptiness. Therapeutic success is measured by the ability of clients to enhance their experiences of meaning in making value-consistent choices and in owning individual responsibility for such choices.

European and American Existentialism

In general, European approaches are more closely aligned with the history of existential philosophy and with either an integration of, or painstaking distancing from, psychoanalysis. American existentialism is closer to humanistic models of therapy. Similarities and differences between existential and humanistic approaches may be particularly difficult to tease out, especially in the American approaches that primarily inform this

Table 2.2   Similarities in Existential and Humanistic Approaches

- Honoring of the subjective experience of the client
- Holistic perspective
- Centrality of therapist empathy
- Process as important as outcome
- Valuing of the whole person
- Goal of enhanced personal awareness
- Salience of "real" rather than "transference" relationship
- Phenomenologically oriented
- Concerns about the human experience and potential, broadly viewed

Table 2.3   Existential/Humanistic Differences

Existential Psychotherapy	Humanistic Psychotherapy
<ul><li>Focus on interaction/process</li><li>Greater therapist activity</li><li>Greater therapist self-disclosure</li><li>Focus on consequences</li><li>Encoding theory/inductive logic</li><li>Centrality of anxiety as growth engine</li><li>Empathy for process</li><li>Attribution of meaning</li><li>Relational and self-actualization as goal</li><li>Acknowledgment of and work with the dark side of human nature</li></ul>	<ul><li>Focus on client/person</li><li>Less active; less directive</li><li>Low self-disclosure</li><li>Focus on client experience</li><li>Decoding theory/deductive logic</li><li>Centrality of reducing client discomfort</li><li>Empathy for client's experience</li><li>Subjective experience</li><li>Self-actualization as goal</li><li>Focus on positive strivings to reach higher levels of being</li></ul>

Source: Shapiro, J. L. (2014a, August 8). Existential psychotherapy: Best evidence. Symposium presentation, American Psychological Convention, Washington, DC.

book and my personal perspective. Some of the similarities and differences can be seen in Table 2.2 and Table 2.3.

American Existential Psychotherapy

Despite the differences summarized above, it is almost impossible to separate existential and humanistic therapies as they are practiced today in North America. Indeed, if it were not for the humanistic movement ("third wave" after psychoanalysis and behavioral), existential may still be something of a rare anomaly in therapeutic practice. Many noted writers and practitioners, including Bugental and Schneider, have self-described or been aligned with an integrated Existential-Humanistic (E-H) orientation.

Rogers

No description of existentially oriented therapies is complete without acknowledgment of the contributions of Carl Rogers. Indeed, he has been called "the first American Existential therapist." Rogers is more commonly and appropriately honored as the most prominent voice in the closely related Humanistic Psychology movement. Humanism is comparable to the positive aspects of existentialism, without the dark side. This point is underscored in the famous Rogers-Buber Dialogue (Cissna & Anderson, 1994). Rogers opined that at the core, human nature is to be trusted, because each individual carries with him or her a constructive quality that emerges. Buber disagreed and replied, "When I come near to the reality of the person, I experience it as a polar reality." The whole person includes what is best in him or her and what is worst. This is the more common existential perspective.

Rogers perceived clients as having a life drive toward self-actualization. Psychological difficulties were interruptions and distortions of the basic process of personal growth. Rogers emphasized the need of humans for positive regard for both self and other. For Rogers, the kind of regard that was essential was that which was offered without conditions. Rogers believed that when positive regard was conditional, it mirrored the *I-it* functional relationships of Buber.

With conditional regard, an individual's self-esteem becomes dependent on expectations set by society, culture, and other people. By contrast, the real self comes from the internal actualizing tendency. The discrepancy between expectations and reality represent incongruity—being out of touch with the real self was Rogers' definition of neuroses.

As the commonly accepted, "third wave" of psychotherapy in America, person-centered work is clearly in opposition to the drive, habit, and symptom orientations of psychoanalysis and behaviorism. From a person-centered perspective, the healthy individual is characterized as fully functioning when he or she is open to experience, living in the present, self-trusting, free to make choices, and creative and flexible in applying values.

Rogers's influence on the field as a whole was profound at the time and continues to be so. His thinking can be seen in humanistic psychotherapy, in therapist training, in the evidence base for therapy, and in his influence on existential therapists such as May and Bugental.

Four individuals dominated the first wave of existential psychotherapy in the West: Viktor Frankl, Rollo May, James Bugental, and Irvin Yalom.

May

Often referred to as "the father of American existential psychology," he was influenced by Kierkegaard's writings and those of his long-time friend, colleague, and mentor, Paul Tillich. In *The Meaning of Anxiety* (1977), he wrote that the experience of anxiety gives impetus for the freedom to act with courage and to live fully.

In the groundbreaking book that he co-edited (May, Angel, & Ellenberger, 1958), Rollo May broke with traditional depth psychotherapy and his psychoanalytic training by arguing that it was essential to see "the patient as he really is, knowing him in his own reality (rather than) merely a projection of our own theories about him" (p. 3). He also presaged one of the most heavily debated cultural issues in the last 2 decades regarding the very nature of how psychotherapy research should best be conducted.

Drawing on the work of Binswanger and Heidegger, May asserted that an existential approach to psychology eschews any pressure to fit a client into a prearticulated theoretical system and warned that "techniques" represented a therapist's avoidance of engaging with the client. Instead, psychotherapy from May's perspective was far more focused on analyzing and understanding the client's unique reality; allowing therapists to enter the client's world and to explore his or her strengths and style of adaptation to the natural trials of life.

Following the philosophical contributions of Kierkegard, Nietzsche, and Pascal, May described existentialism as a way to "cut below the (Renaissance-based) cleavage between subject and object." His approach offered a reintegration of affect and spirit with cognition in understanding clients. May (1977) opined that people are not best understood for their rational capacities alone but as creative emerging selves. This is a bridge between what is abstractly true and what is existentially real.

The need for integration can also be seen today in the "silo" approach, both between and within disciplines in academia, in which hard sciences, social sciences, and humanities are all segregated. Such silos of study lead to the heated debate within modern psychotherapy research between efficacy and effectiveness studies in psychotherapy. Even more germane, May warned against the influence of limiting factor of theory and measurements in controlling data.

For May, an existential, inductive mode of inquiry is far more liberating in promoting self-awareness. Because neuroses emerge from the avoidance of reality, the primary goal of psychotherapy is to counteract it by promoting present awareness.

Finally, May (1969) made a strong case for the reintegration of love, intentionality, and inclusion of values in the practice of counseling and psychotherapy. The integrated self contains both subject and object and focuses far more effectively on the context of the clients' experiences.

Deeply influenced by Tillich and Christian existentialism, Rollo May was a significant transition figure between the European philosophers, psychoanalysts, and American psychotherapists. Two practitioners who were directly influenced by May and who have brought his work to a broader audience of psychotherapists are Bugental (1987) and Schneider (Schneider & May, 1995).

Bugental

Although he and his work had a significant impact in existential psychotherapy, James Bugental is probably more easily defined as an existential-humanistic psychotherapist. He was deeply influenced by both Rogers and May.

In *The Search for Authenticity* (1965), Bugental defined humanistic psychology:

(1) Human beings can be effectively viewed holistically, not in reductionistic terms.

(2) They have choices and responsibilities.

(3) They are intentional, seeking meaning, value, and creativity.

(4) They live and experience life intrapsychically.

(5) They exist in an interpersonal world with awareness of self in context of others.

Each of these could readily fit within a humanistic or existential rubric. However, as Krug (2009) indicates, his focus on the intrapsychic rather than relational realm in therapy brings him closer to Rogers than to Buber and Yalom.

Bugental's signal contributions include exquisite articulations and demonstrations of therapeutic presence and of the use of the here-and-now as a generator of interventions with clients. His articulate and sensitive use of self in the therapeutic relationship allowed for a broader range of both input and responses to his clients.

In the introduction to his *Psychotherapy Isn't What You Think*, he distinguishes between information-oriented psychotherapies and (his) "psychotherapy that centers on the *actual experiencing* of the client in the living moment" (Bugental, 1999, p. xv). For Bugental, and most existential psychotherapists, the therapeutic goal is *life-changing* rather than symptom-altering.

Summarizing existential work in general, Van Deurzen (2010), a chief spokesperson for existential psychotherapy in the United Kingdom, concurred. The focus on client process and his or her subjective experience goes to the "how" of client experience, rather than the more explicit "what."

In Bugental's formulation, the locus of change is the client. The therapist serves primarily as facilitator of the client's process. His method was to engage with the client's grappling with life stress, goal-seeking, and vulnerabilities. Experiential engagement with the client's process supersedes learning any particular facts of the client's life. As much as possible, the therapist tries to share a lived experience of the client's process, bringing his or her resources to bear on dangers and vulnerabilities of the client's life—a connection to Buber's philosophical writing.

The centerpiece of Bugental's work is subjective awareness. In this framework, one can be truly alive if one is aware of self-in-the-world and the limits of human existence. Therapy consists of helping clients gain increasing awareness of their manner of coping and assisting the clients' increases in flexibility and courage. Distinguishing his method from common depth psychology, he described a "let's do it together" in real time, instead of a "whodunit" approach.

One of the most compelling legacies of Bugental's work is his primary standing as clinician and teacher, rather than theoretician. His writing is both personal and up close with the therapeutic encounters. In many case examples on video and in his writing, he demonstrates how he used himself and the here-and-now relationship as a parallel process to increase client capacity to confront anxiety both in and outside of therapy.

According to Krug (2009), Bugental's approach is more humanistic and intrapsychic and less reciprocal than Yalom's and others who define their work as more existential (i.e., Shapiro, 2010). Those therapists and writers follow more closely the Jewish Mystical tradition of Buber and Frankl.

Frankl

Viktor Frankl had an inordinate influence on American existential and humansitic psychotherapy as well as on spirituality and theology in the second half of the 20th century. Sometimes referred to as "height" (versus depth) psychology, Frankl (1959; 1959a) viewed finding or creating life meaning as personal, inconsistent, and idiosyncratic. He promoted the notion that love of something or someone outside the self is the path to transcending human existence. Failure to find this love or dedication causes individuals to turn toward a self-focus and develop symptoms, which in turn, promotes further a spiraling loss of meaning in life.

For Frankl, therapy often consisted of distracting the clients from their self-obsessions and refocusing on a viable other. In doing this, he conveyed to clients an antideterministic, antireductionistic stance in which they may choose the nature of their own existence. Within that relational framework, clients were encouraged to explore what gave meaning to their lives. For

Frankl, the search for meaning was an internal, dynamic creative act, rather than decoding something that was already present.

Like for the other existential therapists, a person's symptoms were viewed as far less a focal point of therapy than an individual's process of being-in-the world, another reflection of Osler's warning about the great physician seeing the person with the disease, not the disease per se.

Frankl's influence on psychotherapy was broad and significant, although the formal practice of logotherapy has been adopted by only a small number of existential psychotherapists. His influence on culture, on spirituality, and on other literature was even more profound. The address given at the presentation of an honorary degree from Santa Clara University to Dr. Frankl began, "Viktor Frankl is a true hero, a man who lost everything . . . but decided none-the-less to say yes to life" (Frankl, 1991).

Yalom

An existential practitioner and prolific writer, Irvin Yalom is credited with two works that both summarized and altered the face of existential psychotherapy: *Existential Psychotherapy* (Yalom, 1980) and *The Theory and Practice of Group Psychotherapy* (Yalom, 1970/2005). In both, Yalom describes a relationship-based approach to psychotherapy in which the real person of the therapist interacts with the real person of the client. Heavily influenced by May, with whom he was an analysand, he described the essence of a client's will (intentionality) as a major component of the therapy endeavor.

Yalom describes anxiety as arising from confrontation with the "givens" of human life: death, freedom, responsibility, isolation, and meaninglessness. The therapeutic goal and process is to stand with the clients and help eliminate their blocks (defenses, symptoms) to facing these daunting yet essential issues. He connects directly with the philosophical tenets of Kierkegaard and the phenomenologists in his encoding approach to human life. The basic assumption is that life has arisen from random events and that there is no predestined fate. Instead, each individual has to create and decide how to live as fully as possible. In his basic text, he queries, "Perhaps we can forgo the question, why do we live? But it is not easy to postpone the question, how shall we live?" (Yalom, 1980, p. 427).

In both professional works and novels, he lays out the salience of the therapist's self-awareness and the manner in which he or she shares himself or herself in the intimate therapy encounter. Most significantly, he describes the uniqueness of each therapy, indeed each session, with clients. In *The Gift of Therapy*, he exalts in the "wonderment" of learning each client's personal story (Yalom, 2001).

Yalom's influence on American existentialism, which he describes as a way of thinking that may be (and usually is, with or without conscious awareness of practitioners) integrated into all forms of therapy, rather than a theory or technique, has been enhanced primarily by the accessibility and popularity of well-written books. He has repeatedly been able to take complex constructs and explain them in easily accessible form.

The Pragmatic Existential Orientation of This Book

It is no surprise that any existential approach might not fit perfectly with that of other clinicians. My personal influences include Erickson, Frankl, May, Rogers, Satir, and Whitaker. However, at the risk of imperfect self-reflection, I view this work as perhaps bridging somewhat the Atlantic Ocean; neither completely American nor European.[6] The core emphases include the primacy of relationship and phenomenology, creation of meaning, self-disclosure, and an active therapeutic approach, particularly around the real therapeutic relationship. My hope is that readers will take it in as it fits personal preferences and skills, modify the approaches for professional relevance, and find personal value in the process.

Notes

1. *Everyday Mysteries* by Emmy van Deurzen (2010) provides a more extensive treatment of the existential philosophers. In *Existential Therapies* (2003), Mick Cooper describes some of the derived therapies in greater depth.

2. In a 1960 paper at the Conference on Existential Psychotherapy in New York City, Tillich commented, "a person becomes a person in the encounter with other persons, and in no other way." Although he placed this conclusion within the framework of "moral self-realization of the centered self," he concluded that such morality was not subject to laws but available only in "limiting encounter with another ego."

3. Although Binswanger was deeply influenced by Heidegger, the connection of his thinking to Buber and Frankl places his work more within the Jewish Mystical tradition.

4. Medard Boss, whose contribution is identified above, is the third therapist who brought existential approaches to psychotherapy with his daseinanalysis. His was likely the most systematic approach of the three.

5. My apologies to those within existential fields of work who find the term *school* distasteful or misleading to individual uniqueness. My intent is purely to help clarify differences between groups of practitioners who share some common attributes.

6. The hope is that it does not disappear into Atlantis or the Bermuda Triangle.

3

Essential Concepts and Themes in Theory and Therapy

The good physician treats the disease;

the great physician treats the patient who has the disease.

Sir William Osler

Existential counseling and psychotherapy are somewhat unique in the panoply of theories of human behavior and healing. The pragmatic existential methods in this book are experiential, phenomenological, and based in the client's subjective experience. Because these subjective experiences are oriented to the here-and-now interaction, the therapist's role is more active and personal.

Rooted in social science and philosophy rather than the natural sciences that highlight discovery and *decoding* of real world phenomena, existentialism is an *encoding theory*. For existential therapists, there is less focus on objective truth to be understood by virtue of carefully planned, progressive, deductive, empirical inquiry. Instead, truth is something to be created subjectively.

Most other theories emerged from deductive science: psychodynamic theories developed out of Freud's physiology training; behavioral theories have a foundation in Watson's social science experiments; even Gestalt therapy, which shares phenomenology with existential approaches, began in perceptual psychology laboratories (cf. Wertheimer & Spillman, 2012; Kohler, 1947; Lewin, 1951, etc.).

Roots

Although origins of existential thinking may be found as far back as the work of Socrates and Confucius, existential philosophy as a field emerged through the work of 19th- and 20th-century European philosophers such as Buber (1970), Heidegger (1962), Husserl (2008), Jaspers (1964), Kierkegaard (1980), Nietsche (1974), Sartre (1943), and Tillich (1952) and religious thought in Judaism (e.g., Buber; 1970; Frankl, 2006), Christianity (Kierkegaard, 1980; Tillich, 1952), Buddhism (i.e., Miller, 2008), and atheism (i.e., Nietsche, 1974; Sartre, 1964). Drawing on these influences and a tradition of rebellion against established order and deductive scientific methods, psychotherapists such as Binswanger (1963), Boss (1979), and Frankl (2006) codified and developed the theory during the post WWII period.

Related Influences

In Chapter 2, four existential schools were delineated. Each offers distinct foci of attention in psychotherapy. The current pragmatic approach shares a kinship with and employs constructs from many existential influences and also other forms of psychotherapy.

Person-Centered therapy (Rogers, 1951) has much in common with the *I-thou* relationship focus of existential therapies. Despite different origins, Gestalt therapy (Perls, 1968), Relational-Cultural therapy (Jordan, 2010), Personal Construct therapies (Kelly, 1955), Narrative therapy (i.e., White & Epston, 1990; Zimmerman & Dickerson, 1996), and to some extent, Motivational Interviewing (Miller & Rollnick, 2012) also share with existential approaches an emphasis on phenomenology, the here-and-now, centrality of the clients' frameworks, personal constructs, and subjective experiences.

Emotion-focused therapy has been described as a combination of existential and attachment theories (Greenberg, 2015; Johnson, 2008). Process-oriented group therapy (i.e., Shapiro, Peltz, & Bernadett-Shapiro, 1997) primarily focuses on an epigenetic development of group process and primacy of the here-and-now.

In the family therapy field, structural family therapy approaches (e.g., Minuchin & Fishman, 1981) that stress the basic family structure and members' work within that frame, Whitaker's (Neill & Kniskern, 1982) existential-experiential approach, and systems-oriented strategic family therapy (Haley, 1963; Watzlawick, Bavelas, & Jackson, 1967) share with existential work the salience of consequences and the intrinsic pull for homeostasis and the status quo in therapy.

It is my strong conviction that pragmatic existential psychotherapy and its unique therapeutic relationship underlie a core of what makes all therapies work, whether or not it is attributed (cf. Norcross & Lambert, 2014; Schneider, 2008; Yalom, 1980).

A Brief Introduction to a Pragmatic Existential Therapy

The nature of existential work, particularly in the phenomenological, here-and-now, real-time moment, makes each therapist and each therapist-client interaction somewhat unique. It is half-joke, half-reality that by definition, no two practitioners of existential work are exactly alike in their approach to patients (DuPlock, 1997). Indeed, the true existential therapist may have quite divergent experiences with each client and from session to session with the same client. This makes a general definition somewhat challenging.

However, there are certain key principles that define the work as existential. Shapiro (2010) listed 12 basic tenets of these approaches to therapy. These are presented briefly in Table 3.1 and described in greater detail below.

Essential to the theory are the clients' examinations and explorations of the true nature of human beings. It is the knowledge of the limits of a person's life that both enervates and enlivens his or her passion to make the most of the life time that is available.

Table 3.1 Twelve Basic Tenets of Existential Psychotherapy

1. Primary focus is on clients' subjective experience.
2. Client's personal attribution of meaning is the reality with which therapist and client are engaged.
3. The therapeutic relationship is the vehicle for healing and dealing with *normal feelings of alienation, meaninglessness, and fears of mortality and the clients' adaptations to those basic human dilemmas.*
4. In the here-and-now context, the therapist is challenged to make explicit what was previously implicit.
5. Therapy is process centered and all content is viewed within the complexities of context.

(Continued)

Table 3.1 (Continued)

6. Through use of parallel process, clients experience the same dynamic in the client-therapist relationship as in outside life.
7. Affective, cognitive, and action realms are grist for the therapeutic mill.
8. Enhanced personal awareness is both goal and method for clients to live more deliberately, authentically, and purposefully.
9. Primary attention is paid to awareness of the constant tension between needs for freedom and security. This relationship between fear (of the unknown) and guilt and stagnation (of the status quo) are viewed at both macro and micro (here-and-now) levels.
10. Exploration in therapy is less on what objectively occurred than on what meaning the event is given by individuals.
11. Anxiety is seen as the engine for change and as a healthy aspect of therapy.
12. Initially, many clients come into therapy with an expressed confusion around their sense that they are doing everything right but feeling unhappy or empty.

Subjective Reality and Seeking Meaning

The primary reality is that in which therapist and client are engaged. What actually occurs in a client's life is important but secondary to what meaning the client gives it and what occurs in the therapist-client relationship.

There are many familiar examples of this, none more poignant than Frankl's descriptions of experiences in the Nazi death camps. Even in the state of extreme privation, ongoing torture, and misery, he described the importance of finding love and meaning in suffering and development of mental spirituality—a place to which the guards could not go. Similarly, many people have not given in to a handicap but instead used it as a way to better inform their lives (cf. Feldman & Kravetz, 2014).

Sometimes Losses Become Victories

One particular patient of mine was diagnosed with a terminal illness and was given only a short time to live by her physicians. After an initial reaction of despondency, she became determined to use the time left in the best possible way; to "take every drop of living out of minutes instead of years." Although the doctors' prognostications were accurate, she described, in one of her final therapy sessions, that the last 6 months of her life were surely her best.

Of course, this happens on a much smaller scale for most individuals. We regularly suffer losses in relationship, career, personal capability, or appearance and are challenged to find new paths and new meaning in life. Indeed, it is the essence of loss and facing new realities that spurs us forward in ways that victories cannot (Viorst, 1998).

As a young girl, Sandra was identified as "a beauty." She excelled in many areas in school but learned early how to trade on her appearance. She won key roles in school plays, modelled swimsuits and undergarments in catalogues, and was "pretty much able to get whatever guy I wanted." At 40, following her second divorce, she was still "playing the looks card." She began trying to correct the toll of normal aging with plastic surgery. When she entered therapy, she was strikingly attractive for a woman her age, but her skills were those of the "pretty young thing."

After several sessions dominated by flirtation with therapist feedback, she began to address the question, "Who am I if I am not beautiful?" As therapy progressed, Sandra was able to discover some tentative answers to that question by exploring herself, below the skin level. She then could begin to build a new life—one that didn't require physical attractiveness as her primary relationship and career skill. She went back to school, finished her BA, and then went to graduate school to begin a new career. When I last saw her, she was struggling to build her new professional identity, but reported, "You know, I feel like I am in the right place for the first time."

Sometimes Victories Generate an Internal Shift

This is not to suggest that only loss, suffering, or failure can provide the impetus for meaning or personal change. Victories can do so also, if we are able to attribute meaning to them.

Cliff had struggled most of his life to keep up with his peers. As a child, he had learning difficulties and was athletically inferior to his peers. At 40, he was just achieving what others had done in their twenties. He was a loyal and relatively effective worker at a company that managed commercial real estate. During a meeting early in 2008 in which the Chief Executive Officer (CEO) was talking about buying two new complexes, Cliff did the unusual. He disagreed and opined that he was scared that the market could burst. To his amazement, his voice was heard, and additional research led the upper management to consider selling instead of buying. They sold four properties before the market crashed in October of that year.

Although he was rewarded handsomely for his insight, the best part, Cliff reported, "I was so high because Jeff (the CEO) and Roland listened to me and took me seriously." This victory and therapeutic encouragement led him to also speak his mind with his family instead of automatically deferring to his wife. Although the first few attempts were "rocky," Cliff later reported that the relationship with his wife and his two sons had improved markedly.

Most meaningful experiences contain a mixture of wins and losses. For example, one of the most exhilarating experiences in life can be parenthood. It may be filled with anxiety, pain, shifts in life priorities, and new vulnerabilities, but most new parents describe the event as both wonderful and life-changing. In a 25-year study I did with expectant fathers (Shapiro, 2014b), one of the most common spontaneous expressions was exemplified by one new dad, who exclaimed, "it's the best thing I have ever done."

Even in the glow of such victories, however, the existential reality emerges that the father's life is pushed psychologically closer to its end by becoming a member of an older generation and the insidious reality that both he and his new baby will someday cease to be.

Who Is the Patient: Disease or Person With Dis-ease?

When therapy is viewed from the perspective of a supplicant seeking treatment from an expert healer, the complaint (symptom) becomes the focus of attention. The patient is "the phobia" or the "depression" and that is the entity that is treated. Treatment, defined in terms of reduction or purging of the symptoms, involves techniques or education.

That is quite different from the current approach. Here, the person-with-a-symptom is the client. Symptoms are not necessarily something to be eliminated. Instead we explore with the client the cost/value ratio of the symptom and most significantly, how the client can endure, grow, and find meaning in the disquiet. Although techniques and skills may be included, the essential aspect of treatment involves the relationship between two individuals working as a team to address the client's concerns, within the client's worldview.

To quote the great Talmudic scholar Maimonides, *"Give a man a fish and you feed him for a day; teach a man to fish and you feed him for a lifetime."* Of course, you may want to help him find tonight's meal while he is learning.

It's the Relationship!

Since Rogers' work in the middle of the 20th century, research into what truly makes therapy work has yielded some poignant indications. According to Shapiro (1987), Norcross (2014), and Norcross and Lambert (2014), among others, the key ingredient in successful therapy is the combination of the match between therapist and client and their relationship.

In existential therapy, everything comes down to the personal relationship between therapist and client. Although it is defined as a real relationship, it has unique rules of engagement. It is essentially asymmetrical—the goal is the client's growth, not mutual growth, and there are professional boundaries and limits on which directions the relationship may go.

Real Versus Transference Relationship

In existential counseling and therapy, the primary goal is to foster *I-thou* moments (Buber, 1966) that create fertile ground for change. The actual relationship between the therapist and client is ideally a deep, present-oriented bond that is explored as experiences arise in the moment. Together, client and therapist explore current issues in the client's life, the impact of core life conditions, and most uniquely, the interpersonal process occurring between them.

Although the relationship may involve considerable projection, it is distinguished from the traditional transference relationship in that what transpires is addressed directly, rather than interpretively, often with mutual self-disclosure. In short, in this form of therapy, *intimacy is considered an antidote to blocked feelings of alienation, isolation, responsibility, meaninglessness, and fears of mortality.*

Existential therapy works in affective (feelings-in-the moment), cognitive (insight), and behavioral realms. The therapist engages with the client to increase awareness at several levels of perceptual, interpersonal, and intrapsychic experience. The client's present awareness in-the-moment is perceived both as goal and method for clients to live more deliberately, more authentically, and more purposefully.

Inductive and Deductive

Most scientific inquiry and approaches to psychotherapy are theory centric. The theory of the therapist governs what constitutes relevant data and explains what they mean through logic and hypothesis testing. In short, deductive approaches begin with the theoretical level and prove "truth" through observing client behavior.

The current approach operates in the reverse manner. Existential therapists observe raw data and generate theoretical notions. In this inductive approach, data precedes theory. The therapist and client engage on a mutual adventure to explore the clients' experiences before putting them into a larger context. This is the essence of encoding versus decoding knowledge.

The philosophical assumption is that whatever occurs only has functional meaning when it is experienced by the person.

This can be seen in the following transcript from an initial therapy session. Note the differences in the nature of the therapeutic relationship and approach between this existential and other, more deductive therapies. The existential therapist (J) is far less a detective looking for some objective truth, than a fellow traveler seeking meaning. J's unspoken thoughts are in *parentheses and italics*.

An Initial Existential Session

Prior to this session, there was a brief phone interview. At the beginning of this first session, I had an opportunity to scan briefly the intake forms filled out by the client. Ella is a 33-year-old divorced woman, a practicing attorney, with no history of mental/emotional disorders in the past. She married her childhood sweetheart when they were in college. They were married for 9 years. She self-reported as a "religious person" who does not use caffeine, alcohol, or any recreational drugs. She had successful experiences with therapy in the past and did not return to a prior therapist, "because I recently moved here and she's 3 hours away." When she came in for therapy, she had not been dating seriously or involved in a primary relationship for the 3 years since her divorce.

J: How may I be of help?

E: I have a lot of anxiety about relationships. My biggest worry is that I will not be able to get into another relationship. I was divorced 3 years ago.

J: (*Intimacy issues may go both ways: Fears of not being in a relationship and being in one—premature to introduce the latter*) So, anxiety about finding a relationship and also a fear of not being in one.

E: More that I won't find one. I am worried that if I do meet someone, I will turn into this little girl, desperate for attention. And then if I don't get the attention, I will crave it and question my attractiveness and value.

J: (*It will be important at some point to consider the marriage, divorce, early attachment and relationship history. . . . Very tempting to go there and explore roots of her current concerns—better to explore from existential perspective*) What if that fear became true, and there was no relationship?

E: (looking a little stunned) Ooh! I would not feel complete without having that partner that I really want. If I didn't have that, there would be a part of me that was missing.

J: Tell me about the part that would be missing.

E: That's hard, it seems a little abstract.

J: Try to talk to me as if I were the missing part.

E: (She laughs, extends her hand, and reaches out toward J.) It's hard, because already in my mind, I am looking for a man and you are a male. I want love that's more than a friendship. I have a number of good friends. I get a lot of enjoyment with connection with my family . . . but I still feel the need for a best friend there always to check in with.

J: *(In most situations the extended hand, nervous smile, and small laugh might have seemed flirtatious—it did not feel that way here—assumption that support is the goal.)* You feel life would be a lot better in a number of ways with that significant relationship.

E: (Chuckle) Even as you say that, I have to laugh. My marriage was very difficult. My life was not better at all, but even with that, I'd like to have the relationship to work on.

J: *(Another temptation to probe the marriage . . .)* It's easy to understand that you'd want that. I am still interested in that part that's missing in you.

E: The part that's missing . . . my own validation of myself. I want someone else to say I'm okay.

J: What's been your experience when someone in the past does validate you?

E: Then I believe it! My mom tells me I am great for who I am. My dad tells me how proud of me he is for my accomplishments. When anyone tells me I am valuable, then I care for and love them as well.

J;   There is a "but" coming. . . .

E: Yeah. Because then a smaller critical voice in my head starts questioning if I am okay, and it grows stronger until someone else can tell me I'm okay.

J: *(Very aware of the rising anxiety in the room)* (After a pause) I just had an experience of anxiety as you were saying that (touching chest)—a tightness in my chest—and what came to mind was a sense of how vulnerable a position that is. I felt more vulnerable—that another voice could be more powerful than your inner voice.

E: (tearful) I want my own voice for sense of self . . . it's so difficult. I do feel very vulnerable letting another person be that powerful. During the divorce, my ex-husband said things that were so hurtful. It's taken me a lot of time to think that I'm . . . not flawed. I still think about some of the things he said to me. They weren't even true. I know that, but . . .

J: Even now, you feel really vulnerable to his criticism.

E: Lately, I have felt a little more like I can own my own identity . . . feel stronger. No, I know who I am when a person criticizes me, I can think, "no, they are wrong, or even if they are right I'm still okay"—but not as strong as I want to be. This is where anxiety comes through in relationships—I absolutely want them to tell me I'm wonderful—but then I'm vulnerable again.

J: That does seem like a very vulnerable place. Giving away a lot of power . . . As if, whoever it is was almost objective in their perceptions.

E: Like they are judges.

J: *(Wondered about going into how this squared with her profession as a litigator, preferred staying with the anxiety.)* It sounds like that when you say it.

E: If I go and talk to a guy I like, and he's not that interested . . . Oh no, I must have come off horribly. I must be unattractive.

J: So, rather than see it as his horrible taste, you see it as your defects exposed.

E: It's getting better, but that's the weak reaction.

J: So what could we do right now that would help grow the voice, of "I like Ella, I respect Ella"—not to ignore the other voice but to balance it somewhat—to cut down on the whipsawing.

E: I don't know . . . probably go through the thought process.

J: *(That last intervention seemed to close her off. Perhaps I got too cognitive and avoided the affect. Want to get reconnected.)* Let me ask you a question, what went on inside just now when I asked you that?

E: I felt a responsibility.

J: *(Back to feeling)* What are you aware of happening inside in your body now?

E: (Very thoughtful and teary, speaking slower)—I don't know if I can put a finger on it or words.

J: Try to take just a moment to focus inside.

E: Another judgment.

J: *(She avoided by becoming cognitive, let's see if it's resistance or just needing a little support.)* Like a sinking feeling?

E: Like guilt.

J: Guilt?

E: Yeah.

J: Wow! Somehow you should . . .

E: Like I'm struggling with something and need to work harder. Sounds to myself like a little kid.

J: That's okay. What does the kid feel? What is your fault, little girl?

E: I'm not appropriate. I struggle to please. . . trying to be perfect.

J: I can probably confirm that you are not perfect. Even though everyone shares that goal, for you it seems more powerful a problem to not attain perfection.

E: Yeah!

J: If you were perfect right in this moment, what would I be seeing?

E: (smiling) Competent, and in my mind I would be all put together . . . animated, outgoing, and attractive, but you know, I really like the part of me that is not all put together. (continuing in a more adult tone) I like coming off as vulnerable and still trying to learn. I do like her, even though I have both sides.

J: *(Want to give her more space to come forth without trying to please me . . .)* (taking an animated stance and shifting seat to be slightly less in front and more beside client) Tell me about those traits that you like.

E: That I like? Animated—I like talking with people and admit the struggle (hands active now), and I like sharing that and it helps them.

J: Are you aware of what you just did (therapeutic amazement voice)? Wow! . . . It was fascinating. . . . You talked about liking something about yourself because it had an effect on someone else. That's fascinating—you seemed very excited.

E: I think that is exciting for me to talk with others, not in the judgmental way, but both of us getting closer. Like being the good girl.

J: And, what's the bad girl part?

E: (laughing and in a flirtatious tone) Well . . .

J: You got a kick out of that.

E: I got a little embarrassed. I wasn't quite sure about where that was going.

J: That's embarrassing. . . . Tell me about her. She has a lovely, impish smile.

E: (laughing a lot) Well—the bad girl . . . she makes decisions on a whim, no planning . . . is very much driven by the moment.

J: The spontaneous side.

E: (She is smiling now.) My brain goes from what I haven't accomplished to just letting it be.

J: Are you aware of what's happening inside?

E: Well, I kind of like it.

J: Your face lit up. You smiled.

E: Like that's the more natural me.

J: So this is a real dilemma—that's the bad part and you are looking for others to say you are good. You are desirable for being good, and you enjoy personally both the good and the bad. This is a real dilemma . . . disquieting.

E: It's because I don't want them to see how I really am. I am really this person that's trying to be real and be loved. I read dating advice online and dating books and my best friend tells me—don't do that—a guy won't like it. I start to think there must be something wrong with me.

J: So let me play back for you what just happened here. I observed you having a little fun with yourself and enjoyed the "real," more complex Ella, and then you went back to "I should." You didn't even change the paragraph. Right in the middle of enjoying some parts of yourself, you shifted suddenly into something you are doing is not okay.

E: (With energy) Yes! And I have anger about it because there's a part of me that believes her. At least a little bit.

J: Are you feeling the anger now?

E: Yes. (In a cautious tone of voice)

J: Tell me!

E: I am thinking of my ex and others shushing me when I was having fun—don't be exuberant. Be proper. Part of me believes that, I should always be considerate, but I am still angry.

J: *(Again, a tease to go historical and find root causes)* (excited, shifts seat again closer toward a side-by-side angle) What does the "bad" girl want to say here?

E: Killjoy. Consider the surroundings, be proper.

J: That's a good description, what would you want to *say*?

E: Figure it out on your own, and don't bother me. I was happy with myself, and now I feel guilty.

J: When I heard that he and others scolded you, my response was a different verb beginning with the letter "*f*" and a pronoun.

E: Yeah. My version of that is 'forget it.'

J: Good! But you are still holding it. Let's talk about right now between you and I—about being scolded or judged.

E: Maybe I *was* wrong. I wasn't being perfect.

J: Let's say that is accurate. You really were not being perfect then, and you are not perfect now. Then what?

E: Inner voice is scolding me.

J: *(Wondering who the inner voice is)* Go ahead and speak that voice out loud

E: You're interfering with others' lives! You are inconsiderate!

J: Ella is really bad! She is so self-centered. And the tiny almost inaudible voice (spoken in a kid's voice) . . . I was just trying to have some fun.

E: Laughing. Yes. That little voice is cute. . . .

J: Tell me what she's saying.

E: (In a small voice) You're cute?

J: (Laughing) So much for cuteness conviction.

E: (Laughing) Am I cute? I am cute!

There are differences here between this form of existential work and the more traditional historically focused, deductive, technique-driven, symptom-centered approach to mend a self-esteem problem, even in the first session. In other forms of treatment, information about her marriage, prior relationships, family, and early attachment would be very interesting and potentially quite valuable. Here, however, rather than analyze or try to get it to change, we try to bring it as live as possible into the current relationship in the present.

Notice the point where I became aware of the loss of connection following a cognitive intervention and quickly went back to a more affective focus. Notice also the teamwork, rather than doctor-patient ambiance. We are doing something together and in the process allowing her to express some self-esteem and positive feelings around the playful "naughty" parts of herself.

Hanging the Unmentionables on the Clothesline

One aspect of the therapy is the therapist making explicit what was previously implicit particularly in the here-and-now relationship. Exploration in therapy is less on what objectively occurs than on what meaning the client attributes to the event.

Earlier, I mentioned my client who has received a terminal diagnosis. We had a long-term therapeutic relationship when she got the terrible news. After telling me what the doctors had said about her condition, she began discussing how her doctor and the specialist who gave a second opinion might be wrong about the extent of her illness. I felt it was important to help her face the possibility. To do this, I took the position that we would have to deal with it together.

J: *(Feeling very sad)* If it is true and you only have less than a year, how would you like to spend that time?" (avoiding all normal conventions when she suggested a possible false positive diagnosis for the second time)

C: Well, I don't believe it. I think the docs are overdoing the diagnosis.

J: If that's right, it'll be a real plus, but just for a moment, let's consider your "bucket list."

C: You mean like jump out of a plane or something? I don't really have a bucket list. Oh, I'd like to see my friends and family more. I'd like to have a good time with my husband and . . . you're going to laugh at this, I always wanted to sing in a choir.

J: What would that be like if you prioritized those things and let go of some of the busy work that takes up so much of your time?

C: I guess, what are they going to do to me, right? If I don't get all the work done, they'll just be firing a dead person, ha, ha.

J: Let's talk about what you really want in your time left, whether it's 6 months or a year or who knows?

By holding her feet to the fire in a firm, gentle way, I asked her to focus more on the end of her life than on her denial of the end. When she did that, her face became animated, and she began to look at what the best possible days would be like, regardless of how few there might be.

This is not an easy task. A therapist who asks clients to face their own deaths in his or her presence must deal with his or her own fears and demons as well. By suggesting that she adapt to what the doctors said, instead of encouraging her questioning of the diagnosis, I brought the end-of-life into the session and offered to deal together with the ultimate loss she was facing. Rather than frightening or disturbing the client, it paradoxically led her to a more positive awareness.

This is similar to the results of studies of supportive-expressive groups for patients with metastatic breast cancer, by David Spiegel and his colleagues (2007). The studies of the group therapy, compared to treatment-as-usual control (educational literature) indicated lower levels of stress, neurotic anxiety, and pain for the group patients. The content of the group discussion was on the disease, distress, and mortality. Although follow-up studies indicated that mortality rates for both experimental and support groups were not different, quality-of-life measures favored greatly the women who were in the group treatment.

Value Conflicts

There are other times when a client's behavior or intention opens the doors for the therapist to "say the unsayable." What is a therapist to do with a client's flirting? What about intimidation? What happens when a client's life issues push on the therapist's personal ones?

These are all important ethical questions. What does a therapist do when there is a values conflict between what is appropriate for a therapist and a client? How do therapists, who are striving to enter the client's world view and perspective, maintain their own values and how do they deal with major discrepancies?

In the 1980s, during the AIDS crisis in the Bay Area, a quiet, reserved client in a long-term gay relationship told me that he believed his partner had a brief sexual encounter on a recent business trip. My client had not been tested and was planning a "retaliatory" weekend with potential for new sexual encounters with other men. Rather than share in his anticipatory anxiety about meeting new partners or the value of breaking out of his introverted shell, I decided to focus instead on his potential homicide or suicide. This was more clearly my value system than the one he avowed, but my personal moral compass would not allow me to do otherwise. By expressing my concerns directly, there was potential for a rupture in the relationship and for losing him as a client.

His response was interesting. He responded not to the death threat but to his surprise that I wasn't down on him for cheating, even as retaliation.

J: Is that what you are mostly concerned about?

C: I really love G, and I don't know he cheated for sure, but I feel like I have to do something.

J: I am struck by how scared and angry you are and how you don't seem to have a way of even confirming what you suspect.

C: If I ask him, what does that say to him?

J: That seems daunting but far less so than dealing with harming yourself or others.

C: I knew you'd make me ask him!

J: (Ignoring the fact that I had not done so) What does that idea bring up for you?

Process Is Content in Context

A focus on process is fundamental and needs to be explored in its full personal bio-psycho-social-cultural context. We really do not know what something means to another person without more fully comprehending the setting for his or her life.

Recently in group therapy, a young woman, Lisa, was talking about her desire to leave her parents' home and build a life of her own. In particular, she wanted to pursue a deeper relationship with a man her parents did not know existed and of whom she was certain they would disapprove. As she told the story, she revealed that her parents were refugees from China who lost everything in Mao's "Cultural Revolution." They worked hard and put great pressure on their children to succeed in school and to maintain the culture of their ancestors in a new country, just as they had.

The man with whom she had developed a relationship was not Chinese and was not in a particularly high status profession. She admitted that they had a sexual relationship for 5 years, but that they could never spend the entire night together. When other group members primarily encouraged her to confront her parents, she became very quiet, and although she seemed polite, withdrew her emotion from the room.

T: Lisa. It seems like the dilemma you have at home is replicating itself in this room. (As the client looked expectantly for more information, he continued.) You were brought up by your parents to be in both worlds, Chinese and American, you are the bilingual generation in your home, with one foot in each tradition. And you are truly a success at being bicultural. Now, in the group you are hearing members of the group support the American side of you, and you hear your parents' voice inside yourself supporting the Chinese side.

C: Yes. It's like a trap.

T: Perhaps, more like a Chinese finger puzzle? The more you try to pull out, the more it holds you tight.

C: So are you saying I shouldn't try?

T: The solution to the Chinese finger puzzle trap is to go into the problem. At this moment, I'm aware of the tremendous pressures on you and how you now are in a situation where the two sides are in balance, at least while you keep your friend Mel out of your parents awareness, and you hold him at what might be a safe distance, because you know your parents so well.

C: But I am still stuck.

T: I think the question I'd like you to explore is, how well being stuck works for you, at least right now?

C: I can't go against my parents, because they would cut me off, and I couldn't finish my MBA.

T: So, maybe as expensive and at times limiting, the status quo is . . . At least for now, you have a sexual relationship and peace with your parents. You just need to keep them separate.

C: I don't know if I want to marry him. There are things I like and things I don't.

T: So that explains one of the good reasons to rely on your parents' rules and customs. It's safer, and you don't have to risk a big mistake.

C: Aren't you supposed to support my leaving home and getting on in my life?

T: What if I did?

C: (Smiling, and then a lengthy pause) I'd reject you as an American who didn't understand.

T: One of the things you are very good at is having one foot in each position, whether it's cultural or personal.

The full context aids the client's burgeoning awareness of a constant process tension between the natural push toward freedom and the often unconscious pull of security. The therapy allows her to experience and explore both macro and micro (here-and-now) level tensions.

For Lisa, the status quo is to have two separate parts to her life. If they were integrated, she would have to make a decision that involved significant loss. Any movement in one or the other direction instigates a pull back to center. The fear and shame about disappointing her parents are on one side and the fear of committing to a life with Mel are on the other. As long as she keeps them in balance, she can continue in her life as it is. As she begins to indicate in the group, she will need to face the fear of the unknown and deal with discord with parents or a loss of the relationship. By staying with the status quo over the long term, she will have a somewhat bifurcated life. However, it is important to note that until she completes her graduate studies, she has a strategy that works, albeit with some discomfort.

What the therapist is doing here is presenting her with her relational process. Later in the group, he will gently encourage her to look at her parallel process in the group—as she asks for help in changing something and rejecting the help as too dangerous, she is unconsciously replicating in the group her inner experience, and by having an unresolvable dilemma, she is effectively avoiding a fuller intimate connection with other members.

The beauty of this process is that it occurred in the group, a setting in which she was able to explore and experiment with both sides of her life, without a major personal risk. Lisa was able to become aware that by being unable to commit to any one person or direction, she was effective at avoiding facing intimacy with her parents, with Mel, with the group members, and with the group coleaders. The emergent questions for her were the extent to which the emotional safety was worth the emotional cost and when and how she could experiment with her dilemma without taking extraordinary risks.

At the end of this exploration, the therapist strongly recommended that she become more aware of this ongoing process in her life and that she avoid making any precipitous decisions, because the method was working. He concluded, "perhaps we can explore in the group any alternative methods that would keep you safe but with less strain, stress, or emotional cost."

Freedom and Security

Both freedom and security needs are basic to human beings. As we develop, each stage is punctuated by periods of going out into the world to assimilate new experiences and periods of making those new understandings part of ourselves by accommodating to them (i.e., Flavell, 1968; Piaget, 1967).

If we were to place the freedom and security needs at opposite ends of a continuum, it is readily apparent that as one gets too far in the direction of either polarity, the other begins to exert a greater pull. Indeed, too much freedom is often experienced as a fear of abandonment, and too much security as fear of suffocation or stagnation.

Existential therapists hold up these contrasting needs and their accompanying dangers to a client. It is often the case that the goal of therapy is to push the freedom—fear of the unknown—envelope but not at the expense of fully losing the equivalent need for security. Sometimes, the therapist is the one who is holding the security, while the client explores the freedom. More often, the therapist is present to hold both sides of the dilemma.

Clients like Lisa, the woman caught between two worlds, become particularly frozen by ambivalence. When they push too hard toward one side of the tension, the opposing force pulls back vigorously, leading to immobility.

At 58 years old, Robert was a manager in a successful company. He was approached by a former coworker to partner in a new business. The opportunity had considerable upside potential and was in an industry that Robert always wanted to try.

After talking to every possible consultant, including a therapist, he remained stuck. One week he'd be sure that he was going to jump to the new opportunity. The next he was finding himself fearful of the risk and drawn to the security of his current job, but then he felt trapped and worried about missing out on his "dream." Each time he got close to deciding one way, the other need, freedom or security, pulled him back into the middle.

His other advisors were adept at clarifying his financial risk and opportunity, the number of work hours it would take either way and other practical considerations but not the conflicting psychological needs. His wife was particularly supportive, telling him she would be on board whatever he chose.

The impasse was going to come to denouement because of a critical deadline, and he was still caught going "from pillar to post." Robert admitted that he would be relieved if someone or something made the decision for him, "like if I got fired."

Once he explored the two contrasting needs and anxieties directly in therapy and acknowledged that he had to make an active choice, he was able to set his future path. The therapist's supporting both needs and acknowledging that anxiety in both directions was legitimate finally gave him the space to make a decision that was anxiety provoking but for all the right reasons.

Existential Anxiety; Neurotic Anxiety

Robert's dilemma brings up another significant aspect of existential therapy—the acceptance of anxiety as a core component of therapy and of life. For this form of therapy, anxiety is seen as the engine for change and is welcomed as part of the therapy.

Existential Anxiety

There is an important distinction between existential anxiety, sometimes called "death anxiety" (Yalom, 1980) or the disquiet that comes from a sense of life as meaningless and limited (Kierkegaard, 1980) and neurotic anxiety. The former is a normal, healthy component of life related to awareness of life's true limits. May (1983) argued that approaching and becoming increasingly aware of one's limits, ultimately death, was the *sine qua non* of growth, freedom, and responsibility.

To existential therapists, it is healthier to face the big questions and to experience angst, than to deny mortality and become stagnant, hopeless, and despondent (Spiegel et al., 2007).

In the experimental psychology literature, the terms *anxiety* and *arousal* (such as system arousal) are used almost synonymously. Results of experiments on the relationship of performance and arousal all follow an inverted U-shaped curve. When arousal is at the lowest or highest ends of the x-axis, performance is poor. When arousal is at the mid points, performance increases. So it is with anxiety in life and therapy.

This is presented in graphic form here. The curve represents a summary of hundreds of studies of learning involving the relationship of anxiety to performance. Note the alternative term *arousal* for anxiety. This is quite concordant with existential notions of anxiety as the engine of growth, rather than something to minimize or eliminate.

Most athletes can describe the way they "psych themselves up" prior to a contest. For most, this means increasing the anxiety to the middle of the performance curve—basically psyching oneself up is equivalent to scaring oneself to a point. Of course this can go both ways. I recall many a pregame bus trip where some of the team members were hopping around, increasing anxiety (arousal), and others were yawning or napping. This latter group

Figure 3.1 The Relationship of Anxiety and Performance

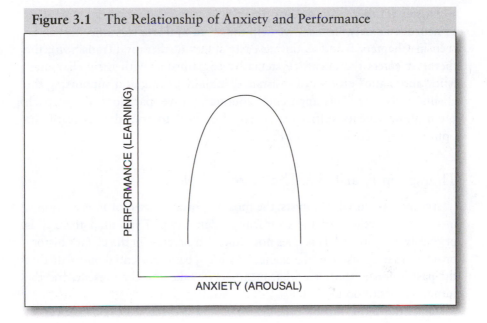

was modulating already too high anxiety to bring it into the optimal range. In managing their anxiety, they were all maximizing chances for a better performance.

Another example of this is the pre-performance theatrical paradoxical injunction "break a leg!" This is not a wish for a trip to the emergency room. It is a way of getting hold of the preperformance jitters and to use effectively the anxiety about failing in an embarrassingly public forum. Therapists often help their clients experience their real anxiety and to use it effectively.

Neurotic Anxiety

In contrast to existential anxiety is another form of anxiety that is deleterious to successful living. Neurotic anxiety arises in defending unconsciously against existential anxiety. Husserl (2008) described this unconscious avoidance as "automatic response," a phenomenon other psychotherapists characteristically refer to as "resistance," "defences," or "symptoms" and that reflects a pressure to return to the status quo.

One major goal of therapy is help clients become more aware in the here-and-now, of their automatic reactions and the underlying pull of security, consistency, and predictability of the status quo. Once aware of their automatic defenses, clients may choose to continue the avoidance consciously or to opt for the freedom to explore, experiment with, and challenge their existential fears of the unknown, which their automatic responses obfuscate.

Existential therapists do not directly treat the symptomatic expression of neurotic anxiety. Instead, we help the client evaluate its value. As will be seen in Chapters 5 and 7, during early stages of therapy (Transition), the therapist enters the clients' systems by empathizing with their characteristic "automatic" process of resistance, initially joining and supporting the clients' resistance. This apparently counterintuitive, paradoxical approach often allows clients sufficient security for them to consider more of the options at the freedom end of the equation.

Therapy in Real Time: The Here and Now

Among existential therapists, the most important focus for intervention is in the shared reality of the counseling relationship. Existential therapy is primarily ahistorical.[1] This does not indicate disinterest in the client's history or what occurs outside in the client's life. It is a basic existential postulate that the past is gone, except for what meaning we take into the present, and the future has yet to occur.

Thus, the most salient time frame is the present. Past experiences of Buber's *I-thou* moments may make current intimacy more available, and future intentionality (i.e., May, 1969) may deeply impact how we function in the present, but the actual moment-by-moment experience of connection and aliveness all occur in real time, in a flow of moments in the here and now.

The successful existential therapist needs to be intensely aware of what is happening in the room between self and client. To best understand and intuit the client's intrapsychic and interpersonal functioning, most existential therapists are aware both of focused attentiveness on the client and their own internal processing during sessions. In addition, great use is made of identification of and awareness of parallel process, in which the client enacts with the therapist the same dynamic as what occurs in outside life.

Work that focuses on the immediate interaction and relationship between therapist and client is the most poignant and the most impactful. Awareness in real time allows the client to choose directions with an appreciation for consequences. When the awareness occurs within an intimate therapeutic relationship moment, the effect may be profound and may be subsequently transferable to the client's back home life.

Attribution of Meaning

In Frankl's (1959a) formulation, the most salient aspect of existential work is to help clients better understand their personal encoding processes and the ways in which they give meaning to life experience. It is a significant yet essential challenge to help people experience themselves as subjects rather than as objects. In *Man's Search for Meaning*, Frankl (1959) famously wrote,

> *Between stimulus and response there is a space. In that space is our power to choose our response. In our response lies our growth and our freedom.*

At 35 years old, Marcus was just embarking on a new career. Although he had some trepidation, he had decided that he would "make something of myself, out of the game." A professional football player, he became aware at age 29 that younger and faster athletes were surpassing him. He came into therapy while he was recuperating from an injury. "When I blew out my ACL for the second time, I knew it was just a matter of time before I was no longer among the employed."

He was referred for treatment with the intent of finding another job, probably as an assistant coach at the college level. He talked a lot about his love for the game and how he really didn't know anything else. "I was one of those Phys. Ed. guys at the U. to get grades that kept me on the field until I went pro. So I got the degree but not the education." He was devoted to his family, especially to the memory of his late grandmother, who was his primary caretaker during his early years. When he was asked what she would say to him now, he laughed and said, "She always said the same thing: 'When one door closes, another opens.'"

T: What does that mean to you now?

C: I ain't gonna be playing football no more, so that door is closed, unless I get a job coaching or something in the game.

T: You seem unenthusiastic about that door. Is there another one?

C: (Bashfully) I'd like to do what you do, only mostly for athletes. Counseling, but also to help them with managing money, because you never know when it'll stop suddenly.

T: There was a lot of energy when you said that.

C: I'd like to be like my grandma, who was always helping out me and everyone else.

T: So your new open door would be to become a counselor.

C: Can you tell me if I could get into a school with my grades?

T: As you wonder about that, what is happening inside?

C: Worries. I don't know if that's a challenge I can win. School and grades are not exactly my strong suit.

T: Tell me about the worries (anxiety), and then we can discuss options.

Marcus was faced with following an old (status quo) script for former players in football; one became a coach once the playing days were over. His dilemma was that something inside was yearning for a new challenge. Ultimately, after a year of remedial work and facing his anxiety of academic failure, he was accepted into a good graduate counseling program and later relished his new career as a counselor/life coach—specializing on work with athletes.

A slammed door like a terminal diagnosis, a divorce, or a blown-out knee isn't the only way that people are pushed to find new meaning. Robert, the business man with the new option, had to choose between two positive options and how he would see himself after a decision.

Any major transition may generate questions about life. Often, clients report confusion around their sense that they are doing everything right but feeling unhappy or empty.

At 45 years old, Carla said that she had "had the dream life . . . I got into a good college, started my career, which has gone well, married a great guy, have two kids that I adore, and I love being a mom. So why aren't I feeling fulfilled? I know who I am as a division chief, as a wife, as a mom, and it used to be wonderful. . . . Now, not so much! A lot of my friends are having a midlife crisis and doing all sorts of things. One is having a new romantic affair. Another left her job and took up painting. This guy I know is always joking that he and I could hook up and run away. I never take him seriously, and I wouldn't cheat on my hubby, but when he talks, I do get some stirrings about a more exciting life."

T: You're asking yourself, now that I'm all grown up, who am I?

C: Sort of. I know I love my family, and my job is stressful but on the plus side.

T: What does it mean to you to have "the perfect life" and still feel like there's something missing?

C: Selfish and guilty.

       In most forms of therapy, that would be a great opening for a therapist to probe either her history or behavior change possibilities. In existential work, however, it may be more important to explore the moment and the meaning she is giving to her life.

T: What if you have been blessed and lucky and are selfish?

C: Yuck!

T: Tell me what it means to you to see yourself as selfish.

C: Like I said, I feel guilty. There are a lot of people who have a lot less than I do.

T: . . . and?

C: I should be happy with what I have.

T: I am blessed with a good career, a great family, a loving husband. If I am not happy with that, maybe I am not satisfiable.

C: (Sarcastically) You been reading my journal? I just should be happy.

T: What does it mean to you that you have so much and it's not enough?

C: My life is just too predictable . . . not creative.

T: One solution to finding your creativity would be to blow up your life like the friend who is having an affair, another would be to recalibrate what in your life brings you meaning and find some ways of expanding that.

C: I want to take a vacation just the two of us, without the kids, but whenever I bring it up, my husband opts for a family vacation. It's been 12 years since we had a week alone together.

T: A second honeymoon?

C: Exactly. He just doesn't get that we are a couple, too. The past several months he is calling me "mom"— not just to the kids.

This evolved into a discussion of how she could tell her husband what it would mean to her emotionally and personally to have a romantic week with him alone, rather than trying to convince him with logic, expressing needs to get him to want what she wanted. The therapist left her with homework for the week to talk to him using the words, *I want*.

C: What good will *that* do?

T: I can't predict the impact on him, but I think it will be interesting to see what it's like for you to state what you want directly.

C: You think I don't ask him directly, then sulk when he doesn't know what to do.

T: That's an interesting idea. It's almost like what's happening here. I recommended that you say what you want and you are questioning my motives and thoughts, rather than agreeing or disagreeing. How do you understand that?

C: Okay. I'll try it, but don't count on him listening.

The desired vacation was less important than her awareness of her pattern of behaving in ways that continue the status quo, rather than risking something unknown. For Carla, the pull of the familiar was particularly tempting because she had filled in all the usual squares for an anticipated "happy-ever-after." The current life transition (mini-crisis) ensued when her current reality failed to match that expectation. The therapist's intervention about her "selfishness" was both disquieting to her and generated the question of what was desirable to her at this point in time.

It is no surprise that prior life adaptations were no longer successful at this life transition. As we age and adjust to life circumstances, novel approaches to finding meaning must emerge.

Carla did not get what she wanted immediately. Rather than risk facing new fears when she went home, she unconsciously opted for the status quo by telling her husband that he was insufficiently romantic. That prompted a familiar mutual-blaming fight. She began the next session,

C: Well. You were wrong. I told him what was wrong, and now we are fighting.

T: *(Very aware that this was the opposite of the homework: She is making me wrong like she does her husband.)* What's that like to be unable to get your husband to do what you want and also to find my advice lacking? That's two people who are not providing for you.

C: Well, I don't blame you. It probably was good advice. It just failed.

T: Well, it did fail in getting the second honeymoon going . . . although it succeeded in keeping things the same.

C: What do you mean?

T: You said that all the appearances in your life were working well and in an attempt to do something new, you ended up back where you started. What's that like for you?

C: . . . it sounds like a defeat.

T: It's only a defeat if you want to risk doing something new. If you wanted to stay safe and secure, it worked pretty well.

C: Are you saying I sabotaged the conversation with my husband?

T: No. I am saying you had a conversation and the result was a very familiar one.

C: So what should I have done (in an annoyed tone)?

T: What would you most like in here right now?

C: I want my husband to come up with the idea. It won't count as much if I tell him.

T: That's a real dilemma. You can get what you want if you ask him, but then it doesn't count, or you can wait for him to read your mind, which I suspect he is poor at doing.

C: Yeah. I want to control my own surprise party. (Laughing)

T: The perfect way to get the appearance of the party right and remove the excitement.

C: So you are saying I should just tell him what I want, let the chips fall, and see what happens.

T: That would be scarier.

Carla began the second session by recreating in the therapist-client relationship a parallel with the one at home with her husband. He is wrong at home, and the therapist is wrong in the office. If this conversation occurred in a balanced, mutual relationship, he too might have taken umbrage. Because of the nature of the therapeutic contract (an asocial relationship), he contains his personal protective emotional reaction and instead of expressing it directly, he uses it to understand how she managed to avoid engaging in a more anxious conversation with her husband.

Parallel Process: *Déjà Vu* All Over Again

When mentors supervise beginning or advanced therapists, it is common for the process that the supervisee is describing to be duplicated during the supervision. This is usually referred to as parallel process. While describing a particularly difficult and resistant client the supervisee hands off the problem to the supervisor in the interaction.

B: I have this kid at Juvie who just does not want any part of the counseling.

S(upervisor): Do you have a recording or notes of the last meeting?

B: It wouldn't matter. Nothing is happening!

S: Well, what have you tried without success so far?

B: Basically everything. Nothing reaches this kid. He just doesn't want to be there and won't talk about what's troubling him.

S: (*Very aware of the help-rejecting pattern replicating in supervision.*) How did you get assigned to such a person who doesn't want help?

B: He requested a male counselor and one who spoke Spanish.

S: So you qualify, but he's unwilling to connect in two languages.

B: Yeah. Well. No. I mean I don't know. We have only spoken English.

S: If you were to describe your frustration in here in Spanish, what would it sound like?

B: *Habla Espanol?*

S: No. But go for it anyhow. You can translate anything important for me afterward.

B: (In Spanish: there was a torrent of words, mostly angry and coming out in a rush.)

S: Even though I didn't understand the words, I sure got the anger and frustration.

B: Well, what can I learn from clients like this kid?

S: Seems like you really empathize with his anger and frustration.

B. was able to express verbally in Spanish in supervision what his client was sharing in their abortive sessions. The supervisor used the replication to help B. discover what was happening in his counseling sessions. Later the supervisor helped him understand that his anger and frustration in supervision was a perfect model and method for understanding his client in sessions.

By dealing with it at a process level in supervision, they could make adjustments without experimenting on the client, who sounded already pretty fragile. She also offered the trainee a window on a way to experience his client by focusing inward.

Another more direct use of the parallel process would have been to ask B. to be his client and the supervisor to be the therapist or vice versa.

Parallel process is not the same as the psychodynamic construct of transference. It is similar in the way the same feelings and events get projected into the therapy or supervision session. The differences occur in how it is identified and approached. If we construct it as the client's trying to resolve the problem by reissuing it in a new situation, then our responses will not be to interpret the projection but to use it in the real relationship. A resolution in the here-and-now relationship may then be able to be applied in some related form to the original issue.

The use of parallel process is essentially an exploration of the metacommunication that occurs in all interactions but especially in meaningful, more intimate ones. Therapy is a rare opportunity to address some of the nuances of the communication process. An implicit aspect of in-depth therapy is that the therapist has the right to comment on what is happening in the room and to describe the implication of clients' behaviors and words.

The Goals of Existential Counseling or Psychotherapy?

Bugental (1987) describes this type of therapy as "life-changing," but what does that mean? Isn't eliminating a phobia or alleviating any symptom potentially life-changing? In a sense, every challenge in life, whether one surmounts it or is negatively impacted, can change the course of life. Ella's divorce was life-changing in some ways, but the manner in which it impacts her will be what she does subsequently. What meaning will she give to the event? How will she adjust? In what ways will it impact her future in or out of primary relationships?

The Method Is the Goal

The kind of therapy presented here is designed to create and nurture a process of change in the manner of relating to self and others. Existential therapy often does result in symptom changes, but that is secondary to a client developing a process in which he or she may address his or her life challenges by the acceptance of his or her reality and the courage to face fears of the unknown.

In existential therapy, the goal of the therapy mirrors the nature of the therapeutic interaction. This is quite different from, say, psychopharmacology or behavior therapies. The action of pill taking or learning new habits may have a host of specific results, but the end goal is to stop.

Many forms of treatment consider the therapeutic relationship a precondition for change. In existential work, the intimate *I-thou* relating, search for meaning in life and facing life's demons with courage is precisely the preferred process to transfer into everyday life.

Note

1. There were several moments in the case study of the first session with Ella that I considered the importance (and seductiveness) of her history, before refocusing on the present.

4

Existential Counseling and Psychotherapy

Strategies, Qualities, and Methods

You gain strength, courage and confidence by every experience in which you really stop to look fear in the face.

You must do the thing you think you cannot do.

Eleanor Roosevelt

Techniques in therapy are usually defined as specific procedures in which the therapist guides, directs, or helps the client reduce symptom occurrence or severity, alter habits, change thinking patterns or affective reactivity, or to gain insight into the origins of particular concerns. By contrast, existential therapy is guided by a long-term strategy in which meaning attributions are explored in the context of a unique interpersonal relationship.

The therapist is far less of string puller than a wise and trusted companion, collaborative senior teammate, experienced psychological guide, and philosophically informed witness to clients' increasing understanding of their personal manner of adapting to anxiety and search for meaning in life. Existential therapy occurs within a unique relationship in which both therapist and client are engaged in a quest for awareness of the vagaries of a specific human life; to explore "concerns that are rooted in the individual's existence" (Yalom, 1980, p. 5).

Anxiety: The Engine of Change

"Existential psychotherapists take the experience of anxiety to be a fundamental 'given' of being-in-the-world" (Spinelli, 2007, p. 317). Existential anxiety arises when facing the unknowns in life and is best appreciated by the therapist as a healthy accoutrement of the pursuit of life's meaning.

However, there is a contrasting anxiety that pulls individuals back toward the familiar, the secure, and the status quo. When clients avoid or defend against facing their fears of the unknown, with symptoms, resistance, or denial, they are responding not to the healthy existential anxiety but to its obverse: neurotic anxiety.

Neurotic anxiety is defined, in this framework, as thoughts, behaviors, or emotions that keep individuals in the status quo instead of facing those fears associated with freedom. Neurotic anxiety operates more automatically or unconsciously to preempt making choices. Facing healthy existential anxiety may involve choosing a re-adjustment in the balance of freedom and security-seeking to feel more comfortable and effective in life.

There is no direct attempt to treat or diminish these neurotic symptoms in existential work. Instead, the therapist and client explore together the relative success of the behaviors in maintaining security. Those consequences are then explored vis-à-vis the costs in limiting the client's experience. If a client defends successfully against the natural anxieties and the givens of existence, he or she may feel safe but also may be living in a world that emulates an emotional solitary confinement. The therapy strategy is to hold both sides of the tension up to the client and allow him or her to explore options in balancing needs for security and freedom.

C: I want to phone this woman I just met, but I am worried that she'll just reject me.

T: Your fantasy is that she'll say no, won't remember you, decline when she sees your caller ID?

C: All of the above.

T: So what if any of those happened?

C: Then it'd be over and no chance for recovery.

T: So it's risky.

C: Yeah. I want to ask her, but I want a guarantee, too.

T: (Holding up both sides) This is not an easy decision. If you ask and she rejects, you are alone and probably hurting. If you don't ask, you are alone and maybe feeling guilty. (*And if you ask and she accepts, then you need to face that dilemma—best to address later.*)

C: So what do I do?

T: (Summarizing consequences) Well, one thing is clear. By avoiding asking her so far, you have successfully protected yourself from possible hurt, and you have been safe with things-as-usual. You may not like the way they are, but at least it's a familiar discomfort.

Note that in this short vignette, the focus is not on causes but on consequences. This is an important aspect of the method. Questions involve exploring what is occurring, how the client is responding, and examining his choices and the outcomes of those choices.

Ahistorical Focus

One unique aspect of existential therapy as an intrapsychic approach is that it is ahistorical. Rather than explore the rationale or reasons for a particular symptom or client upset, the data for sessions is the present, and by inference, the future. In this formulation, implying or discerning motivation is far less basic than exploring consequences. The end result of behavior and the cost of maintaining or changing are more primary foci.

Existential therapists are much more interested in descriptions of *how* things are working, rather than *what* caused them. The therapist's response to Carla in the previous chapter was not about self-defeat, (although she could easily be viewed as an adept saboteur in her marital relationship). Instead, the therapist focused on the outcome and benefits of her behavior (security). While exploring consequences, therapist and client are together examining both what is occurring and what is positive about the behavior, thoughts, or emotions. By focusing on the client's strengths at achieving some goal, even if it is discrepant from what she claims she desires, the inference conveyed is that she has a choice.

Based on popular conceptions of what psychotherapy is and does, many clients come to therapy with a belief that an intrapsychic archeological dig into long lost memories or unconscious experiences will yield some truth about the genesis of particular symptoms or reasons for debilitating habits. There is certainly some potential value in this kind of inquiry and exploration. However, existential approaches eschew such detective work in favor of the present phenomena and their meaning. This is not to suggest that history is unimportant, but that it has less to yield than in other orientations.

For existential therapists, dreams, memories, slips-of-the tongue, and childhood experiences are salient primarily in how they play out in the present. We accept memory as useful, primarily in how it provides a template for personal attribution of meaning.

Memory as Creative

It has been demonstrated in many experiments that memory is far more an act of creation than is popularly believed. All memory is necessarily selective and often conforms more to the current ego state than to the one when the memory was originally laid down (Buchanan, 2007; Scheflin & Shapiro, 1989). Indeed, accuracy of memory is affected seriously by the recall process, the context in which it was created, and manner of retrieval.

In existential therapy, the objective verifiability of particular recall of past events by a client is by far secondary to what it means to the person today. A client's memory of even traumatic events is worthy of consideration, but how it is impacting the interaction between client and therapist or between clients and their significant others is essential. Thus, interventions often drift away from "What do you remember?" to "What's happening now as you recall this?"

Memory and the Here-and-Now

Louis (40 years old) reported that he came into therapy at the insistence of his wife because of his inability to have any emotions or tell her what was happening inside. Early on, we established that he did in fact experience a host of emotions, but that he seldom if ever put words to them (alexithymia). However, in sessions he was able to describe his anger and irritation, as well as tender, loving feelings for his wife and their three children.

After 2 months of therapy, he began to tear up about a news item about a child being molested by a clergyman. The session went slowly with long pauses between client and therapist speaking.

J: That seems to be hitting you very hard.

L: (After a delay) I don't know why this one is so rough ... maybe, because I was an altar boy at the same church, when I was a kid.

J:　(Matching delay) So it hits close to home. What images does it conjure up for you?

L:　(Weeping and speaking in almost inaudible voice) I never told anyone about it. I really can't talk about it.

J:　(*Assuming he was molested as a child*) It seems so painful even now. Almost like you feel deeply for what the little girl in the news is going through.

L:　I was molest . . . (weeping again), you know as a boy by a neighbor when I was around seven or eight. I never told anyone, except in confession. The priest told me it wasn't my fault, gave me absolution, and told me not to talk about the neighbor to anyone. He was doing his best, but it was like it was my sin.

J:　(Also teary) That sounds dreadful even now (bringing back the present).

L:　I think it might be the reason why I can't, you know, tell my wife about my past or why I am sometimes not very intimate with her.

J:　(Refocusing on the here-and-now) Tell me what it's like to be telling me.

L:　It's okay! You can't tell anyone, right?

J:　So it feels okay to tell me, but then you jump to worrying that I might let someone else know. How do you understand that worry?

L:　I'm so ashamed.

J:　(*It will be important to do something later to address his lack of fault in being victimized, but it's important to hold this moment between us.*) Tell me about the feelings of shame.

L:　I wanted to tell my dad, but I worried that he might kill the guy and go to prison. They are both gone now. The guy who did it was stabbed by his wife, and my dad passed away a few years ago.

J:　I am aware that you may not have told your dad, but you are telling me.

L:　Yeah. I am worried about something happening to my kids.

J:　That is very scary. What can we do to help them avoid an awful experience like that?

L:　I have to warn them, but I don't want to go into details.

The present-moment focus and use of parallel process (replication of the outside dilemma with the one developing in session) allows therapist and client to work on the issue within the immediate, frequently changing, client-therapist relationship. There was no chance for the client to undo his feelings of past shame. However, in the present, a similar process between therapist and client could be faced and worked through.

The therapist here brought the reporting into the present relationship. When experiences are shared as they occur in the here-and-now, opportunities for clearer comprehension of issues, the impact of consequences, and ability to effect changes are enhanced.

Turning Report Into Reality

By bringing the here-and-now into primary focus, the therapist can experience the client in real time without the distance and filters of her or his report on events. When it occurs within the therapist-client relationship, the material is less biased by the client's memory, personal receptivity, level of embarrassment, or capacity to relate events clearly. It also allows the therapist to experience more fully what the client is discussing or describing. This effect is magnified in group therapy, in which multiple reflections are available in real time.

For example, there may be a considerable difference between a client's description that he is confused by others' apparent avoidance of him and the experience of his intimidating presence in the session. Craig is in his late twenties and has had a series of short relationships and jobs.

C: It happened again this weekend. My friend and I went out to this brewery, and we met some girls, and it was going well, and then both of them were paying attention to my friend and pretty much ignoring me.

T: *(Recognizing her personal discomfort at the word "girls" to describe women in their twenties)* How do you understand that?

C: (Raising voice) I don't know. I just don't take what they say and flatter them. I will tell them if something is amiss. You know, he just listens to them, but if they ask a dumb question, he just goes along. I ask a clarifying question back.

T: Say more about your understanding of how you end up on the outside.

C: There isn't much more to say. I think I've been quite clear. I am surprised that you don't get the picture.

T: (Feeling a sense of intimidation and pressure) Maybe it seems to you that even in here you are not fully understood.

C: I think a guy would understand.

T: *(Feeling both irritated and pushed away)* Let's try something here. How might it look if I did understand like a guy would. What would we be saying to each other? I'm not a guy, so what would I need to understand?

C: (Lowering intensity) I know. I just don't know how to talk to girls. My jokes don't go anywhere, and I don't chit-chat well. I am better about serious conversations.

T: Good. Let's not chit-chat. Seriously, what would you like right now?

The description of last weekend's events was clear, but the way in which his anxiety manifests itself to push others away was far more evident when enacted in the consulting room. When that occurs in real time, it can be dealt with far more effectively.

The therapist here did not directly confront his intimidating and demeaning relating. Instead, she recognized her personal disquiet and then used that knowledge to bring his behavior and attitude more into the moment as a joint effort.

Asocial Interventions

All therapeutic approaches make use of asocial responses. To some extent, this is what underscores the therapeutic ambiance as unique (Young & Beier, 1998).

In any phenomenological approach to therapy, there is an assiduous and consistent use of asocial responses by the therapist. Therapist interactions are designed to break the expected social norms for conversation. The deliberate use of asocial responses alters the form as well as the content of interaction by removing predictability. When he or she responds in an asocial manner, the therapist creates a new context in which the client can be more conscious and creative in the relationship.

Even something as apparently innocuous as a client's asking, "How was your weekend?" may be treated sometimes as an important component of the therapy. Stephen, in his mid-30s, is a salesperson.

C: Hey Doc. Good to see you. How was the weekend?

The normative social reaction is well-known: "Fine. How was yours?" But what if Stephen's use of the social norms was also his characteristic manner of avoiding, rather than making, connection? In that case, the therapist might forego the social norms and query (in a very asocial manner).

T: You are interested in how my weekend was.

C: Yeah. Just saying hey! Mine was great!

T: And where are you now?

C: Okay, I guess.

T: There seems a drop-off from the weekend to here. What's happening for you now?

Although the example seems a little strained, it is important to note that by responding asocially, the therapist is able to shift to a more meaningful, here-and-now interaction rather than a less genuine wondering about her weekend. When she got beyond the socially automatic reaction, by responding in an unexpected manner, there was far more reason for Stephen to attend and to react more authentically.

In any normal social environment, there are normative responses to someone expressing anger, for example. We might avoid the person entirely, try to calm him or her down with reason, or let the person know in other ways that his or her reactions are inappropriate for a given situation.

How different that is in a therapy session. In the face of a person nonverbally expressing anger by gesticulating wildly or taking with a loud voice, a therapist might respond with empathy, "you're feeling angry!" Instead of the distance that anger usually produces, it opens an opportunity for connection.

Beier and Young (1984) wrote, "Therapeutic intervention provides the patient with a new experience which does not follow the old silent rules (that guide interactions in social contexts)" (p. 8). When silent rules are not followed, it opens up the interaction to new creative experiences. When that can occur in a safe, supportive, respectful, nonthreatening setting, the uncertainty encourages clients to engage less automatically and more thoughtfully. Disengagement from normal discourse with a focus on the client's subjective world in the here-and-now enhances the client's sense that the interactions need greater attention and are more important.

When the developing relationship is atypical and requires greater attending, it is often more absorbing for the client. That sense of engrossment or intense engagement makes the endeavor seem far more real and significant. Indeed, even a simple question about the prior weekend can become an opportunity for growth and more authentic communication.

Working From Within

The intimate connection between the client and therapist allows for increased empathy for the client's experience at both content and process levels. Existential work begins with a deep, hopefully nuanced understanding of the client's subjective experience in his or her world. This involves sensitivity to client values, beliefs, feelings, behaviors, and manners of coping as well as the multiple contexts in which the client lives.

When the therapist moves from an opposite to a shoulder-to-shoulder orientation, he or she opens opportunities to experience the client's world as the client experiences it. From this vantage point, accurate empathy, therapeutic attunement, and an enhanced therapeutic alliance are more likely. In addition, when the therapist approaches from the same perspective as the client, he or she will be more quickly aware of any ruptures in the therapeutic alliance and will be better suited to correct them. This kind of empathy enhances intimacy and makes the pathway to *I-thou* moments more likely. In existential work, much of the time in therapy is spent in recalibrating this moving access to the client's inner workings and search for meaning.

The importance of being on the same side as the client may be especially important when the therapy is not completely voluntary.

Jan was not an easy client. A fifth-grade teacher, she was referred to therapy after a few explosive arguments at work with another teacher and some parents. On the initial phone interview, she stated, "It's either therapy or being put on administrative leave."

C: So what do you have to teach me? I know, calm down and stop saying provocative things to parents even though they really deserve it.

T: Let's take a step or two back here. I can't recommend that you calm down or stop anything until I know what you want.

C: I like the teaching and most of the kids and want to be left alone from these helicopter parents, who think they know how to teach. They should actually try being in a classroom with 11- and 12-year-olds.

T: It is very disturbing to be told how to do your job, especially by someone who doesn't know what the job really is.

C: Yeah. That's right!

T: Is this something new? What seems to be happening now?

C: It is very new. I am not accustomed to be criticized for my teaching . . . (long pause) well, I guess I should have been better prepared for this group of parents. They destroyed the fourth-grade teacher last year, and the third-grade teacher from 2 years ago transferred out of district.

T: There's a lot of evidence that these parents are a real problem, but am I correct in hearing that you are frustrated partially because you could have been better ready for them.

C: Yeah. But I don't know what I could have done differently. They are relentless in trying to get the school to change for their little darlings.

T: So are the kids a problem also, or is it only the parents that you'd like to be sent to the alternative school?

C: (Laughing) Or Juvie Hall!

T: (Laughing also and joining with her) We probably can't transfer them into "juvie." Maybe we could figure out some way of better protecting you from their acting out.

C: I like that. Yes. They are just like acting-out children.

T: So how have you dealt with smart-assed, oppositional kids? That may give us some clues.

C: Well, I can't send parents to detention or the vice principal.

T: That won't work. I'm more interested in how you could be better protected from their intrusions and disruptions of your classroom.

The therapist turned Jan's disinterest and frustration into an exploration of self-care in a difficult situation. She kept bringing the discussion to what the two of them might do together and never questioned Jan's subjective reality. She also upped the ante a bit when she described the helicopter parents as "smart-assed" and "oppositional."

Facing the quandary is far easier when a supportive, encouraging, confident, experienced companion is along. When the therapist here tried to serve as that trusted partner and consultant, Jan could face her very real dilemma, explore her automatic blocks to addressing them directly, and find more creative solutions through enhanced awareness of her personal wants and needs.

Any client may initially block this form of an enhanced connection and intimacy when his or her internal anxiety spikes and he or she is pulled back to the safer, (albeit unpleasant) status quo. At that point, the therapist continues in the attempt to stay within the client's process by being empathic with both the misery of his or her situation and his or her current inability to escape in a viable manner. Once there, the therapist can redirect the client to explore the meaning of the current impasse.

In *My Voice Will Travel With You: The Teaching Tales of Milton H. Erickson*, Rosen (1982) described Erickson's method of connecting so closely with the client's unconscious mind that altered states of consciousness could be elicited. So it is with existential work. The client is seen as having an inherent capacity for attribution of meaning and for choosing how to deal with life events. *Existential therapy is designed primarily to work with the clients from within to help them identify their blocks to the goal and to find their personal paths of a more meaningful life.*

It is essential to understand that the therapist's challenge is to help the client find his or her path from within his or her worldview and current way of being. The method begins with acceptance of the client and the client's manner of doing things. It begins with the client's current state of being, not where either the client or therapist hopes he or she will be. Once thus attuned to the client, the therapist can be there in his or her system and focus on those personal defenses, limiting beliefs, and behaviors that pull clients in the opposite direction of their stated goals. The therapist may clarify, from the client's perspective, his or her intrinsic values, beliefs, myths, and emotions that provide meaning.

Specific methods for determining a client's stylistic manner of psychological self-protection are detailed in the next chapter.

The Benefits of a Positive Psychology

As focused as it is on life's distressing givens, existential therapy may also be viewed as being nested within the rubric of positive psychotherapies. Rather than illuminate the deficits of human nature or of a client's pathology, existential methods orient primarily around a client's strengths and ego functioning. The goal of this treatment is to identify, activate, and most significantly, join the unique worldviews and strengths of individuals and to help them bring those strengths to bear on the aspects of life that keep them stuck in a mode that is overly restrictive or emotionally costly.

It is important to distinguish between those goals of positive psychology identified by Seligman (2002) that lead to authentic happiness and those which emerge from simplistic notions like the power of positive thinking. A modest change in orientation, motivation, or attitude is quite unlikely to alter essential existential anxieties of living.[1] As Schimmack (2008) indicated, direct efforts to increase positive emotions do not necessarily decrease negative emotions. Quite the opposite in fact; direct attempts to increase positive emotions often not only have a very short shelf life but also may actually result in an increase in negative feelings.

By contrast, joining with the client and working as a team increases the likelihood the client will make the internal shifts to create meaning in life and thereby approach what Maslow (1968) famously called "self-actualization." This existential notion of "life-changing" therapy (Bugental, 1987) reflects the philosophy of the ancient Greeks, such as Socrates and Plato, whose notion was that happiness emerged from self-knowledge and finding deeper meaning.

Seligman and Csikszentmihalyi (2000) identified positive human functioning as an interaction between bio-psycho-social orientations in life. One major implication of positive psychology is a primary emphasis on the present with potential to instill hope for the future through facing fears and finding meaning (cf. Shapiro, 2012). Because memory tends to conform to the current ego state (Scheflin & Shapiro, 1989), exploration of past causes is considered less useful than awareness of the current moment and the immediate relationship. In general, the discrepancy between expectations and experienced reality supersedes in importance the content of specific memories.[2] Present implications and consequences of events as remembered are considered more significant than the actual occurrence.

At 55 years old, Sid has been unemployed for 3 years. He is discouraged and close to despairing that "anyone will ever hire someone my age." A former manager in a food service business, he sees younger people getting jobs for which he applied. The therapist is in her late 60s.

C: I think I am out of touch and probably over the hill. When I apply for jobs, they are always asking for computer skills.

T: What's that like to be over-the-hill?

C: I think I just blew it when I took the package from (my last company). Now I can't get back in. I just thought that the deal would go away, and I'd make as much leaving as working.

T: You looked down right now, what are you feeling?

C: Stupid.

T: *(Letting the judgment versus emotion stand)* You made a blunder 3 years ago and feel stupid now, because new positions do not seem like they are in the cards.

C: Well, actually it wasn't a blunder. My friend stayed in the company, and she got downsized without a package.

T: It seems like you read it correctly; damned if you stay and damned if you leave. It seems like that is still the case now. You want to work and use those excellent skills you have, but they ask about other (to you) less relevant skills.

C: (Angrily) Yeah. What the hell does SQL and RSS have to do with managing food services?

T: Your anger about being put in a dilemma now seems very real.

C: It's real all right. Do you know what those things are?

T: What if I said I did not?

C: You're just as outdated as I am.

T: And what if I said I did know RSS and SQL?

C: Then you couldn't understand my problems.

T: Either way, we can't be on the same page, and you are isolated from me as well as others.

C: Yeah. I do seem to be alone here.

T: What would be the risk of being understood in here?

Positive Psychology Retrospective

Perhaps most important in focusing on consequences is the notion that the primary impact of what has gone before is that it has constructed the present. In a recent book (Shapiro, 2012), I argued that it is essential for the therapist and client to recognize that past decisions were not necessarily erroneous just because they are no longer working. Many decisions that were correct at younger ages wear out with increasing age and changes in life contexts. The therapist can help alter a client's negative self-impression by focusing on the client's successes and current skills that got them to this stage of life, rather than what errors were made.

By exploring with clients their pattern of adaptive choices in life, a therapist may help them appreciate what is going right in their lives and how to bring those strengths and skills to bear in the current life crisis. Methods of identifying client strengths and using them through the construct of resistance are the focus of Chapter 5.

Maximizing Therapeutic Effects

The goal of existential therapy is to empower the client to be responsible for his or her own choices and to face future events in life with greater strength and courage. When the therapist serves as a highly skilled, professional "teammate" in a real relationship, rather than a more distant expert with techniques or manuals, the client gets to experience those possibilities during the treatment. The therapist serves as a temporary representative of others in the world and allows the client to experiment with a variety of interactions while in a safe environment. This makes subsequent transfer of the experiences in therapy to back home life far easier.[3]

Hope

In addition to therapist skills and strategies, there are a host of nonspecific factors that improve the likelihood of client success. As Frank (1961) indicated, the most important factor in successful healing is the capacity to instill hope. When the therapist enters into a client's system and framework, he or she is indicating intrinsically that the effort is worthwhile and there is reason to anticipate a positive outcome. There would be no reason to make an intimate connection with a client who is a lost cause.

Grounded hope (Feldman & Kravetz, 2014) is also conveyed inherently by a basic belief that meaning may be derived and choices made despite apparently desperate circumstances (Frankl, 1959). This is communicated less by any specific intervention than by the process of the therapist's striving to connect meaningfully and skillfully to join in the client's subjective reality.

If, as Frank (1961) suggested, a major aspect of a client's distress is a sense of demoralization, the therapist's deep connection, respect for, and caring about the client and his or her life-as-lived, is a counteracting trend.

Consequences: Is It Working Out the Way You Hoped?

Another nonspecific factor, closely related to hope, is the therapist's expectation that the client will make good decisions. His or her willingness to explore together with clients discrepancies between conscious desires and outcomes indicates an expectation that clients will engage in actions in their own best interests. The very act of attending to consequences instead of attributed motivation opens the door for the client to reexamine unconscious needs.

By giving the results back to the client either as a mild confrontation or in the form of therapeutic amazement, the therapist is gently offering the client an opportunity to explore what is happening in a data-first, inductive manner.

C: I just think that maybe I am too intellectual, and people are put off at work.

T: Just so I understand correctly, you think that you come across as too smart for others at work, and they feel threatened?

C: Yeah! Like just this week, Betty asked for my help with a programming problem. I found a major glitch in her code, but when I showed her, she seemed more upset than thankful.

T: So you felt used or. . . ?

C: Not really used. I guess I wanted credit, and I didn't get much. She probably won't mention my troubleshooting when she gives the corrected code to the manager.

T: If I remember correctly, a few sessions ago, you described Betty as a person who you were attracted to and who was very appreciative of your bringing her coffee. I think you said that you were embarrassed that she told others about your thoughtfulness. Can you help me put your two experiences together?

C: You have too good a memory! (Smiling) Do you remember everything that all your patients say?

T: It's hard to know right now if you are happy or unhappy that I remembered the coffee incident. Is this like the ambivalence you experience about Betty's reactions to you?

C: That's what I do when I like someone. I think I find ways to prove that they don't.

T: It is somehow safer to believe that I remember everything all my clients say, rather than caring for you, and it's also safer to believe that Betty may not be that into you. What do you suppose you'd have to face if you believed that Betty liked you, too, or that I experience you as important to me?

C: (Long silence seems very emotional)

T: About three feelings just seemed to flash across your face. What are you aware of?

C: I got real anxious, because if someone likes me and I like them, they could reject me later and it would really hurt.

T: So at the risk of remembering more that you said, this could be like what happened with Ali.

Often distress is proportional to the discrepancy between intent and behavior. The therapist's approach is essentially to comment on that difference. To reframe slightly, *"you say you want to achieve your goal, and what you have been doing is this. Let's look together at how this is going and you get to evaluate your method with me."* Often, when security is at risk, the behavior and consequence is far more telling than the stated wish.

Although most often the healthier goal is for the client to face the fears of the unknown, the therapist does not judge which end of the tension the client leans toward. Instead, the therapist's job is to notice that the client is doing something that moves toward freedom or security and reflects with the client the extent to which that serves him or her.

Therapist Self-Disclosure

One characteristic that may minimize a client's sense of pathology is the therapist's presence as a person. By sharing their reactions in the process, therapists normalize clients' experiences and encourage them to pursue alternative paths.

Therapist disclosure also underscores the value of the client as a person and fellow struggler in life. That sense of being valued is a significant plus in feeling supported and in making changes.

In existential work, process self-disclosure is essential. A therapist sharing feelings in the moment may well enhance the connection and deepen the person-to-person experience. It is important to note that disclosure of details of a therapist's life can be irrelevant or even detrimental to the client's personal experience.

Trust in the Therapist's Ability

Because the nature of existential therapy is unique and intimate, the therapist can expect to be tested. He or she must appear to be trustworthy and capable. A therapist inspires confidence in clients by demeanor, ease with difficult conversations, and by conveying a sense that he or she is up to the task.

The therapist's confidence, empathy, acceptance, and caring all enhance the client's sense of safety while traversing new emotional ground. Many existential therapists have noted that this is an approach ideally practiced by mature therapists. Certainly life experience goes a long way toward inspiring confidence in clients. Similarly, the capacity to hold troubling levels of both client and personal affect will inspire a sense of faith in the process.

Existential Methods

The essence of the therapy is facing the human condition and creating meaning. Often the process does limit, reduce, or eliminate symptoms, but symptom frequency and strength are not a direct focus of attention, unless they are so debilitating that therapy can only proceed until they are mollified. The inherent assumption is that any attempts to manipulate change in client attitude or behavior, regardless of the positive intent, may paradoxically lead to increased anxiety and a corresponding pull toward continuation of a suboptimal status quo. This is more likely to occur when the therapist is viewed as an outside presence, pushing to force or induce a change in the client, instead of being *with* the client. Change initiated from without is characteristically contrary to the natural path of healing and minimizes helpful placebo effects of treatment.

In summary, the existential method requires that the therapist keep attuned to his or her personal beliefs, theories, biases, and assumptions. Without such awareness, there is a risk that the therapist will inadvertently impose his or her personal adaptations to life on the client; in Buber's terms, treating the client from an *I-it*, rather than an *I-thou* perspective. Optimally, the therapist emphasizes and explores the client's immediate conscious experience as it unfolds in the context of the intimate client-therapist relationship. Finally, the therapist's focus is on process and description of what is occurring (the plane of perception or data) rather than on derived interpretations from theory.

Notes

1. For a more detailed critique of the limitations of the "positive thinking" perspective, see Ehrenreich (2009).

2. One exception may be in treatment of trauma survivors and clients suffering from certain forms of Post-Traumatic Stress Disorder (PTSD). They may in fact benefit from specific content memory recall and exposure in a safe setting. The therapist dealing with the client who had been molested as a child determined that the current process was more important.

3. Transfer of training as a major component of the termination phase in therapy is explored in depth in Chapter 7.

5

The Centrality of Resistance in Counseling and Therapy

What you resist, persists.

Carl Jung

Why is it that clients do not always respond as counselors and therapists desire? Regardless of the apparent sophistication, elegance, and research evidence of psychotherapeutic interventions, they do not always have the desired effect. How is it that when clinicians do everything "by the book," the results fail to reach or only approximate the desired outcomes?

Every viable client who voluntarily comes in for therapy is conveying the honest message, "*Please help me. I really need your help.*" What is not said aloud, but must be understood, is the unspoken codicil, "*Of course you understand that I need to fight you every step of the way.*" There are many reasons for this, but the most essential is anxiety about change. Another way to interpret this apparent double message is that the client wishes to stay the same and have the therapist alter the universe to make the client's life better.

Bugental and Bugental (1984) dramatically referred to the anticipation of change as "a fate worse than death." They were not the original authors to recognize the natural fear of change. Dostoevski wrote, "Taking a new step, uttering a new word, is what people fear most" (1917, p. 1). Tillich (1952) described this core existential anxiety as related to the conflict that arises between the tendency to preserve what is and the resourcefulness to strive for what could be. In short, resistance is the natural outcome of the tension between security and freedom: the status quo and the unknown.

When the client is ready and willing to change, therapy usually proceeds quickly and effectively. Many of the crucial theoretical divergences involve the methods to prepare the client to be in that open, highly motivated state. For many clients, solutions to most problems, personality issues, or self-defeating patterns are well-known. They just cannot make these life-changing or even behavior modifying shifts without assistance. A great deal of the time in therapy then is devoted to preparing the client to overcome personal resistance to change.

Historically, resistance has been perceived as a problem in therapy progress; something that has to be endured as nontherapeutic time in sessions. Many systems of therapy provide rationales and methods to avoid, analyze, ignore, take a step-wise approach, slog through, or patiently wait until the client relinquishes behaviors that go against therapeutic progress. It may be a necessary obstacle to "the real therapy," but resistance per se is not the "good stuff."

Resistance in This Existential Framework

In most perspectives, resistance is reflected by the client's inability or refusal to comprehend and meet therapists' healing insights or directives, the opposite of the current viewpoint. In relationally based existential work, resistance is considered the therapist's best friend. Rather than a block to therapeutic goals, or a counter to therapeutic work, it is a most useful component of the therapeutic process. In this model, resistance is considered to be

(1) within the client as a reflection of the fear of change; not as a block to the therapist,

(2) an inevitable component of the therapy and is likely generated by therapeutic interventions as well as client fears of the unknown, and

(3) something to be honored and respected as a pathway to understanding client strengths.

Thus, resistance is to be experienced by the therapist as a client's expression of ego strength, which usually operates somewhat like a global positioning system (GPS) to the area most available for therapeutic work. Client resistance is an indicator of client strengths, which are available to be used jointly to address client weaknesses and needs. When clients block, avoid, or otherwise don't respond to a seemingly well-timed and apparently appropriate therapeutic intervention, they are likely using their best skills to defend against the risks of facing the unknown. At such moments, the therapist's job is to experience the resistance in the moment, identify the strengths being exhibited, and to recognize what anxiety is being defended. Once the therapist is aware of these, he or she needs to embrace the defense and use the client's strength by joining the resistance in both content and process.

The essence of this approach is that it fosters effective encounter with both neurotic and existential anxiety. This methodology takes the concept of resistance to a different level, and although the procedures described in this chapter are unique in some ways, they are consistent with Yalom's (1980) writing on clients facing the givens of human existence and May's (1969) discussion of the daemonic and negativity as essential components of intentionality—a core construct in his approach to existential psychotherapy.

Before exploring these atypical and counterintuitive pragmatic approaches to identifying and joining characteristic styles of resistance, it is useful to explore first historical and alternative viewpoints.

A Brief History of Resistance and Healing

The phenomenon of resistance is hardly unique to counseling and psychotherapy. For centuries, a host of methods have been used to facilitate change for those in need. Some methods involve distraction; others immersion. Often, the most powerful process involved was a belief that powers greater than the client were responsible (i.e., Frank, 1961; Frazier, 1890).

Rituals, Ordeals, and Witnessing

Healers, shamans, kahunas, elders, witch doctors, and medicine men created elaborate rituals to help clients change presumably without their own volition. Rituals, drugs, and trances were all common devices to allow ailing members of a culture to experience less anxiety in altering their behaviors, thoughts, or emotions.

These methods have changed in content but still work their "magic" through similar processes today. Rituals, ordeals, and other manner of suspension of disbelief are common antiresistant approaches employed to address modern-day dilemmas.

Up to 5 million pilgrims a year come to Lourdes in France for miraculous healings. In fact, some find the experience curative, but what is particularly fascinating is that the extent of the cures is directly correlated to distance travelled. Thus, a pilgrim from San Sabastian in Spain (2 hours by car) is likely to have fewer benefits from the waters than one from Paris (5 and one half hours by high-speed rail) and significantly less than a pilgrim from Honolulu. Apparently, enduring the ordeal alters expectations.

Eminent hypnotherapist Milton Erickson frequently recommended that difficult clients trek up Camelback Mountain in Phoenix near his home office as part of their therapy. Many of his clients reported, "I found myself halfway up the mountain one morning before my session with Dr. Erickson, and I began wondering if my hike was due to a posthypnotic suggestion." One significant aspect of this attribution is the belief that they were complying without full volition. Some more powerful force had taken over and prescribed beneficial actions.[1] Just as for their primitive forebears, the belief that their will had been temporarily overtaken by some philosophically consistent greater force was an essential component of healing. In the 1970s, comedian Flip Wilson captured the notion well with his iconic line "The devil made me do it."

Don't Even Suggest It's That Easy!

An ordeal in psychotherapy may often be a positive inducement to change. A therapist who hears a client's concerns and responds that a hopefully positive outcome will require some hard work is far more likely to see him or her return for another session. Conversely, a therapist who conveys to a client that the solution is "simple" may never see the client again. A few years ago, I was interviewed on the phone by a potential client. After a briefly describing his needs he asked,

C: So now that you know, do you think you can help?

J: I can't promise anything at this point, but I understand how rough things have been, and I am willing to work with you on giving it a good try.

C: I called another therapist, and he told me he'd have everything up to snuff in 6 weeks with his special program. Do you have the experience to match that?

J: I do not have a 6-week program, and in fact, from what you have told me, I suspect that it would take far longer.

C: Yeah. That's what I thought, too. I'd like it all fixed in 6 weeks. I don't think he really understood the depth of the dilemma. Can you see me this week?

J: Yes, but as much as we both would like a 6 week program or even less, we cannot plan for anything that short.

C: My grandma used to say, "Do it right, don't do it quick."

The interesting thing about this particular client was that he came into the second session having decided to face, rather than avoid, a very difficult decision. In effect, he had actually turned a crucial corner in his therapy in a few short weeks. He stayed in longer to "be sure I made the right decision. I count on you to hold my feet to the fire, if I try to stray." For him, the notion of a quick solution was unacceptable, even though he was able to find one himself. What was more important was his desire for empathy for his plight and someone to walk with him on his arduous journey. This client needed someone to honor his resistance and ambiguity and reassure him that the problem was substantive enough to justify his internal turmoil.

An instantaneous assessment and technique-centered cure might have actually been slower, because it carried with it an embedded metamessage that the client was foolish not to see an obvious answer. This client would have entered treatment feeling less secure, more reliant on the powerful therapist, and less confident in his personal ability to face and deal with change. In short, the more certain the therapist, the more resistance is likely to be generated, and the less the client is capable of making desired change himself. Counterintuitively, an ordeal, or empathic support for the difficulty in problem solving, strengthened the client's resolve.

Maximizing Placebo in Psychotherapy and Counseling

Jerome Frank (1961) identified four features common to healing across cultures:

1. Faith in the healer's ability, confidence, empathy, acceptance, and caring: This experienced, knowing ambiance enhances client hopefulness.

2. A setting "aura" conducive to hope and expectation of help (i.e., sacred ground or a qualified office): The setting accentuates a disengagement from normal life exigencies and maximizes a sense that it is a place for healing.

3. A rationale or philosophy that explains health, illness, and normality: The myths involved are compatible with the seeker's worldview (i.e., faulty attachment, learned habits, demonic possession). Within such a belief system, if prophesied cures fail, the belief is maintained, often strengthening hope for future cure.

4. Any form of therapy that reduces demoralization or promotes grounded hope allows for a reduction of alienation and closer connection with others. Treatment is often successful when it is emotionally arousing.

Applying this template to modern-day therapy suggests that whatever format of therapy is used, many extratechnique stimuli deeply affect the therapeutic outcome. Therapists who maximize their "placebo impact" through environment, ambiance, attention, and real engagement with clients are likely to have greater success. These presumably extratreatment phenomena all work to prepare, or dissuade, the client to change.

When it comes to resistance, a therapist's asocial responses (Beier & Young, 1984) and acceptance of the client's desire to avoid change create a far less predictable environment, one in which influence may be more keenly felt. If a therapist honors, even savors, the client's attempts to create distance, the closer they become. Thus, when a client's internal antichange codicil does not have the usual impact of reinforcing the familiar and status quo, it opens a door to the therapist to join with the client from within, in a uniquely ego-syntonic manner.

Resistance Across Theories

All forms of clinical work allow in some ways for resistance, although the term itself connoting an unconscious process is anathema to some theoretical schema.

Psychodynamic Theories and the Adaptive Nature of Resistance

Freud (1900/1952; 1915) introduced the term *resistance* to describe an adaptation to anxiety. For Freud, resistance was an unconscious mechanism that kept both unacceptable instinctual impulses and unresolved intrapsychic conflicts from awareness. He further elucidated the construct with a significant insight. Because resistance was *adaptive* in reducing anxiety, it would be quite robust. Modern existential, psychodynamic, and psychoanalytic thought may differ on the particular core fears or whether instinctual impulses are being defended, but the notion that resistance is adaptive still provides understanding of, and direction for, therapy.

For decades, psychoanalysts and other dynamically oriented therapists have considered working with resistance to be a cornerstone of treatment. Within these approaches, developing insight into the resistance and working it through the transference/countertransference relationship at several levels of unconscious depth is a core component of treatment.

Some psychodynamic authors, particularly those promoting short-term dynamic therapies, took quite aggressive approaches to eliminating instead of analyzing resistance. Davanloo (1999), for example, used the term *head-on-collision* to attack the underlying anger in resistance. Sifneos (1973) focused more on the anxiety but also recommended meeting client resistance with emotional flooding. Both approaches are at odds with existential principles of joining.

Cognitive and Behavior Therapies and Resistance

Most therapists in the cognitive and behavior camps have historically viewed therapy as a learning experience. Basic assumptions include the belief that clients are rational, and given the proper circumstances and instruction, will opt for logical decision making. Habits can be progressively improved and changed with practice, and the core responsibility for change rests on externally applied contingencies, mostly supplied by the therapist-as-teacher. Considerations of unconscious motivation and resistance to desired change do not fit well with objective logic or rational decision making. Thus, *resistance* as classically defined makes little sense and is generally considered irrelevant to treatment within these modalities.

Client missteps or failures are considered primarily as noncompliance with programmatic therapeutic behavior shifts. Noncompliance such as avoidance or improper completion of between-session homework is assumed to be a failure of proper therapist instructions.

Even those who use terms like *resistance*, consider it only as a block to successful therapy. In general, this view correlates with the notion of electrical resistance: the force that blocks or slows the conductance of current. Usually such resistance is corrected by increasing the width of the wire or other conductor or by finding an alternative way of reducing friction to allow ease of passage. There is a logical and external adjustment that fixes the problem.

So it is for cognitive and behavior therapies: the locus of responsibility for client change is the therapist. Any noncompliance is considered to be the patient resisting the therapist or the therapist's instructions, not as resistance to change within the client. Thus, effective resolution involves the therapist being more creative or effective.

In 1980, DeShazer, a cofounder of Solution-Focused Family Therapy, took this notion to its logical extreme when he famously declared "resistance is dead." His hypothesis was that a teamwork approach between a therapist and family and a positive expectation of change on the part of the therapist would obviate the clients' pull toward homeostasis *against* the therapist. From his perspective (an interesting combination of cognitive behavioral therapy [CBT] and family systems approaches[2]), resistance is reduced to the refusal by the clients to take in the therapists' perspectives. The "dead resistance" was that of a fight between therapist and clients. DeShazer did not consider resistance as a reflection of an internal process involving facing fears of the unknown.

Cognitive Behavior Therapy

Arguably the most common form of therapy today, CBT has an interesting relationship with resistance. Westra, Aviram, Connors, Kertes, and Ahmed (2012) indicated that for practitioners of CBT, resistance in therapy is important to "prevent, identify and minimize." They wrote, "resistance is an interpersonal phenomenon that is heavily influenced by the therapist, and sustained client resistance can be considered *a clinical skill error*" (p. 163) [italics added].

For CBT in general, the onus for "fixing" the noncompliance belongs with the therapist, not with the client or interaction between the therapist and client. A therapist-centric locus of change requires that adjustments involve a redefinition and reconstruction of contingencies and reassessment of therapists' approaches.

Beutler, Harwood, Michelson, Song, and Holman (2011), writing more generally than from the purely CBT framework, reported poorer outcomes of therapy when ambivalence-like resistance occurs. They concur with often reported conclusions that noncompliance (and more classically defined resistance) diminishes with nondirective styles of therapy. However, although they recommended enhancements to the therapist-client interactions as resistance reductive, the responsibility for change remained with the therapist.

Exploring attunement to the interactional patterns, Beck, Rush, Shaw, and Emery (1979) concluded that an increase in positive therapist reactions to clients, both behaviorally and emotionally, would enhance outcome. More recently, Judith Beck (2011) has also recommended greater emphasis on the therapist-client relationship. However, within both of these frameworks, noncompliance or resistance, defined as occurrences of "counter-control behavior" or "negative cognitions" may be rectified not in the relationship but in the therapist.

In general, CBT focuses more on the technique, often including manualized treatments based on symptoms, rather than therapist-client interaction or influence. If the client is nonconforming, it is advisable to alter the instructions until a set can be found to which the client will not resist. Resistance is not deemed adaptive. Unconscious ambivalence about change and avoidance of intrapsychic conflicts are not considered.

Variations Within CBT: Motivational Interviewing

CBT is an increasingly large umbrella. Many other techniques have been adopted into the CBT family. Motivational Interviewing (MI), an approach that began primarily as a method to treat addictions, does address resistance more directly. As with any approach to addiction treatment, noncompliance is a major and ongoing concern. Miller and Rollnick (2012) define MI as "a collaborative conversation style" designed to strengthen a client's motivation and commitment to change, particularly with regard to self-destructive behaviors. MI is employed when normative and anticipated client ambiguity is highest, especially during the earliest (precontemplation and contemplation) stages of therapeutic change[3] (Prochaska & DiClemente, 2005).

Moyers and Rollnick (2002) focused on this dimension of generalized client resistance to change. They argued that client ambivalence about change and the manner in which the therapist addresses the ambivalence will enhance or reduce the likelihood of success.

MI employs techniques that involve "rolling with" the resistance to tip the balance of ambiguity away from the status quo and toward change. A predominant notion of MI is that of close teamwork instead of a conflict between a therapist pushing for change and a client pushing back against the desired change.

In this manner, MI breaks with the majority of CBT approaches by focusing more intensely on the client's choices, rather than on the therapist as locus of change. This strength-based perspective is more directly respectful of the clients' abilities to find a path to success. Miller and Rollnick (2012) also promote compassion for the client and recommend the therapist having "your heart in the right place so that the trust you engender will be deserved" (p. 20).

Some of the techniques of MI approximate aspects of the existential approach that follow. However, the existential approach pushes the envelope further with regard to multiple levels of resistance to change and in the strength-base of interventions.

Other Variations

One form of CBT that addresses resistance directly is Acceptance and Commitment Therapy. ACT involves accepting reality as a given and encouraging a client's commitment to living with both reality and his or her key personal values.

Another variation, Dialectical Behavioral Therapy (DBT), explores with the client aspects of skill-building failures through "functional analysis." This involves a careful investigation and assessment of what occurred, specifically what went off track, and when it deviated from the planned program. The therapist and client together explore the events, thoughts, and feelings that occurred to interfere with successful completion of homework. Any discoveries of secondary gain or benefit of noncompliance require a shift in approach.

Although the secondary gain construct is used, it is usually referred to with regard to "automatic thoughts" without considering these phenomena unconscious. This provides a partial bridge to Husserl's (1931) notions of automatic response that correlates with neurotic anxiety.

Resistance Between and Resistance Within

To approach resistance in psychotherapy, it is essential to distinguish resistance that arises from internal ambivalence to change from conscious and deliberate noncompliance.

Opposition, obstinacy, obstructionism, refusal, and rejection may be present in any therapy environment, especially when counseling is mandated by parents, the court, a spouse, or so on. Those working with adolescents, particularly those "in the system," are very familiar with the very conscious stance of refusal, even at the client's personal expense.

As indicated previously, noncompliance is the sole component of resistance in several approaches, particularly CBT. By contrast, for current purposes, resistance is best understood as an unconscious phenomenon (automatic responding). The client is mentally defending against the fear of change and the anxiety of facing the unknown. The client's defenses support the status quo portion of the freedom-security equation. If the client is perceived as resisting change, instead of resisting the therapist per se, the therapist may take a far more supportive, less confrontational stance. In fact, it is uniquely heuristic to experience resistance as the client's unconscious ambivalence. When therapists recognize that clients defend with strengths rather than weaknesses, they can view true resistance as the client's unconscious mind requesting aid while simultaneously pointing to the best bridge across the anxiety-filled moat. By signaling both the anxiety and the best method for the client to address it, resistance is essentially the therapist's best friend.

It is desirable for the therapist to use enough "press" (Bugental, 1987), "leverage" (Yalom, 1990), interpretation (i.e., Portuges and Hollander, 2011), or relational intimacy (Shapiro, 2010; 2014a) to activate client resistance. Once it is present, it is to be honored and respected as the unconscious indicator of the client's ego strengths. With that handle, therapy may work optimally.

Existential therapists share Freud's belief that anxiety-fueled resistance is adaptive but focus somewhat differently on client anxiety at facing the givens of human existence. Rather than analyzing the resistance to develop insight, existential therapists use the anxiety-based energy toward the development of intimacy and the creation of meaning.

In Figure 5.1, the primary approaches to dealing with resistance are depicted (regardless whether the construct is named, where the locus of change resides, or how it is perceived). Psychodynamic approaches involve helping the client trigger the wall of resistance and then analyzing its

Figure 5.1   Theories of Resistance

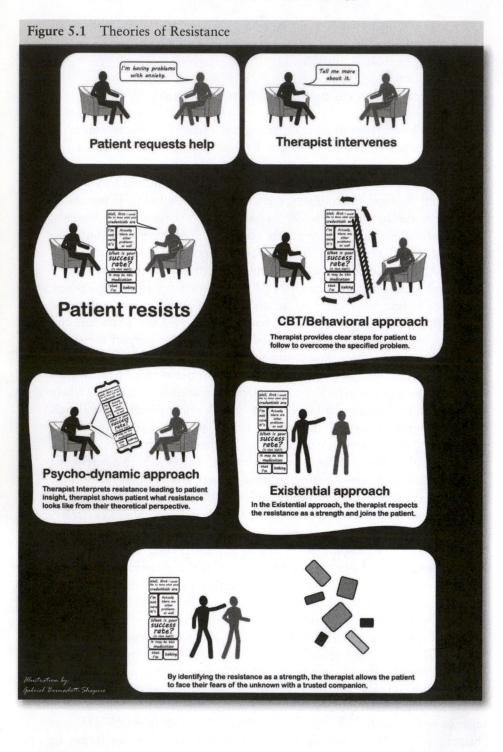

components to allow for client insight. Although they do not deliberately attempt to elicit resistance, when confronted with the resistance wall, CBT and other behavioral approaches find ways to build in progressive steps through, around, and over the wall.

The existential approach is designed to get the client and therapist on the same side of the wall of resistance and to use the wall for support in moving into unknown territory. There is no specific desire to remove that support.

A Pragmatic Model of Dealing With Resistance in (Existential) Counseling and Therapy

If resistance is a manifestation of an internal struggle between the guilt of the status quo and fears of the unknown, it is fueled primarily by the pull of the security and corresponding avoidance of substantial anxiety related to change and to freedom. The method to be detailed in the tables below necessitates a close therapeutic relationship with the client. It requires the therapist's awareness of the here-and-now moment and his or her capacity to join with the client in the client's process. In some ways, working with resistance demonstrates the therapist's deep respect and empathy for the client's being-in-the-world process and is emblematic of the strength of the existential approach.

When the therapist joins a client more fully in his or her retreat from freedom and acceptance of the status quo by joining his or her unique manner of expressing anxiety, it paradoxically opens the door for clients to feel safer exploring more fully their existential anxiety and confronting the neurotic anxiety.

Approaching resistance in this manner is a cornerstone of existential treatment as it fosters attempts to create *I-thou* moments with the client. When the method is used in an authentic manner within an intimate therapeutic relationship, it has the potential to enhance the subject-to-subject phenomenological experience and allow the therapist and client to approach the here-and-now ambivalence as a team.

The current approach to resistance in therapy begins with certain assumptions that emerge from the deeply phenomenological work of Binswanger (1963), Boss (1963), Frankl (1959a), Husserl (2014), and Spinelli (1997).

It is essential to acknowledge here that Frankl (1959a) employed a related construct, *paradoxical intention,* as a therapeutic technique. He did it so intuitively that others who later adopted the technique misunderstood its usefulness and scope (i.e., Haley, 1963, 1976). *Paradoxical intention* applied to resistance works consistently well. However, when applied to behavior in general, the impact is more random.

A client's resistance unearths the protective strength fed by his pull to emotional security. By identifying and understanding the manner in which a client is effective in self-protection, a therapist has a window into clients' unique coping skills. This allows the therapist to connect and be with the client, in both content and real-time process in a uniquely ego-syntonic manner.

Within this existential framework, awareness of the givens of human life (isolation, meaninglessness, freedom, and especially mortality) produces useful, beneficial (existential) anxiety. Counteracting awareness of this existential anxiety are unconscious defensive reactions that prevent facing the fears of the unknown. These automatic protective responses (Husserl, 1931), often referred to as symptoms or neurotic anxiety, are uniquely useful in reaching a client.

Systematizing Intuition

A therapist who is oriented toward assessing the clients' strengths through resistance may identify and effectively use the client's momentary style of expressing neurotic anxiety. The methods per se are not novel or unique. They have been employed in clinical settings for decades by clinicians who have been deemed particularly intuitive. Specific studies of such therapeutic masters as Viktor Frankl, Milton Erickson, Carl Rogers, and Carl Whitaker have highlighted this underlying mechanism. For these master clinicians, identifying and joining resistance just seemed natural. What is unique here is the manner of categorizing the style of client resistance and consciously joining with that resistance in a systematic manner. Although this approach may have wide-ranging application within other theoretical frameworks, both the approach and the rationale behind it, are essentially existential.

This method changes the equation. Rather than experience resistance as nontherapeutic time in therapy, or as something to be avoided or endured, it embraces resistance as the path to the client's process, indeed the way to his or her heart.

When clients resist a particular intervention, they are defending against anxiety by using their strengths. When the therapist comprehends the strengths of client, he or she understands the optimal way to reach the client. The therapist's job is to

- identify those strengths,
- recognize what the client is defending within himself or herself,
- discern the extent of neurotic anxiety generating the defense,
- embrace the defense (honoring the client's process and strength), and
- join the resistance.

Resistance Styles

In the chart below, a six-fold classification of resistance styles is offered. They do not represent any form of pathology. They are adaptations to anxiety that pull toward the status quo. Each represents considerable strength.

It is essential to understand that the importance of any of these styles is *in the moment*. They do not necessarily reflect personality or trait patterns. In this form of therapy, it is only important to be aware of the nature and style of resistance in the here-and-now. At another moment in time, the nature of the resistance may be quite different. Thus, this method is most useful in the process of therapeutic interaction.

Resistance to influence and avoidance of change may be demonstrated cognitively and affectively. In cognitive forms of resistance, the client uses thoughts, words, language, intellectual logic, and confusion to ward off the potential for change. Affective forms involve the use of emotion, either by flooding the environment with excess feeling or by withdrawing feeling to the point of disconnection.

The second dimension locates the defensiveness in the relationship. There are three loci: external, internal, and away. External defenses involve moving against the intrusion at a distance. To use a castle analogy, these defenses are across the moat and in the perimeter, away from home. Such defenses are fairly aggressive. Internal defenses allow the therapist inside the walls and even deeper into the depths of mazes, confusions, or intrapsychic quicksand. Here the person supporting the requested change is mired and cannot find much ground to maneuver. Finally, away defenses are those in which the client indicates, often in nonverbal ways, that he or she may have left his or her body in the therapy room, but at least at the moment, his or her consciousness is elsewhere.

If these seem somewhat akin to sympathetic nervous system activation for fight, freeze, or flight, it is no accident. The fear of change is threatening to the ego, and the defenses are similar to life-threatening reactivity. They also mirror Horney's (1945) depictions of movements (toward, away, against) that underlie attempts to deal with neurotic needs.

Table 5.1   Characteristic Resistance (Defense) Styles

	Cognitive	Affective
Internal (maze)	Cognitive Internal	Affective Internal
External (perimeter)	Cognitive External	Affective External
Away (dissociative)	Cognitive Away	Affective Away

As the tables in this section indicate, each style has positive attributes and potential deficiencies.

The Cognitive External Style

When clients are defending their personal status quo with a cognitive-external style, they may seem suspicious, questioning, argumentative, and distant. At times, they may seem more like a prosecuting attorney than a client seeking therapist help. The point of contact is away from the client, and the push is against the therapist intellectually.

Table 5.2 Cognitive External Style

Positive Attributes	Deficiencies
• Well defined cognitive, logic, and analytic systems • Good troubleshooting skills • Quick assessment of novel situations • Early warning of danger • Ability to see through obvious to underlying motivation	• Generally poor access to feelings, especially vulnerable feelings • Suspiciousness • Lack of spontaneity • Often rigid adherence to internal beliefs • Some lack of attention to apparent facts • Antagonism and blaming

T: When we ended last week, you mentioned that you wanted to get into the ongoing battle with your family. Does that make sense today?

C: I guess as a therapist, you have to hone in on mother, right? (Wary, distant, pushing against the therapist)

T: I was just wondering if that was worth continuing or if there is something more present for you.

C: You can't weasel out of it that easily. Do you want to ask about my mother or not? Let's not play games here.

At this point, the therapist is probably back on his heels, wondering what is occurring and what in the relationship between them is so threatening as to need so much more distance. If he were to probe further, the attack would likely increase with a corresponding reduction in possibility of change.

What if instead of pushing against or withdrawing, the therapist *joined* the resistance? He already knows that the client is being defensive in the moment. He also knows that the form is external and cognitive. The path to joining might well be in those realms.

T: (smiling) So. You are thinking that because I'm a therapist, I see talking about your mother as a dog might see a bone—can't resist.

C: Well, don't all of you think everything is about mothers?

T: (Very cognitively) The question on the table before us is whether we should pursue my agenda or yours. How will we negotiate that?

C: Well, you are the expert. You will probably choose.

T: On the other hand, you are paying for the therapy time. How would you call the shots?

C: I want to talk about my childhood, because it is coming up a lot with my son. I just don't want you to think that's all there is.

T: Just to be sure we are on the same page, what else is there that I might miss in my delight at delving into your childhood?

C: I saw you in the store last weekend, and I didn't come up to say hello and wondered if you had seen me also and ignored me.

T: Had I seen you and ignored you that would have been hurtful. Let's talk about that first.

The client was pushing the therapist away, an interesting parallel process to the thought that the therapist may have deliberately ignored him. By understanding that the client had to work in a suspicious manner, and by joining him there, they were able to use the energy to get to an important matter quite readily.

Joining Cognitive External Resistance

(1) The therapist begins with the expressed thoughts, skepticism, doubts, and suspicions and only slowly moves toward any underlying feelings.

(2) Working with the content expressed, the therapist openly explores his personal motivations for the interventions or questions.

(3) The therapist begins by initially respecting and supporting the perimeter boundary, entering only with client's clear welcome and, even then, with proper hesitation.

(4) All interventions meet the client in the here-and-now. In this case, being cognitive and only moving toward the affective on invitation.

The Affective External Style

When clients are defending their personal status quo with an affective-external style, they may seem emotionally overreactive. They keep distance from the therapist by flooding the room with excess feeling and apparent volatility. At times, they may seem to be having a tantrum or meltdown. The point of contact is away from the client, and the push is against the therapist emotionally. Once the client has flooded the entrance bridge and filled the moat with emotional monsters, he or she can focus on the therapist's inability and avoid his or her internal fear of the unknown.

Although it may seem a bit contrived, I am using the same vignette here to make comparisons between the styles more comparable. In the real world of therapy, there might be far less concordance of content with different resistance styles.

Table 5.3   Affective External Style

Positive Attributes	Deficiencies
• Easy access to feelings • Able to express wide range of feelings • Intuitive • Impressionistic • Able to shift attention focus readily • Spontaneous • Able to be theatrical; role play	• Poorly defined cognitive/analytical skills • Global responsivity • Naïve • Poor differentiation of detail • Unable to keep to long-term planning or delay gratification • Poor discrimination of subjective and objective reality

T: When we ended last week, you mentioned that you wanted to get into the ongoing battle with your family. Does that make sense today?

C: (In a loud and emotional voice) My family! My family! What is with that? I am trying to get my life in order, and you bring up my family!

T: (In a level, empathic tone) My question about how we left off last week seems very upsetting.

C: (Increasing intensity) Upsetting? It's outrageous! Are you trying to devastate me by adding so much to my plate?

As in the cognitive external example, the therapist is probably taken aback by the intensity of the moment, wondering what is occurring and what in the relationship between them is so threatening to require so much more distance. If he were to probe further, the emotional volatility might increase until the therapist is sufficiently pushed away.

Again, the therapist may pull back, defend his innocence, or preferably, *join* the resistance. He already knows that the client is being defensive in the moment to avoid internal anxiety. He also knows that the form is external and affective. The client is showing the path to connection.

T: (Raising his voice slightly) Here you come in with so much going on, and I just add to it by bringing up the past as well.

C: (Still aroused, but tone is slightly modulated.) It's like I can't win. You always have to bring up more to deal with. Well, maybe enough is enough!

T: (With emotion in tone) You are trying to do the best you can, and here I am making it seem like you'll never catch up. That seems unfair. What would *you* like to address today?

C: At this point, I don't even remember.

T: Well, perhaps we can trust your feelings. What are they saying now?

C: I am having a lot of feelings about how I am parenting my son. It brings up the awful feelings I grew up with. No matter what I do, nothing ever seems right.

T: So when I suggested where we focus, it brought up all those feelings again. You don't feel that you can be right with your son. You didn't feel you could be right as a child, and now you feel that you can't even be right in here. That sounds dreadful. Do you have any sense of what might have precipitated this vulnerability?

C: I saw you in the store last weekend, and I didn't come up to say hello and wondered if you had seen me also and ignored me.

T: Had I seen you and ignored you that would have been hurtful. Let's talk about that first.

The client was pushing the therapist away, parallel to the feelings that the therapist may have rejected her. By understanding that the client had to work affectively and by joining her there, they were able to use that energy to get to the relational issues in the room. By going into her emotional language, he was conveying at a nonverbal level that he was willing to respect her processing at the moment. By joining her in her affective mode, he was also indicating that to continue to be more emotional in the moment would paradoxically increase closeness.

Joining Affective External Resistance

(1) The therapist begins by reflecting the client's content concerns at approximately matched levels of affect in as empathic a manner as possible.

(2) Therapist adopts the client's pacing, attitude, and orientation.

(3) The therapist matches the high level of affect, slowly guiding the client to a more modulated balanced expression of cognition and affect. By accepting the boundary and joining the client there, he demonstrates respect for the client's process.

(4) All interventions meet the client in the here-and-now. In this case, being affective on invitation and only later on invitation, moving toward the cognitive.

(5) Developing teamwork at emotional levels may seem at times chaotic and unstructured until a working trust can be established.

The Cognitive Internal Style

Unlike defenses that push against the therapist on the perimeter, internal styles of resistance involve inviting the therapist into the psyche's inner workings and then creating an unmapped maze. This form of protection provides immobility by having too many options to consider. There is no apparent attack, no monsters, but there is a surfeit of frustration available.

When clients are defending their personal status quo with a cognitive-internal style, they may seem unable to make decisions, overly concerned with details and perfectionism. Although they seem to be consistently compliant with the therapist, no change is evident. At times it may seem like they are stuck in quicksand. The point of contact is inside the client, and interventions are often met with excellent reasons for inaction.

Table 5.4 Cognitive Internal Style

Positive Attributes	Deficiencies
• Well defined cognitive, analytic skills • Attention to detail • Ability to consider all options before acting • Ability to acknowledge self at least vis-à-vis inward focus • Nonimpulsive • Assessment of internal reality	• Generally poor access to feelings, especially vulnerable feelings • Suspiciousness • Lack of spontaneity • Often rigid adherence to internal beliefs • Some lack of attention to apparent facts • Antagonism and blaming

T: When we ended last week, you mentioned that you wanted to get into the ongoing battle with your family. Does that make sense today?

C: Yes. I've been thinking about that all week. It's quite complex. (Apparently compliant, with a negation coming)

T: Can you share some of your thoughts this past week?

C: I don't think I ever told you, but I know I told my doctor. I was a bed wetter as a child. I think it was until age 10. No, maybe nine, no wait, my mom said it was 10, but I remember not going on sleepover camp when I was 11.

T: What about the battle with your family brought it up?

C: Well, there are several things. They want to come visit, but it upsets my wife because they always tease and embarrass me.

T: About the bedwetting?

C: No. Wait it was 10. I remember now.

At this point, the therapist is trying to track, wondering what is occurring, what the relevance of bedwetting is, and why the client is creating so many blocks to connection. If he were to probe further about the bedwetting or the impending visit, it may not be relevant. The more they go down one train of thought, the greater the distance.

How might he *join* this resistance? He is aware of the client's defensive distancing. He also knows that the form is internal and cognitive. The path to joining might well be in those realms.

T: There is so much to consider here. As I hear you discuss the bedwetting, the visit, the relationship between your wife and your family of origin, I am struck by all these intertwined topics.

C: Yeah, and that's only scratching the surface.

T: (Very cognitively) Perhaps it would serve us to consider all the possible variables here and decide if we are best suited to discuss them one at a time or all together. How might we even decide how to progress?

C: Well, you are the expert. You could choose.

T: On the other hand, you are paying for the therapy time. How would you call the shots?

C: I don't know. Everything seems so entangled.

T: I would agree with you, and choosing one method (all together or individually) would leave the other method untouched. We might miss something important.

C: Okay. But where do we begin?

T: I have an idea. It may not be the best starting place at the moment, but we could always switch if we need to. . . . Can we talk for just a moment about how what we are doing together makes you feel like you can't do it right?

C: I saw you in (the store) last weekend, and I didn't come up to say hello and wondered if you had seen me also and ignored me.

T: (Staying with the defensive style) Gee. That's a lot to consider. I might have seen you and ignored you. I might not have seen you. If I had seen you, I might not have wanted to violate confidentiality. If I hadn't seen you, was it just that I was preoccupied or was there some unconscious reason why I hadn't seen you? What have I missed?

C: Yes, that's right. I thought all those things.

T: That sounds like some burden to wonder about. What did it mean to you that you went unseen by me in the store?

C: (Hesitantly and with a questioning tone) . . . that you wouldn't want to be seen with me?

T: And what would *that* mean to you?

The client was avoiding the therapist, in parallel to his worry that he may have deliberately ignored him. By understanding that the client had to assess all the possible ramifications, and by listing all the ones he could think of, the therapist was joining him in his process to address the here-and-now more readily. Somewhere in the relationship is access to the client's fear of freedom.

Joining Cognitive Internal Resistance

(1) The therapist begins by reinforcing the reality that a decision is difficult by joining with the multiplicity of options and slowly moves toward affect, meaning, and decision making.

(2) Often the therapist will initiate examination of unconsidered options that might on the surface seem to complicate matters.

(3) The therapist enters the internal maze and only slowly allows for movement, once momentary security has been achieved.

(4) Initial interventions will be cognitive and often confusing. Movement to attribution of meaning and/or feelings is on invitation or agreement and is often generated by mounting frustration in the lack of movement in therapy.

The Affective Internal Style

When clients are defending their personal status quo with an affective-internal style, they may seem particularly underreactive. They keep distance from the therapist by withdrawing emotion from the room with what may seem like a temporary depression. At times, they may seem to be nonresponsive or very slow to respond. The point of contact is within the client, and the maze here is affective (on the surface, a lack thereof). It may seem that the client has invited the therapist into a room and then pumped out all the oxygen. Without air, there is little opportunity to explore any other anxiety.

Table 5.5 Affective Internal Style

Positive Attributes	Deficiencies
• Ready access to certain feeling states • Particular sensitivity to negative emotions • Understanding of multiple levels of emotional depth • Willing to focus inwardly • Nonimpulsive; unlikely to get into trouble by spontaneous action	• Lack of differentiation of external cues • Lack of access to positive feeling states • Poor attention to detail • Unable to act decisively • Nonspontaneous

T: When we ended last week, you mentioned that you wanted to get into the ongoing battle with your family. Does that make sense today?

C: (Long pauses between utterances with quizzical expression) My . . . family . . . I guess (sigh) . . . that'd be okay.

T: (In a level, empathic tone) You don't seem enthused about that. Is there a more important place for us to begin?

C: (Very slowly, sighing and showing a pained expression) No . . . it doesn't matter, I guess . . . it's okay.

As in the cognitive internal example, the therapist is probably taken aback by the low level of intensity of the moment, wondering what is occurring and what in the relationship between them is promoting so much distancing. If she were to probe further, the client might slow down even more and be increasingly elusive.

Again, the therapist may pull back, defend her interest in the client, probe for signs of depression, and (assuming that there are no reasons to expect a depression here) preferably *join* the resistance. She already knows that the client is defensively holding on to the status quo in the moment. She also knows that the form is internal and affective. The path to joining is likely in those realms.

T: (Slowing pace, exhaling noticeably, and dropping tone) It . . . seems . . . almost like . . . discussing this . . . is almost overwhelming.

C: (Still with low affect with long pauses between utterances) It's like I can't win. . . . There is so much. . . . My family . . . my wife . . . nothing helps!

T: (With slow empathic slowly paced tone) You are trying to do the best you can, and here I seem to be adding to the number of issues . . . (long space) like there's almost no way to get going, let alone get on top of things. What would be possible to address today, perhaps not your family?

C: (Sighing and exhaling) At this point, I don't even remember.

T: (Sighing and exhaling, slow pace—multiple pauses) Well . . . perhaps we . . . can trust your feelings. . . . What are they saying now?

C: I'm worried about my son. . . . He's stressed out and seems like I was as a kid.

T: So when we talk about your family and how you are almost immobilized, it's a double whammy with your empathy for him. It must feel exhausting. Do you know what's happening in here to make that happen again now?

C: This may not mean anything, but I saw you in (the store) last weekend, and I didn't come up to say hello and wondered if you had seen me also and ignored me.

T: Had I seen you and ignored you that would have been another situation that leaves you not knowing what to do. Let's talk about that first.

The client was avoiding the therapeutic process by being stuck. No matter what the therapist offered, it seemed like too much. The parallel process here was the similarity of back home dilemma and the therapeutic relationship. The potential of a nonmeeting at the store precipitated a host of dilemmas.

Understanding that the client had to work in a feeling-centered, questioning manner, the therapist joined in the multiple dilemmas and with very low affect. By staying there with the client, she was not able to be defeated. Once that became evident, they could work as a team to get to the relational issues in the room. By going into the client's (low) emotional language, the therapist was conveying at a nonverbal level that she was willing to respect the client's processing at the moment. In an apparently paradoxical manner, the therapist's enervating approach actually energized the client and brought them closer.

Joining Affective Internal Resistance

(1) The therapist begins by affective acknowledgement of complexity and depth of emotion.

(2) The therapist adopts the client's pacing, attitude, and orientation.

(3) The therapist matches low key, slow affect, and emotional ambivalence and confusion.

(4) All interventions meet the client at the present moment. In this case, being affective and respectful of the depth and complexity of the client's dilemma and only later moving toward the cognitive—on invitation.

(5) Developing teamwork at low emotional levels may seem at times like the therapy is moribund and unstructured, until a working trust can be established.

The Cognitive Away Style

Clients defending their personal status quo with a cognitive-away style will seem more distant from the therapist. There is an elusive quality that makes it hard to pin down any basis for connection. They seem to offer only parts of themselves at any given moment. Because there is safety in reduced intimacy and contact in the therapeutic session, the point of contact is away from the client almost as if the therapist and client are observing some objective event as spectators.

T: When we ended last week, you mentioned that you wanted to get into the ongoing battle with your family. Does that make sense today?

C: I guess that would be as good as anything (distant, apparently disinterested).

Table 5.6 Cognitive Away Style

Positive Attributes	Deficiencies
• High tolerance for ambiguous situations • Ability to perceive a wide variety of perspectives • Ability to function in nonsocial context • Not powerfully affected by rejection • Ability to "act," role play effectively, and be experimental in novel situations • Not adversely affected by past	• Poor coordination of here-and-now • Lack of coordination of affect and presence • Emotional coldness • Inability to make lasting, sustained, or intimate contact with others • "As if" quality to relationships • Poor access to feelings

T: I was just wondering if that was worth continuing or if there is something more present for you?

C: (Thoughtfully) No, not really. If you think it's worthwhile. . . .

T: (Going for any affect) What did it feel like when I just brought it up?

C: I was kind of expecting it. I was very upset when you said it last week, but I worked it out myself during the week, so it's okay now.

At this point, the therapist is faced with a dilemma. The topic is important only in the past. It is no longer an issue in the present, yet there is no other experience that the client is interested in addressing. So the therapist can deal with the client with nothing to work on or deal with something to work on that presumably has been resolved. The choice is between client absence and a lack of anything meaningful to discuss.

How might the therapist *join* this style of resistance? He already knows that the client is being avoidant. He also knows that is away and cognitive. The path to joining might well involve requesting that the client be less present by role playing, one of the most common techniques in psychotherapy.

T: I'm interested that you were able to handle the discomfort at what I said so effectively. Would you tell me what you did to be so successful?

C: I'm not sure. Maybe I just put it out of my mind and attended to other more pressing matters.

T: (Very cognitively) The ability to get over hurts is something that you have been interested in addressing, and here you did it yourself. It would probably be of value for us both to see the method in action and be able to replicate such success in the future.

C: (A little warily) Well, you are the expert. How do we do that?

T: Let's try just a brief experiment. Let's imagine we were back in time to last week. What do you recall that I said?

C: You said that what I was dealing with at work seemed similar to what is going on with my boyfriend.

T: Imagine that we are time travelers, and it is a week ago in session. I'll begin. "You know Jean, I wonder if the situation at work is similar to Ryan's anger directed at you." Is that close enough? (Client nods) Now just react the way you did last week, only out loud.

C: I don't like when you connect the dots that way. It's like you're blaming me for things that others do to me.

T: Good job! You are feeling irritated with me for blaming you when you feel like the victim here.

C: Yeah. I'm pretty upset by your taking their side.

T: Like I don't care for you. I'm only looking for connections.

C: I saw you in (the store) last weekend, and I didn't come up to say hello and wondered if you had seen me also and ignored me.

T: Had I seen you and ignored you, it would have been another example that I don't really care. What's that mean for you in here?

The client was resisting the therapist by offering either presence (with nothing to talk about) or affect (which was no longer present). This is analogous to the thought that the therapist ignored her at the store last week. By understanding that she was defending against intimacy by acting as if she were not in the therapeutic relationship, he was able to go with her strength by recommending role playing: Be here, but don't be fully here. This allowed her the space sufficient to engage in the anxiety provoking question of his caring for her.

Joining Cognitive Away Resistance

(1) The therapist begins with the acceptance of the client's difficulty in being fully present. Early verbal interventions are supportive of clarifying and maintaining the separation.

(2) Understanding that the client is more comfortable and able to deal with intimacy in an "as if" or pretend fashion, he recommends role playing, role reversals, or other psychodrama-inspired techniques—allowing the client to act in the present in an imaginary (once removed) form.

(3) The therapist begins a slow movement from there-and-then to here-and-now as trust builds through his willingness to offer a format in which the client feels less threatened.

(4) If the client is comfortable expressing affect indirectly, the therapist approaches him or her with an ostensibly indirect method to comply with therapy and also to use his or her strengths.

The Affective Away Style

When clients are protecting their personal status quo with an affective-away style, they may seem very tense and jittery during the session. They keep distance from the therapist by appearing nonverbally volatile, as if they are ready to either bolt from the room and from therapy or on the verge of emotional impulsivity. At times, they may seem unable to interpose a cognition between a feeling and (potentially dramatic) action. A therapist confronted with this defense often feels very tentative, "like all of a sudden I have stepped into a room and the floor is all eggshells." The point of contact is on the tenuous ambiance in the room and a stance of mutual spectators who are sizing up together some impending disaster.

Table 5.7 Affective Away Style

Positive Attributes	Deficiencies
• Spontaneous • Feelings connected closely with behavior • Here-and-now orientation • Practical intelligence • Able to size up situations and act quickly (i.e., emergencies)	• Poor judgment • Lack of cognitive aspects in decision making • Discontinuous experience of the world • Reckless and arbitrary • Nonreflective; often illogical • Poor long-term concentration

T: When we ended last week, you mentioned that you wanted to get into the ongoing battle with your family. Does that make sense today?

C: (Leg jiggling and furtive glances toward windows and walls near therapist—no eye contact) I don't know why we have to get into that. The past is past.

T: (In a level, empathic tone) Would something in the present or future be more useful to you?

C: (Continued signs of agitation) No. I guess I just don't feel like talking today.

This leaves the therapist in a conundrum in which she is being told that the client does not want to talk, but the client's nonverbal behaviors indicate that there is something going on.

Although the agitation is not at the level in which she might be concerned for her own safety, she is worried about what is occurring for the client. Any probing might drive him further away. She might pull back and let the client come forward at his own pace, but also wants to engage sufficiently to indicate that she is present and interested. Recognizing the affective and away quality of the resistance, she can join it by focusing on both.

T: (Moving up her pace to begin to mirror the client's agitation and avoiding eye contact) It seems like you'd prefer to be anywhere else but here right now.

C: Not anywhere!

T: (Still avoiding eye-to-eye contact looking up as if thoughtful) So as tense or uncomfortable as this seems, there could be worse situations to be in. That is strangely reassuring to me—probably less for you.

C: (Rapidly) Well, like the dentist.

T: Yeah, that can be worse. How might we spend our time here? I promise no drilling.

C: (Laughing and leg jiggling slows) Okay, no drilling. I could use some nitrous though.

T: So if we did have some nitrous, what would that feel like?

C: Floating. No care in the world.

T: (Fleeting eye contact) It's funny that you should mention "floating" on nitrous. The last time I had dental work done with nitrous, I had this amazing combination of dreams and ideas floating in and out of my mind. The thoughts were both kind of out there and somehow poignant. I was almost regretful when I came down, and of course my sore jaw added to my regret. If there were no risks of drilling here and you were on nitrous, what might we discuss?

C: This may not mean anything, but I saw you in (the store) last weekend, and I didn't come up to say hello and wondered if you had seen me also and ignored me.

T: What was it like just to see me in another place, let alone if we spoke? It's another situation that leaves you not knowing what to say or do.

C: (Agitation dropping somewhat) I didn't want to talk there either.

T: Had I seen you and ignored you that would have been like I was dissing you. Could we briefly talk about that? What's it like to be in here talking about the hard things and not being sure if I care at all?

Joining Affective Away Resistance

(1) Work begins with therapist's early internal recognition of patients' pressure for imminent action.

(2) It is of value to express empathy for tense, difficult "walking on eggshells" feel in the room.

(3) It is best to avoid direct confrontation. Often the use of indirect and metaphorical approaches or storytelling is most beneficial.

Joining Must Be Authentic

Jordan (2010) wrote that growth-fostering relationships "lessen the suffering caused by chronic disconnection and isolation" (p. 23). A disingenuous or manipulative relationship will do the exact opposite. It is insufficient to recognize the client's resistance style. The therapist has to find comparable feelings and reactions in himself or herself to be able to genuinely to relate to the client's resistance. A therapist who knows that the client is fearful of and is resisting certain change cannot join with the client unless he or she can tap into his or her own fears of facing the unknown (Stanislavski, 1989).[4] Being aware of those personal concerns will make connections with the client far more poignant and team-like. This does not mean that the therapist has had to suffer the same content as the client, but that he or she understands and is empathic with the client's fears about losing the status quo for some unknown future. Accessing the therapist's personal self and engaging in the real relationship can be the core factors in change (i.e., Gelso, 2011; Markin, Kivlighan, Gelso, Hummel, & Siegel 2014; Norcross, 2011). By contrast, attempts to fake it or pass in the client's culture or experiences will likely seem phony and fail.

It Seems Counterintuitive. Why Does This Work?

Consider the radical notion that resistance does not demand that the therapist fight through the wall, analyze the wall for windows of insight or building steps into and around it. Instead, it is the client's way of informing the therapist how to join him or her and using the wall as a back support to set out on a new journey as a team.

When the resistance is designed to block the therapist from encouraging the client to change, attempts to avoid or attack the resistance will inevitably refuel it. Even if there is an appearance of compliance in the session, the pull of the status quo will reassert itself in force between sessions and subsequently reemerge as strong as ever. However, when a therapist joins the client's process of resisting, the therapist is demonstrating caring, respect, and empathy. In a manner that seems paradoxical, the therapist is offering to hold the resistance and the anxiety for the client, to allow him or her the opportunity to explore change more safely.

From this perspective, the proper timing for any intervention involves an acute sensitivity to the client's psychological strengths. It may seem incongruous or ironic, but the best indicator and pathway to those strengths is the nature and viability of a client's defensiveness.

A client's resistance is emblematic of the protective strength fed by the pull to emotional security. It offers the therapist a window into clients' unique ego strengths. Taking this further than the many therapies that encourage empathy with the *content* of a client's interactions, the current approach of joining resistance is an expression of empathy for the client's *process*.

Clara and the Wedding Invitation

Clara, a 38-year-old divorced woman with two children and a successful professional career, was in therapy to "move on after my husband left me." Her progress had been slow but steady, permeated with considerable ambivalence, including a few "late night meltdowns, when I called him to come over for sex and tried to get him back."

Approximately a month before this session, she had discovered through the children that he was planning on marrying a woman he had met about 6 months after their divorce. For several sessions, she was extremely tearful and confused about whether to attend the wedding, "for the kids." She was also extremely upset that the new woman in her ex-husband's life was "attractive, successful, and very nice to the children. I just can't hate her, but I can't abide her being a mother to the children either."

This interaction occurred about 20 minutes into the session.

C: (Through weeping and tears) I just can't decide what to do. What should I do? Will it scar the children if I don't go? What if I go and can't handle it? My God, what will I do? What should I do?

This was a repeat of prior sessions in which the therapist was supportive, understood the dilemma, and expressed empathy of an impossible situation. On frequent occasions, they just sat together. The problem was coming to head, because the wedding was this upcoming weekend. The therapist determined that the resistance at this moment was clearly affective and had primarily external qualities. She began trying to find the level of despair in herself and began expressing it to Clara.

T: (Very emotionally) This is an almost impossible situation! If you don't go, that will lead to worry about the kids and I suspect about wondering about what is going on all afternoon. If you do, it could be very painful for you to see them marry or try to be happy at the reception.

C: (More distraught) Oh. The wedding! I haven't even thought about the ceremony. She's some kind of orthodox religion, and I know that will be a real problem for me. My boy said it was a 2-hour deal. I'd have to see the kids be in that! But if I don't, well, I'm going to have a miserable Sunday next week either way.

T: (With emotion in her voice) It's a terrible dilemma. No good way out. It'd be easier if they got married while you were away somewhere.

C: I thought about going to Maui with my friend, but then I worried that I might ruin a perfectly good vacation. (in a very loud voice) I will not let that woman ruin Maui for me!

After four repetitions of this interaction, the therapist decided to join the resistance by upping the ante on holding to the status quo.

T: (Raising her voice, talking rapidly) You know, as I think of it, you just can't make a decision about what to do. Either way it's so risky. It's too much pressure, and having such an event in your face would be horrendous. Even if you only went to the reception, it'd be a nightmare!

Following a lengthy silence after the therapist's "outburst," Clara sighed and said,

C: I have thought about this a lot. I don't want to disappoint you, but for me, not knowing is worse than knowing.

T: (Not fully matching the new calm) So, how will you begin to protect yourself? What if it becomes too much for you? This just seems very dangerous.

C: I think I will go, but just to the reception, and I will bring my friend for support. That way, if I have to leave, we will just go.

T: (Skeptically) That might work, but if you do leave, how will the kids get home?

C: Good catch. I'll ask my sister-in-law to be available if they need a ride home.

T: Will she be able to do that?

C: She actually offered to take them and bring them home. (After a silence) If I need to call you on Sunday or come in on Monday, will you be available?

T: If you call on Sunday, I'll call you back. We could schedule a Monday meeting right now.

When the therapist was willing to join with Clara's high level of affect, Clara was able to find her inner calm and describe a potentially viable plan of action. Clara's resistance to coming to terms with her ambivalence became more workable only when the therapist took on the affective component. That allowed Clara to face her very real dilemma.

This could be interpreted from a systems perspective (Clara needed a certain amount of emotion in the room, and when the therapist took over some of it, she could feel safe being more rational), from a psychodynamic perspective (Clara felt more fully understood and was able to lean on the therapist to come to a decision), or from a humanistic perspective (Clara felt accepted for who she was without pressure to change, so was able to make a decision). However, the therapist described it as "empathy for the impossible emotional situation. I felt my own distraught feelings when I have had to make a choice between two bad alternatives and let those flow into the moment."

She also acknowledged that she chose to take the "can't decide" position. "I just knew that I had to bring my full feelings into the situation and join her in the full dilemma. I was confident that'd she'd come to sort it out today and just needed my holding up the status quo (no decision) so she could face what she had to."

The Case of Thomas

Thomas is a 33-year-old second-generation Chinese-American man. He initially was referred by his physician for psychosomatic problems.

About 6 months prior to the therapy, he instigated a painful break-up of a relationship. He has a history of daily marijuana use when he was in his twenties, but claims to be only an occasional weekend user now. He has a responsible position at a high-tech company. This interaction occurred in the fifth session.

C: I am having trouble sleeping and am getting more and more irritable.

T: When did this start?

C: This week.

T: Any idea about what prompted it?

C: (In an irritated voice) Well, aren't you full of questions today? I don't know what started it. If I did, I'd get it to stop.

T: (Hearing the irritation and the client's impulse to not discuss the issue he brought in) So this is frustrating. Not only are you irritated by the lack of sleep, but my questions are also annoying, because there is no clear answer.

C: (Calming down) No, it's not the questions and answers. I just need a good night's sleep.

T: Is there something we could do here to help promote that?

C: Do you have any sleeping pills?

T: That'd be a good question for your primary care physician. Maybe there is something on your mind that is getting in the way of a good night's sleep. Lack of sleep can be even painful, well beyond irritable. . . . I know you've already probably rounded up the usual suspects, but perhaps there is something that your mind is tossing around.

C: There is one thing, but I can't imagine that it would cause sleeplessness.

T: (*That sounded seductive, best to let him bring it up. Let's see what happens when I go away from it.*) Well, if you think it's not a factor, we could look elsewhere for alternatives.

C: It's these thoughts about my ex-girlfriend that keep coming up. I know that she was bad for me, and that the break-up was my idea, and it was miserable, so why can't I recall how bad that was when I try to sleep?

T: Is it about her per se or loneliness or just a riddle that needs to be solved?

C: There you go with all the questions again.

T: (*So I've been seduced twice into following his lead and he is defend-ing—cognitively and externally—by questioning and dismissing what I am doing.*) (joining) My questions seem off today. Mostly what I am aware of is the frustration in the room, and it's hard to get a handle on it. At the risk of another ridiculous question, do you have any ideas about how we might get our heads around this?

C: (Laughing). No. It's been really lonely this week.

T: Lonely and no relief in sleep is a painful combination. (*Instead of pushing him to the next level, taking the process back to reinforce empathy with his position*)

C: I heard that she is going out with this guy.

T: That's got to be troubling. (Normalizing)

C: No. I broke up with her, so it shouldn't bother me (resisting cognitive external again)

T: (*Stay empathic and go to the cognitive—let him come to the affect.*) Even though you don't want to be with her, it doesn't quite fully diminish the news.

C: Why is that? It doesn't make any sense.

T: I can think of a few strange ways—you know how I have those kinds of strange thoughts—why you may be upset. I'm interested in your analysis.

C: Maybe I think that if she is in a relationship before me, maybe it was all my fault.

T: (*That seems loaded, let me go with it.*) What do you think when you examine that rationale?

C: I am pretty competitive and egocentric. . . . (after a silence) I don't think that's it. I am very competitive, but I think it's something else.

T: (*Stay cognitive here.*) You seem to have given this a lot of thought, but competitiveness may not be the answer.

C: Is it normal for me to remember the good parts and forget the bad parts?

T: You tend to focus on the good, and your optimism at work has helped you get ahead. There is something else here. I wonder if we could get our heads around this.

C: (After a long silence) I was in the emergency room last Tuesday. I thought I was having a heart attack. They said my heart was fine. It was a panic attack.

T: That sounds scary. What's it like to tell me that?

C: I haven't told anyone else.

T: This is really important then. I am honored that you trust me with that information.

C: I met this girl a few weeks ago. She's really different. She's quiet and reserved—here's the joke—she's Irish. So I am the talkative Chinese guy with the quiet White girl.

T: How was that for you?

C: (Hesitant, then pause) . . . you didn't ask about the panic attack.

T: What would you like me to know?

As usual, the resistance here was inconsistent. When it did come, approaching him from within the resistant frame was the only useful access he offered. As the session progressed, he disclosed more of his anxiety. Three sessions later, he was able to directly confront some anxiety-based erectile difficulties with the woman. It is important to note that joining the resistance was the most effective method for his progressive self-disclosure. He would push the therapist away whenever he was close to opening up additional vulnerability. When the therapist joined in the method, the more vulnerable side emerged. His sleeplessness dissipated over a 2-week period as they addressed a host of anxiety-laden issues.

Think France in the Early 1940s: Join the Resistance!

The method described here is consistent with other existential approaches and matches the intuitive interventions of many master therapists. The uniqueness of this approach lies in the categorization and systematic application. In all cases, the goal is to identify resistance, recognize it as anxiety about change, and join it sensitively and carefully.

The approach to joining resistance reflects the core of the pragmatic relational-existential method described through the book:

(1) Empathize deeply, and join with the client in his or her personal manner of being-in-the-world.

(2) Identify the client's strengths from the way he or she protects himself or herself in the moment.

(3) Help the client use those strengths to address his or her areas of concern.

(4) Work together as a team to address anxiety.

(5) Help the client separate neurotic and existential anxiety and honor the latter.

(6) Stay as much as possible in the here-and-now relationship.

In many ways, resistance stands as a core of the existential-relational approach.

Notes

1.   A testament to the power of the phenomenon was that the assumption that Erickson had secretly inserted the suggestion contradicts a core tenet of Ericksonian hypnotherapy: that the method is predicated on eliciting something from the client, rather than interjecting the therapist's will.

2.   Family systems approaches have been typically divided into structural and strategic camps. Although all systems approaches share many commonalities, the structural approach grew out of psychodynamic, and the strategic approach was more informed by behavioral theories.

3.   See Chapter 7 of this book for detailed information on stages of therapy and therapeutic change.

4.   Named for Constantin Stanislavski, Method acting, which became popular in the 1930s, involves actors eliciting their personal emotional memory to convey true emotion. There is a combination of empathic observation and expression of emotion that is experienced as genuine. This oft-described ability to cry on cue is actually the actor responding to some sad events in her or his own life. Thus, the tears are genuine, albeit mediated.

6

Using All the Data

How Do Therapists Know What They Know?

> *Someone within you will always be a stranger.*
>
> "The War You Left"
> by Joy of Cooking

Understanding and relating to clients in the manner described in previous chapters is no easy task. Attempting to create an environment for *I-thou* moments, joining clients through their strengths, and helping them create meaning requires insightful observation, intuition, and an ability to communicate effectively.

Like all of the "talking cures," relationally based, pragmatic, existential psychotherapy is built on communication skills including

(1) the ability to accurately perceive the full messages expressed by clients,

(2) the capacity to use internal indices of understanding and meaning, and

(3) the skill to reflect that information back to clients in a usable manner.

The Nature of Human Communication

Human interaction involves a host of interwoven factors. In addition to the content of the words spoken, there are vocal, relational, and contextual indicators that may alter or even reverse the full message.

Mehrabian and his colleagues (1967; 1967) concluded that 90% or more of the meaning in a verbal exchange is conveyed by nonverbal aspects of communication. Although subsequent studies have brought the absolute percentage into question, there is no doubt about the extensive nonverbal components in communication.

Even within the "talking cure," much of the verbal information we absorb is understood in a social context, impacted by how it is said and the state of the receiver. Argyle (1988) summarized the impact of the nonverbal components of communication to be more about the relationship between the speaker and listener than about the passing of information. He noted that the nonverbal components express affect and attitudes about the relationship, manage better the interpersonal cues, preserve one's personality, and keep the communication within cultural bounds.

All human communication relies on contextual and cultural factors. Thus, although the words may be identical to those written in a book, the message that the therapist decodes involves several factors.

Verbal and Nonverbal Communication

Recently, I overheard two of my graduate students during a class break:

E: (In an irritated tone of voice) I can't believe that he texted me this kind of message.

P: Maybe he was in a meeting or something and just wanted you to know that he was thinking of you. Maybe he remembered that you were in class.

E: No, he should have called. Now I can't call him and have to text him back.

P: Maybe you should wait before texting him back. He'll get the message.

The interchange contained subcultural inferences:

1. Texting and vocal communication are not equivalent.

2. There are subcultural conventions about when each is proper.

3. There are rules about responding to a text with a text, instead of a call.

4. There is an expectation that the interval between return text messages carries similar meaning for all parties.

Imagine the potential for relational conflict if the text sender was from another culture, unaware of these unspoken rules. Imagine he was like me, proud to be able simply to successfully send a text message.

In therapy, tones of voice, phrasing, spacing between words, emphasis on certain words, posture, and facial expression all contain important cues for understanding what the client is trying to convey.

Nonverbal Characteristics

Nonverbal components of messages

1. are culturally bound and far more context-specific;

2. communicate affect, attitudes, and values in the situation;

3. are often perceived as more powerful, reliable, and trustworthy; and

4. may emphasize, deemphasize, or even contradict aspects of the verbal message.

When verbal and nonverbal data are congruent, qualifiers tend to go unnoticed. However, any discrepancies between the two create ambiguity, which generates anxiety and necessitates further exploration to read the whole message accurately. In social situations, it is common for the listener to decrease anxiety by quickly resolving the discrepancy—often by choosing the anticipated message as the accurate one. For the therapist, it is essential to read the contrasting implications and to hold them both up for the client.

For example, the client may be relating an event that seems very painful but doing so while smiling at the therapist. Rather than combine those or choose one of the messages, the therapist may provide feedback:

T: What you just told me seems like a painful loss, yet you seem to be smiling while you describe it.

C: I guess I don't want to cry.

T: The smile allows you to tell me about the pain but not have to re-experience it here?

C: If I let myself, I just break down.

T: What if you did let it out here?

C: (Getting teary and then with a grin on her face) You only have one box of tissues.

T: What if I had another box?

Here the therapist responds to the double message by reflecting back to the client that he is aware of both. Rather than resolve them, he honors both components.

Nonverbal Messages Sent From Therapists to Clients

In addition to reading the client's nonverbal communication and receptivity, it is important for a therapist to have insight into what she or he communicates without words. Openness, comfort, or tension may be conveyed simply by body posture.

Do the therapist and client mirror body position? Erickson (1978), speaking about using hypnotherapy, described how he would try to orient his body, the pacing and spacing of his words, and his breathing rate to the client's as a way of enhancing the relationship and the influence of his interventions, stories, and trance inductions.

Physical Appearance and Dress

One of my colleagues, a Bay Area psychiatrist, always wears a bow tie and jacket to work. Another local psychiatrist could challenge Hillary Clinton for her closet of professional pant suits. Many male therapists wear ties when working. I wear an open collar dress shirt and slacks. In Santa Cruz, California, a few years back, one local psychologist wore shorts and a tie-dye shirt while working. Each of these is conveying both what makes them personally comfortable in the work environment and what their clients might expect.

Because of the intensely personal nature of existential work, style, appearance, and dress express "this is who I am." Congruence between a client's and therapist's appearance may make a connection more likely. As I write this, I am over 70 years old and have a full white beard. One of my colleagues has opined that with the right kind of red suit, I could pass easily for

Figure 6.1   Gender-based Demand Characteristics for Female and Male Therapists

It is important to note that female therapists often have a greater challenge than men in dress and appearance. Aside from the wider array of choices for women, they may be more readily judged by their appearance and women's appearance is more typically sexualized in American culture. For this reason, most women, particularly younger ones, have to dress more "professionally" than their male counterparts.

It is just a reality of modern life that a man can wear the same attire to work and to dinner; not always so for women.

Aging does mitigate this somewhat and brings to mind the lovely poem "Warning" by Jenny Joseph: *"When I am an old woman, I shall wear purple."*

Santa Claus. It's hard to estimate the positive impact on clients. Although this may be out of the client's conscious awareness, it can impact the necessary feeling of finding someone who is likely to understand.

Therapist Age

Characteristically, clients report feeling most comfortable with a therapist who is older than themselves. This age expectation can be an issue at times, particularly for newly licensed therapists. How comfortable will a 50-year-old married client feel about discussing relational issues with a 26-year-old therapist? It's a question that arises frequently in training.

One of the real advantages of this field, and existential work in particular, is that therapists hit their peak much later than those in other professions. Several years ago, I had the opportunity to have an extended conversation with renowned family therapist Carl Whitaker while driving him from the airport to his hotel prior to a presentation. As we discussed psychotherapy in general, he revealed, "You know, the older I get, the less resistance there is to whatever I say to families; one of the (perquisites) of aging." The statement really struck me. It could be that he was just so much more adept and less ego involved when he encountered resistance after years of experience, but it could also be true that clients are less likely to resist someone who looks like a grandparent. I might add that it was one of the few times in my life that I was grateful for rush hour traffic on Highway 101. It gave me a far longer chance to visit personally and alone with one of the experts in my field.[1]

Office Ambiance: Contextual Cues

Regardless of particular technical skills a therapist may have, clients will respond differentially to the ambiance in his or her office. Many years ago, I shared an office suite and waiting room with Virginia, a very fine therapist, whose office décor was noticeably different from mine. My office was replete with bookshelves, a few art objects I had picked up on my travels, large comfortable reclining chairs, and a sofa. Virginia's seemed more like a Victorian drawing room. She had delicate china, frills, and fringes on the chair covers, small seats with upright backs, and shawls over the small love seat. It should not be much of a surprise that her clientele was almost entirely adult women. I observed a few times when she did conjoint couples therapy, watching the male member of the couple freezing momentarily in the doorway, wondering I guessed, if there was a place for him to sit. When she and I conversed in her office, I had the same feeling I had when visiting my children's elementary school classrooms with the miniscule chairs that looked like they might not bear my weight.

On the other hand, when she visited my office, she seemed to almost disappear in my large reclining chair. My clients were usually men or couples. Obviously, she and I were appealing to somewhat different populations of clients.

The impact of the office environment was brought home to me vividly when I was in training. One of my clients was a young woman who was dealing with both relational and career concerns. One day, we both arrived at the appointed hour only to discover that the clinic office was closed for a Canadian holiday. I recommended that we each drive to my university office and meet there. A few days later, when I played the tape of the session for my supervisor, he commented, "Something is very different here . . . More social interaction . . . less depth . . . it's almost as if you were meeting at a different location." Amazed at his intuition and perceptiveness, I immediately told him what had happened. He responded, "My guess is that you have more personal things in your university office, and she was responding to those! There will be a readjustment next week, when you are back at the clinic." It was one of those powerful intern-learning moments.

No one space or décor will appeal universally. In existential work, in which the relationship is so vital, congruence between the space and the therapist's self is an excellent beginning. A discrepancy between a client's expectation and the actual office appearance may be sufficient to reduce the likelihood of a second session. If the client expected a "light and airy" ambiance and found herself in a dark "man cave" office, she may feel sufficiently out of place, regardless of what was discussed.

Metacommunication

In addition to awareness about the content and context of communication, therapists need to attend to additional relational messages that are also being transmitted. Bateson (1972), Haley (1963), and Watzlawick, Bavelas, and Jackson (1967) argued that all communication carried with it additional (meta) components that delineated how each message that passed could redefine the relationship between the parties.

For example, a client may ask a predictable question in therapy: "Exactly what is existential therapy?" "How long have you been in practice?" "Can we renegotiate the fee?" Of course, he or she is interested in an answer to the query, but in addition, the client is asserting, *"I am announcing my right to ask you a question."*

If the therapist responds directly to the content, he or she is, at a meta-level, agreeing with the client's assertion. If the therapist responds instead with a statement, such as, "you are wondering about my ability to help you," he or she is simultaneously opening up the discussion of client motivation or anxiety and declaring disagreement with the client's meta-assertion. The therapist is affirming that he or she is the one who gets to ask questions and, in addition, is asserting his or her right to interpret what the client is saying.

This may seem overly complex, but awareness of metacommunication offers therapists another window into the meaning of client verbalizations by focusing less on presumed intent and more on consequences.

Why Consequences?

Because consequences often reveal the client's opting for the status quo, they have a significant place in existential interventions. When the therapist and client together recognize an unfolding here-and-now process that has an inevitable consequence of apparent security and protection from facing fears of the unknown, the client may begin to confront the implications consciously.

Understanding metacommunication is best accomplished by attending to the unique internal reaction each person has to any interaction. As a therapist, I may not be immediately aware of a client's motivation to keep interactions in the session safe, but I can be aware of feeling pressured to accept the options the client verbally offers. Experiencing that consequence, I have the option to adjust. Often there is a parallel between what the client is relating and the interpersonal process in the session.

C: I met this woman last weekend, and it was going well, but she was playing these games . . . talking about how men didn't take her seriously, and she was trying to stand up for herself.

J: Where did that leave you?

C: Well, you know, I want to meet someone who is good enough for me, and she was smart, but I just don't like the game playing.

J: *(Is he saying that we are playing games here?)* And . . .

C: Well, I just crushed her at her game. I asked a lot of questions and really pinned her down to defend her position. After a while, she left and I went home.

J: *(This may be a status quo victory in here also. I am feeling cut off by his words and cavalier attitude about his "victory." I'll approach intellectually.)* So, a bit of a Pyrrhic victory?

C: Let me recall, is that where he won the battle, but everyone died?

J: Yes. You went out to the party to meet a woman and to attempt a new relationship and you were successful in several ways. You met someone at least a little bit interesting, and somehow you managed to get home alone without her number.

C: You know that's not what I want!

J: I do know that. *(Staying with consequences)* I am just struck by how effective you are at staying single . . . in this case, by refusing to play her games by attacking her vulnerability.

C: I just think that I need someone who doesn't play games.

J: *(He is holding to his position. The metamessage here is he needs to be right and maintain control. What if I focus on what would happen if he relinquished control?)* I agree that game playing is not what you want or need and if pushed, you can be devastating at it, but I wonder if you'd engage in a few moments of speculation here about that woman? (Client nods assent.) Imagine for a moment that she plays those games because she is anxious and that you were to devise a strategy to get her to be more real. How might you approach the situation? Talk to me as if I am her.

After a few minutes of role play, the therapist wondered again aloud, being careful to acknowledge C's need to be in control,

J: So if we are right here, and it's purely supposition, let's imagine that she gave you her number. What would that force you to deal with?

Communication and the State of the Receiver

Regardless of how well we communicate, there is room for misunderstanding based on the state of the receiver and by what he or she expects to hear. In any relationship, there is, at times, a discrepancy between what is said and what is heard.

Confirmation Bias

It is common for individuals to gather, interpret, and remember information that confirms their biases or expectations. Thus, an expectation that the other person will be hostile or disagreeable will increase the sensitivity to anything that may hint at negativity. There may be a lower threshold of doubt or less willingness to suspend critical thinking or disbelief while searching out those confirming messages. Once they are perceived, it adds to confidence that the bias was accurate and increases the likelihood of further discoveries.

Confirmation bias (Nickerson, 1998) is particularly strong with emotionally charged issues or a sense of threat around a deeply ingrained belief. In general, the emotional state of the receiver, especially anxiety, may exacerbate confirmation bias.

Self-Esteem of the Receiver

The way a client feels about herself will often determine what parts of a message are heard. For a person with low self-esteem, almost any message may be reinterpreted through the unworthiness lens.

When she came into therapy, Alicia, 29 years old, was a successful marketer and graphic artist for a biotech firm. She had been at the company for 5 years and had received progressive promotions. Although she may have been slightly above her preferred weight, she was fit, had an open, attractive face, and dressed stylishly. She claimed that she had been "lucky at work, but unlucky in love." Early in therapy, she described prior relationships, focusing particularly on her high school sweetheart, who had left her for another girl during their junior year. She was convinced that his new girlfriend was smarter, more athletic, and prettier.

A: I'll never have a good relationship. Guys just don't like fat chicks.

T: And you see yourself as "fat."

A: I'm sure you can see that.

T: What's important is what you are seeing.

A: Well, I have tried about every diet possible, and they never work, and I will probably end up a spinster. I can see that you are married and very pretty. I am fat and ugly and single.

As she went on to describe failed relationships with men as an adult, she also indicated that although her bosses and coworkers appreciated her at work, she considered her performance subpar.

One man she met recently told her he thought she was beautiful and witty.

T: What was that like for you to be called beautiful and witty?

A: Oh, I figured he was just trying to get me into bed.

T: And . . .

A: Well, I didn't succumb to his flattery . . . but he called back and asked me out again. I think there may be something wrong with him.

T: Any ideas what that may be?

A: I Googled him and checked him out online. There wasn't anything obvious. He has no arrest record, is an occasional social drinker like me, and we like a lot of the same music and activities.

T: And he was okay not rushing into a sexual relationship.

A: Yeah, so I wondered if maybe he was gay or nonsexual, but he kissed me on our third date and he was into it.

T: The impression I get is that the biggest red light here is that he sees you as attractive.

A: (Laughing) Yeah. What's that Woody Allen line about not wanting to be in a club . . .

T: I think it's Groucho Marx who said something like, "I wouldn't want to be in any club that would accept someone like me for membership." I wonder what you would have to deal with if he saw your flaws, and he was attracted to you anyhow.

The obvious goal was to find a way to open the communication channels by having the client *risk* removing her "fat and unwanted" filter. Assuming that it was somehow functional, the therapist decided not to challenge directly the perception of low self-esteem. Instead, she focused on the challenge of being accepted despite the "obvious flaws." This way, the client's defense against either abandonment or suffocation in a relationship might be addressed.

Her therapist needed to understand how Alicia selectively perceived input and worked with her by adding bandwidth that allowed Alicia to explore her world from a perspective in which the low self-esteem filter was more porous. This is far more effective than directly providing contrary evidence to try to change Alicia's mind. Alicia's self-deprecating filters would have blocked the message, and she would conclude that the therapist was not very perceptive.

Therapist Confirmation Biases

Clients are not alone in filtering input. Perceptions and understandings of what clients are communicating may be filtered greatly by the theoretical and cultural frame of the therapist. Thus, a psychodynamic therapist might tune into historical antecedents of current behavior, a cognitive behavior therapist may see disordered thinking, and the existential therapist may look for what is occurring in the moment.

For Alicia, the woman with low self-esteem, each theoretical set of filters might generate different data, and those might in turn lead to different approaches. Some therapists might want to focus historically on the trauma of being rejected by the high school boyfriend or on earlier attachment issues that may have generated her low self-esteem. Others, through use of Socratic questioning and directed work on the cognitions that go into the low self-esteem, might look at opportunities for thoughts or behaviors that could counteract the low self-esteem. By definition, each unique theory brings with it filters to highlight what is important (separating wheat from chaff) and methods to address the identified issues. Thus, therapy with Alicia, or any client, may seem radically different across therapists.[2]

The Therapy Context and Communication

In any communication, meaning conveyed is impacted by the entire milieu. In therapy, all communication occurs in a special environment with unique rules. Therapy is essentially a one-sided relationship, focused on the client's needs. Unconditional positive regard (Rogers, 1951) is possible only in such an unequal relationship. A therapist may have personal reactions, but they are used primarily to better adjust to and understand the client.

Although perceptual acuity is important for all therapists, it is mandatory for existential therapists, for whom everything important is occurring in the here-and-now. Accepting the import of communication in the moment requires attunement to multiple levels of input. For this form of therapy, there is far greater reliance on rapport than report and on meta-communication, because of the immediate impact these may have on the here-and-now therapist-client relationship.

The Psychotherapy Context

At the beginning of a session, there is a transition from normal social or business interaction to the asocial interactions that occur in the consulting room. It is somewhat analogous to a person who is bilingual and bicultural. A client may be speaking one language and using one cultural framework on an ongoing basis, and then when the situation shifts, he or she may reorient to the second language.

It is not just the words that are translated, the whole culture shifts, along with behaviors, meanings, and inferences that may not fit in the first language.

Linguist Benjamin Whorf (1956) opined that because of linguistic differences in grammar and usage, speakers of different languages conceptualize and experience the world differently. In short, there may not be categories within some cultures and languages for experiences that are intricately delineated by those in others. It is useful to recognize therapy as a unique cultural context.

Therapists' Processing Systems: The Use of Self

The plethora of communication and contextual variables are understood by therapists through their theories and intellect, their well-developed perceptual skills, and some less obvious, yet significant means of processing input, both within and between sessions.

Because existential therapy is so oriented to the moment and to what is occurring in the here-and-now, the therapist needs to be particularly well attuned to all that the client is offering or presenting in real time. The effective therapist is acutely perceptive in discerning what the client is experiencing and in understanding the nonverbal modifiers.

Content and Process: Revisited

As described above, the content of a message sent from client to therapist comprises the words alone, as if they were written down on a blank sheet of paper, texted, or appear on a computer screen. That content, embedded within the current relationship between therapist and client, is considered the *process* of communication. Understanding the content-in-context process involves a multiplicity of data sources, some involving cognitive and sensory perceptions, some linear, others intuitive.

Linear Sources (Empirical/Observable Data)

Linear data include whatever the client brings to the therapy moment that may be observed or reasoned, based on the therapist's orientation. A well-trained therapist pays very close attention to the observables that the client brings to the moment. Both verbal and nonverbal cues are almost automatically integrated into how a clinician approaches a client. Sources of data may include several qualifying aspects of clients' communication styles. Do they make eye contact? Do they sit up at the edge of their chairs while talking? Are they animated? Do they keep their smartphones on to look at text messages during sessions? Do they look around the consulting room for distractions? Sometimes, it is the therapist's keen perception of minute cues that makes a significant difference in both understanding clients and intervening clinically.

Other sources of linear data, such as intake information, a client's previous therapy, and the referral source also impact understanding and point to an intervention approach.

When Fred first entered therapy, he listed several former therapists. Naturally, I asked him why he chose not to return to one of them. His response was quite important in formulizing the therapy moving forward.

F: Well, you know how therapists are.

J: What in particular?

F: They all wanted to talk about my "sainted Irish mother" and could not believe that my relationship with her was fine.

J: So if I want you to leave therapy, all I have to do is bring up issues with your mother.

F: You got it.

J: What other issues may be off-limits?

F: That's it!

Within those parameters, set by the client, the I was well-advised. After 2 years of therapy, Fred introduced the matter of his mother once he was certain that I was able to work from within his protective system.

Nonlinear (Intuitive) Sources of Data

Several years ago, I owned one of those large, rotating satellite dishes. It could receive hundreds of channels from 36 satellites in geosynchronous orbit. Most of the channels received were quite familiar to broadcast and cable subscribers today, but that wasn't all that was travelling to and from the satellites. Television and FM radio signals share bandwidth. With the proper decoding, I could receive additional "hidden" uploads and downloads. For example, when my dial was tuned to receive television station WGN in Chicago, I could adjust settings to also receive a subchannel, WFMT, an impressive Windy City FM station that featured primarily classical music and the Saturday Night "Midnight Special" program of folk and blues music.

It was all a matter of what my equipment was set to receive. This is a remarkable metaphor for the way therapists interpret what their clients are saying. It has long been clear to psychotherapists that multichannel communication occurs all the time. Master therapists have a wide bandwidth of multiple inter-woven channels. Many are nonlinear, subjective, less rational, or intuitive. Often the messages from all channels are consistent. When that occurs, there is little notice of many subfrequencies. However, when the messages do not coincide, such as the simultaneous broadcast of a Chicago Cubs game on the TV chan-nel and a Tchaikovsky festival on FM, the discrepancy becomes quite evident.[3]

The Inner Life of Therapists

When a plumber goes out on a first job, he has that large tool box with all sorts of implements of his trade. The clanging sound of the wrenches, clamps, and hammers are reassuring, even for apprentices. When therapists ply their trade, the major tools are internal capacities—no comforting clatter of metal on metal. Of course, even novices are aware of and somewhat prac-ticed in empathy for client content, certain listening and reflective skills, and theoretical approaches, but these are primarily cognitive capabilities. What makes master therapists unique is the development of their capacities for understanding and accepting data from a host of internal sources.

Nonlinear sources of data are often referred to summarily as therapist intuition. These include the therapist's awareness and use of her or his own feelings, auditory and visual imagery, symbols, dreams, metaphors, stories, and therapist free association. In addition, the ambiance created by the clini-cian as a person and by the setting is influential.

Reverie

Psychodynamic theorists and therapists, such as Bion (1962), Ogden (1997), and Quatman (2015) use the term *reverie* to describe unconscious processing that includes kinesthetic, visual, and auditory imagery as well as fantasies, ruminations, and daydreams. Defining the process, Quatman wrote,

> *we are the recipients of a level of access to the inner experience of the other, and ultimately an understanding of the other that could only be yielded by a co-creational process, and that is, at the same time, both a mystery and a gift* (2015, p. 135).

The Brain and Communication

The budding field of neuroscience is identifying how our brains mirror each other in subconscious ways and how feelings are transmitted between people at primitive brain levels. It is something similar to the oft-repeated refrain that dogs can "smell" fear and respond by automatically becoming more aggressive.

Neuroscientists such as Panksepp and Panksepp (2013) have shown that empathy, particularly for fear, occurs between rodents and other submammalian species. Solms and Panskepp (2012) and others analyzing what they call "neuro-psycho-evolutionary data" have also suggested that lower brain functioning assists in providing the energy for construction of higher forms of cognition. Finally, Panksepp and Biven (2012) provide an archeology of the mind in which they provide the connection between neurobiology and emotion based on brain loci.

These significant findings of modern technology reaffirm classic experimental studies by Schachter and Singer (1962) and clinical inferences postulated by Berne (1969) and others for decades: Although all this occurs in nanoseconds, affect precedes cognition. Nowhere is this more obvious than in emergency situations. When the sympathetic nervous system activates, it is initially for fight or flight, only secondarily does cognitive functioning take over to make reasoned decisions.

This has important implications for clinicians. If significant sources of data are carried on nonlinear, subconscious channels, it opens up a potential gold mine for clinical insight. When two individuals can communicate, unconscious mind to unconscious mind, the number of channels on which we are connecting may increase dramatically.

The notion of unconscious transmission of important communication has been codified in part in Jung's conceptualization of a genetic collective unconscious. For Jung (1959) all humans carry an identical psychic system of a collective, universal, and impersonal nature.[4] Whether this level of psychic connection is inherited or is shared in social ways, it is a significant component of therapeutic connection.

The recognition of either congruence or disconnection of linear and nonlinear communication allows therapists to approach and enter a client's system with greater empathy, caring, and accuracy. Often described as "intuition," or clinically as "attunement," it reflects input from the therapist's feelings, auditory and visual imagery, and context-specific information.

Feelings (Kinesthetic Imagery)

A therapist's emotional reactions during sessions are a source of nonlinear data. At times during a session, the therapist may well experience anger, sadness, joy, or any other emotion. These may be an important indicator of what is happening at a less observable level in the room. When therapists are aware of their own feelings during sessions, they may better discern what clients are saying or not saying at any given moment and help the clients become similarly attuned to their own affect during interactions.

C: I know it's normal these days, but I still think it's not wise for our daughter to be living with us since she graduated from college.

T: What is the part that is troubling about it?

C: Well, she might become unmotivated and just hang out with us and never use her education.

T: When you said that, I picked up a lot of sadness in the room.

C: It's me. I was crying last night when I thought that I had failed as a father, and now she might pay for that.

T: I can see a tear, so it's sad in here also. Tell me about the sadness.

In this case, the therapist's personal sadness allowed both the therapist and the client to be more present and to work on the important issue of his fears of failure as a father. The therapist accurately picked up the sadness coming from the client at an emotional level underneath his words. In this example, the affect experienced was an accurate reflection of the client's state. It isn't mandatory that the feeling is accurate to be effective. Often the emotion labelled by the therapist is corrected by the client.

The following occurred during the seventh session with a client, a mature man who is very cognitive and rational in his approach to life. His work as a computer engineer made him successful at work and supported his natural rational approach to his life. He was describing what seemed to be a very distressing circumstance at work: to identify two members of his team to lose their jobs and to convey the bad news that they would be the next victims of the company's downsizing. He was talking about how he had argued with his boss to keep his team intact and provided excellent data to support his argument.

As he talked on, his body seemed to be almost immobile and his jaw seemed clenched.

T: What does that feel like?

C: Well, you know how this economy is. The truth is that our profits are down, and we are a little heavy in personnel. The problem is that the fat is in other divisions. We are already lean, and we are the only profit center in the whole company.

T: Yes, but what are you feeling now?

C: Well, you know there's a lot of injustice in this world, and this is only one example.

T: Well, I am aware of feeling a lot of sadness right now as we sit here. I'm wondering if I am picking up some of that from you.

C: No. I don't think I am sending off any sadness. Of course the situation is sad, but I am keeping my job. (As he said this his voice was raising.) I'm just really pissed at my boss for being so foolish and not fighting for us with the vice president.

T: So perhaps some anger is what I am sensing.

C: I am very irritated and resent being put in this situation where I have to choose and deliver the news and that S.O.B. gets off like it wasn't his fault. (As he said this he began to tear up.)

T: Let's stay with the anger a moment. What does it mean to you that your carefully supported arguments were ignored?

The therapist used her well-honed affective receptivity to discern what was going on inside her client and she put it out in a nonthreatening manner. Her initial appraisal of the feeling in the room may have been inaccurate. Corrected by the client, it became an effective intervention. It is also possible that she was accurate, but he was unable to deal with the sadness, at least until he expressed directly the anger, a more comfortable emotion at the moment.

In some situations, kinesthetic imagery may be directly conveyed to a client. Ellen had been suffering from some serious posttraumatic stress disorder (PTSD) following a sexual assault while she was on military duty. She had followed through as best as she could with the command structure and ultimately decided to leave the service when her term was up. This was a change in her long-term plan of being a career officer. She first came into therapy with me 3 years after her honorable discharge. As we talked, she indicated that she was all too familiar with being pushed around and physically mistreated as she was growing up.

E: I've been going to this women's support group at the Veterans Administration (VA), and this week we are to make a list of people who have harmed us and think about how we could confront them.

J: What's that like for you?

E: It's okay. The other women are all very supportive, and we all have lots of issues.

J: What are you thinking about right now?

E: I need to go and confront this old teacher at my high school who almost raped me when I was around 15.

J: That sounds very scary.

E: Well, someone has to tell about her. I know that I'm not the only girl she accosted.

J: (Responding to his own feelings) I just got a real chill when you said that.

E: (After what seemed like a 2-minute silence, Ellen became very emotional.) I don't want to cry in here.

J: Do you know what's making you feel teary?

E: You are feeling *my* chill. It's like death and everything is still and cold. When I was over in Iraq, I sometimes got the same chill when I was alone on guard duty.

J: So what we are experiencing here is terror.

When we faced together the actual emotion in the room, we became more able to communicate about what was happening in the now instead of the report of her homework assignment or pressured plans of action.

Other Generators of Feelings

The specific emotion being experienced is not always clear. Perhaps a therapist will get a sense of what is going on in the room by noticing that he or she is feeling uncomfortable and taking a few moments to check in. Being aware of one's own feelings while also listening closely to a client involves a certain level of trust in one's own unconscious processing. Of course this means a therapist must be aware of any personal issues he or she is bringing into the room.

I reported previously on an event that occurred in group therapy several years ago. I was one of two coleaders of a group that was about to begin a marathon (15 hour) session. At approximately 2:00 a.m., 7 hours before the group was to begin, I was surprised by the abrupt break-up of an important relationship. Without question, my emotional capacity was both sensitized and compromised by what I carried into the group session (Shapiro, Peltz, & Bernadett-Shapiro, 1997).

Without my competent cotherapist, I would have been far less able to trust my emotional reactivity to clients. It would have been easy to project my own emotional tumult into clients' dealing with troubled relationships and, in the process, potentially miss what they were communicating.

A very different kind of situation occurred for me with a client whose regular appointment was at 1:30 p.m., right after lunch. Although the client was a very bright, engaging, and attractive 29-year old woman, we went through a number of sessions during which all the emotional oxygen seemed to drain out of the room. As I tried to focus on her, I found myself sleepy and struggling to stay awake. At first I assumed that it was a post-lunch, blood sugar issue and began by scheduling my lunch after her session. I also increased the airflow and lowered the air temperature in the room. Finally, and with dread of insulting a patient by suggesting that she was "boring me," I engaged in the following intervention.

J: As you were talking just now, I became aware that I was losing a lot of energy. I'm wondering what it's like for you in here?

C: I am feeling pretty low today also. Maybe you are just picking up on my tiredness.

J: That may be it, but can we take just a few minutes of your time to discuss what is happening in here?

C: Pretty much the usual. I've been tired all week . . .

J: (Getting even more exhausted) Perhaps there's something we are not discussing.

C: (Suddenly looking embarrassed and blushing) I've been having this dream about you for a few weeks. It's upsetting I think.

J: Would you be willing to share the dream?

C: It's mostly images. Although nothing ever actually happens in the dream, it feels very sexual. I woke up one time very . . . aroused.

J: What about the sexual aspect of the dream is unsettling?

C: You know, I have a real problem with sexual relationships. Whenever a sexual relationship gets close and personal, I lose interest.

J: You can be intimate or sexual, but when they are combined, it's threatening, and so you find a way out. So . . . in here, when our relationship becomes sexual in your dreams, it is more threatening and you pull back by removing the energy in the room. What's it like to be discussing it now?

C: Anxious, scary. My mind is racing to other topics.

J: What if you tried to be with the anxiety for a few minutes, knowing that this relationship will not be physically sexual?

In this case, my increasing tiredness turned out to be reflective of the client's emotional withdrawal. To use terms she later expressed, encapsulating her separation of intimacy and sexuality "I am pretty good at leaving my body here, but sending my mind elsewhere!" By paying attention to the disquieting feelings of my own drowsiness during session, I was able to open a valuable door for discussion and in the process became quite energized and focused.

Emotional sensitivity is not the only access to unconscious indices that help identify a more accurate understanding of client-therapist communication.

Visual Imagery

It is very common for individuals to represent their world through visual imagery. They *see* what is happening in their *mind's eye*. Therapists often employ visual imagery to understand what their clients are expressing, to theorize what it means, discern what is important, and when to intervene.

Many therapists experience what their clients are saying visually. While a client is describing an event in their present or past, the therapist may picture something from his or her own life or history. These visual images may provide another level of connection to the client as well as potentially novel interventions. During one point, a client was describing her continuously troublesome relationship with her significant other. As she began to rehash the "can't live with him; can't live without him" material from prior sessions, the therapist intervened.

T: I just had the image of Charlie Brown trying to fly his kite. No matter how many times he tried, it always ended up in a tree.

C: Are you saying I'm like Charlie Brown? I guess I do feel that way often, especially when he tries to kick the football, and Lucy pulls it up no matter how many times she promises not to.

T: That may be more accurate, but I wasn't picturing you as Charlie Brown. I was seeing you as the kite—at the mercy of the wind, the trees, and of course whoever, in this case Kyle, has the string.

C: You may be right. I often think that I don't have a mind of my own. I just do what others do and go where the wind takes me.

T: (Reflecting on how controlling the client seemed in the therapeutic relationship) I know that's how you describe yourself in romantic relationships. Is it also true with your friends and at work?

C: No. I am the go-to person at work. I know where I want to go and how to get there. I guess sometimes when there's a large group, I'm a follower with my friends, but Julie and I are definitely equals.

T: So this is important. It looks like the situation with Kyle is the aberrant one. What is there about you and him that causes you to be so subservient?

C: I'm afraid that if I don't do what he wants, he'll dump me, and I'll be alone.

T: Tell me about your worries about being rejected.

The shared image, initiated from the therapist's unconscious, allowed the therapy to move to a deeper level rather than traverse familiar patterns. This is not to convey that there is magic in the art of therapy. It is acknowledging that the way a therapist represents client input may be in the form of imagery, rather than more linear sentences.

A similar example occurred in a group therapy session with a client who was demeaning herself and presenting herself as particularly unappealing. Despite members' disagreeing with her, it was a visual image from my cotherapist that changed the ambiance.

C: Basically, I am just a stick in the mud, never wanting do anything, just a drudge going to work and back to my apartment.

T: I just had this image of you (it happened last week also). I visualized you as a young bird, perched on a tree limb. You are about to spread your wings and fly away, but you hesitate to look around and leave the tree and nest behind.

C: I'd like to be that bird and soar into the air and see where the winds take me.

T: What would that look like in here? What might you do differently right now?

C: It makes me scared.

T: It is scary! Try to describe what is so risky here?

After the session I asked my cotherapist about the image. She replied, "I first had it the first night of the group when she introduced herself. Then it came up several times later, so I just thought I'd share it now and see what might happen. Worse come to worst, she would have just rejected it and stayed stuck."

Auditory Imagery

In addition to kinesthetic and visual processing, some therapists are primarily auditory in the way they represent perceptions in their worlds. Such individuals are prone to understanding how things *sound* and to activate their perceptual world around auditory input. I am personally aware, for example, of an almost constant music track running in my brain. It's not dominant, but when I feel stuck with a client, I can sometimes tap into the music. As surprising, and bizarre, as it may seem, the music often indicates to me what my unconscious mind is processing. For example, during a session that seems stuck, I might find myself paying attention to the Volga Boatman theme or another dirge.

Indirect Use of Auditory Input

Unless I am working directly with a musician or a client who also processes the world in an auditory manner, I will not share that image directly but take in the understanding of what's occurring in the moment from the dirge-like representation. I can then reflect back to the client a sense of despair, depression, or sadness.

At 45 years old, Ken was unemployed and was running out of his benefits. He reported that he had two interviews during the past week. Although he seemed unenthusiastic about either, he seemed to be emotionally level on the surface. However, the session seemed to be going in circles. I took a moment to tap into my own unconscious processing. I became aware that the music I was hearing was an old blues number, "Nobody knows the trouble I've seen." Like many "slave songs," it's a song about isolation and hope only through divine presence.[5]

K: So that's basically the way things have been going. Not really much different this week

J: *(If nobody knows his troubles, how can I convey that?)* I am getting a sense that you are feeling very much alone and that nobody really understands you, even here.

K: Sounds like you've been reading my journal!

J: Tell me what it's like to feel that even your therapist doesn't understand.

K: Well, now you do. I just feel like I'm losing my manhood the longer I am out of work.

Often therapist's inferences can be off target. Had I misread the input from my own internal processing, the next few interactions may have gone like this:

J: I am getting a sense that you are feeling very much alone and that nobody really understands you, even here.

K: No, I don't think so.

J: So what would be a more accurate description?

K: I think I am holding in a lot of anger. I am being screwed after having spent my life being a good guy.

J: Let's talk about this anger.

The lack of concordance between my interpretation of how the music was informing me wouldn't necessarily slow down or inhibit the progress of therapy. It just allowed the client to correct me with his subjective experience in a way that we could work. In fact, the opportunity for him to correct me and move ahead may be facilitative in helping him feel more in charge of his life, at least in this moment.

Notice that I did not share my personal auditory imagery with him. For one thing, that was my unconscious, not his. Ken might respond with confusion, upset, and misunderstanding about my listening to old blues songs in my head during his session. I used the information from my unconscious processing to reconnect with him on a more relational plane.

Direct Expression of Auditory Imagery

With some clients, it may be possible to share the imagery directly. I was working with Nick, second violinist in a good symphony orchestra. He believed that he should be first violinist, but he never seemed to move up, even though he reported that he was technically the better musician. As he described his work and home life, he seemed to be constantly busy; ever focusing on what needed to be done. When he asked about what gave him pleasure, he paused for a long while and then said, "Getting things done well." Meanwhile, as I checked in while we were together, the music in my mind varied from active classical pieces to some very busy rock and roll.

J: When it comes to music, you are keen to make each note technically right, just as the composer wrote it. When it comes to your relationship with your wife and children, you take a similar approach, trying to be the best you can be.

N: What's wrong with that?

J: Nothing, except you seem frustrated at having too much to do in a day.

N: Maybe if I just worked smarter.

J: Perhaps. *(Focusing on the music theme)* I was wondering if you were composing your life these days, what piece would be the score.

N: Hah! Probably something from Tchaikovsky.

J: That's funny. When I tune into the soundtrack I have for you, it alternates between Rimsky-Korsakov's "Flight of the Bumble Bee" and the Beatles' "Helter Skelter."

N: Funny you mention it. I've been listening a lot to the "White Album." Maybe I am going at that speed.

J: Are you aware of any music that would describe this moment?

N: Well. You mentioned "Flight of the Bumble Bee."

J: A few sessions ago, you mentioned how pleased you were that the symphony was playing the "Jupiter" this season. What would happen if you began playing Mozart in your mind right now?

Long pause.

J: (Noticing that his breathing had slowed and that he seemed more relaxed in his chair) What's happening?

N: I love that piece, It's in (the key of) E, which always makes me feel more connected.

J: It's good to be in your comfort zone. What could we do to help keep you in Jupiter's orbit, instead of flying around like a bumble bee, desperate for the next flower?

We were subsequently able to connect around his near frenzy to get things right, and in the process, losing his sense of direction and personal center.

A truly magical moment occurred several sessions later. He reported that he had been offered an opening for first violinist in a well-regarded touring orchestra. As we explored it, he was tortured between the opportunity and the security of his current position. Somewhere late in the session, he turned to me and said,

N: Okay. You're the musical genius, what's playing in your head now? Probably "Revolution Number 9," right?'

J: (Taking a few moments to check in—*Do I want to share this, it seems out of left field?*) You know, this may sound really weird, it's a great old fiddle tune, "Orange Blossom Special." I don't know if you know it.

N: (Looking stunned) I don't know how you knew that. That was the first song I ever mastered on the fiddle. It made me want a career as a musician. I heard it as a kid by Vassar Clements. I spent hours comparing that to the Flatt and Scruggs and Charlie Daniels versions. I bet you never saw me as a bluegrass guy—all the (other) three B's (Bach, Beethoven, and Brahms). Haha—my little secret. Did you know that when I "slum it," I jam with a local bluegrass band?

J: So somehow, I picked up on your playful side. What does that side want? Do you want to hop on a train like the Special or Wabash Cannonball?

N: I really do want to try the first violin job. I just get so scared about leaving my comfort zone.

J: If you did take on that challenge, you'd be like that kid trying to master such a tough song as the "Orange Blossom Special." Let's talk about the risks and what it'd be like being challenged like that.

I cannot say definitively what linked my auditory unconscious to his. Perhaps any response to his request might have been facilitative. The fact that the particular tune was so personally meaningful to him opened a door for us to explore the boyish side of his personality, a part of him that he (and his family) enjoyed only rarely. It is possible that the music was an amazing coincidence, but given the substantial data indicating the close psychoneurologic connection between music and emotion (i.e., Habibi & Dimasio, 2014), it is also possible that we had made that unconscious connection.

Symbols

Many therapists are drawn to various mythologies or art forms that hold meaning. When a client is describing repeated relationship disasters, it's not hard to connect with a myth like "Tristan and Isolde" or "Romeo and Juliet."[6]

By bringing it to the myth level, the client and therapist may be able to get a better handle on events without confronting them (and the accumulated resistance) head on. Many therapists report using Jungian archetypes, Greek and Far Eastern myths, or religious imagery as a way to understand and reach clients.

Therapists are not alone in using symbols to represent complex emotions. A client's personal symbols of meaning may be excellent keys to their personal values, unconscious life, and attribution of meaning. While working with Vietnam-era veterans, it became clear that one of the blocks to moving on was retention of symbols from the war. One retired infantry master sergeant, who had seen considerable combat, frequently described how when he looked at his medals, he felt "undone." He brought them in to sessions, and as he described them, he became very tearful. He had been told by friends and members of his (VetCenter) PTSD therapy group to lock them away and not keep them in clear view.

After a few weeks of exploration, during which he always carried the medals with him, the following interaction occurred,

C: My group told me again that I should dump the medals. I know they're right, but I can't do it.

J: What would it mean if you put these away?

C: I don't know. I just can't do it.

J: Instead of doing that, may I ask you to do something very difficult?

C: (Suspiciously) You can ask . . .

J: Could we talk about each of the medals individually in here?

We began a very painful experience of a few sessions, which we arranged on three back-to-back days, so I could monitor his reactions. Although there was no suicidal ideation, I was concerned about how agitated he might have become. After a halting start, he actually became calmer as he described what occasioned each medal.

In the third of those meetings, we began to talk about what the medals meant to him.

J: It seems like while the medals keep part of you in Nam, which is problematic, they also keep you connected to comrades and buddies.

C: (Sobbing) My only connection to those who didn't make it back.

J: Getting rid of them, means forgetting the sacrifices and horrors you faced.

C: It's more than that. I also did some things that I didn't know I was capable of doing, and I don't want to ever see that side again.

J: So the medals keep you from looking at the hell that was around you and even in you.

Once we had broached the symbolic meaning of the medals, we explored how he could remember without torturing himself. His solution, which emerged from his VetCenter group, was to find the loved ones of those killed in Nam and offer them the medals in memory of their family members.

Although I did not share this symbolic ideation with my client, once I got to experience his pain at both keeping and losing the medals, I could connect with personal experiences of holding onto objects to prevent facing old abandonments and new fears.

Representational Systems

Clients and therapists alike tend to represent their perceptual lives primarily in visual, auditory, or kinesthetic ways (Bandler & Grinder, 1975; Rosen, 1982). The construct was derived from careful observation and codification of Erickson's "intuitive" methods of joining clients. In the example above, I was able to use my auditory processing with that of my clients. With a client who represents his perceptual world more visually, it would have been more facilitative to intervene using visual imagery.

Clues to a client's primary representational system may be found in their construction of language. A person who primarily uses visual imagery might say things like, "Well let's *eye* the options you have from several perspectives," "I can *see* what you mean," or "That approach *looks like* it might . . . "

Auditory indices may involve statements such as "it *sounds* like it may work," or "you're not hearing me." Kinesthetic representations often are expressed as "I know what you mean, but it just doesn't seem to fit," or "When you said that, it felt right."

Note how the therapist shifts representational language to match the client's.

T: As you talk about the situation with your friend, I envision a battlefield with each of you on opposite sides of a chasm. (Visual description)

C: It's more like I just feel sick inside. (Kinesthetic)

T: (Adjusting to the kinesthetic image) It feels like a really big loss with no sense of how to break the impasse . . . almost a sense of dread or inevitable loss.

The shift represents the therapist's attempt to be more empathic, including the client's method of perceiving her world. Similar enhanced empathy may be reflected in the use of client metaphor.

Metaphors and Stories

Clients use metaphoric representation frequently to express complex experiences. The images or stories are often personal and relate to something that has significant meaning. Empathy and joining a client's manner of creating personal meaning may open new intimacy and abilities to discuss matters in greater depth.

C: So I knew if I just keep pushing through it, I can get the situation to work through sheer force of will. Like I am the engine that keeps my whole company going.

T: How is that going so far? It seems like it has been a successful strategy in the past.

C: Not that well, yet. There are some administrators that just keep blocking progress by constantly retracing old ground.

T: So you are frustrated by their interference with your drive to push through the problems. How will you get around those difficulties?

C: I am like a big old truck. I have a lot of energy, a full tank, and a big hemi overhead engine.

T: (Joining in the metaphor) Pedal to the medal has been effective historically. I worry that this time, someone has jacked up the rear end, and your wheels are off the ground. Maybe we either need to find an alternative strategy to pure stick-to-it-ive-ness or figure out how to modify the truck to front-wheel drive.

C: (Smiling) Do you know Star Trek? This sounds like the "Kobayashi Maru" dilemma.

T: (Smiling also) Maybe we need to reprogram the test computer like Kirk did! We know that what normally brings you success is not working because the context has changed. I don't have a specific answer, but I wonder about changing the approach rather than just trying to floor it.

C: I do have this one wild idea.

T: I like those . . .

In addition to joining the client's metaphor, the therapist is also indicating a team approach by inserting the personal pronoun *we* instead of *you*. In that way, she is enhancing the notion that together they will find a solution using the client's strengths.

Therapists are well advised to allow themselves to become absorbed in the client's metaphors as a way to connect in deeper ways. One client, who was particularly fond of baseball metaphors, was facing the potential failure of his business during the Great Recession of 2009.

C: So here I am, two outs, bottom of the ninth, nobody on, and down by two runs.

J: And from what you've described earlier, the accountants are closers like Mo Rivera.

C: That's funny! Yeah! They are trying to *close me down*, and they are also tough to beat.

J: Two runs down and you at the plate, you just got to get on base. You can't hit a sacrifice fly with nobody on third and two out.

C: I know that selling out at below-market price is a futile sacrifice.

J: How might you get on base right now? Any ideas about how you might walk, "take one for the team," maybe even a catcher's interference?

C: Okay . . . More flexible thinking. Maybe I am getting in my own way here.

As I entered his metaphor, I was drawn to my personal identification with the 2004 Red Sox who were in a similar situation against the Yankees in a playoff series. My images were dissimilar from the client's, but we could meet emotionally.

Often, stories can generate powerful interventions. Milton Erickson (Erickson & Keener, 2006) was a pioneer in using story, metaphors, and light trances to move clients onto productive paths. The content of Erickson's stories was generated, in large part, by his own unconscious receptivity and their manifestations in internal metaphors and narratives. His stories had special meaning to him and the manner in which he made sense of his clients.

For those of us who are parents or are in touch with our own childhood stories, a savored children's story may come to mind, illuminating the process in the room. Working in Silicon Valley for example, the story of the *Little Engine that Could* (Piper, 1930) is a frequent visitor, especially with very ambitious clients, who trade in most of their life for career advancement. Another children's story, *The Runaway Bunny* (Brown, 1942), helped the therapist comprehend at a metaphoric level a way to understand and subsequently assist a woman in dealing with the empty nest, her own aging, and postmidlife development. When working with clients for whom a particular story has meaning, an indirect shift to an alternate story may be more impactful than a more direct confrontation.

Free Association

That classic method to better understand the client's unconscious within psychoanalysis may also be a two-way phenomenon. The therapist's free association may provide a window into his or her own unconscious processing and inform his or her deeper understanding of the client. The interaction between the therapist's and client's free association may elicit novel insight.

Diamond (2010), exploring modern psychoanalysis, describes how the unconscious processes of the analyst may enhance intrapsychic change. He uses the phrase "therapist's mind use" to explore direct unconscious to unconscious communication.

The Value and Dangers of Self-Data

The advantage of using both atypical perceptiveness of linear clues and of enhanced attunement or intuition by a therapist is clear. However, equally clear is the danger of reifying such perceptions. There is a realistic worry that the therapist's perceptions may be more related to self than to the client. There are two interrelated warnings about such formulations:

(1) The importance of therapist self-knowledge and awareness

(2) A mandate that self-data must be treated heuristically, generating hypotheses to be tested, rather than as revealed verities

Know Thyself

Given the unlikelihood (or desirability) of a therapist's ability to emulate science fiction characters to conduct a Vulcan mind-meld, the best protection a therapist has against overconfidence in unbridled self-reference is self-awareness. A therapist has to be attuned to emotional states, thoughts, and life events that are present in her or his own life.

For example, a therapist going through a divorce may see a client's marriage through somewhat negatively tinted lenses. Similarly, a client's decision to engage in behaviors that are contrary to the therapist's moral, religious, or ethical standards must be explored from the client's reference point, not the therapist's. It's an ongoing challenge to listen closely to a client's wish when it is incongruent with one's personal internal processing. Personal therapy, consultation, and/or supervision of cases are ongoing needs for all therapists. Awareness goes a long way to minimize prejudice and limit perceptual/theoretical filters while exploring another's life.

Recent political "Balkanization" has added to the social, religious, cultural, and moral differences in value systems. Clients are likely to say things that the therapist will want to rebut, rather than understand—a decidedly nontherapeutic endeavor.

One of my supervisees was confronted with a third-generation American client who was pregnant and contemplating an arranged marriage that required a religious conversion and in-laws whom she described as "Indian Right Wing Tea Partiers." These values were anathema to the therapist, and she was torn between "trying to save my client from this fate" and empathic understanding. Although she was a novice counselor, she recognized her conflict as serious. It took several sessions of self-exploration before she could contain her personal feelings and work successfully from the client's perspective.

Later in supervision, she described being surprised that the client was initiating discussion of a number of alternatives when the therapist was "hearing" her with less personal obstruction. At least one way to describe this phenomenon was that the client had been reading the therapist's discomfort.

The Aware Therapist

In any interaction between people, there is often a great deal occurring that is conveyed in multiple channels, both in the individuals and between them. Existential therapy that is intensely oriented to the here-and-now relationship requires enhanced sensitivity to a host of possible linear and nonlinear communication parameters.

In addition to perceptiveness of the complex context within which content is embedded, knowledge of the internal state of the sender and receiver provide valuable entrances to far more comprehensive understanding of the client. From that more extensively informed vantage point, the healing effect of the therapist-client interaction and *I-thou* moments are increasingly likely.

Notes

1. Among others for whom I got to be the transportation were Carl Rogers and B. F. Skinner. I frequently recommend to graduate students that they volunteer to make the airport runs when visiting speakers come into town. It's an amazing opportunity.

2. The proposition that clients have theories as well and the importance of matching therapist and client is addressed in Chapter 8.

3. A baseball fan might opine that a blues festival and a Cubs broadcast might have some affective synchronization.

4. Bell proposed a corresponding theory of quantum entanglement in particle physics in 1944 (Kaiser, 2014).

5. The Paul Robeson (1925) version can be heard at https://archive.org/details/Paul-Robeson-collection-111-120

6. This particular myth about love unattainable or separated seems amazingly cross-cultural. Among its many variations are Native American stories that inspired the rock and roll song of "Running Bear and Little White Dove"; Chinese and Burmese lore, depicted in the Tiger Balm Gardens in Hong Kong; and the Bing Crosby–Ingrid Bergman film, "Bells of St. Mary's."

7

The Four Epigenetic Phases of Psychotherapy

Observe due measure, for right timing
Is in all things the most important factor.

Hesiod

Like most human endeavors, patterns and procedures in therapy occur in something of a predictable, progressive manner. Timing interventions to client readiness is the essence of clinical success. Seasoned therapists often describe the bulk of therapy time as readying the client to be available for a few quick interventions, whether those are insight-, action-, or relationally oriented. One of the biggest errors new therapists make is to engage in major therapeutic methods prematurely.

Intrasession Arc

There is both a predictable trajectory to the entire process of counseling or therapy and a corresponding miniprocess within each session. Bugental (1987) offered a seven-stage progression within each session: opening, transition, first work phase, transition, second work phase, transition, and closing. It is important to note that within sessions, transition stages (testing the waters) consistently precede jumping into the next stage of therapeutic work.

Many others have described the early connecting/reconnecting of therapist and client as a build-up to whatever level of depth and progress is possible in the specific session and finally a closing, involving a reduction of the intensity and increased ability to resume normal life consciousness.

Existential therapy always tracks the clients in their world. When the clients are checking out their level of trust, the therapist is there with them. When they are divulging important information, the therapist is receptive, and when they are ready for specific intervention, the therapist recognizes the moment and attempts to intercede in useful ways.

The Trajectory of Therapy

The current chapter is focused on the overall treatment trajectory across sessions. Many authors have described stages for the course of therapy from initial contact to termination and follow-up. One fairly generic model identifies relationship building, assessment, goal setting, interventions, termination, and follow-up.

In his classic *On Becoming a Person*, Rogers (1961) identified a process model with seven interlinked stages of therapeutic growth for a client, progressing from more rigidity to full-functioning and self-actualizing.

Table 7.1   Carl Rogers' Seven-Stage Model of Therapy Process
Stage 1. Rigid thinking, judgmental, unwilling to self-disclose
Stage 2. Slight loosening but very low personal responsibility, tendency to look for ways to blame others, sees self as a victim
Stage 3. More willingness to talk about self—often with third person reference, better access to past feelings than present ones; Rogers saw this as a primary step to entering therapy.
Stage 4. Able to acknowledge deeper feelings—often past events, can take responsibility for events, sometimes a "wry humor," some initial trust issues with therapist
Stage 5. Feeling more connected to and accepted by therapist, able to explore deeper current feelings, therapist role to provide opportunity for deeper experiencing of feelings, less denial

(Continued)

Table 7.1   (Continued)

Stage 6. Full experience of deeper feelings in present, enhanced awareness and meaning possible, cognition and emotion more integrated and congruent, better self-care
Stage 7. Effecting change personally in and out of therapy, greater sense of living in the present, awareness of further changes and desirable possibilities, enhanced empathy for self and others

For Rogers, therapy involved the creation of a relevant environment for clients to make these progressive, inexorable shifts. Consistent with his client-centered approach, he viewed the steps more as guideposts along a long journey rather than discrete stops. His method required empathy to the current client stage of growth, which opened doors to ensuing stages. Although there are seven stages here, therapy proper truly began with Stage 3—essentially a five-stage process.

Taking a more experimental approach, Prochaska and Norcross (2001) described a six-stage trans-theoretical change model based on psychotherapy research.

Each stage contained an identification of a time period and necessary tasks to promote change. Although they approached change from a different perspective, their trajectory lines up fairly well with Rogers' formulation.

Table 7.2   Prochaska & Norcross (2001) Progression of Change in Psychotherapy

Stage 1. Precontemplation. No intention to change behavior in the foreseeable future; problem is only in others' eyes.
Stage 2. Contemplation. Client may be aware of the problem, but has yet to commit to make changes.
Stage 3. Preparation or "baby steps." Client has some intention to act and likely some unsuccessful attempts to ameliorate situation.
Stage 4. Action. Clients modify behavior, experiences, and environment to alter their lives and experience. *This stage tends to be longer term and more intense than the prior ones.*
Stage 5. Maintenance. Clients engage in practice, consolidation, accommodations, and relapse prevention.
Stage 6. Termination. Change occurs independent of the therapist.

Prochaska and Norcross (2001) defined appropriate therapist roles for each stage and issued a strong warning that therapists be careful to identify client readiness and to avoid treating all patients as if they are in the action stage. They add, "The vast majority of patients are *not* in the action stage" (p. 447). This has very important implications for counseling and therapy.

Hackney and Cormier (2001) identified five stages in therapy: (1) rapport and relationship building, (2) assessment/problem definition, (3) goal-setting, (4) initiating interventions, and (5) termination. It is important to notice that in their formulation, intervention (Stage 4) comes only after all the preparation work.

Stages in Multiperson Therapy: Couple, Family, and Group

Because process and relationship development are essential in existential psychotherapy, family and group therapy models provide unique understanding of the overall trajectory.

Renowned family therapist, Carl Whitaker identified three stages for family therapy: (1) engagement, (2) involvement, and (3) disengagement (Connell, Mitten, & Bumberry, 1998). Although he was addressing the process in family therapy, there is a significant emphasis on preparing the client prior to encouraging difficult cognitive, emotional, and behavioral shifts.

The trajectory from preparation to termination is especially clear in the group therapy literature. Because of the relational complexity of group process, many authors have designed ways to track the development of group process.

Battegay (1989), Corey and Corey (1987), Fiebert (1963), MacKenzie (1990), Schutz (1967), Shapiro (1978), Toseland and Rivas (1984), and many others offered predictable trajectories of therapy in which progressive stages are built upon achieving success at preceding ones. The described stages are remarkably similar across orientations.

Shapiro, Peltz, and Bernadett-Shapiro (1997) and Corey, Corey, and Corey (2013) describe a remarkably similar progression of phases through which groups normally traverse. The model is quite useful in exploring the trajectory of learning or change in individual existential therapy.

A Four Phase Developmental Sequence

Therapy is defined here as a natural four phase developmental process. Each phase provides heuristic guidelines to be used by the therapist in identifying

Table 7.3 A Sample of Models of Group Process Trajectory

Battegay (1989)	Dreikurs (1951)	Tuckman (1965)	Dies (1985)	Henry (1981)	Schutz (1973)	Shapiro (1978)	MacKenzie (1990)
Exploratory contact	Establish relations	Forming	Preparation	Initiating	Inclusion	Introduction	Engagement
Regression	Interpret dynamics	Storming	Early sessions	Convening	Control	Learning the rules	Differentiation
Catharsis	Patient's understanding	Norming	Transition	Formation	Affection	Therapy proper	Working
Insight	Reorientation	Performing	Working	Conflict		Termination	Termination
Social learning		Adjourning	Termination	Maintenance			
				Termination			

156

proper timing for trust building, confrontation, and interventions. Progressive phases of the therapy are characterized by different foci of resistance. The identified phases may be used both as a normal arc of the entire across-session process and a trajectory within sessions.

It is essential to note that the process is rarely linear. There are jumps ahead and regressions to former stages of process. Often a retreat in level of intensity is preparatory to a client's confrontation with new fears of the unknown. The therapist's goal is to travel on the client's path and go at the client's speed, not to keep the client on a predetermined track or order.

Because we are exploring existential work, we are using a relationally based set of stages that emerged from group therapy process studies (Shapiro et al., 1997), rather than a technique-centered, more step-wise behavioral model. The current model coordinates well with the Prochaska and Norcross (2001) stages of change.

The four interlocking phases in an ongoing (and often quite nonlinear) therapy are

1. Preparation—getting the client into the consulting room ready to engage in the change process.

2. Transition—joining with the therapist to best use what he or she has to offer. This phase characteristically includes several distinct tests of trust.

3. Treatment—working directly on the creation of meaning, development of insight, and behavior change within a close, intense, and meaningful relationship. This is the phase during which the therapist is likely to recommend

Table 7.4   The Shapiro et al. (1997) Stages of Group Therapy Model

Stage	Tasks
Preparation	Bringing clients to the therapy consulting room, screening Development of working therapy diagnostics
Transition	Discovery of what this therapy and therapist can offer Building trust through asocial interventions, testing
Treatment (Most Theory-centric)	Interruptions in normative neurotic anxiety/automatic processing Psychological experiments to facing fears of the unknown Focus on attribution of meaning
Termination	Saying aloha and dealing with this and other losses Transfer of training

experiments designed at exploring the tension between freedom and security and the attendant anxieties of living with the status quo and facing the unknown.

4. Termination—transfer of training from the therapy session to real (back home) life and dealing with loss and parting; allowing the client to continue on the path on his or her own.

This process is envisioned as both *inevitable* and *ideal*: inevitable because successful completion of each previous phase is considered prerequisite to dealing with subsequent stages and ideal because many courses of counseling and therapy fail to progress through all the stages.

The Value of a Predictable Process

Effective therapists shift with the ongoing process. The starting point for successful therapy is empathy with the client as he or she is, in the moment. It is not where we want the client to go.

Therapeutic interventions that are effective at one phase of therapy are often deleterious at others. It is axiomatic that clients need to know their current state of being and the extent of their personal resources prior to embarking on new life paths. Perhaps the therapist and client both know the solution to a yet unresolved problem, but being able to engage on that new path requires readiness and sensitive timing.

If the therapy process is in the treatment phase, direct interventions, be they meaning-centric, insight-oriented, or pragmatic recommendations for experimental thoughts and behaviors, may be quite successful. However, these are likely not to be useful during transition, when the primary focus may be on testing, trust building, and resistance.

These phases cannot be effectively envisioned as a turn-by-turn global positioning system (GPS) map. They only get us to the right neighborhood. Unique streets, roads, lanes, and blind alleys must be individually discovered— often on a trial and error basis.

Preparation

For most clients, preparation begins with some identified need for change. Most often there is intrapsychic discomfort, interpersonal conflict, or a referral from another interested party. Although some clients relish the luxury of psychotherapy, most view a referral with some disquiet; the mental equivalent to a referral to a periodontist or proctologist. Thus, a majority enter therapy with both hope and ambivalence, limiting early compliance.

The Initial Phone Call

The initial contact is usually by telephone. Unless it's an agency or larger clinic, therapists will return voice mail messages personally. Therapists have different phone styles and may want to accomplish varying goals during that initial phone call. At the very least, it is essential to ascertain if there is a connection between what the client wants/needs, what the therapist can offer, and whether there is a time when they can actually meet. Client ambivalence can make that unexpectedly difficult.

Some therapists have very lengthy and detailed intake forms. Some offer a "loss-leader" free first appointment as a way to better get the right clients into counseling. Neither is recommended for therapists who are working with an existential framework. Lengthy histories and descriptions of symptoms may deter early connection and relationship building. They signal a greater professional distance than is characteristic for relationally oriented therapists.

An initial free evaluation session can be problematic for four reasons. First, it is frequently a difficult psychological shift to an often significant fee for service after there has been a no-cost session. Second, it establishes the therapist as "marketer." This can cause a therapist to oversell in a first session to convert the client to a paying status. Third, the initial session is more of an evaluative "blind date." If a client is unsure that the therapist is acceptable, the therapist may artificially inflate his or her "first impression" with social charm. Finally, it indicates that the therapist is not respectful of his or her own time—curiously the only commodity that is being sold. Such devaluing can be poor modelling for a client, especially one with low self-esteem.

This therapist is returning a phone call to a prospective client, the same day it came in.

T: Hi, I'm calling for Rob.

R: This is Rob. Who is this please?

T: I'm Dr. Smith. You left a voice mail message. Is this a convenient time to talk?

R: Yeah. Thank you. I want to get into therapy and work on some issues that are popping up.

T: Can you give me a very brief sense of the issues you'd like to pursue?

R: My relationship with my girlfriend is deteriorating after many years, and at the same time, I am having some problems at work.

T: Can you tell me how you got my name?

R: You saw my cousin's husband many years ago, and it seemed to help him a lot. So my cousin suggested I call.

T: Okay. I have openings on Tuesday morning at 10:00 a.m. and Thursday afternoon at 1:00 p.m.

R: I can make the Thursday. I'll just do a late lunch hour.

T: Do you know where I'm located?

R: Yes, I think so. Are you still downtown in that white building?

T: Yes, on the second floor, suite 201. Please come in about 15 minutes early to fill out the paperwork.

Some therapists prefer a lengthier phone interview during which they obtain more data on the prospective client's history, background, prior therapy, and so on. In addition, they may wish to provide "frame" information about the therapy. For example, "We will begin and end on time. Sessions are for 45 minutes, and my charge per session is $180." or "I am on the panel for XX behavioral health. If you have that insurance, your copay will be around $20 to $40 per session. You'll have to check with your human resources department or insurance for the exact amount."

The Initial Session

Some therapists prefer to read whatever referral charts are available prior to the first meeting. My personal preference is to meet the person and develop a personal impression before I read the chart. For me, reading in advance may bias my first impression, and I will lose out on valuable personal reaction information. From a relational existential frame, I prefer to experience the client personally before I discover how others have perceived him or her.

Whitaker called this "the first blind date." What kind of relationship will begin as a result of the information offered or withheld and the manner in which it is presented? What kind of early relationship chemistry will begin?

Like many blind dates, the therapist-client pairing is not always easy or optimal. Sometimes the chemistry is just not right for either or both. If the therapist is aware of a likely poor working alliance, it may be best to refer the client to a professional who is better attuned to this client's particular needs. The disconnect may be due to the content of the client's issues, therapist concerns, or the style of presentation or communication.

Thus, for example, a therapist with hearing difficulties may be hard pressed to work with a client that drops his or her voice or speaks extremely softly.

Similarly, if the client's issues coincide with those the therapist is currently personally working through, it may be suboptimal.

Sometimes the client is asking for an approach that is not part of a therapist's comfort zone or theoretical perspective. It makes more sense to quickly evaluate what the client is seeking and make a determination than to engage a client for a few sessions before breaking off the relationship.

C: (On the initial phone call) I am looking for Eye Movement Desensitization and Reprocessing (EMDR) and cognitive behavioral therapy (CBT) for my post-traumatic stress. Do you do that?

T: (Evaluating) Can you give me a brief description of what the problem is?

C: I was bullied as a child, and it is coming up again at work with my boss. I want to learn how to let go of the past and relax more when she is on the warpath.

T: So you want EMDR and CBT as a way to develop techniques to reduce your stress.

C: Yeah, but I do not want to discuss my childhood or my mother or do any long-term navel-gazing. I read on the web that those therapies work in 6 weeks. That's what I want.

T: Okay. Thank you for being so clear. I don't work with those approaches, but I will be happy to refer you to a therapist that does.

C: So you won't see me.

T: I work in ways that might be quite opposite of your goals. I can refer you to colleagues who are excellent professionals and offer what you are seeking.

C: Okay. Oh, and I need an appointment either after 7:00 p.m. or on Saturday.

T: I'll give you a couple of names. Be sure to tell them of your time requirements.

Resistance During Preparation

Although clients will use those forms of resistance that are consistent with their ego strengths, there are some general forms of resistance that emerge from early ambivalence. Even self-referred clients often have questions about the risks of the entire enterprise. Their strong pull toward the status quo may conflict with an initial attempt to get into a process that encourages change and comes with a corresponding surge in anxiety.

Specific forms of resistance may be cognitive (asking about the therapist's orientation, requesting a reduced fee, offering only a small, often inconvenient window of available time, requesting the therapist credentials, etc.). They may be affective (bursting into tears or shutting down during the initial phone call or first session). Many a clinician has had the experience of dead silence and wondering if the phones were still connected. "Please let me know if you are still on the line." Sometimes, the initial ambivalence is expressed through anger, especially if the client is there involuntarily. For example, they may forget their payment. Ambivalence-oriented resistance may also present as "away," such as when a client is a no-show or comes very late for the initial session.

After assuring that he'd be early enough for the paperwork prior to the first session, one client came 25 minutes into the allotted therapy time. This left the therapist with a dilemma. Should she break her rules and see him without the paperwork, extend the session into her usual between session break, or end at the usual agreed upon time regardless? Similarly, the client may divulge a major, possibly traumatic issue as he reaches for the doorknob at the end of the session or after the session is over, take an inordinately long time writing the check, asking questions the whole time.

Should she hold to the rules to provide a more secure frame? These are hard questions for a clinician to answer on a first meeting. Whatever her approach, it is likely premature to directly confront the client's ambivalence. Any intense early intervention may turn the ambivalence into client flight. If there is an unanticipated threat, he may scurry back to the status quo, sans therapy, avoiding the risk of change. She needs to respect the ambivalence, hold it in mind, and link it to later events as therapy progresses.

Transition

When the first session begins, the preparatory phase of therapy gives way to the early stages in the transition phase. This is often instigated by the usual therapist openings, "How may I be of help," "What brought you in today," or "You mentioned on the phone that there were two areas you'd like to explore. How would you like to begin?"

During the transition phase, the client gets to set viable outcome goals and become prepared for the kinds of change that are possible in existential work. These goals may vary widely from symptom relief to "life changing." It is essential that the client and therapist find mutual ground and comfort with available methods.

Together, therapists and clients set the stage for the treatment that is to come. Trust needs to be established, tested, and progressively grown. Clients need to learn how to get what this therapy has to offer. A working alliance is established and the relationship goes through some "growing pains." In comprehending the strengths of a client, in-the-moment shifting resistance patterns are identified, and the therapist will attempt to increase trust by joining these patterns.

Trust-building during transition essentially determines whether the treatment will establish a productive working alliance in which major life issues may be addressed and confronted.

Therapist Limitations

Somewhere during preparation or early transition, a therapist has to determine whether there are potential problems that could lead to poor therapy outcome. Every therapist has limits. They may be educational, training, or personal, but there are clients and issues for which each of us is unprepared or ill-suited. A recent informal survey of 25 counseling psychologists and marriage and family therapists yielded the following areas of counselor disquiet: domestic violence, death and dying, rape, loss of a child, eating disorders, sexual dysfunction, PTSD, couple or family therapy, and men's issues. It is no surprise that the particular area of discomfort for one was the exact area of specialization of another.

In the 1970s, Carl Rogers famously disclosed his discomfort discussing both sex and aggression. His particular discomfort did not make him a poor therapist. By being aware of limitations, he was working effectively within those constraints. His clients found ways to address their needs through avenues in which he had expertise. It would have been different had he been unaware of his own sensitivities.

That of course, is the crucial concern. Therapists need to be aware of their strengths and weaknesses. It is ethically questionable for a therapist to work out personal limitations with a client in need.[1] Thus, for example, if I am very uncomfortable with clients who exhibit Axis II (personality) disorders, it is incumbent on me to work with a client with a borderline personality disorder only under close supervision and with additional training.

Some restraints are theory distinct. For existential therapists, a focus on eliminating the symptom, dealing with long-buried historical psychodynamics, or teaching the client new skills are typically out of the active arena of therapy. This doesn't mean that the therapist will ban the introduction of such discussions from the therapy, but he or she will guide the client to focus more on the present. Symptom mitigation may occur primarily as a result of the client's growth through the relationship with the therapist and challenging his or her fears of change.

None of these limitations may be sufficient to close out therapy progress, but they will restrict a client's disclosure or how he or she may relate.

The Initial Interview

Most clients respond to the therapist's invitation by describing the problems that instigated their coming into therapy. They often have hypotheses regarding the reasons for their angst and discomfort. The client's theory about causality and change is often useful in adjusting the nature of approach. For example, the client may have a perspective that when bad things occur, he or she must have been responsible and deserved the outcome. Some clients reveal value systems with their personal theory. For example, a client may believe that hard work or an ordeal may be necessary for change. These are all important cues for the clinician's development of a treatment plan.

The initial interview is designed for continuing evaluation of the potential working alliance, diagnosis, and case conceptualization. It begins when clients enter the waiting room. Sometimes ambiance in that space has an unpredicted impact. Is it a quiet place? Are there many people and staff about? Are the forms readily available? Is there music playing and, if so, what kind of mood does it set? Are there the usual doctor's office magazines? Are they relatively up to date? Is the lighting subdued or bright? Clients make a number of primarily unconscious judgments in that time and space.

When the therapist appears, he or she welcomes the client and also may make judgments. Has the client completed all the forms and taken a moment to close her eyes and get settled, or is she texting, holding the forms in her lap, and balancing a large beverage? Clients also make initial note of the extent to which the therapist appears to be as envisioned.

T: Hi. I'm Stacy. Are you Judd?

C: (With voice trailing off) Oh, hello. I somehow thought you were older.

T: Come on in. We can talk about that.

Sometimes the way the therapist and client are dressed makes an interesting impression that can impact the first session. If the client's internal picture of the therapist is of a mature woman in conservative professional clothing with her graying hair in a bun, he might have some major recalculations if the actual therapist is dressed fashionably in maternity clothes and appears to be in her early thirties. What is important here is the discrepancy between expectation and reality, rather than the actual appearance of the therapist.

The therapist's office also lends itself to anticipations. For example, what are the implications if the office is dark in wood tones with all walls lined with bookshelves containing books and artifacts if the client expected light and airy? What are the assumptions that may be made based on the posted degrees and licenses?

Diagnosis

From an existential perspective, diagnosis is somewhat different. The goal is not to form a DSM or ICD diagnosis and plan a treatment based on that symptomatology. Instead, the therapist will assess the possible relationship, the ego strengths of the client, the client's dominant defense style, and an exploratory plan of approach with this client. The evaluation of a client's strengths is in sharp contrast to approaches that begin with the symptom mix. This is an evaluation of the person, who is exhibiting a particular anxiety imbalance, rather than a symptom-centric approach (i.e., "the phobic").

For existential work, an important component of diagnosis includes an assessment of the client's contrasting pulls between fear of the unknown and guilt of the status quo. Often, therapists will begin to understand the client's unique tension by focusing on consequences, rather than trying to assess motivation.

Case Conceptualization

The initial therapeutic interview leads to a preliminary case conceptualization that may be shared with the client. It serves as a starting point from which the therapist assesses the client's capacity for change, the impediments to those changes, his or her levels of intellectual and emotional capabilities, potential risks of the treatment, symptom manifestations, and the strengths in the clients' support systems.

T: (At the end of the first session) Let me briefly summarize what I have heard from you and what I may be able to offer. You have described a situation where you have "checked all the right squares," but your life is no longer giving you the same kind of excitement as before . . . (waits for some positive indication or clarification). It seems that while you have been doing the things you are supposed to do, you have somehow lost sight of what you might want. The obvious solutions like a marriage breakup or quitting the job are not either appealing or feasible.

C: Right. I am feeling very stuck, and I also do not want to go back on the antidepressants that I tried 2 years ago.

T: Well, let me tell you what I can offer. We can meet weekly for the next 3 months, and together we can try to find a way to deal with what seems like a very real dilemma. You are coming in early enough to be able to make some changes that may not be as drastic as the ones you have already considered.

C: So no immediate answers?

T: No. If it were that simple, you would have figured it out yourself a long time ago. This is something we can grapple with together and between us, come up with some ideas.

C: I can do that. If it is possible to get an appointment around the noon hour, it'd be easier for me to get away from work.

T: I think that might be possible in a few weeks. I will let you know as soon as it is available. In the meantime, could we meet at this time next week?

The Early Transition Process

In describing the events that precipitated the call for an appointment, the client may lay the culpability on others, on historical mistreatment or trauma, or on how they are currently victimized by an unreasonable relationship in family, at work, or in their social group. Given their accounts and attributions of causality, the overriding (unspoken) message to the therapist is, "*the world is not working right for me. I'd like you to rearrange the way the universe operates so that I can keep doing what I have always done, but get far better outcomes.*" Most therapists hear this unspoken request as akin to the definition of insanity frequently attributed to Einstein, *Doing the same thing over and over and expecting a different result.*

Thus, the initial challenge for the work is to realign the locus of change from the environment to the person. Regardless of accuracy, this is often not what the client wants to hear.

In the first session, Tomio, a 59-year-old engineer, married for 25 years to a successful pharmacist, mentioned that the relationship was becoming intolerable because of his wife's emotional "explosions."

C: So when she went nuclear again, I just withdrew and waited for it to blow over.

T: Is that a strategy that has worked in the past?

C: Sometimes. But it isn't working now. She just gets more angry.

T: So you are doing what you've learned is often successful, but this is either one of those times when it is not working, or there has been a change and it will be increasingly ineffective.

C: Yeah. That's what I am thinking. Do you think you could see her with me and get her on some medication or something to calm her down? I can't imagine what life will be like in 6 or 7 years when I retire and we are together 24/7.

T: It would be your first choice to find a way to use chemicals or something to get her to change.

C: I came up with four options: (1) get her to change, (2) find a way to adjust to her, (3) leave, or (4) keep going with what I am doing.

T: (This is a characteristic early transition intervention—Note that it is about planning and developing a teamwork approach—it joins with the client's primary logical way of functioning and is not confrontive.) That's good rational thinking and gives us a starting point. At least for now let's put option 3 on the back burner . . . we can always come back to that if need be. Let's also not try to get another person to change. That seems frustrating and likely has a very low probability of success. Number 4 is not desirable, because that's not working now. That leaves us with number 2—you making some personal adjustments. Do you want to describe which changes you have already considered or tried and discarded . . . no sense going over unsuccessful ground.

Notice at this phase of therapy, the therapist primarily is trying to build an alliance. Even though she suspects that Tomio's withdrawal of affect may be contributing to his wife's reported volatility, it is premature to dig into that. She will also return to his concern about a postretirement future. For now, her focus is on creating teamwork and getting him to become more responsible and able to deal with his current dilemma. She begins within his preferred cognitive frame of reference, by working with his four options.

This single interaction with Tomio will not be sufficient to effect change, but the pattern of listening, empathizing with both the content and process of the client, willingness to begin with his analysis of the situation, and focusing in on what may be fruitful will help the client build a more trusting relationship. She also is demonstrating one of van Deurzen's (2010) "golden rules" accepting "adversity, anxiety, confusion, paradox and life's dilemmas" (p. 317). The focus is on developing the courage to face them and learn tolerance and endurance.

During this period, therapists gauge clients' openness and resilience. Clients need to learn to respect and trust the therapist and to become open to facing anxiety and fear by leaving their comfort zone. The central task for this phase of treatment is to prepare the client for treatment. This requires at least two processes:

(1) the development and testing of the special trust possible in a therapeutic relationship, and

(2) determining possible outcomes with this therapist-client combination at this time.

Testing the Trust Levels

Before delving into sensitive, shameful, or anxiety-provoking issues, clients will want some assuredness of the therapist's capacity to handle them. During transition, a series of tests occurs that place trust in a realistic perspective and push the therapist's limits. With each successful test, the area within which the therapy may be most productive becomes clarified.

Let's See How She Handles This One

Clients are generally not foolhardy. Before they will trust the therapist with core pain and sensitivity, they offer a small corner of a problem to the therapist to see how he or she does. If the therapist shows comfort, empathy, caring, and competence with that component, the client will progressively disclose more central concerns.

During the first two sessions, Christy described a weekly pattern of going out drinking with friends, meeting "the wrong guys," and engaging in some risky sexual behavior. She also talked about her woe of becoming 30 years old with no long-term relationship prospects. The therapist listened and was empathic. He also wondered aloud with her about the effectiveness of bar hopping with a group of women as a strategy for meeting "appropriate" men.

Of course, he did not give her dating advice. Yet, in the ensuing third session, Christy reported,

C: So I took your advice and stayed home this weekend and just cleaned my apartment and talked with a few friends. I didn't go back to the bars when my friends went.

T: (Not what I recommended. Is this about "parental" permission?) How was that for you?

C: Well, to be honest, I expected that I'd feel really lonely and guilty for missing a chance to meet someone, but I actually felt okay. Of course, I am no closer to that relationship I want.

T: What's it like to tell me that?

C: (Laughing) Just checking to see if you felt guilty about my doing it right, but no "Prince Charming."

T: So. No prince, no white stallion, no sudden romance. What does that bring up for you?

C: Well. It's no different either way . . . I did get a call from a guy I met a few weeks ago at my spinning class.

T: And?

C: Well here's the thing. I don't know what I'd do if I went out with him and it didn't work out. . . . I also don't know what I'd do if it did. How do you like that?

T: Well . . . that's a real dilemma. Risking love is vulnerable and scary, no matter how it works out. Do you know what the larger risk is for you?

Christy went from practical steps to stopping doing something that wasn't working to beginning to look at her fear of intimacy. She offered the larger issue only after he passed her first test.

Shapiro et al. (1997) designated this phase of group therapy as determining the shape and size of the room in which therapy may occur. They described two major tests for the therapist: a test of the ceiling and a test of the floor.

Testing the Ceiling

The ceiling test involves the intensity with which the therapist is in his or her comfort zone (i.e., how much direct client anger can be tolerated). Because counseling and therapy are designed to reduce rigidity and promote change in thought, affect, and behavior, the process can often lead to substantial reactive volatility. Once clients begin to re-experience pain in their lives in the present, there is often an outpouring of expressed emotion. Just as for extreme thought or behavior, high levels of affect may serve to test the capacity of the therapist to handle certain levels of emotional intensity.

How comfortable can a therapist be when the client is expressing deep sadness or high levels of anger? How well can a therapist tolerate a client who is shutting down, apparently too depressed to talk?

As clients test the therapist's ability to handle atypical levels of emotional expression, he or she may well be confronted with his or her personal comfort limits and relative levels of safety. Clients and therapists need to find the emotional levels in which fruitful work can be done. If a therapist feels overwhelmed or intimidated by the manner of a client's expression, the therapist's personal defenses will be engaged and the interaction between them impacted. In such a situation, the therapist may be ill-suited to focus on the relationship, the client's needs, or even the importance of the threatening process.

A therapist does not have to be able to accept all levels of expressed affect. What is necessary is to let the clients know the therapist's comfortable range and limits. Because the affective volatility is a trust test, a clear indication of the therapist's limits will often actually calm the client.

When I was an intern at Hawaii State Hospital, I was assigned an inpatient male who was brought to the hospital by the police after several violent incidents. A Polynesian man, approximately 6'4" and 300 pounds, he had an imposing appearance. We met in a small office with two chairs. During the second session, he got up out of his chair and began pacing. My experience of him was that he was looming above me. At that time, my mind went to escape possibilities and how to get help from the attendants. It was not easy to listen to him while having such thoughts. At some unconscious level, he apparently discerned this and became even more agitated.

The session ended, and my subjective experience was that I had dodged a bullet and escaped. Objectively, I realized that what I tried to do was to calm him down, but the discrepancy between my subjective state and my words apparently worked paradoxically. My supervisor, who had watched the session through a two-way mirror, immediately pushed me to describe my own feelings. Naturally, I felt somewhat defensive and acted as if I was fine with the encounter, until he told me that it was scary for him to watch. My initial reaction was to wonder why he hadn't intervened to protect me, but it was also quite a relief to know that he shared my emotional reaction.

After we discussed my personal feelings, he wondered aloud whether the client might have been experiencing something similar. Although he was not physically intimidated, he certainly had to be concerned about his incarceration, potential long-term commitment, and loss of freedom. My supervisor, recognizing the parallel process of testing in the therapy and supervision, empathized and left me to figure out what to do before my next session with the patient.

About 5 minutes into the session, the patient again got up and began pacing in the same (to me) menacing manner. This time, I told him that I felt very uncomfortable with him standing and my sitting. To my surprise, he looked more worried than angry. Taking that cue, I continued,

J: Would you be okay with us walking and talking in the garden behind
       the building?

       He smiled and asked if that would get me in trouble.

J: The thing I am worried about is someone else overhearing our confi-
       dential conversation.

C: Oh well, maybe we could go outside, "talk story" (Pidgin for chat).
       And then come back in (and) talk more?

In reality, we were out in the garden for about 5 to 10 minutes of our
scheduled 50-minute session and then back in the office and in chairs.

When I communicated my emotional comfort limit, instead of being provocative, it had an unanticipated calming influence. At some level of consciousness, he was testing to determine what aspects of his experience would
be acceptable. Once he knew what my limit was and that I was endeavoring
to accommodate his need to be standing and moving, he felt that we were
coming to a place where we could talk casually and also seriously.

Of course, as an intern, I was still worried about what my supervisor
would think about my removing him from the interaction while we were
outside. Again reflecting parallel process, he simply inquired if there was
anything that happened out of his earshot that I wanted to explore in supervision. I replied that the guy just talked casually and very generally about
his family and neighborhood until we got back in to the office. It was there
that he opened up much more of his fears of being committed and kept in
the hospital.

My supervisor then said that "it seemed like he had to find out if you
would listen to him as a person without probing questions, before he could
trust you to know how scared he was." I was aware that, in addition to that
moment being a terrific lesson on how to do therapy, he was showing me
that my fear of being evaluated would be ameliorated by his being understanding of what I needed (another parallel process).

Several weeks later, I asked him why he hadn't just told me that I could
be innovative and walk with the client and he very kindly replied that his
solution might have been different than mine and what was important was
my struggling with my own genuineness and congruence with the client.

Test of the Floor

The floor test requires a determination of appropriate and inappropriate
topics to bring into the consulting room. Therapists in general will avoid
treating someone who is not in the room.[2] Discussing one's sister-in-law's

addiction is probably outside of productive work. Discussing one's personal reaction in the moment to the addiction and what it means to the client is likely well in bounds.

If a woman is complaining about her husband's behavior, the therapist is usually limited to discussing how she may adjust, rather than how they together could devise a strategy to change his behavior.

Alice first came to therapy with a problem about her partner's drinking, which she called "alcoholism." She claimed that she wanted the therapist to help her devise a plan to get her partner, Marie, to stop drinking altogether. She had previously been to Al-Anon and two other therapists for help with this problem.

T: This seems very important and frustrating to you, that you cannot seem to affect Marie's drinking. You've tried two other therapists and Al-Anon, and now you are here with the same goal.

A: Well. She doesn't even think she has a problem. So I think the first order of business is how to convince her that she's alcoholic.

T: I wish I had that kind of magic wand and could convince her of anything. What I am most concerned with right now is your discomfort and what we could do to address how you are coping with her drinking.

A: Well, how do you usually get people to stop drinking?

T: Let's focus for a moment on your frustration with her behavior, with everything you've tried, and even with my inability to change another person.

A: I am frustrated. It's like nothing I do will work.

T: What if there isn't anything you can do to change her drinking? What implications are there for you?

A: I just have to get her to stop. I have alcoholics in my family, and I know what that leads to.

T: So if things remain how they are, you see a dark future for yourself.

A: For her. Not so much for me.

T: What future *do* you see for yourself?

Notice that the therapist is experientially informing Alice that what is going on with someone not in the room is not something he can affect. Instead, what is relevant is what is happening inside Alice.

Many clients will test more than once the capacity of the therapist to work on an impossible (or highly improbable) task. With this perspective, the therapy can only deal with the client per se and her present experiences. When he directs her back to the room, he is passing the test, because now they can work on those things that can be changed.

Many years ago, I had a client reveal to me that his goal in therapy was the return of an arm he had lost in combat in Vietnam. It was only after I told him that we both wished that was possible and refocused him on his feelings of being incomplete as a person, that the therapy was able to move forward. What was interesting about this client was that he returned to the same test, the request for his limb to be returned, before he trusted me sufficiently to address several new challenges in his life.

Later, he told me that my willingness to wish with him (as if from the inside) made a huge difference. Everyone else basically just told him to "get over it and adjust."

The Help-Rejecting Complainer

Sometimes either test takes the form of the client as help-rejecting complainer. The client requests advice or assistance, and then when it is offered, the client lets the therapist know that each recommendation must inevitably fail.

Patti came to therapy to find a way to leave the married man with whom she had been having a long-term affair.

P: I know I should leave him. It's a dead end. He'll never leave his wife, you know.

T: So you are looking for some support in getting out.

P: Yeah. I gotta do it. My friends all tell me to leave. Even his friends tell me there's no future.

T: Have you tried being unavailable at a time when he is likely to phone?

P: Yeah. That doesn't work. He knows that I am always with my cell phone.

T: What about taking some time out to get away and think or just a temporary break for a week or two?

P: What if he finds someone else or goes back to his wife? He keeps telling me that he's not having sex with her. If I am gone, maybe he will.

T: So you don't trust him.

P: Of course I trust him. I am crazy about him. His wife is very cold to him.

Notice that whatever the therapist recommends is met with a prediction of a negative outcome. To pass this test, the therapist has to refocus away from how Patti should leave this situation and refocus on what is occurring in the room.

If the therapist suggests a tactic to effect the leaving, it is likely to end up in the ongoing verbal quicksand. Recommendations or strategies may work better in the treatment phase of therapy, once trust is established and the client's resistance to any change is somewhat moderated, but not during tests of trust in transition.

Instead, the therapist needs to empathize with the dilemma, balancing both sides.

T: Basically, what you are saying is that you are in a very difficult predicament. Any choice that you make will be both helpful and painful.

P: How do you mean?

T: Well if you decide to stay, you have all the benefits of being with someone you are crazy about and also getting lots of the good parts of the relationship, without having to do the chores of a full-time life together. You also get the expensive gifts and vacation weekends away, and you have all the problems and heartaches of being with a married man part-time and knowing that he is not exclusively yours.

       If you leave, then you have your freedom and a respite from the pains of his returning to his wife, regardless of the nature of their sexual relationship, but you will miss him and the relationship you have will be gone.

P: So what should I do?

T: This is a tough decision because so much is involved. It seems unlikely that any snap decision will work, because either way there's something lost.

When the therapist empathizes with Patti's process and holds the dilemma with her, it obviates Patti's need to use that quandary as a test of therapy and avoidance of change.

Experiential Learning in Transition

Once clients determine the possible limits for therapy, they will adjust to try to fit into that range. The point of note is that this learning must occur *experientially* to build the trust. Regardless of verbal instructions, the only way to truly believe the limits is to test them. This testing is rarely conscious or planned. It is just learned as a part of relational trust-building process. Even though therapy is a unique, boundaried, one-sided relationship, trust builds slowly and through experience.

Working together, client and therapist determine the shape and size of the emotional space. Above the ceiling are levels of pressure and affect that are intolerable, and below the floor of the room are those matters that cannot be effectively dealt with in the particular form of therapy. Once the room/context is temporarily settled and the relational trust has grown, treatment can begin.

It is important to note that there are commonly new tests or a revisit to the older tests prior to each new level of depth or intimacy in the therapeutic relationship. This was demonstrated clearly in my work with the combat veteran who had lost an arm. When the therapist recognizes and anticipates the testing as part of the ongoing relationship, he or she can join the client's journey to new possibilities. The therapist's acceptance allows the client to put the test in abeyance until the next anxious voyage into the unknown.

Therapist Trust Building

While the client is testing the therapist for levels of trust, the therapist is assessing the client's capacity for interpersonal, intrapsychic, relational, and instructive interventions; potential for intimate connection; tolerance of self-disclosure; ability to focus on process; best timing; and methods to activate each.

Like trust building, these are also characteristically learned in a trial-and-error experiential process. As the therapist intervenes, he or she will discover methods that propel a client forward and also what inhibits the process. In this way, the therapist learns to adapt to a client's language, manner of expression, metaphors, preferred representational systems, level of optimal anxiety for best receptivity, and so on.

Transition and Resistance

Resistance is most common and intense during the transition period in therapy. The risks of change and confronting fears of the unknown are formidable. It is unwise to enter into that realm without a trusted companion—an experienced therapeutic Sherpa for the daunting trek. The unconscious goal of resistance during transition is trust in the therapist as that valued companion and trusted guide.

Clients will test the levels of trust with their most effective tools, whether they are approach or avoidance, cognition or affect, closeness or distance.

When these occur, therapists are best advised to recognize these client methods as pulling toward the status quo, empathizing with them, and ultimately joining them. Trust is built by accepting not only what the client says but also his or her manner of communicating.

Treatment

The techniques involved in existential psychotherapy are detailed in several sections throughout this book. For this exploration of the trajectory in therapy, only a few of the methods are highlighted. The entire array of methods is available in actual sessions.

In the pragmatic existential approach described in this text, the relationship is the healing element. Thus, the entire course of treatment is a therapeutic enterprise. Within such a model, it may seem remarkable that a single phase of the process should be identified as the one in which the major impact occurs.

Although it is clear that the entire process has varied levels of impact, the bulk of the major change-oriented interventions occur during this treatment phase. Successful therapy involves getting the person to the room (preparation) and preparing them to be receptive (transition) before offering them the desired methods of change (treatment). The final phase (termination) consolidates the new learning.

In an existential frame, the core of the treatment phase is about creating meaning, accepting the vicissitudes of human life, making choices, using anxiety to foster growth, and so on. The data used are subjective experience and the relationship. This therapy is far less focused on what happens to individuals than on what it means to them and how they react. Nowhere is this more elegantly presented than in Frankl's (1959a) descriptions of his concentration camp experiences.

During the treatment phase, the therapist joins with the client within the latter's subjective reality and highlights discrepancies between what the client claims he or she desires and what is occurring in his or her life. The therapist will underscore the status quo (both content and process) and gently encourage the client to take some small steps to face the fears of the unknown. It is important to remind therapists learning this method that facing the fear and determining how to draw meaning from the consequences is far more healthy than being counterphobic. A woman who is phobic about heights does not have to challenge herself by parachuting from an airplane or looking over the edge of the Sears tower in Chicago. What is useful is to encourage the client to explore the consequences and implications of the fear and to look at the risks of letting go of some parts of the fear.

A classic example of this is the person who cannot commit to a relationship because of a fear of rejection. The existential therapist explores the implications of that potential rejection and might recommend what Yalom (1990) elegantly calls a "thought experiment" in which the client considers the resultant anxiety, if the rejection did not occur.

C: I guess by any standards, I am a loser when it comes to relationships. It's been one rejection after another. I don't even want to try again.

T: *(Thinking that the client is asking for encouragement to try again)* What is it like to be a relationship "loser"?

C: I'll never have a partner. Never have a family. Go through life alone.

T: When you picture that scenario, what does it mean to you that you are and expect to be a loner?"

Under normal circumstances in a relationship, what the client expects to hear is encouragement and reassurance. (i.e., "When the right guy/gal comes along . . ." or "You are smart, successful in work, and respectful. You'll find the right partner. It just hasn't happened yet.")

In response to such reassurance, the client might feel a little better but will soon point out that this hasn't happened and that he or she has no sense that it might. By contrast, when the therapist makes the asocial response— "what's it like to be a loner?"—the client is encouraged to explore his or her personal meaning attribution and perhaps discover some aspects of self that are forestalling in advance any possible suitors. The therapist cannot fix up the client with a likely partner or encourage the client to seek partners in new places. Instead, the therapist's job is to help the client activate his or her personal capacities to explore the fears of change and to examine what dangers lurk if a relationship were to upend the status quo.

In addition, the therapist and client are building what is hopefully an emotionally and intellectually intimate relationship. The very existence of such a relationship, however contrived by the context, contradicts at some levels the "loner" appellation. The process by which the person reduces that apparent incongruity will also create opportunities to understand his or her attribution of meaning and to look more realistically at personal ability to form and stay in a consequential relationship. In short, the confrontation between the thought of being unable to be in a relationship, in the context of an important relationship, can create a shift in a self-defeating self-image.

C: I think the only relationship where I have never been rejected is this one.

T: What sense do you make out of that?

C: Well, I am paying you to listen to me whine.

T: In what ways are *you* different in this relationship?

C: I am honest and . . . not trying to impress you.

T: So the difference is that here you are more fully yourself. Hmm . . . I wonder what implications that has (Therapeutic amazement).

C: You are saying that if I am myself, I might not get rejected.

T: I am wondering about the difference between getting rejected or accepted for who you are versus what image you might want to portray? I am guessing that getting rejected when you are being open and vulnerable would be harder to stand.

C: But then at least I wouldn't have to keep up the façade. Did you notice that the last two times I came in here I didn't wear any make-up?

Treatment Foci

In the treatment (working) phase of therapy, the clinician adjusts his or her focus as needed in a number of realms:

- Concentrated presence as both method and goal
- Attention to client and therapist awareness
- Use of parallel process (the equivalence between what is occurring between client and therapist and what client is describing about his or her life outside of therapy)
- Exploration of ongoing tension between a push to freedom and often unconscious counteracting pull of security at both macro (life span) and micro (in the moment) levels
- Honoring existential anxiety about the basic givens of life and using it as engine of growth
- Confronting neurotic anxiety (often described as symptoms) that keeps clients from existential anxiety
- Finding ways to extend intimate relating and applying them to out-of-therapy life
- Saying the unsayable
- Finding true fulfillment rather than appearing to do things right
- Relating to the client's manner or style of attributing meaning to life problems
- Confrontation of discrepancies
- Seeking greater meaning is the *sine qua non* of treatment

Confrontation and Encounter in Existential Therapy

One prime therapist technique is *confrontation*. This involves pointing out incongruities in the client's presentation of self and allowing him or her to examine both sides of the message as real. What comes to mind here is F. Scott Fitzgerald's observation,

The test of a first-rate intelligence is the ability to hold two opposing ideas in mind at the same time and still retain the ability to function.

In existential therapy, the goal is to hold opposing thoughts in mind and examine the truth of both. Rather than be blocked in attempts to resolve what seem like incompatible sides of self, the therapist is engaged in honoring the full complexity of a person.

Three Steps Forward, Two Steps Back

Therapy does not occur in a linear manner. There are leaps forward to new tests of the fear of the unknown and retreats to the status quo and security. Often, a regression in therapy may indicate that the movement is going too fast or a sign that the client is about to introduce a new level of

---

Figure 7.1   What Is Confrontation in Existential Psychotherapy?

Confrontation is often envisioned as an aggressive challenge, disputing the facts or conclusions that a person might draw. Many students watching an old "Gloria" video of Fritz Perls or a 1970s-style encounter group with a non-professional leader, such as the Synanon addiction approach, conclude that an "in-your-face" approach characterizes a true confrontation.

Actually, from an existential perspective, confrontation is common, but far from aggressive and never a challenge of another's perspective. In this approach, a "heavy confrontation" usually involves holding up a mirror to a client and requesting assistance in understanding the discrepancy.

Sometimes the discrepancy is between two different client statements. A therapist might query, "Joe, I'm a little confused here. A few minutes ago you said that you are devoted to your children and are a 'pushover' when they want something. Then you just reported that the children, particularly your daughter, were annoying, out-of-control, undisciplined and that you just need to 'escape' the house on weekends. Help me understand those apparently different experiences."

Other times it is a discrepancy between verbal and nonverbal messages. The therapist might say, "You are saying something that seems very sad and frustrating, and at the same time you are sitting back with your hands behind your head and smiling as you say that. I am confused as to how I might put those together."

Notice that in both cases, the therapist offers the apparent contrasting messages back to the client and requests clarification. She is not saying that one of the messages is incorrect; she is indicating that she wants to understand the client's full experience better.

She may also offer her personal process experience. "You just told me something that seems painfully sad. And you are smiling as you say it. I wonder if I am more sad than you."

depth or topic. Signs of resistance are valuable indicators for the therapist to explore more closely what is occurring in the therapeutic relationship and to be increasingly open to the new direction or old ground the client is traversing. When the therapist joins with the resistance, it allows clients to feel safe enough to explore mutually more complex and deeper components of their subjective selves.

Resistance in Treatment

During the treatment phase of the therapy process, resistance is characteristically about the client's internal fear of change, something Bugental and Bugental (1984) likened to "a fate worse than death." As clients challenge the status quo of their lives, anxiety arises and the natural pull is back to security and doing things the way they always have done them, despite the costs. As the clinician and client work together to encourage some modest experimentation in life, anxiety rises and often takes the form of resisting change: by or through cognitive questioning, affective overemoting, or behavioral failing.

When the therapist is aware that the resistance is to change in the moment, the therapist can make adjustments in support, empathy, or recommendations of various forms of experimentation. It is essential to understand that facing the fears of the unknown is valuable. Overcoming them may not be.

Facing Fears in Treatment:
The Waimea Rock Challenge

Several years ago, when I was practicing in Honolulu, I had two individual clients (Anita and Sam) who were approaching their fiftieth birthdays with some angst. Each personally decided to test their fears on a large rock that juts out into the ocean at Waimea Bay on O'ahu. Characteristically, it is teenage boys who test their masculinity by jumping off the top of the cliff into the ocean swirling below, not middle-aged folks on a personal quest.

Anita drove to Waimea Bay, climbed up on the rock, checked to see that the tide was in, held her nose, and with a running start, leapt into the Pacific Ocean. She returned to therapy the next week exhilarated and delighted with herself. She described the event as "life-changing."

Less than 10 days later, Sam made the same pilgrimage. He climbed up on the rock. Three times he went to the precipice, looked down at the ocean, and walked back from the edge to consider the leap. After the third time, he slowly climbed back down and drove home. In his next therapy session, he described the event with evident satisfaction. Forgetting that I had not suggested such a test, he asked if I considered him a failure. Before waiting for my answer, he asserted, "*You know, I knew I could do it, but that wasn't me. I need to deal with my demons in other ways.*"

From an existential perspective, both were quite successful in facing a real fear. For Anita, who was generally very conservative, facing such a great danger was a turning point toward several less dramatic positive changes. Thankfully, her impulsive leap had a safe outcome. Sam, whose life was filled with incautious risk taking, found it exhilarating to recognize danger and focus on the value of avoiding unnecessary risk.

Each faced existential anxiety and tested themselves. Had the desire to jump been a function of neurotic anxiety and resistance, either might have forgotten to fill the gas tank and run dry before leaving Honolulu or developed a sniffle that precluded being in the ocean. Neurotic anxiety, the fear of fear, keeps individuals locked in the status quo.

Termination

The final phase of therapy involves two factors: transfer of training and saying goodbye. It's best when the therapist and client mutually agree that the present work is complete. Optimally, it occurs when the client has learned how to be courageous in the face of personal demons and dilemmas and can address them without the therapist. Sometimes clients come to a particular resting point in their life-journey and decide to leave therapy, at least temporarily.

Termination can occur for many reasons however. Financial considerations, third party (insurance) limitations, breaks in the process because of work or life events, illnesses, and moves can all prompt a premature termination. Some clients become fatigued at the hard work of therapy and want a temporary or even permanent break. Finally, sometimes the therapy stalls and there seems to be diminishing returns in continuation. Terminations may be temporary. Many clients will return at a future date to address a new problem, just for a checkup, to reassure themselves that the therapist is still there, or to find strength to address a new crisis.

Regardless of the reasons and manner of the termination or break, it is important that the therapist initiate a discussion of the two major issues of ending or pausing a relationship: saying goodbye and transfer of training to the client's "real," out-of-therapy life.

Although the focus on termination comes in the final weeks of treatment, the relationship is designed to be temporary from the very beginning, and when successful, the therapist's goal is to become anachronistic in the life of the client. It is an unbalanced, asocial relationship that is focused not on mutual needs but on one person. Once he or she develops a working alliance with a client, effective therapists are always pointing toward the client's independence from the therapy relationship. The influential family therapist Carl Whitaker (1988) told me that he always began the first session taking notes with a clipboard in his lap. He believed that the clipboard block was symbolic that the relationship, however intense, was ultimately temporary.

Transfer of Training

Termination is successful when the client and therapist explore what has been learned and how it can be used in daily life. If the translation to real life is not accomplished and solidified, the therapy may be limited to contexts like the unique therapeutic relationship.

T: Let's review what have you accomplished here and how you can use it.

C: Well, the biggest thing is to be aware of when I pick a fight with my wife, it usually means that I am anxious about our closeness.

T: So when you remember that, what can be different?

C: What I hope I'll do is just to tell her that I am getting anxious and to ask that we go more slowly.

T: What would you be hoping to get in response?

C: Well, what I am worried about is that I'll be vulnerable, but knowing her, she'd probably like that I am telling her what I am feeling.

T: If I recall, when you did that a few weeks ago, she responded with a lot of respect and understanding.

C: She actually told me that she comes on so strong because she is anxious also.

T: So being aware of what is happening inside and communicating that sounds like a plan. Not to be a wet blanket, but what would happen if she didn't respond well?

C: I hope I'll be able to just keep at it.

Saying Goodbye

The second aspect of termination is dealing with loss and endings; saying goodbye. There is no question that Americans in general are far more comfortable with hellos than goodbyes. A hello is a beginning, marking untapped potential. We tend to avoid endings as a prototype of death, the final goodbye.

Because of the discomfort, many are loath to acknowledge that a relationship is actually ending. Resistance at termination usually focuses around issues of abandonment, isolation, loss, and mortality.

1. Denial: "Well, this isn't really over, I can come back if I need to, right?"

2. Anger and rejection: "Well, it will be good to have my Wednesday morning back and the money I'll be saving."

3. Weaning: "Why don't we plan to meet again about every 3 to 4 weeks, just to make sure it's going well?"

4. Attempts to change the relationship: "I wonder if we could be friends in the future. You know, get together for a cup of coffee or lunch sometime."

5. Developing new symptoms: "I know that we are quitting, but the past week I've been noticing my anxiety getting much worse, and I can't sleep through the night."

Like resistance at all other phases of therapy, these involve the fear of change and the unknown. Therapists need to contain them and work with the clients on maintaining courage.

Sometimes, clients are not alone in feeling a loss of the special intimacy of a therapeutic relationship. Therapists also may have difficulty letting go of a relationship that has been powerful and successful. In some ways, it may feel like launching a child. One wants them to do well on their own, but there is still a desire to remain in touch.

When this feeling of impending loss is troubling at an unconscious level, therapists may subtly avoid their own fears of loss by engaging in interactions such as re-engaging, creating more dependence, or trying to convert relationships from professional to personal as a way to prolong their roles in clients' lives. Social media can provide a conundrum in this effort. To what extent is it acceptable to "friend" a former client on social media such as Facebook or LinkedIn?

The place for therapists to work through these losses is not with clients but in their own personal therapy or supervision. The extent to which therapists know themselves and their personal needs for reassurance will reduce unconsciously generated actions to hold on to contact. To be effective at the kind of intimate depth work involved in existential therapy, one is well-advised to be involved regularly in personal therapy and supervision.

This is true for even the most experienced practitioners. During my final years in practice, a client who I had seen years before came back into therapy. He is a fascinating and brilliant man, who was dealing with his own age-related change at work. Our backgrounds were remarkably similar, and the issues that we had to confront in life were almost parallel. I looked forward to sessions with an atypical anticipation. He worked hard in therapy and was very appreciative. As termination of our therapy approached, my own retirement from practice was not far off. I was very aware of missing the relationship and contact. There was an eerie parallel in my personal therapy: As I talked about my sense of loss of this relationship and of my preparing for retirement from my practice, my therapist was becoming more frail and shortly later passed away. Thankfully, that loss enabled me to grasp the importance of savoring the psychological intimacy I had shared both with my client and with my late therapist. Had I avoided confronting either loss, I could have missed out on the opportunity for personal growth.

The Small Town Phenomenon

If a therapist practices in a small community or rural area, he or she is likely to run into former clients in other settings. One therapist recalled how a client showed up in the shower with her at the only athletic club in their community. Another found that when his regular internist was on vacation, he was unexpectedly confronted with a client for his annual physical exam. In small communities, people often have varied roles. Clients may be one's gardener, dentist, realtor, or banker. One therapist discovered that he was on the same matchmaking dating website as a client, and her name was recommended to him as a potential match. Normally, psychotherapists prefer anonymity; when that is simply not feasible and there are likely to be dual relationships, it is mandatory that it be discussed in session.

One of the real advantages of an existential approach is that the potentially confounding roles may be confronted directly, with room for both the therapist's and client's awareness and experiences. In my personal life, I have worked in both small and large communities. I have also seen several therapists as clients. In the smaller professional community (Honolulu), any time I went to a professional meeting or event, I would be in contact with several current and former clients. During the event itself, compartmentalizing was the best method, but often it would require some earnest discussion, especially if there was anticipation of the event.

At one such event, two therapists were debating their theoretical and practice differences for a mental health professional audience. Although they had major differences in approach and the debate got quite heated, they demonstrated professional respect during the question and answer section at the end. In response to a query from the audience about who they would see as a therapist, each was gracious enough to identify his debate opponent. During a discussion after the event, they realized that each was seeing me privately. Both had a need to discuss their feelings of "guilt" in the next session.

The sessions in which these events occurred went well and opened up some interesting issues about privacy and image. Fruitful interactions may occur precisely because of the small town experience. A more dramatic experience occurred when the play *Equus* came to town for a few showings. It was an event naturally attended by most of the mental health professionals on the island. At the showing I attended, there were five current and 11 former clients in the lobby. It was a time for reflection both about the powerful play and the multilevel relationships. It also prompted many sessions of discussion.

Such an occasion would be very unlikely in a larger community.

C: I just heard that I will be giving the keynote address at the meeting next month.

T: We should discuss this. I am slated to be the emcee and will probably be introducing you. How do you feel about our interacting in a public environment?

Experience With Termination

Although the avoidance of loss is a major factor in the difficulty of the termination process, lack of experience is another difficulty. I recently asked a class of advanced graduate students in a practice-oriented program how many first interviews they had seen or done in their coursework to date. The answers ranged from a dozen to 25.

When I inquired about the number of terminations, most of the class of 25 said "none." The highest number was two. These students were about to go into internships in which they would be doing primarily short-term counseling with regular terminations.

It is clear that training in closing, and even middle stages of therapy, is not as complete as the early stages. Academic semesters and quarters are not well structured for such learning, and often professors are themselves more comfortable teaching early skills. When we consider that symbolic termination begins in the first session and that the measurable outcome of our work depends on effective transfer of training, that is a serious deficiency.

Effective Termination

When termination goes well it is a bittersweet experience for both client and therapist. There is a loss of a very special relationship intermixed with a commencement of a new stage of more independent life. Accepting and facing that loss is part and parcel of the existential therapy experience and, like an adult child leaving the nest, it can become a prototype for clients moving forward.

A few years ago, I received an email from a client I had seen over a decade ago. He wrote,

> *I don't expect you to remember, but this is the 10th anniversary of our last session. I wanted you to know that I am doing well—I did marry the woman (LOL)—and we have two children. My life really turned around and I am most grateful. It was very painful on Friday mornings at 9 a.m. for several months. At first I was angry and sad that you were not there anymore. I felt like I was missing my best friend in the world and frequently wondered what you would say at times, but I slowly realized that I basically knew or could imagine what you would say. I was carrying our brotherhood along with me and was doing well on my own. There have been bumps on the road, but all in all I have coped well. So thank you. Oh BTW, my wife, who you never met and who was with me as a girlfriend during those dark days, thinks you're a miracle worker.*

Secondhand transference aside, the benefits of a successful termination were that he could live effectively on his own, address his personal issues, and deal with the exigencies of his life. His ability to experience anger and sadness over the loss of the relationship is exemplary of a positive adaptation.

Follow-up and Evaluation

Obtaining feedback and detailed evaluation of any procedure is incredibly useful and can allow for future adjustments and tweaking that will improve delivery of services. Outcome results measured at termination, 6 months following, and a year after termination would make a major difference in how we explore the true evidence base for treatment. Sadly, few studies contain such follow-up measurements. Those that do generally demonstrate that interpersonal, existential, and psychodynamic approaches are as effective at symptom reduction at termination and have longer-lasting positive outcomes than technique-based, symptom-oriented approaches.

As difficult as it is to do follow-up studies in a lab setting, it is much more complex practically and ethically for clinicians in real world practices. Follow-up studies of psychotherapy risk both patient confidentiality and iatrogenic effects of the contact itself. Recontacting a former client could inadvertently indicate to him or her that you are encouraging him or her to come back into therapy.

Often such approaches are hamstrung by so many ethical and pragmatic considerations that true follow-up data are likely to miss some far more personal impact of the therapy. A clinician's subjective determination of how well a treatment went may be of value, but client and objective data round out the picture and would help develop a true evidence base.

Notes

1. Sometimes issues come up unexpectedly in therapy and cannot be avoided. In such situations, the more ethical response may be to work with the client while getting supervision and simultaneously working on the personal issues in the therapist's own therapy.

2. Some therapists make an exception to this policy when the client is a child or dependent elder and the therapy involves parenting or caretaking.

8

Show Me the Evidence! What Is the Proof That Existential Therapy Works?

There are more things in heaven and earth, Horatio, than are dreamt of in your philosophy.

Shakespeare—*Hamlet* (1.5.167-8)

Establishing an evidence base for existential psychotherapies is challenging. There are some traditional studies that demonstrate comparable or superior results for existential and related experiential methods, and they will be reviewed briefly here, but there are few programmatic approaches that address "life-changing therapy."

Much of the deductive hypothesis testing that fills professional journals is focused on technique-centric methods that are predominantly symptom-oriented. On many levels, the bulk of this research is irrelevant to the methods and goals of existential therapy. In this chapter, the reasons for this discrepancy are explored, some relevant evidence is provided to support an expanded use of existential methods, and the important question of the relative contributions of art and science in clinical work is addressed.

Some Realities for Clinicians

There is no question that discerning and demonstrating positive evidence for any treatment is desirable. Existential counselors and psychotherapists want to engage in best practice and to use methods that are scientifically established and noniatrogenic. Practitioners who view each client and situation as unique embrace the need for tried-and-true methods that can be applied effectively with clients. However, these clinicians require valid tests on appropriate variables.

Fiscal Considerations

For many therapists, there are substantive financial implications. Neither they nor their clients will get reimbursed by third party payers, whose agents determine whether a treatment for a particular symptom or symptom cluster is "medically necessary," and if so, which treatment is likely to get the client out of therapy most quickly. In the United States, United Kingdom, and several continental countries, specific psychotropic medications (in the "formulary") and Brief Cognitive Behavior Therapy (BCBT), preferably in a manualized form, are the primary choices for all emotional and behavioral ills. Practitioners using other treatments have to convince provider relations that an alternative is preferable.

Short-term economic goals of large insurance carriers or a National Health Service can be inimical to more effective, longer-lasting treatments. The primary objective is a speedy end to treatment, with measurable benefits. That external pressure to truncate treatment or to find methods that suit well the quarter-by-quarter bottom line ethos may well provide a spurious, short-sighted savings at potentially high human cost and intermediate or long-term economic loss.

For example, a series of studies conducted in the 1970s at the military Family Life Centers in Hawaii at Pearl Harbor (Navy), Ft. Shafter and Tripler Army Medical Center (Army), and Hickam (Air Force) bases indicated that the return on therapy for service military personnel and their families yielded approximately six dollars in savings for every one spent on therapy. Moreover, from a fiscal perspective, it was clear that recidivism is far more expensive in the long run than a lengthier successful initial treatment (Shapiro, 1978a).[1] Similar results have been reported by Lorig et al. (1999), Cummings, O'Donahue, and Ferguson (2003), and Cuijpers, van Straten, Hollon, and Andersson (2010). At least a few studies have indicated that the long-term outcome was better with relationship centered/ experiential group therapy (Shapiro, 2010a).

Similar findings have been reported in recent meta-analyses. Szentagotai and David (2010), reviewing studies for several mood disorders, indicated that despite a slight increase in upfront cost for the added treatment, there was no significant financial downside in adding psychotherapy to psychophar-mocology. Miklowitz and Scott (2009) showed that relapse rates consistently declined over a 1- to 2-year period—a considerable savings in human suffering and financial cost. McHugh et al. (2007) also demonstrated that the initial cost of psychotherapy (cognitive behavioral therapy; CBT) for panic disorders was more than offset by greater longer-term effectiveness of the treatment.

Preaching to the Choir: The "Hegemony" of CBT[2]

In most large institutional settings and among insurers, the general belief is that CBT[3] is *the* answer, if the first choice of psychotropic medication fails. Most modern therapists adjust to this either by adopting CBT methods; translating psychodynamic, existential, or humanistic therapies into CBT terms on progress notes; or making those frequent, seemingly interminable justification arguments with the insurance giants. It is not unusual for reim-bursement to be withheld for months or even permanently if the therapist uses alternative language, even after the treatment has been authorized and, in some cases, completed successfully.

Why the Monopoly of a Single Approach?

There are several rationales for this apparent theoretical hegemony. First and foremost is the fact that CBT has been the most studied form of psychotherapy and is the easiest to describe to lay persons. CBT is primarily educational and takes a "practice makes perfect," successive approximations methodology. It also targets the presenting symptoms and can show that, with treatment, those clearly specified symptoms can be reduced in occurrence and severity.

At this point, there is a long history of the study of this particular modal-ity. The plethora of efficacy studies in academic laboratories and the smaller but increasing number of effectiveness (real world) studies have real value in better understanding how symptoms may be manipulated and altered for the relief of a patient's discomfort. These studies have been replicated and found to be reliable under laboratory conditions.

Secondly, CBT is described as a brief treatment modality. Short term, rather than longitudinal, studies are far easier to conduct in academic laboratories. This is especially compelling for aspiring academicians completing doctoral dissertations and for faculty in research institutions, whose research grants, tenure, and promotion are judged in large part by quantity of clean, straightforward, publishable studies. One unfortunate outcome of this push to publish is a separation of professional journals along theoretical lines. Thus, some journal editorial boards are biased toward the academically favored CBT approaches.

Third, psychotherapy is a unique field that crosses disciplines that are more competitive than cooperative in what seems like a battle for supremacy. CBT has been successfully shown to be equal to, or superior to, the current psychiatric trend of medication-alone treatment.[4] Several studies also show the advantages of combining the CBT with chemical intervention.

In a sense, CBT and psychotropic medication are predicated on similar premises: diagnose, reduce, and/or eliminate the presenting symptoms. That premise encourages the use of straightforward, equivalent outcome measures that allow for simple and clear comparisons.

However, as Heatherington et al. (2012) and Levy and Anderson (2013) have strongly indicated, this monopoly, like all others, precludes or co-opts alternative perspectives, and results in a loss of "significant intellectual diversity" (Levy and Anderson, 2013, p. 211).

Alternative Goals for Counseling and Psychotherapy

CBT may well be a treatment of choice if specific targeted behavior change is the primary reason for psychotherapy. However, in cases where symptom alleviation is not the objective, measurement of that outcome may provide an inaccurate or misleading indicator of success.

What if a therapist and client agreed on the goal of increased courage to face a number of life's exigencies, rather than to do away with or manage the client's acrophobia? When the goal of therapy is life changing rather than behavior modification, a very different treatment approach may be indicated. One of my graduate students recently encapsulated this issue in my Existential Psychotherapy class when she asked,

> *Why would you want to explore and savor anxiety, which is obviously uncomfortable for the clients, when according to Prof. X. in another class, you can do away with it or reduce it to less troubling levels with CBT or mindfulness?*

Her well-intentioned question opened an important discussion on the true and often divergent goals of therapy. In response, I asked her, "Are we talking about existential anxiety or neurotic anxiety?" The remainder of the class involved a quite energetic exploration of the meaning of a *symptom*, what goals there were for the treatment, and what best suited therapist abilities and client needs.

"Include Me Out"[5]

Existential therapists have characteristically eschewed as irrelevant the symptom-based efficacy studies. There are political, philosophical, and clinical motivations for this avoidance.

Heated, seemingly interminable political debates between clinical and experimental psychologists have roiled psychology departments for decades, with each side declaring their own righteousness and attributing either naiveté or the demonic to the opposition. Although all agree on the desirability of evidence-based practice, clinicians question the applicability of laboratory efficacy studies to guide practice, and experimentalists accuse clinicians of ignoring research. The questions revolve around both what constitutes evidence and turf wars.

One of the primary battles is the debate around the primacy of technique or relationship. Existential therapists and scholars commonly find themselves on the relational rather than the technique side of this culture war. Because existential therapists do not necessarily view measurable behavior change and mollification of symptoms as a particularly preferred treatment outcome, they consider even reliable measurements of those results to be of little interest. Many in the existential camp might well argue that a simple shift in behavior may be more obfuscating than facilitative in reaching the desired goals of greater courage, flexibility, finding meaning, and ability to make better choices when faced with important life realities.

For many who call themselves existential or humanistic therapists, the question of proof that their approaches actually work is both ridiculous and insulting. Nobody who has shared the psychological skin of another; experienced the growth in cognitive, behavioral, and affective flexibility; and achieved a general shift in outlook would find such a question as relevant: "Just look at the client, that's all you need to know." Today, however, such subjective and qualitative indices of success are often relegated to secondary status when compared to therapies which have numbers to establish the evidence base.

Give Him a Fish or Teach Him to Fish

From the pragmatic existential viewpoint presented in this book, therapy narrowly focused on behavior change is essentially what Maimonides considered offering a fish dinner to a hungry person, without providing the means for him to learn to fish and to feed himself. Here, the goals and measurements of existential therapy and CBT diverge significantly. Cognitive therapists may legitimately aver that they are teaching cognitive skills, but their success is measured in shifts in intensity or elimination of targeted behaviors. Establishing an evidence base for whether or not the man had dinner tonight is far less complex than a longitudinal study on his increasing skills to provide for himself and his family.

Faced with a choice of approaching solely the target behavior, or of having treatment plans dictated by an insurer, many psychodynamic-, humanistic-, and existentially-oriented private practitioners have opted out of the system and do not take third party payments. In my personal private practice, I chose to provide my clients with an "insurance-ready" statement but did not join any provider panels.

The risk of making this kind of choice is twofold: (1.) accepting the possibility of a less than full practice and (2.) catering to an upscale population of clients who could pay out of pocket. In part, I was able to support this level of "integrity" because by the time managed care took center stage, I had a mature practice and a full-time university position.

A Lack of Fit Between Efficacy Studies and Existential-Humanistic Therapy

There are six major reasons why psychodynamic, humanistic, and existential therapists would have difficulty buying into symptom-centric goals and the contingent methods that lead to success in that realm.

1. Definition of the Problem

Existential and CBT therapists define the reason for therapy differently. For Bugental (1999) the goal of existential therapy was "life changing," rather than symptom altering. For van Deurzen (2010) existential therapies focus on the "how" rather than the "what" questions—the central concern being the client's subjective experience. Spinelli (1997) describes his existential-philosophical model as exploring and clarifying the client's being-in-the-world, rather than ego-strengthening or symptom removal.

2. Opposing Views of the Locus of Change

In efficacy studies, the independent variable of note is technique. The client and the relationship are secondary. The locus of change and the responsibility falls on the therapist, not on the client. Failures are viewed as mistakes by the therapist in getting client compliance.[6] For the existential therapist, the locus of change is the client, and the relationship is seen as a more significant change factor than any technique.

Evidence-Based Relationships

The September 2014 issue of the journal *Psychotherapy* was devoted to papers exploring the therapeutic relationship. Summarizing their own work and decades of research by others, Norcross and Lambert concluded,

> *The contribution of the relationship to patient success is similar for all psychotherapies studied . . . Effective psychotherapy cannot, and does not, exist without a positive relationship.* (2014, pp. 398–399)

Considerable research evidence (i.e., Norcross and Lambert, 2014) shows that treatment effectiveness is dependent on the relational context in which it occurs. The salience of these findings for existential therapies is powerful. The therapeutic relationship may be insufficient for desired changes, but it is the necessary *sine qua non*.

It is interesting to recall a passing comment made by pioneering behavioral and strategic-oriented theorist Jay Haley. At the second Erickson Evolution of Psychotherapy Conference (1986), he was asked by a therapist in the audience whether he would take her on as a client after the conference. He replied, "You know, you'd be better off with one of my students or my wife. They are warm. As a therapist, I am more of a cool tactician."

3. A Very Different View of Human Nature

Efficacy studies are based on reductionism. As a theory based in explanations of habit, behavior development, and causality, CBT fits well.

Because problems are considered to be learned, new learning can eliminate the disquieting symptom and produce behavior change. The core notion is that a change in one aspect of a client's thinking or behavior is necessary and sufficient to move forward. There is no space for a construct that a symptom (as per the dictionary definition) represents something else that may not be observable to the healer. The anxiety or depression is the point of interest, just as the torn knee ligament is to the orthopedic surgeon.

Existential therapies look at the whole person and eschew any attempts at reductionism. The basic notion is that the whole (person) is greater than the sum of his or her parts. Thus, treatment for specific behaviors or parts of persons, (essentially arguing that the whole is equal to *some* of its parts) is anathema to treatment. It is the person with a torn ACL, not the knee, who is the patient.

4. Different Aspirations for Clients

Efficacy studies focus on freedom from discomfort. Existential therapies focus on how to create meaning from anxiety and how to learn to face anxiety in the pursuit of freedom.

The Client

One of the major concerns for humanistic and existential therapists is awareness of the client's perception and his or her experience. Several studies have demonstrated the significance of the client's perception in determining outcome, particularly the client's perception of the therapist's caring for him or her. Notice it was not the therapist's belief in how much he was conveying the core conditions, nor external observer impressions from videotape analysis. It was how the client felt. This is a strong statement regarding the centrality of relationship over specific theory or technique. O'Hara (1986) additionally warned that the key was not simply therapist empathy for the client but empathy for the relationship they share.

It seems just a little arrogant for therapists to believe that therapeutic change may be independent of client personality or beliefs. Wampold (2001), echoing Lambert's (1992) work, underscored the significance of the patient's contribution to psychotherapy outcome. Bohart and Tallman (2010) argued that clients are the most salient factor in therapeutic success and warned about the tendency toward "therapist-centricity" in studies of therapy.

Client–Therapist–Technique Match

One factor that has gone relatively underconsidered is that therapists are not the only theorists in the consulting room. Clients have personal theories about human nature and change, although they may not easily articulate them. In a small and curious study, Shapiro (1987) concluded that some clients were behaviorally oriented while others were psychodynamically oriented, at least based on the level of sexual activity in which they engaged while sexual stimuli were projected on a screen. This bimodal curve brought into question the extent to which the match between therapist and client on personal and theoretical grounds might be more salient than the technique or stimulus per se. It is likely that some clients respond best to more deterministic, reductionistic approaches and others to more humanistic, whole-person, phenomenological approaches. The major determinant of success here might well be the match.

In a major policy statement (2013), the American Psychological Association Presidential Task Force on Evidence-Based Practice concurred with this assessment, *variations in outcome are more heavily influenced by patient characteristics for example, chronicity, complexity, social support, and intensity—and by clinician and context factors than by particular diagnoses or specific treatment "brands"* (p. 321).

Norcross, Beutler, and Levant (2006), summarizing decades of psychotherapy research, argued persuasively for the interaction effects of the context of treatment, the patient, the therapist, the relationship, and the techniques of treatment. It is only when we consider all of these separately and together that we may make confident conclusions about what causes the therapeutic change. Their conclusions match well with the basic ideographic definition of psychotherapy as the study of the individual.

5. Efficacy and Effectiveness Studies

Although there is little debate about whether or not psychotherapy works (i.e., Seligman, 1995; Wampold et al., 1997), there is considerable disagreement about approaches, desirable outcomes, the specificity of "active ingredients," qualifications of therapists offering service, and how much therapy should conform to a manual for treatment.

Over the past several decades, a multitude of researchers have tried to tease out the crucial variables that govern positive outcomes. Two broad types of studies have been used: efficacy studies and effectiveness studies. The terms, which may seem counterintuitive, were adopted from pharmacological research.

Efficacy (Laboratory Studies)

Efficacy research focuses on the performance of an intervention under ideal, controlled circumstances (high internal validity). The best controlled and replicable efficacy studies involve the manipulation of a single independent variable and preferably few measured dependent variables. By contrast, effectiveness studies measure performance under (high external validity) "real-world" conditions (Nathan, Stuart, & Dolan, 2000). For existentially oriented therapies, real-world studies are far more relevant. Efficacy studies are of interest only heuristically, for their potential to generate new hypotheses.

The strength and weakness of efficacy studies is random assignment to experimental and control groups, strict inclusion criteria (often excluding data from subjects who have more than a single presenting problem). The goal is to, as cleanly as possible, connect a specific diagnosis with a corresponding treatment. To accomplish this, manuals are used for therapist responses to assure equivalent, and as much as possible, identical treatment. Outcomes are "often assessed on a short-term targeted basis, typically focused on changes in symptoms rather than on more global changes in personality or quality of life" (Nathan et al., 2000, p. 965).

Effectiveness (Real-Life Studies)

Effectiveness research is designed to measure outcomes across broader populations of clients in real-world settings. These studies include clients who present with comorbid pathology or chronic conditions. Treatment is far more based on clinical issues and clinical judgment and is adjusted during the course of the therapy based on client reactions and needs rather than progressively as in a manualized approach.

In efficacy studies, nonspecific factors, such as placebo effects, are a nuisance to be eliminated as much as possible. In effectiveness studies, they are part of the overall treatment. For existential therapists, these nonspecific elements are essential components of the relationship and the therapy.

6. The Unique Issues for an Inductive Theory

The most significant lack of fit for existential approaches lies deep in the basic philosophy of science. In a world of deductive logic and decoding methods, existential psychotherapy has an uphill climb, because the data are applied in a very different manner.

In studies of therapy outcomes predicated on deductive logic, testable hypotheses are generated by the theory. Data is collected and analyzed to confirm or deny the null hypothesis. Did the data support the prediction or not? Can it be replicated?

This scientific method, common in most natural sciences, has yielded a host of testable and replicable "truths." We no longer question that the earth travels around the sun, doubt the pull of gravity, or question the composition of a water molecule. Most theories of psychotherapy follow this logical scheme. The whole is broken into component parts for analysis.

How Theory Can Create Data

When exploring complex human behavior, deductive approaches have some difficulties and limitations. Two primary aspects of theory are highlighting relevant information and connecting meaning to those data. An effective theory filters out much that could be significant when viewed from an alternative perspective. In short, theories of human behavior create[7] the data, and in so doing, become restrictive and sufficiently rigid to render them unavailable for what legendary philosopher of science Karl Popper (2002) called "falsifiability."

Another noted expert in the philosophy of science, Thomas Kuhn (1970), distinguished between normal science that follows this deductive paradigm, and *revolutionary science* that overturns the basic conceptualization.

Existentialists have ever identified with the latter, representing rebellion against the common order of things. For existential philosophers and therapists, deductive logic and empiricism are not the guiding principles to be used to discern the human world. Rather than decoding the mysteries of the universe, an encoding approach begins with data and develops into theory. The initial assumption is one of chaos to be experienced, accepted, and comprehended subjectively. Data are only significant within the context of the perceiver. For the phenomenologically oriented therapist, the entire enterprise is an exercise in wonder and discovery, to the extent possible without preconceived notions.

Within this frame, each encounter is somewhat unique, and the immediate relationship in the moment between therapist and client is more significant than change-oriented techniques. Pre-set theoretical limits or instruments are anathema to understanding the life-as-lived experience of another person. The approach recognizes the basic engineering principle that form follows function rather than precedes it.

The Law of the Instrument (Kaplan, 1964)

Deductive logic and theory are not the only limiting factors for inductive approaches. The available measuring sticks also have built-in biases and restrictions. Einstein is credited with noting,

Everybody is a genius. But if you judge a fish by its ability to climb a tree, it will live its whole life believing it is stupid.

Understanding that the measuring stick itself creates and limits data is a powerful insight in comprehending study outcomes. Many observers across fields of inquiry have noted that once the instrument is determined, the available data are impacted or controlled.

Warning about the need to be cautious with one's tools, Mark Twain is commonly credited with the quotation,

Give a boy a hammer and everything he meets has to be pounded.

For example, if an investigator was challenged to measure behavior change with reference to a nominal scale (he or she can count but not order incidences of occurrence), the instrument of choice would focus attention on the number of times an event occurs. The investigator could statistically measure that count versus another and begin to formulate a conclusion that one treatment led to greater or fewer incidences and also determine the probability that such a discrepancy would occur by chance.

Those data could be replicated and build confidence that one treatment actually correlated quite well with statistically significant greater or fewer occurrences of the target behavior (or symptoms). Voila! Here is "proof" that one treatment is superior to another (or more typically, superior to no treatment) in affecting the number of times a specific symptom occurs. Those numbers may even hold up over several trials or multiple locations and perhaps be useful in formulating a treatment model.

Here's the problem. There are two major assumptions that truly bias the data and the conclusions that can be drawn. First, the theory on which the experiment is based has pre-ordained that more or fewer incidences are desirable. Second, the instrument we have to collect data was limited to prespecified observations. In this way, the expectation of a certain outcome simultaneously confirms our theory and inhibits the development of opposite formulations.

In a stunning example of favoring instrumentation, Chambless and Crits-Christoph (2006) conclude that the wise approach is to use what is currently available, rather than explore more openly.

> *Of all the aspects of psychotherapy that influence outcome, the treatment method is the only aspect in which psychotherapists can be trained, it is the only aspect that can be manipulated in a clinical experiment to test its worth, and, if proven valuable, it is the only aspect that can be disseminated to other psychotherapists.* (p. 199)

Because their capabilities for training, clinically manipulating, measuring, and testing are circumscribed by techniques of treatment, they recommend that study and generalization of alternatives is out of the realm of "*only*" acceptable and should be avoided. Although their intent is likely in the pursuit of "good" science," it paradoxically may lead to the exact opposite result by restricting the data that can be measured.

The great physicist of the 20th century, Albert Einstein,[8] is commonly attributed with opining an opposite notion that statistical significance is quite different from life changing:

> *Not everything that can be counted counts,*
> *and not everything that counts can be counted.*

A witty take on this phenomenon is comedian Steven Colbert's forced-choice query:

(a) George W. Bush great president,

(b) George W. Bush, greatest president

Although it is intended as humor, the point is well made. The assumptions behind the question and the instrument itself determine the outcome data.

Because the measure doesn't allow for any other possibility, it violates a basic principle of the philosophy of science. Any restriction on what data are observed, collected, and interpreted reduces the possibility of alternative evidence. Historically, anything that falls outside the common field of view and measurements is pejoratively labelled "unscientific." Reducing therapist variability by using manuals for treatment may make studies cleaner but not necessarily more valid or useful to clinicians or clients

Existential Therapy: Instrumentation and Outcome

An existential approach to measurement eschews initial predictions, hypotheses, and determined measurements. Instead, the experimental approach involves beginning with the widest possible array of data collection methods and develops hypotheses that lead to theorizing about the meaning.

Deductive methods might well miss positive or negative data, simply because they don't look for them or have a convenient tool for measuring them. If we are to measure properly how existential therapy impacts outcome, measurements need to include process as well as a far wider array of outcomes. Herein lies a basic incongruity between existential psychotherapy and a manualized, technique-driven, symptom-oriented approach to measure evidence. For example, one goal of most existential therapy is to help clients learn to develop courage to face core human conditions, such as the limits on one's life span. A relevant methodology might involve a measure of that variable, unrelated to decreases in symptom incidence.

In addition, by definition, existential therapists define each therapeutic encounter within and between clients and sessions as unique. Within that framework, replicability (except at a process level) may reflect more a failure to connect with the client's individual being-in-the-world than an instance of success. Attempts to severely control independent variables are anathema to the goals of the kind of life-changing therapy that is described in this book, and there is serious question whether it is possible if desired.

Stiles (2009) argued that suppositions of equivalence across therapists using manuals are demonstrably flawed. Krause and Lutz (2009) also showed that the assumption that everyone within a treatment group receive identical treatment is "drastically violated" and that in "outcome-relevant treatment, therapist and patient input variables or types causally influence each other" (2009, p. 74).

Furthermore, there is the existential question, do deductive efficacy studies give in so far to the demands of the status quo that they supersede any needs for freedom? From the existential inductive perspective, the dependent variable data derived from measuring variations in specific symptoms may be countable, replicable, and statistically significant, but it doesn't offer much clinical validity.

The prejudice toward numerical values that can be statistically manipulated to produce probabilities, effects, sizes, and levels of significance may be an example of the Law of the Instrument. The clean data are compelling, whether or not they are truly measuring valid goals of therapy.

Is this an impasse? Are the methods of deductive scientific inquiry not appropriate to measure a basically inductive approach? Is it as futile as trying to evaluate the taste of a peach using only a weight scale?

Psychotherapy: Art, Science, or Hybrid

The six categories of discrepancies between the avowed goals of existential psychotherapy and the deductive scientific method are daunting, but there is another even more basic question about the nature of psychotherapy. Is it truly a science or might it be more of an art form—an issue that has been explored over the years in the journal *Voices: The Art and Science of Psychotherapy*?

If therapy, at least in part, were considered an art form, it would alter the way in which we consider the outcome. The *Mona Lisa*, the statue of *David*, or the ceiling of the Sistine Chapel may be copied but never replicated. There is something of the artist that infuses the work and makes each piece one of a kind, inspired by the artist's state of being at the moment of the individual brushstroke.

Imagine someone approaching Van Gogh and requesting another "Starry Night." Even performance art is somewhat different each time. An actress might say the same lines each night in a play, but her personal state of being will cause her lines to be delivered inevitably with a somewhat slightly altered inflection. As a former folk musician and performer, I can personally attest to the fact each time I sang the same song in front of an audience, the output was affected by my personal emotional and physical state of being and the nature of receptivity I sensed from the audience. I might add that this may have been imperceptible to me at the time of the performance but was clearly noticeable on tape review.

Our perception of therapy as art, science, or some intricate combination determines what can we learn from quantitative evidence and what remains in the more subjective qualitative realm. Evidence of success tied to reductionistic approaches does not account for the whole person. There are certainly those professionals who would prefer a clear separation of art and science, willing to use the form of evaluation that best suits their personal interests, but segregation may provide clarity at the expense of accuracy.

Denoument

Fortunately, that dichotomy may not need to be set in stone. There are means to study what occurs in therapy and how such practices affect outcomes.

Before reviewing some of the studies that allow us to rethink evidence, there are a few significant aspects of scientific inquiry that bear understanding:

(1) All true revolutionary scientific breakthroughs have occurred at least in part in an inductive manner. Someone noticed something and began to study it without contemporary bias. This was true for Galileo, Einstein, Pasteur, Curie, Darwin, and a host of others whose discoveries led to theories, which in turn generated testable hypotheses. In short, inductive logic preceded and was the creative spur to deductive logic.

Within our own field, Freud's (1911-1915) initial observations preceded his theorizing about innate drives, his hydraulic model, and application of deductive methodologies: originally hypnosis and subsequently free association. Each subsequent theory of personality, behavior, cognition, and affect had similar roots.

Where would existential thinking be without Kierkegaard's observations of anxiety, Frankl's comprehension of meaning that emerged from his subjective experiences in the Nazi concentration camps, Heidegger's sense of being-in-the-world, or Rogers' focus on the person in psychotherapy? Each of these innovators broke from contemporary deductive logic by noticing something from a far more subjective perspective.

It is imperative that we respect both historical consensual truths and creative narrative discoveries. In his exploration of metapsychology and interpretation in psychoanalysis and psychotherapy, Donald Spence (1982) described the differences and connections between what he called narrative truth and historical truth and the implications for research. The former underscored the personal construct phenomena that are necessarily the data that are the core of individual therapy.[9]

A complete understanding of the nature of psychotherapy will require new conceptualizations and a focus on both kinds of data.

(2) Referring to psychotherapy as an art as well as a science actually puts it squarely in the realm of medical practice. As precise in measurement and refined in technique modern medicine strives to be, the effect of the healing presence remains a significant factor in outcomes for most clients. Indeed, the effects of placebo (inert or non-specific substances that produce positive results) remain a powerful aspect of medical healing. Several neuro-psychological studies investigating placebo effects indicate that expectation of a positive result activates brain centers differentially (i.e., Wampold, Imel, & Minami, 2007; Qiu, Xu, & Sackett, 2009).

Thus, just as for the relationship in psychotherapy, the relationship between physician and patient is also a significant factor in change. This strong relational factor is also significant in education. According to a recent finding by the executive director of Gallup's Education Division, two variables were most predictive of post-college success: a mentor who cared (relationship) and a relevant internship (Busteed, 2012; Friedman, 2014).

In their extensive exploration of psychotherapy as both art and science, Hofmann and Weinberger (2007) concluded that like most other areas of health care, psychotherapy requires a synthesis of scientific technique and artistic expression. They argued that regardless of the size and number of brushes and colors on the palette, effective therapy works best when the tools and scientific methodology are synthesized with (individual) creativity.

What Is the Evidence for Existential Approaches?

It is daunting to consider the complexities of measurement of outcome for therapies that are so singular and uniquely based on the here-and-now moment, so dependent on the relationship, and focused on inductive logic. It is easy to see why many practitioners have opted for the "include me out" approach, focused on rigorous case-study methods of inquiry (i.e., Stiles, 2009) or railed from the sidelines while the economically driven third party payers have determined that only certain specific, short-term, "medically necessary" (primarily CBT) procedures have an acceptable evidence base. These methods are simpler and easier to replicate and provide numbers that can be then used as justification for continuance or termination.

However complex the variables in existential work may be, it is important that outcome and process criteria are explored and measured on a variety of instruments. The first questions are whether such studies have been already done and how to improve their relevance for the future.

Early Studies: Carl Rogers, Scientist

It may seem surprising to many outside of humanistic psychology to recognize that Carl Rogers was one of the most significant researchers and innovators in evaluation of counseling and therapy. Goldfried (2007) refers to Rogers' (1957) original article and call for empirical testing as "a revolutionary break with the past." While developing client-centered psychotherapy in the 1950s, Rogers carefully delineated several factors that were essential in successful treatment. These necessary "core factors" for personality change included *empathy, genuineness (congruence), and unconditional positive regard.*

From the late 1950s and extending through the 1970s these constructs were explored in a variety of studies. Scales were developed and tested in the clinical and academic communities. In the 50 years following Rogers' original observations and challenge for empirical research, there are over a thousand citations and hundreds of studies.

In the early years, the core conditions were studied empirically with clients of almost every diagnosis, including schizophrenia (Rogers, Gendlin, Kiesler, & Truax, 1967) and in a variety of settings (i.e., Barrett-Lennard, 1962; Truax and Mitchell, 1971). Truax and Carkhuff (1965) demonstrated outcome differences for therapists who measured high and those measuring low in these factors. Carkhuff and Berenson (1967) and Barrett-Lennard (1962) developed reliable scales to measure "accurate empathy." They were both used in empirical studies and adopted for training basic skills to novice counselors.

Indeed, it is a tribute to Rogers's inductive discovery of the core conditions that the "helper" skills are used today in almost all programs that train graduate students and even lay therapists.

The Next Wave

For a while, after the 1970s, the number of empirical studies on these core conditions diminished. Instead, they were assumed to be essential components of all therapies (Watson, 2001). The core conditions are reflected today in constructs such as attunement, therapeutic alliance, emotional intelligence (Goleman, 1995), mirror neurons, and neuropsychological studies (Decety & Ickes, 2009; Decety and Lamm, 2009; Siegel, 1999).

Bohart and Greenberg, (1997) noted the importance of empathy for affective as well as cognitive states. Close intimate understanding of a client's world also takes a central role in therapy described by Elliott, Watson, Goldman, and Greenberg (2003). Hubble, Duncan, and Miller (1999) showed the extent to which a therapist's empathic understanding was essential for client progress.

In their meta-analysis on studies of empathy, Elliott, Bohart, Watson, and Greenberg (2011) concluded that therapist success was correlated with higher levels of the three interlinked skills of empathy identified in neuroscience research: affective simulation, perspective taking, and emotional self-regulation. They also reported that client characteristics and impressions of the therapist's empathy contributed significantly to the outcome. In brief, across all types of therapy measured, clients who felt understood at deeper levels by their therapists were more likely to have more positive outcomes of therapy. The premises and model of pragmatic existential therapy in this book are at least indirectly supported by these data and conclusions. Bottom line: It's the relationship!

Beyond the Core

Those variables first noted by Rogers in the 1950s had the advantage of being both outcome and process oriented. As researchers and therapists have become more sophisticated in exploring evidence for relationally based therapies, a new set of possibilities has emerged.

The 2006 Presidential APA task force on evidence-based treatment opened the door to a wider array of inquiries than the more limiting Empirically Validated (EVT) or Empirically Supported (EST) named movements. In EST/EVT methodologies, treatment and disorder specificity predominate. Thus if a client suffers from a phobia, the assumption is that CBT is the most appropriate approach to the treatment, based on the plethora of prior efficacy studies.

There is no reason to question the viability of cognitive behavior therapy to treat specific phobias. However, one must consider the assumptions that are being made to support the decision to use this treatment. First, it is assumed that the phobia is specific and limited. Second, it is assumed that the term *symptom* truly means behavior, rather than its dictionary meaning of "representing something else." Third, it must be assumed that for this patient and this clinician, no alternative methods may be equal to or superior.

From both research and clinical perspectives, each of these assumptions may be suspect. As a clinician, I have an ethical/moral obligation to treat the patient. Unlike in laboratory efficacy studies, if a client's clinical picture is more complicated, he or she still deserves attention and treatment, rather than being dropped from the study or removed from the data pool.

Studies of the Therapeutic Relationship

In many ways, the "real" client-therapist relationship is the *sine qua non* for existential therapy. With Buber's *I-thou*, Rogers' core conditions, and Gelso's (2011) research on the real relationship as backdrop, it is clear that mediating variables fall within the phenomenological experience of therapist and client interaction. Techniques that might be successful in reaching the mutually determined goals of therapy occur in a very unique relational context.

There have been a large number of studies on process variables in the counseling setting. For example, *therapeutic alliance*, originally a term of psychodynamic therapies, is now generalized to almost any form of therapy and related to outcomes. Safran and Muran (2000) concluded that treatment methods and relational acts are inseparable. Research that honors either technique or relationship as superior effectively misses the crucial fact that in practice these are inextricably intertwined (Norcross, 2011).

Although it is important to weigh both technique and relationship, from an existential frame, technique or tactics are only relevant and effective within a larger relational framework. Throughout the past decade, researchers have been demonstrating empirically what Norcross (2014) has called "evidence based relationships (EBRs)." Norcross and Lambert (2014) summarizing meta-analytic studies observed a "remarkable consistency" in the connection between a host of common relational variables and outcomes across populations of clients and types of therapy.

These studies expanded the earlier results on Rogers's core conditions. Clients who experienced their therapists as higher in empathy and congruence had superior outcomes to those whose therapists were seen as lower in these constructs. The authors repeat an oft-noted observation that Rogers, Frank, and Buber argued more than half a century earlier, "relationships can heal" (Norcross & Lambert, 2014, p. 400). As Greenberg (2015) also indicated, the therapist's attitude, pacing, facial, tonal, and other nonverbal behaviors and characteristics create a therapeutic climate in which change will have the greatest likelihood of occurring.

As was described in Chapter 6 of this book, this has implications for therapist orientation, behavior, and training. All other variables (i.e., symptom severity, chronicity of problem, cultural norms, and consequential gains) being equal across samples, the more connected the therapist is to the process of the client and to the interpersonal process between them, the better likelihood for therapeutic success.

Norcross (2011) summarized treatment/training recommendations to include the creation and cultivation of the therapy relationship as the primary goal, regular monitoring of patients' impressions of the treatment and therapeutic relationship, inclusion of evidence-based relational techniques along with evidence-based treatment methods, and individualized treatment to each client. These recommendations are fully consistent with the pragmatic existential therapy methods in this book.

Hard Data: Decoding Studies and Existential Therapy

Having made the strong argument that typical Randomized Controlled Trial (RCT) outcome studies are not well-suited to existential methods, it is interesting to consider what kinds of relevant results have been attained. In general, for the reasons listed above, there have been few direct studies of the existential approach. As Vos, Craig, and Cooper (2014) note,

> the widespread reluctance to engage in the current quantitative methods is based on beliefs that the reductionistic and dehumanizing nature particularly of the efficacy studies is anathema to the core existential beliefs. (p. 3)

Efficacy studies are by definition technique- rather than relationship-driven, focusing on what Buber referred to as the instrumental (*I-it*) relationship. Furthermore, it is challenging to operationally define complex constructs such as meaning and to control for treatments with such complex variables.

Despite reluctance and even antipathy, there are areas of research that have tested existential or existentially-related variables. Results uniformly indicate that existential methods are at least equivalent to CBT methods and may have longer-lasting results. However, because of the relatively incompatible nature of deductive hypothesis testing and existential inductive methods, most of the comparisons are somewhat indirect and remain out of the efficacy domain. Case studies and qualitative research on these existential approaches do indicate substantive positive outcomes with real-life clients. However, to date, evidence for relationship-oriented, phenomenologically based therapies have been generally overlooked by researchers who are primarily focused on learning-based techniques.

At least five groups of studies have explored efficacy and effectiveness of existential and existential-like therapies: emotion-focused therapy and other humanistic-experiential approaches (Greenberg, 2015); comparisons between methods that focus on existential-meaning themes (Vos et al., 2014); psychodynamic (Shedler, 2010); existential group therapy (Shapiro & Diamond, 1972; Diamond & Shapiro, 1973; Shapiro & Gust, 1974); and CBT-like studies that have added existential components (Gebler & Maerkler, 2014).

Existential-Like Studies

Greenberg and his associates employing Emotion Focused Therapy (EFT), a blend of affect, relationship, phenomenology, and attachment, have shown consistent significant effect sizes favoring the treatment (Goldman, Greenberg, & Angus, 2006; Johnson, Hunsley, Greenberg, & Schindler, 1999). Greenberg (2015) defined EFT as a

relationship, characterized by the therapist's presence and the provision of empathy, acceptance, and congruence, as an affect-regulating bond. Over time, this interpersonal regulation of affect is internalized by the client as self-soothing and enhances the capacity to regulate his or her inner states. (p. 350)

This relationship per se is seen as therapeutic and it provides a platform on which interventions may provide optimal processing of affect. To be effective, the therapist becomes as fully immersed phenomenologically with the client as possible.

The question of efficacy and effectiveness has been the subject of several quantitative and qualitative studies. In their comprehensive review of research on "humanistic-experiential" therapies (HEPs), Elliott, Watson, Greenberg, Timulak, and Friere (2013) explored outcome and process measures that were characterized by

(a) a belief in the curative value of the therapeutic relationship,

(b) the centrality of client's subjective experience,

(c) empathy in which the therapist attempts to join the client in his personal experience of the world, and

(d) a belief that the authentic relationship, within therapeutic boundaries, provides the client with validation at an emotional level.

Because these overlap with the existential approach described in this book, this research is considered quite relevant.

The results, based on a meta-analysis of nearly 200 outcome studies, and using standard measurements and practices, indicated that based on both quantitative and qualitative indices, these HEPs were effective and equivalent to other (i.e., CBT) methods.

Elliott et al. (2013) came to the following conclusions:

(1) HEPs were associated with large pre-post client change immediately following treatment and at early and later follow-ups.

(2) These results held in RCT studies with standard controls (wait-list or treatment-as-usual).

(3) Comparisons to other therapies were statistically equivalent on outcome measures.

(4) There were no significant differences on the characteristic outcome[10] measures between HEP and CBT approaches.

The results held over an array of diagnostic categories. Conclusions were that HEPs were "efficacious" in treatment of depression, chronic medical conditions, and interpersonal problems and possibly so, pending more studies, in treatment of anxiety[11] and psychoses.

Existential Meaning-Themed Studies

In a meta-analyses of 21 RCTs of existential therapy (1,792 participants), Vos et al. (2014) concluded that individual and group therapy that focused on meaning in life showed large effects on positive measures of life meaning and moderate effects on psychopathology and self-efficacy at both post-treatment and follow-up. The studies emulated as much as possible the CBT efficacy studies with manuals, laboratory controls, and waiting list ("care-as-usual") groups.

Their analysis indicated that when similar methods are employed, independent variables that are focused on existential themes are comparable in outcome to characteristic CBT, mindfulness, and ACT approaches.

Studies of Psychodynamic Therapy

Shedler (2010) provided a compelling argument for the equality or superiority of psychodynamic methods. He summarized an extensive exploration of meta-analyses:

Effect sizes for psychodynamic therapy are as large as those reported for other therapies that have been actively promoted as "empirically-supported" and "evidence-based." In addition, patients who receive psychodynamic therapy maintain therapeutic gains and appear to continue to improve after treatment ends. (p. 98)

He identified seven features that distinguish psychodynamic from CBT-manualized approaches. These include foci on (1) affect and expression of emotion, (2) exploration of fantasy life, (3) interpersonal relations, (4) the therapy relationship, (5) exploration of attempts to avoid distressing thoughts and feelings, (6) identification of recurring themes, and (7) discussion of past experience (developmental focus).

All but the final one are shared by existential therapies, albeit often in a somewhat different manner. Implicit in both psychodynamic and existential approaches is that the primary focus is not symptom remission. Shedler (2010; 2011) argued that success involved the relief of symptoms but more significantly the development of positive capacities and resources. These may include

> *the capacity to have more fulfilling relationships, make more effective use of one's talents and abilities, maintain a realistically-based sense of self-esteem, tolerate a wider range of affect, have more satisfying sexual experiences, understand self and others in more nuanced and sophisticated ways, and face life's challenges with greater freedom and flexibility.* (2010, p. 100)

The overlap with existential therapy is surely sufficient to bring the latter under the umbrella of significant effect sizes reported for these treatments.

Group Therapy Studies

In the 1970s, building on methodology from earlier studies (i.e., Shapiro, 1970; Shapiro & Ross, 1971, 1973) in Ontario, Canada, my colleagues and I at the University of Hawaii studied over 70 different brief, term-limited therapy and training groups.[12] Researchers explored both process and outcome dependent measures including paper and pencil measures, ability testing, measures of self-actualization, external observers' reports, contemporaneous Galvanic Skin Response (GSR), and video analysis.

In several such studies, experientially oriented, phenomenological approaches were compared to what are now called psycho-educational (CBT) group approaches and wait-list control groups. Among the populations served were college and graduate students, teachers, counselors, firemen, police, incarcerated juveniles and adults, military personnel, and Hawaii State agriculture personnel.

When groups were conducted by experienced licensed professionals (primarily psychologists) from a variety of theoretical orientations, results indicated that while all groups showed improvement, the existentially oriented groups were significantly more impactful, promoting superior outcomes on multiple measures in each of the studies (Shapiro & Gust, 1974). Changes on behavioral measures such as hypnotic susceptibility (Shapiro & Diamond,

1972) and preferred outcome measures such as locus of control (Diamond & Shapiro, 1973) showed similar results. Of even greater significance was that the differences between groups increased in follow-up measures.[13]

Equivalent results on similar outcome measures were reported by Foulds and Hannigan (1974, 1976) in Gestalt-oriented groups at Bowling Green State University in Ohio.

CBT Studies With Existential Components

The fifth index of effectiveness can be found in a few recent studies which have included existential variables and methods in the mainstream CBT studies. Much of the work has employed group treatment and centered on phenomena such as grief and loss, cancer treatment, and chronic pain—all obvious existential issues. Therapy was not done from an existential framework in these studies. Instead, a few sessions of existentially oriented themes were added to standard CBT-manualized approaches.

Breitbart et al. (2010), working with advanced cancer patients in group therapy, used a standard, structured, manualized, psycho-education approach with themes that were related to finding meaning in life and coping strategies. The approach was similar in many ways to the "cognitive-existential" approach of expressive supportive group therapy reported by Kissane et al. (1997, 2003, 2007). The groups of women with either early stage or metastatic breast cancer were time-limited, manual-directed, and focused on relevant themes for grief, loss, and cognitive management. In both studies, patients showed improvement, but in the Kissane studies, the overall effect size was small. In general, expressive-supportive groups with a focus on cognitive techniques, over more relational ones, have been shown to be less effective than other existential approaches in outcome studies.

Gebler and Maerckler (2014) focused on the meaning-centered and relational aspects of existential therapy in their study of clients with chronic pain, by adding a few sessions of existential themes to the standard CBT group treatment. One of the most beneficial aspects of their study was that it included 3 and 6 month follow-ups to the posttest data collection. The results favored the group that had the existential themes over the CBT-alone group (same number of sessions), particularly at follow-up measurements. "The integration of an existential perspective leads to significantly lowered pain-related disability than the classic cognitive behavioral group-program" (p. 155). They also noted that the effects were magnified for patients who had a more spiritual orientation.

Whither Existential Therapy?
Research in the Current Environment

These few studies are interesting but hardly conclusive. However, the fact that existential themes had to be inserted into standard CBT treatments does speak to the ubiquity of CBT for both efficacy and effectiveness studies. In a sense, the researchers could be creative but had to do so within the current orthodoxy. It would be very interesting to compare true existentially oriented groups to the classic CBT and hybrids. Of course, that would force a nonmanualized approach. Manipulating and measuring relational depth and the extent to which clients felt the therapists' caring might very much favor approaches that consider the relationship as the primary healing element (i.e., Cooper, 2013; Knox, 2013; Knox and Cooper, 2010).

This next step seems very important for the credibility of existential therapies in the current economic environment. There is every reason to expect that RCT and deductive hypothesis testing will remain what Cooper and Reeves (2012) have called the "gold standard." What would be more appropriate, especially for studies of existential approaches, would be a "platinum standard." There is room for such studies in the field and sufficient indices that a broader, more inclusive approach might allow for far more comprehensive representation of the varieties of effective methods of psychotherapy and counseling.

Diamond and Shapiro (1975) recommended a model experimental paradigm for continuing group therapy studies. A slightly updated version for group or individual therapy is depicted in Table 8.1.

Equivalent designs would allow for direct comparisons of a variety of theoretical approaches without pre-ordaining any particular method. When the primary goal is "life-changing" there is an obvious need for more longitudinal studies, more approved qualitative methods, and designs with adequate attention-placebo control groups.

In addition, it might be possible to begin to match best therapies with individual clients. It would add specificity to Luborsky, Singer, and Luborsky's (1975) clarification of the "dodo-bird effect"—that all therapies help some individuals. Such studies might eliminate the "winner-take-all" ambiance between so-called hard versus soft or relationship versus technique approaches.

A Curmudgeon's Perspective on Outcome Research[14]

The time is right to explore in depth the how, why, and for whom existential therapy is most appropriate. Existential therapists have an opportunity once again to be the true rebels and demonstrate the value of the methods to the nonbelievers.

Table 8.1   A Model Experimental Paradigm

	Experimental (Process) Group	Attention-Placebo Group Psycho-Education	Wait List Control Treatment-as-Usual
Step 1	Determine goals Designate comparison groups	Determine goals Designate comparison groups	Determine goals Designate comparison groups
Step 2	Application and screening	Application and screening	Application and screening
Step 3	Pretesting*	Pretesting*	Pretesting*
Step 4	Random Assignment	Random Assignment	Random Assignment
Step 5	Experimental (existential) treatment with qualified professionals *Process measures recorded*	Control (psycho-education) treatment with qualified professionals *Process measures recorded*	No treatment
Step 6	Posttesting on pretest measures Subjective qualitative measures Determination of demand characteristics (interview)**	Posttesting on pretest measures Subjective qualitative measures Determination of demand characteristics (interview)	Posttesting on pretest measures Determination of demand characteristics (interview)
Step 7	3 to 6 month follow up (all measures)	3 to 6 month follow up (all measures)	3 to 6 month follow up (all measures)—depending on setting and ethical treatment, best group to date may be offered***
Step 8	1 to 3 year follow-up	1 to 3 year follow-up	1 to 3 year follow-up
Step 9	Report results to group members and professional community	Report results to group members and professional community	Report results to group members and professional community

*In a best case scenario, each data collection period should include paper and pencil tests, self-report, behavioral observations, external observer reports, and clients' beliefs/values regarding what leads to personal change. Qualitative process measures begin within group and are analyzed independently by researchers who are not group leaders.

**Statistical analyses (independent of therapists/leaders) should occur at steps 6 through 8.

***If group with best measured outcome is offered to wait list controls subsequent follow-up data collection may be extended for this group at and after group termination.

The Control-Group Challenge

Over the past decade, major shifts have occurred in psychological research. There are some advances. Statistics have become more complex and hopefully more meaningful (i.e., effect size versus simple statistical significance), and meta-analyses combining studies to generate larger sample sizes and to correct for single study errors are common and seem useful. However, one aspect of research seems to have gone in a quite different direction. Most RCT studies have lost sight of the attention-placebo control groups.

The contrast between any therapeutic treatment and "treatment-as-usual" (a euphemism in most studies for no treatment) is not clear proof of superiority of the treatment in question. There is no guarantee that the same results could have been attained by a similar number of hours of attention or even a regular gift of peanut butter cookies. That may seem a harsh assessment, but I have been around long enough to recognize the loss of an important aspect of objective scientific investigation.

Although some issues around random assignment can be fixed mathematically with meta-analyses of numbers of studies, we cannot clear up the lack of relevant control groups by larger numbers of studies. We may get statistically significant results, but they may not be meaningful. I am reminded of a local merchant during my youth who often stated, "I lose money on every sale. I make up for it in the volume!"

The Nose in Front of My Face

As an academician, I have worked almost entirely in graduate programs since 1969. My primary role has been training clinicians at the masters and doctoral levels in mental health fields. In addition, I have regularly consulted with and trained professional clinicians. The total number exceeds 3,000 different students.

There are some inescapable observations and conclusions garnered through those years. First of all, as for most human traits, not all clinicians are created or developed equally. Some are simply better equipped or learn more effectively than others. Even after graduation and the lengthy internship required by the State of California, some new clinicians are qualitatively more effective with their clients.

Some take to the training avidly and relish in human connection with others. Others are more technically oriented and want the best possible diagnostic tools and counseling methods to effect client change. Some come to comprehend process in therapy. Others stick with observable behaviors. Some enter with and/or develop a greater capacity to accept others' ways of life.

Second, although exposure to an array of theoretical orientations has an obvious impact on capabilities, and the training itself often leads to impressive self-insight and broad competencies, students' core values seem to indicate which kind of psychological theories they will be most comfortable with in the long term.

There are three inescapable conclusions about research that must be drawn here:

(1) Nonequivalence of therapist competence inevitably introduces variability into studies that attempt to control methods, clientele, or techniques. Attempts to control these differences with manual-based interventions cannot fully account for differences in warmth, empathy, and genuineness (accidentally) conveyed by the therapist. It's irrelevant whether these are considered the active ingredients or placebo effects. They are potential confounds that are communicated to clients that are picked up at many levels of consciousness, and they make a difference in outcome.

(2) Clients are not equally responsive to all therapists or therapeutic approaches. What is best for one client may be fairly ineffective for another. Some clients are best reached with behavior-first methods, while others respond only to insight-first. Some clients are more cognitive and others more affective. As explored in Chapter 5, clients protect against change in a variety of personal ways.

(3) Cultural factors (broadly defined) play a huge role in how well a therapist-client connection may develop. Age, sex, and culture-of-origin of therapist may have differential effects that have little to do with the theory being tested.

Implications

Any studies of therapy outcome must take into account not only the quality of therapeutic care but also the therapist's experience, the client's expectations, the client's value system, and the client's primary manner of processing perceptions. Without these considerations, studies will be inevitably biased toward those variables that can be manipulated simply and for which there are readily available measurement tools. The limitations of "one size fits all" techniques are obvious.

Furthermore, studies conducted in lab settings, primarily with graduate student "therapists," may be subject to several biases that obviate the obtained results. In most programs, students are usually trained primarily in certain circumscribed methods. They may develop some competency in treatment delivery of that singular method, but when the results are compared to application of alternative approaches in which their training is minimal, any results may be severely compromised.

In general, doctoral students trained in CBT are conducting CBT studies based on a diagnosis or presenting symptom, rather than clients who would choose this method or this therapist. Furthermore, because this is the dominant theory and approach favored by academicians and because it is so much more straightforward and easier to study in short, publishable articles, it has an appeal that may affect both the scientific alternatives and the likelihood of those studies being published. Indeed, because the approach is believed, though not proven, to be more economical, there is additional pressure to eschew alternative approaches, such as existential therapy.

This is the exact opposite of how the scientific method is supposed to operate. The most notable aspect of revolutionary science is how a long tradition is broken by those pioneers who inductively found data and alternative approaches to the reigning authority and bureaucracy. Newton's Law of Gravity has held sway for centuries, but new studies indicate that all matter does not fall to earth at 32 feet per second. Particle density and other intricate factors may alter the speed of descent. That new "fact" may be disconcerting, but we must be open to such possibilities.

In our field, the notion of the salience of the relationship is over a half century old. Yet it is still less recognized than it need be to fully comprehend what occurs in a therapy setting. This is particularly germane in existential therapies.

As Norcross and Lambert (2014) summarized,

The therapy relationship makes substantial and consistent contributions to psychotherapy outcome independent of the specific type of treatment. Moreover, efforts to promulgate best practices or evidence-based practices (EBPs) without including the relationship are seriously incomplete and potentially misleading. (p. 399)

To study psychotherapy without attending to the relationship is equivalent to ignoring hydrogen in studying the chemical composition of water.

Notes

1. The conclusions of effectiveness of a variety of treatments were contained in a report to the Commander-in-Chief of the Pacific Air Force and Admiral of CINCPACFLT. It was used for internal military purposes and to enhance the scope and number of offered treatments for military personnel and dependents at several centers on Oahu. The document was not published.

2. The term *hegemony* to describe the current political climate in the field was used by Rutan, Stone, and Shay (2007) and again by Shedler (2010).

3. Cognitive therapy was combined with behavior therapy in the last quarter of the 20th century and has continued to expand as it encompassed many facets of other modalities (i.e., motivational interviewing, ACT, schema therapy, mindfulness meditation). However, as these approaches expanded, combined, and evolved, the behavioral base focus on the symptom has remained fairly stable.

4.   The medication orientation, the psychiatric "hegemony," is so ubiquitous among medical school training programs, residencies, and new psychiatrists, that the some members of the American Psychiatric Association have recently begun a "Special Interest Group" for psychotherapists.

5. This delightful play on words is attributed to Al Smith, four time governor of New York and presidential hopeful.

6. This was explored in Chapter 5 with regard to resistance, but it also is more general for CBT efficacy studies.

7. This is less of a problem for existential therapies, which find such creation of prime interest and worthy of focus. By contrast, deductive theories make the assumptions that the data represent true findings in the real world, rather than a convenient comprehension of the subject. This is obviously much less of a problem for sciences which investigate nonsensient beings.

8. This quotation or a very similar version is also attributed to William Bruce Cameron (1963, p. 13).

9. Some of the divergence of narrative truth and historical truth may be mitigated in couple, family, and group therapy, in which consensual reality interacts with personal constructs.

10. This is a very salient factor, because common measurements were focused on CBT-defined measures such as symptom reduction, which are more added effects than the primary thrust of existential work.

11. Some forms of anxiety per se may be considered positive rather than negative in existential approaches. Thus, measures to reduce or eliminate the experience may be inappropriate.

12. Replications using computer homework software were completed with training groups and PTSD groups in the 1990s (Bernadett-Shapiro, Peltz, Bischoff, Shapiro, & Kovachy 1999).

13. A more comprehensive treatment of these studies can be found in Shapiro (1978) and Shapiro (2010a).

14. My curmudgeonry is geared to confronting and informing colleagues with Santayana's warning about learning from history or having to repeat it. In this case, the famous Hawthorne Electric Company study. I am not (yet) the kind of curmudgeon who is shaking his cane in the air and chasing younger faculty out of the lab.

9

Beyond the *I-Thou* Dyad

Group, Couple, and Family Therapy[1]

> *The self is only a self because it has a world,*
>
> *a structured universe, to which it belongs*
>
> *and from which it is separated at the same time.*
>
> Paul Tillich, 1952, p. 87

Because of the significance of relationships and context per se, some of the most common and effective forms of existential psychotherapy involve simultaneous treatment with small groups of clients.

In group, couple, and family therapies, there are unique opportunities for clients to confront core existential anxiety in their searches for *I-thou* contact. Questions about meaning, intimacy and isolation, loss and freedom, and responsibility often appear more in the foreground in the roiling concoction that combines both therapeutic and naturalistic relationships.

It's the Relationship(s)!

Meaningful relationships should occur within the consulting room, but they are far more important when they happen out of the therapy hour. A therapy session may last for an hour. There are an additional 167 hours a week of contact for a family sharing living space or for a couple sharing a bed. One essential goal of therapy is to make the 1 hour anachronistic in the clients' lives.

Buber (1957) called "entering into a relation" a fundamental principle of human life. He argued that humans cannot be isolated in their search for meaning. For Buber, man is always in relation—"there is no I without a thou." In his classic debate with Carl Rogers (Cissna & Anderson, 1994), Buber opined, "Life is meeting." Boszormenyi-Nagy and Spark (1973) bridged this concept into "contextual family therapy," postulating that the goal of family therapy should be fashioned around the process of interaction, rather than individual constructs such as reality, effectiveness, self-actualization, or habit.

The Freedom-Security Tension

According to Minuchin (1974), the well-functioning family supports progressive autonomy while maintaining mutuality and safety. Haldane and McClusky (1982) refer to the process of coming to terms with one's self, within the world of family life, as a core existential challenge. Buber called this essential struggle in life "differentiated relatedness" (Medina, 2010). Existential psychotherapy encompasses that primary relational dilemma by focusing on the tension between the needs for freedom (independence) and security (the status quo).

Symptoms as Strength

One of the founders of family systems therapy, Virginia Satir (1967), identified constructs that could be effectively employed in strategic and structural family work and existential psychotherapy. She underscored the functional value of symptoms for the ongoing family functioning. This perspective goes far beyond the notion of secondary gain. In existential approaches, the meaning of a symptom and its consequences offers a perspective on client strengths and on the expression of neurotic anxiety.

Individual and System

There is also considerable overlap in some family systems and existential approaches in diagnosing and effecting change. In addition to the centrality of relationships, essential tensions and the value of symptoms, both approaches have a present and future orientation, a focus on interaction, and a clear comprehension of the limits of individual freedom. Recognition of these common factors promotes employment of multiclient existential therapy.

Because existential therapy is primarily about relationship and the relational context, there are potential advantages of group, couple, and family approaches over individual modalities.

Unique Advantages of Multiperson Therapy

Within an existential frame, several benefits can be maximized because of the intensity and functionality of here-and-now, real-time intervention strategies. Among the benefits of simultaneous treatment are economics, universality, opportunities for altruism, minimizing the self-perception of pathology, connectedness, vicarious learning, experimentation, dilution of transference relationships, and so on (Shapiro, Peltz, and Bernadett-Shapiro, 1997; Shapiro, 2013; Yalom, 2005). These advantages are summarized in the box below.

BOX 9.1: UNIQUE ADVANTAGES OF MULTIPERSON THERAPY

Economic Advantages: A single therapist or therapy team sees more clients per hour. In addition, multiperson therapies tend to be of shorter duration in number of sessions than individual ones.

Universality: There are increased opportunities for connectedness and a sense of shared experience and problems along with a reduced sense of isolation. A client's understanding that there are skeletons in everyone's closets often opens avenues for experimentation.

Multiple forms of learning: Learning occurs by active doing or vicariously through others' work.

Minimizing subjective experience of pathology; maximizing hope: Receiving help from another member underscores that someone "just like me" may effect change—a symbolic indication that the problems do not require intervention by an expert.

Altruism: Helping others allows clients to feel better about themselves. Something so uplifting counteracts low self-esteem.

Opportunities for safer experimentation: On the "cultural island" of multiperson therapy, clients may experiment with novel behaviors or attitudes and get feedback within a less risky, more nurturing environment.

Dilution of transference relationships: Although existential therapy focuses on real relationships, the group environment allows for unconscious projections onto several individuals at once, not just the therapist.

Enhanced transfer of training: Particularly in a natural group, small interventions may have far-reaching impact. Any change by a member in a connected system requires compensatory shifts by others.

Recapitualizing the family dynamic: Particularly in groups of strangers, every significant other in life is symbolically represented (S. R. Tillich, 1972). Thus, there are opportunities to work out conflicts and dilemmas without having to face powerful responses pulling toward the status quo.

The Major Advantage: Real Time, Real Interactions

In multiple person therapies, clients interact with each other, as well as with their professional therapists. While the professional therapist-client relationship is bounded by professional ethics and focused on the client, client-to-client interactions take into account the feelings, thoughts, and experiences of each person. These interactions occur openly in real time. The therapist has the opportunity to note what impact the client's behavior has on others who are not specifically advocating solely for his or her healing, growth, and development. Relationships with others occur within the perceptions of the therapist, unfiltered by clients' self-reports.

In individual existential therapy, most of the material discussed involves the client's subjective experience and what occurs in the unique, empathic, nonjudgmental therapeutic relationship in the here-and-now. Reality testing is limited to the unique relationship and setting.

By contrast, on the "cultural island" of the group process, both subjective and objective realities coexist. The client has an opportunity to be heard with therapeutic empathy and also to be confronted with the impact of his or her behavior on others, who are there for their own needs, not the client's. When the group is effective, reality testing and feedback can be offered in safety and be a powerful impetus to new awareness and significant changes.

Similarly, in couple therapy, while both members report to the therapist about what is occurring in their lives and the interaction between them, they also replicate the event in process in the presence of the therapist. Commonly, couple therapy begins with each partner offering a litany of sins perpetrated by the other. They then turn to the therapist as if he or she was the judge and request a "ruling" on the relative righteousness of the two subjective perspectives. In existential work, the therapist will then explore with them what they want from the relationship, the consequences of continuing the emotional and perceptual tug-of-war, meaning around intimacy and distance, and the process in the room.

Walt and Peg have been married for 6 years. They had two children in the past 24 months. She instigated the appointment "to get him to help more around the house." He came in reluctantly and expected to "be ganged up on by Peg and the therapist."

P: I am home all day with the two kids, and he comes home and won't even take care of them while I make dinner.

W: I just need a short break from work to change my clothes and relax before I can be with the kids.

P: Well, I don't get a break. Either I cook dinner and have the two of them getting into trouble, or he cooks the dinner, and I continue my day of 24/7 time with a toddler and an infant.

W: You know, I wanted to wait to have the second one. You were the one who insisted that we try again when K. was one.

P: (With an angrier tone) So now you are punishing me because WE have two babies!

W: I'm not punishing you. I offered to make dinner when I get home, except when I have my late meeting on Tuesdays. I play with them every other night. I put R. to bed most nights after you nurse her. I offered to give you a weekend day off. And don't forget I am working full time and supporting the whole family.

P: Yeah, big deal. You put them down some nights after I have had them and nursed them and changed them and got up at 5:00 a.m. Why can't you get up when they do?

W: Because, all I can do is get them and bring them to you for nursing . . . and then I am a wreck at work. (Turning to the therapist) I suppose you are going to side with her now and tell me to do more.

T: (Focusing on process) I am mostly aware of how you are both feeling depleted, and neither one feels supported, during a time of stress.

P: Well, I need more help!

T: (Pre-empting Walt's reply) I think you both need more help and a respite from two kids in diapers and far more work than you can handle. The most striking thing here is that neither of you seems to be experiencing any sense of teamwork or respite from the constant demands.

Note that the therapist avoided taking sides and used the content of their complaints to focus on the process in the room and at home. She also underscored how much both were in need of relief. Subsequently, they will likely refocus on their common experience of isolation, fantasy that life will always be so, and on working together to try to alleviate some of the stress.

The Need for a Here-and-Now Process Focus in Multiperson Therapy

In individual therapy, there are essentially three entities to monitor in the room: (1) the client, (2) the therapist, and (3) the interaction between them. In couple therapy, there are seven: Each client (1, 2); the client relationship (1-2) the therapist (3); each client and therapist interaction (1-3; 2-3); and the three-way interaction (1, 2, 3). In a family of five, that number is increased geometrically to 120, and in a group of eight clients with two cotherapists, the permutations of interactions are near astronomical. There is no way for any therapist to be aware of everything occurring at verbal and nonverbal levels in that complex stimulus soup.

That is the pragmatic argument for a process, metalevel, or systemic focus. There is simply too much going on in the room to take it all in, to evaluate each for salience and to respond. A couple, family, or group process may be very complex, but it does occur in the here-and-now and allows for interventions that promote change. Within most systems, there is a homeostasis that keeps the system functioning, albeit often not always optimally for all members. When the balance is interrupted, often the stability may be maintained by scapegoating, shunning, or pathologizing a particular member in an attempt to bring back some equilibrium.

As one of his parents averred during the third session of treatment, "We'd be fine if John (age 16) didn't act so much like an adolescent. It's like he has no judgment." Others joined in to agree and embellish with stories of John's judgmental lapses and paradoxically added fuel to John's symptom fire. John took the opportunity to begin arguing with his "perfect" sister; both confirming others' pejorative perceptions of him and playing well his assigned role in the family drama.

Had the therapist focused on the content of John's many transgressions and attempted to work out some contractual agreement for his future behavior, he might well have missed entirely the process that at the moment, the family may be able to function only when they have defined roles as "good" child and "bad" child. Instead the therapist posed the following:

It seems clear that you see John's 16-year-old behavior as troubling and that you all, including John, seem to think that if he changed, everything would be better. . . . Indulge me in a fantasy for a moment. Let's say that John is now in his twenties. He's graduated from college, and his prefrontal lobes (pointing to his own forehead) have matured sufficiently to greatly improve his judgment. And let's imagine that everything else has remained the same. Just take that in for a moment, and then let's talk about what would happen in the family right here in this meeting.

In this intervention, the therapist began by acknowledging their perceptions, added some normalizing about John's age-related behavior, and refocused the family on what anxiety they might have to face if they did not have the John-as-scapegoat problem holding the family together. He was not surprised when the "perfect" daughter said,

By the time John and I are out of college, our parents will be divorced!

Her assertion placed the process of scapegoating as a family adaptation to marital discord. John's sixteen-year-old behavior was an effective diversion to avert potential family disruption and give the parents a common challenge they could address together. Even John was convenient and willing, at least unconsciously, to play his role just as everyone else was. Once the awareness was in the room, the therapeutic attention was refocused away from the teenaged son and more onto the anxiety about maintaining family existence.

Because there is so much occurring simultaneously in the room, a process focus allows significant interactions to be brought into the here-and-now, where they can be more effectively addressed. When he attends to process, the therapist has the opportunity to observe the consequences of actions, as well as the presumed intentions. These additional data allow for interventions that do not attribute blame but instead underscore success (maintaining the status quo; avoiding the feared unknown) and cost (unhappiness and stagnation). In the family example, scapegoating John kept everybody from exploring the far more frightening potential marital break-up.

When the therapist focuses on the interactions and consequences, he is intervening in an asocial and unexpected manner. This approach replaces the attribution of blame with functional anxiety and greater vigilance, which offer opportunities to face the underlying fears and to experiment with novel behavior and new learning. Thus, the more complex the endeavor becomes, the more likely it will respond to a relational, process, existential approach.

The Two-Pronged Characteristic of Multiperson Therapy

In couple, family, and group therapy, there are two progressive foci of intervention: communication work and structural work. Effective communication is a necessary precondition for successful interpersonal interactions. Getting clients to say what they mean and to hear accurately what is said is crucial. In small groups, clear communication is far more complex than in a one-on-one individual therapy setting.

Once communication is clarified and other members of the entity understand one another clearly, the need for any additional work may be illuminated. When the obfuscations and misconstruals of others' meanings are eliminated, the nature of emerging anxiety is clarified, and the clinician's direction becomes evident.

Sometimes, in couple and family therapy, clear communication is both necessary and sufficient for success. These therapies are usually brief (10 to 12 sessions) in duration. In other cases, clarifying the communication may expose far more significant problems. These *structural* problems usually require long-term therapy (a year or longer).

Characteristic structural problems often involve a perceived betrayal, loss of trust, addiction, domestic violence, significant psychopathology, or a third party exerting a major influence in the couple or family.

When Ken and Sylvia came into therapy, it was a week after his discovery of her 6-month-long extramarital affair with a mutual friend. They described a 20-year history of misunderstanding, verbal battles, and what she described as "his refusal to see what had happened to my life." After several weeks of stabilizing the situation, discussing options, and dealing with his hurt, anger, and feelings of betrayal, they agreed that the marriage was worth trying to save, "at least for the children." She first cut off sexual contact, then agreed to stop seeing the other man entirely. The situation in sessions was tense, but a working alliance slowly developed.

As the sessions unfolded, they described a high-profile college courtship during which "everybody expected us to get married and have a successful family." They were both standouts in their high school and colleges, young stars in their respective fields, and both had gone on to advanced degrees and well-reimbursed careers. When the first of their four children (in 6 years) was born, she became a stay-at-home mother, while his career flourished. They were both devoted parents and agreed that they expressed more affection for the children than for each other.

About 3 years prior to the therapy, she had essentially ended their sexual relationship, reporting "and he knows why."

T: (Turning to him) Can you elaborate on what caused this?

K: No. I don't have a clue. I just know that she turned off and started to come to bed way after I was asleep.

T: (*I'm guessing that he had an affair*) So, you don't know. Did you ask?

K: Well, I tried to a few times, but she just said that I know why.

T: (Turning to Sylvia) Would you let me know the reason? Ken doesn't seem to.

S: He should!

T: Perhaps . . . I'd appreciate it if you'd let *me* know.

S: His sister!

K: Which one?

S: Kathy, of course. She told me that he had a reputation as a great lover in school, before we met. I was astonished, because it wasn't great between us, ever.

K: (Stammering) What about our honeymoon? You said it was terrific.

S: That was in 1985. What about recently?

T: (To Sylvia) You were hurt by what Kathy said. And you wanted to experience him as a more passionate person.

S: Uh huh.

T: How did you try to convey that to him?

S: I knew that he wasn't interested in me anymore because I gained weight with the pregnancies. All he said was that he thought weight gain was normal, and it didn't matter to him.

K: (Addressing the therapist) I told her I was still attracted to her.

S: (To the therapist) I didn't believe him. I still don't.

K: Based on what?

T: You wanted him to somehow be more attuned to your feelings about your pregnancy weight?

S: Duh! It's like he couldn't see that I was distressed. I am 20 pounds heavier now. It's like he didn't even notice.

T: If he had noticed, what would he have done?

S: Understand that I didn't feel sexual with the extra poundage . . . and try to show me he cared in other ways.

K: Like what? Like foreplay or something?

T: (Interrupting, as she rolled her eyes). Tell me. Ken can listen.

S: Like loading the dishwasher after dinner.

K: I don't believe this. You told me to help the kids with homework after dinner, and that's what I do. I can't be in two places at once.

S: You see what I have to deal with. No wonder I am not interested.

T: (To Sylvia) You want him to know what it's like to have your life trajectory changed from being a scientist to being a mom, and you want him to know without telling him directly. I am guessing that it's frustrating that he is not a skilled mind reader. (Turning to Ken) You are trying to please her by doing what she says, but somehow are missing what she wants. I know this is unfair, but would you be willing to tell me what you would like from Sylvia right now?

K: I can't believe that something my crazy sister said could bother anyone. Consider the source!

T: (Turning to Sylvia and reframing/interpreting) He feels bad that you took to heart something that Kathy said. He doesn't think her perceptions are reliable, and he certainly doesn't feel unattracted to you. Before you respond . . . (Quickly turning to Ken) How close was that?

K: Yeah. That's all right.

S: (To T) Well he could have said that at the time!

T: What is it like to hear that now?

S: It feels better, but why can't he say it directly to me?

T: You both have a choice here. Savoring a small positive or finding ways in which it is imperfect. It's kind of like him missing the message that loading the dishes is foreplay.

Although it was clear that the relationship had at least two significant structural flaws (breaking off the sexual relationship and the affair), the therapist began with communication, knowing that unless they could truly speak a common language and understand each other's needs, the far more anxiety-provoking structural work would be impossible.

The Value of Miscommunication

In the therapeutic context, failures of communication may well serve to protect the individuals from facing more frightening existential anxiety. For

Ken and Sylvia, this ultimately meant him facing his fears of isolation and abandonment, her anxiety about a lack of meaning in her life, and their combined concerns with aging and mortality.

According to Whitaker (Neill and Kniskern, 1982), her affair could, in one way, be construed as their unconscious joint effort to find intimacy and meaning in their relationship. From this perspective, and in a "two-by-four to the head" manner, Sylvia was unconsciously showing Ken his complicity in the affair and offering him an opening to make things better. Although a therapist cannot blame the cuckolded partner for being party to the affair, it is important to keep in mind the positive consequences of the discovery of this affair: more communication, direct expressions of (admittedly painful) emotion, and a 2-year commitment to therapy and the relationship.

Extramarital affairs are an extreme measure to try to fix a marriage. It is always best to institute change prior to such an event. Shapiro (1984) has noted that therapy, instituted at an earlier escalation than an extramarital affair, characteristically is of 2 to 3 months' duration. After the affair, it is a year or more. For Ken and Sylvia, it was over 2 years before the relationship was on more stable and stronger footing.

Unique Therapeutic Interventions

Most of the counseling and therapy work with couples, families, and groups follows the same progression as individual therapy. Existential approaches are typically focused on process, the here-and-now, neurotic and existential anxiety, and intimate relating. There are, however, some unique methods when there is more than one client.

The Therapeutic Triangle and Three Stages of Couple Therapy

There is a common three-stage approach in existential psychotherapy with couples, families, and groups.

Stage One: Enactment

Initially, the therapist encourages "enactment" (Minuchin & Fishman, 1981). Particularly useful with couples, families, and groups who have enduring connections outside the therapy hour, enactment involves creating an environment in which the clients replicate outside-the-office communications.

Interactional patterns, even arguments similar to the ones at home, ensue and escalate during sessions.

For the existential therapist, this enactment phase is primarily diagnostic. He or she can observe how communication works to create distance instead of closeness, how individuals project and imagine a partner's supposed motivations, and how it maintains the intimate (status quo) equilibrium. For Ken and Sylvia, this can be seen in her assertion that he knows why she retreated, and he asks about it in ways (mostly indirectly) that push her further away, rather than closer. Having observed these patterns, the clinician can determine where, and in what ways, to intervene.

The Fight. For most couples and families in therapy, distrust, disconnection, and *I-it* interactions are manifold. To protect against the anxiety provoked by potential *I-thou* intimacy, most couples, families, and even workplace groups, develop fairly effective, predictable, automatic avoidance mechanisms. Although they are less fruitful than *I-thou* relationship moments, they are more reliable and predictable.

One well-known manifestation of this phenomenon is *The Fight,* a well-practiced battle, unconsciously designed to create distance and maintain the status quo. The fight operates as if it were a well-rehearsed play. Every line is known and recited with verbal and nonverbal perfection, right down to the final name calling, insults to family-of-origin members, door slamming, storming out, retreat to another room, or an apparent "agreement to disagree." *The Fight* usually emerges at times when one or more members of the family are feeling needy or vulnerable, potentially available for an *I-thou* contact.[2] Instead of facing the risk of this relational existential anxiety, *The Fight* emerges from neurotic anxiety, offering predictability and retreat to the familiar and safe forms of disquiet.

Because this manifestation of neurotic anxiety involves more than one person, it represents both individual and systemwide participation. Thus, interventions are best delivered at the interactional rather than intrapsychic level.

Before trying to help the clients alter the sequence, the clinician must observe the full enactment. Having experienced *The Fight*, and observing each member's characteristic auto-avoidance pattern, the therapist may insert herself into the ongoing progression, interrupting the sequence by providing alternative lines for the drama. In so doing, she turns the well-rehearsed play into an improvisation. If she has fostered an empathic, therapeutic relationship with each of the members, she can refocus the clients' attention to consequences of the battle, instead of attributions of each other's motivations. The revised goal is for the clients to face a moderate amount of the anxiety of unpredictability as they carefully experiment with alternatives, with support from all members of the system.

Stage Two: Therapeutic Triangle

Normally speaking, triangulation is considered a problem in couple, family, and group member functioning (i.e., Bowen, 1985). However, in the example of Ken and Sylvia, the therapist deliberately created a triangle, directing communication through herself, rather than having the clients communicate directly with each other. As she inserts herself into the interactional flow, she can serve as a universal translator, reframing what is said and offering it to the partner in ways that alter both the (undesirable) distancing consequences and the source of the message. Sylvia will accept the therapist's "apology" for Ken far easier than Ken's less clear attempt. Ken will hear from the therapist that dishwasher loading is foreplay, something he could not take in from his wife. Not only does the therapist translate the message into a meaningful language for the listener, but she also models a different kind of communication, one that begins with active listening and ends with a more clear direct statement of "want."

Stage Three: Extraction With Influence

In the third stage, the therapist turns it back to the clients to communicate directly. Three of the most often stated words in a therapist's lexicon here are, "Tell her that!" In this stage, the therapist encourages the clients to engage with each other in a manner that may allow for *I-thou* interactions. It is common for couples in this third stage to report in therapy that "we did a Dr. X last weekend." Laughing, they report that they were getting into an old pattern, and then one queried, "What would the Doc say now?" They both knew the line, said it to each other, chuckling at their shared private joke and mutual success, and then proceeded to follow the new internalized dictates for effective communication. In time, they will own the new communication without need to attribute it to the therapist.

Characteristic Methods

To effectively use the unique opportunities available in multiperson work, existential therapists primarily focus on joining with clients in their interactions and the therapeutic process. Two strategies that foster connections involve bringing the clients into the therapist's real time mental processes: therapeutic amazement and magnifying emotions.

Therapeutic Amazement

An interesting collaborative strategy, requiring apparent naiveté by the therapist, may be particularly useful in getting the clients to reassess their opposing goals. Therapeutic amazement brings the clients into the therapist's mind as he or she comes to awareness of a pattern without obvious sophistication.

Carl and Sophie have been living together for 6 years and were planning their wedding. They described a recent evening during which they had a romantic dinner and made love. Soon afterward, they began talking about the anticipated honeymoon trip and the wedding. That's when the argument began.

S: Each time we start talking about the wedding plans, Carl shuts down, and we end up in a fight.

C: I don't shut down. I just have no opinion about flowers or canapés or colors of bridesmaids' dresses.

S: Well, it seems like you don't have any interest in me.

C: Babe, that's not true. I love you and can't wait to be married. I just can't deal with the wedding planner.

S: Gail is my good friend, and she is giving us a great deal.

T: (Confirming some enactment) Is this how it goes at home also?

C: Pretty much.

T: (Therapeutic amazement—sounding slightly confused) So let me get this straight, you are feeling really close and connected and start talking about your future, and a sequence begins between you, and at the end you are feeling distant. Interesting!

S: What do you mean? We just went from one pleasure (lovemaking) to another (wedding).

T: (In a halting, questioning tone of voice) So, it would seem, but somehow . . . the whole interaction went from a warm afterglow of a great evening to an unhappy morning. It's almost as if—correct me if I get this wrong—the intimacy was so good, and then you both collaborated in creating a very effective distance.

C: I felt fine. It's just the incessant wedding planning.

T: I am not questioning either of your reactions to the topic. . . . I don't know . . . it's just the timing. It almost seems like when you feel vulnerable and open, somehow, you get closed and distant. Help me understand this.

S: Well, I was feeling like I needed to get up, but I didn't want to do it before he was ready.

T: How would telling him that you needed a break be hurtful?

S: Like he'd think I wanted to get away or didn't love him or something.

T: Tell him that directly.

This led to a more open discussion of the cost-value of their fight versus the fear of providing or experiencing rejection. They were able to discuss openly with one another, whether the status quo (here the predictable effect of the disagreement), avoidance of the fears, and truncated intimacy has a better payoff. For Sophie and Carl, it began to open an opportunity to get closer and reach their actual desire instead of being safely frustrated.

Magnifying Emotions

Sometimes clients seem unaware of the pain they are experiencing, or they have an unconscious pact to keep interactions as civil as possible. At such times, the therapist may embody the apparently hidden affective components, helping them hang the dirty laundry on the clothesline. Van Deurzen (2012) calls it "making the implicit explicit" (p. 37) and what many have described as "saying the unsayable."

In a family therapy session, the parents were talking about the very sad experience of deciding to put down the family dog. They discussed it at length, logically and actually quite empathically, as all evidence was that he had an incurable cancer that was causing him almost constant pain. I knew the event was to occur during a break week between sessions, so I was prepared for it in the postmortem meeting. As they spoke about the dog, it almost seemed that logic was the sole component of their experience. Even the two children, Katie and Zack, were sitting in the office as if nothing momentous had occurred in their lives.

At one point Katie, the teenaged daughter, turned to me and said, in a sarcastic tone, "Okay, what's next?"

I was quite sad about the loss, and my eyes were obviously moist, so I replied, "I never met Max, but I am very sad about your family's loss."

K: Well he's a dog, and we didn't want him to suffer. He was almost 10.

J: I am sure that you did the right thing, the kind thing . . . *and* I am feel-
      ing sad.

      There was a noticeable silence in the room for almost 2 minutes. Then
      the youngest family member spoke.

Z: I am feeling sad, too. I miss him. (Tears began to well up, and he went
      to his dad for a hug.)

At that point, everyone started to shed tears.

The therapist's sharing his own sadness and holding to the feelings in the
face of logic allowed them to begin a more active and complete mourning
for the loss of their family member of the past 10 years. For Zack (age 9),
the dog had been present his entire life.

Another example occurred in a group in which Craig, a 66-year-old man,
revealed that in the wake of a federal investigation, his company had forced
him to resign from a senior executive position, even though he had been
exonerated and was identified as the person who tried to rectify a problem
caused by others. He expressed sadness and frustration, because "I am not
ready to retire and play golf, and nobody wants to hire an old geezer."

Members of the group tried, to no avail, to reassure him. He accepted
their "kindness" but continued to talk about how they don't know "what it's
like in my industry when there is a taint on your reputation." One woman in
the group acknowledged that it would be very hard to get another position
and expressed how unfair that all was, because he was being scapegoated
by the board of directors.

Craig responded, "That's another thing. I appointed three of them, and
there was only one vote in my favor."

One of the two coleaders (T1) intervened with the observation, "that
makes it a betrayal as well as a rejection."

C: (Backing down and actually sliding his chair back a few inches) No.
      Not really. They were doing what they had to do to save the company.
      They really didn't have a choice.

T1:   They couldn't have fought for you instead of *abandoning* you?

That term was particularly powerful, because Craig had earlier described
his birth parents putting him up for adoption when he was 3 years old and
of abusive adoptive parents. He "escaped" when he was 18 to join the
Marines.

C: (Looking sad) They just did what they thought was in the best interest of the company. They didn't see any options.

T1: So it's not *Semper Fi,* like the Corps.

C: (Sardonic laugh) No, in business, you just leave the dead and dying out on the battlefield and cover your own ass.

T1: Is there one person on the Board who you feel should have protected you more?

C: Yeah. Cary. I brought him up in the business, brought him onto the Board, and now he won't even take calls from my wife or me. He could have stood up.

T1: So that's really a disloyalty.

C: Yeah, I stood up for him and took a few hits when he was going through a messy divorce, and my wife and I got his son into rehab for a drug problem.

T1: So your feeling toward him is . . . ?

C: Well, he's not a strong person. He is probably doing the best he can.

At this point, several members of the group expressed feelings and perceptions about Craig and his situation, and a few shared similar experiences of betrayal from friends or family, each one with lingering anger toward the people who let them down.

T1: Several people (listing names) seem to get a bit of what you are experiencing, and they are all feeling anger for you and toward the people who wronged them. It's hard to see your anger?

C: Well, it is what it is.

T1: Would you be willing to try a short experiment?

T1 set up an empty chair and asked Craig to tell (an imaginary) Cary what he was feeling. Craig was only able to ask questions about why he was so let down. After about 5 minutes, the coleader T2 asked, "May I try something?" (Toward Craig and T1) Receiving an affirmative reply, he got up and moved his chair behind and to the right of Craig's.

T2: (Placing his hand on Craig's shoulder after asking permission to do so) Okay. I am going to be Craig for a few minutes. (Turning toward Craig, he added) You don't have to do anything, just see how this may fit for you.

T2:   (Speaking as Craig)[3] Cary, I am so pissed at you for betraying me that I'd like to take you out to the woodshed and give you a good whuppin'. After all I have done for you over the years, you saw me in a vulnerable moment, and instead of trying to help, you just jumped on the pile. I am FURIOUS! (said with a real angry tone of voice) You screwed me over. Well SCREW YOU and SCREW the whole Board. You are cowards in my book! (Turning toward Craig) How close is that?

C: That is not anything I could say to him.

T2:   That's fine. You haven't, but what are you feeling as you hear that?

C: Yeah, I would like to take them all out to the woodshed and let them know there are consequences to their actions. I am really angry. I guess I don't know what good it does to say it.

T1:   (Very empathically) You don't have to express it to them, but unless you acknowledge it, it could eat you up inside with frustration. Doing it is separate from knowing what you are feeling.

C: (Loudly) Well SHIT! I AM ANGRY. My wife has been carrying all the anger for both of us. She'll be glad to know I am on board.

T: It's important to share your feelings with her, so that she can be freer to support you. You don't have to confront anyone, but it's worth knowing.

Using this as an affective bridge (Shapiro et al., 1997), other group members started to talk about unspoken emotions. They praised Craig for his courage and for opening the door for them to disclose their own feelings more directly. The cotherapists monitored Craig while they encouraged the other members to share more of their experiences.

This is provided as an example of magnifying emotions. It is more leader-intensive than many other interactions. In the group setting, when members can provide the impetus for each other, they may benefit by experiencing altruism, a minimizing of a personal sense of pathology (receiving help from non-professional), easier transfer of training to back home life, and feelings of universality.

Interactional Intimacy

In individual existential work, the therapist strives as much as possible to relate from inside or beside the client. He or she attempts to create an *I-thou* interaction with acceptance and working within the client's personal framework. In multiperson therapies, interventions are designed to occur from inside the interpersonal interaction as well as within individuals.

To the extent possible, the members of the group, couple, or family are viewed through a process perspective. Interventions are conceptualized on the interactional level. This allows a therapist to express acceptance of and even admiration for the consequences of clients' collaboration, before helping them explore whether the predictable outcomes are worth the effort. Ideally, through the therapy, they will discover how to work in ways that hopefully extract a much lower overall emotional cost.

From this orientation, not only do individuals have existential challenges, their combined units do as well. Couples, families, and group members may move in concert to express a group-level resistance, a group level of symptomatology, or demonstrate other behaviors motivated by neurotic (avoidant) rather than existential anxiety. Often, these phenomena may only be observed or addressed at a process or group level. Resulting interventions address existential anxiety at a system rather than individual level.

In two case examples in this chapter, the therapist explored interactional teamwork. Instead of a focus on Sophie's introducing wedding planning at an apparently inopportune moment, the therapist called attention to the couple's effective distancing. Similarly, even in addressing Sylvia's affair, the initial focus was on the impressive success of the couple's miscommunication.

On the surface, this may seem unfair to the apparently "innocent" spouse. However, the client here is the entire unit; not the individuals within the unit. Addressing attention solely to the identified patient may actually disrupt, rather than heal, the couple or family. It could have the impact of supporting their continuing avoidance, creating external moral judgments, missing the subjective phenomenological experiences and characteristics of their relating, and failing to help them heal interactions that are harmful.

When Groups Are of Strangers

Interactions in an ongoing natural group, such as a couple, family, or in-house organizational group, can be fairly obvious and, in most instances, involve fewer people.[4] The most common form of group therapy is comprised of members who are strangers to one another. In these groups, therapists have the opportunity to observe and subjectively experience relationships, from first impressions, through early attempts at connection, to cooperative alliance. Collaboration in group therapy is unique, because there is no final goal of doing something unified together (Shapiro, 1978). Instead, the purpose is for members to connect and through their budding relationships, help one another deal with individual meaning.

Subjective experiences, relating in the moment with other members and group leaders, provide the opportunity for enhanced self-reflection in an environment in which both bounded feedback from therapists and unbounded feedback from other members is available.

A 60-Year History

The existential core principle (Buber, 1966) that therapy is relational in nature makes group therapy a unique environment for interpersonal encounter and change. There are myriad opportunities for discovering and expressing oneself and practicing personal integrity in this setting.

Existential approaches to group therapy, counseling, and encounter have been described since the middle of the 20th century. Hugh Mullen (1955; 1992) was an eloquent and frequent challenger of objectivism in therapy, providing a clear description of the subjective, phenomenological approach. Combining and contrasting analytic and existential tenets, Mullen and Rosenbaun (1967) espoused an early model for existential therapists in group. Hora (1959) also provided examples of the uniqueness of the existential group therapist. The most influential and far-reaching existential group therapy model appeared in Yalom's (1970) first edition of *Theory and Practice of Group Psychotherapy,* the standard text in the field for many years. It is profoundly existential in orientation. My own practice of existential groups and studies of group outcome began in the late 1960s. My first textbook, *Methods of Group Psychotherapy and Encounter,* (Shapiro, 1978) explored subjective, phenomenological approaches to groups.

An interesting combination of different levels of multiperson therapies is presented in Coche and Coche's (1990) description of couples group therapy. In their clinical model, they combine the closed couple dynamics with the group of strangers. Although they describe their systems approach as "seat-of-the-pants eclecticism" (p. xvi), there is much that corresponds with existential constructs. Judith Coche[5] (1990) elaborated those in her paper on resistance in existential marital therapy.

Although existential group therapy has never been comparatively popular by comparison to other approaches, most borrow nonetheless significantly from existential approaches (Yalom, 2005), and the research on evidence-based relationships (Norcross, 2011) has a distinctly existential flavor.

Distinguishing Characteristics of Existential Group Therapy

Among the characteristics that define existential multiperson therapy are:

(1) The therapist is present as a person, not as a distant expert or transference screen. This is also linked to therapist self-disclosure. Carl Whitaker's (1988) referred to the therapist as "the most experienced patient in the group."

(2) Therapists exhibit an abiding respect for subjective experience: emotions, fantasies, and so on. These are treated by the therapist and, in time, by other group members as valid phenomena for understanding.

(3) Respect is conveyed for the whole person, who may have symptoms.

(4) There is an awareness that the clients' unconscious minds contain pushes for love, courage, altruism, and creativity as well as violence, revenge, narcissism, and anger.

(5) The curing factor is the deep (*I-thou*) bi-directional relationships between clients and therapist.

(6) It is believed that the therapist is changed by clients as well as the reverse.

(7) Therapists foster a basic imperative for all humans to seek meaning in their lives and that each person's meaning is unique.

(8) Therapists show a willingness to allow the client to "be" who he or she is without a need to fix or alter that from the outside. The best change follows internal demands and is consistent with the client's values.

(9) The therapy setting should allow for relationships and interactions which enlarge awareness of the immediate experiences occurring in the room.

Losses and Choices

Schneider and Krug (2010), promoting an integrated existential-humanistic approach, summarize many of these factors by focusing on exploration of the centrality of clients' reclaiming and re-owning the losses in life. Clients are encouraged to be more present, identify the ways that they engage in self-blocking, and assume greater responsibility for freely made choices.

Each new choice requires relinquishing something that previously held value. These "losses" are faced best when therapists encourage expanded awareness and ways-of-being in daily life. Groups are particularly effective at addressing those goals. As clients in groups discover the impact of their choices on others, they are allowed the space and opportunity to experiment with alternative ways-of-being. When they choose to try something new, or stay the same, others can provide them with estimates of the psychological costs of each movement toward freedom or security. Although a similar process of awareness of choices to take or avoid risks will occur in individual therapy, in group it is witnessed by others. The significance of witnessing on both the observed and observer is hard to overestimate.

The family, couple, or group environment may be uniquely effective because of this "closer-to-real-life" situation. Learning goes beyond understanding from the professional therapist; it involves the risk of true reactions from others who are also risking others' judgments to their giving and receiving feedback.

Effectiveness of Existential Multiperson Therapy

Most of the evidence for therapy was covered in Chapter 8. The evidence base for multiperson therapy outcome is consistent with findings of individual work. However, complexities and differences between researchers and clinicians are exacerbated in the multiperson therapy arena.

Unique Difficulties Associated With Group, Couple, and Family Research

(1) The absence of adequate control groups is quite problematic when considering couples, families, or groups of clients.

(2) Outcome measures are even less standardized than for individual therapies.

(3) There are few longitudinal studies; this is a particular concern for existential and psychodynamic work because there is often a hibernation effect of increasingly positive results (Shapiro and Ross, 1971; Shedler, 2010).

(4) Comparisons between groups of different sizes make comparisons of actual treatment difficult to assess. For example, what is the difference in nature and amount of therapy for a family of three and one of eight?

(5) The length of treatment (one session to 50 or more) is inconsistent across studies.

(6) There are significant questions in published studies regarding the level of sophistication and training of family or group therapists, particularly in studies conducted in academic settings. Unless the therapists are experienced and well-trained in existential therapy, cross-theory comparisons are moot.

(7) Interactionally based interventions require a different set of dependent variables than either intrapsychic or behavioral measures. Lebow (2000), who focuses on circular causality in family therapy, argues poignantly against linearly based instruments, common in deductive approaches.

(8) Because of the complexity of multiple interactions in group therapies, far more sophisticated process measures are needed (Burlingame, Fuhriman, & Johnson, 2004).

(9) Although many consider RCTs to be the gold standard, they are limited in measuring treatment common in existential multiperson therapies. There is an increasingly recognized need for case study and n=1 studies to add to necessary depth to analysis (Carlson, Ross, & Stark, 2012).

(10) Frequently, family or group therapy is nested in a comprehensive treatment program. True measures of effectiveness of individual components are best determined when the treatments stand alone.

Indices of Evidence

Despite the daunting array of difficulties, some studies do indicate the primacy of multiperson therapies, especially those with an existential orientation. Group therapy outcomes have been summarized by Barlow (2010). Shapiro (2010a) focused especially on process-oriented groups, including RCT studies. Excellent reviews of the advantages of family therapy can be found in Shadish and Baldwin (2003), Sexton et al. (2011), and Goldenberg and Goldenberg (2012) who conclude,

> As for couple and family therapy, there now exists considerable research-informed evidence that this modality is effective for virtually every type of disorder and for various relational problems in children, adolescents and adults. (p. 457)

Why Existential Couple, Family, and Group Therapy?

The core of existential counseling and therapy is true relationships with an *I-thou* method and purpose. Existential therapy with individuals has a unique focus on real relationships between client and therapist. Multiperson existential therapy offers clients the opportunity to pursue that goal with fellow members of a couple, family, or group of strangers. Methods used in these formats are similar to individual work but have some added advantages including relatively unbounded real-time feedback. Whether clients using these methods attain *I-thou* moments, striving for them is especially useful in finding meaning in life.

Notes

1. Some consider couple therapy to be a subset of family therapy (i.e., Goldenberg & Goldenberg, 2012). However, marital therapy and marriage counseling preceded family therapy by decades. Contemporary authors who consider couple work as a distinct, related area of interest include Gottman (1999) and Gurman (2008, 2010).

2. This fight may be so ubiquitous and familiar, clients are usually able to recognize and describe it readily. I have often opined to couples that the fight is so familiar and predictable, it may occur at their home when they are out.

3. The technique, which is also referred to as alter-ego or "doubling," comes from psychodrama and is quite useful in existential group therapy.

4. An exception may involve large families or family of origin sessions as described by Framo (1976) in which multiple generations of a family are brought together for sessions—an "it takes a village" approach.

5. As a college freshman at Colby College, my classmate, Dr. Judith Milner Coche, was as influenced as I was by Viktor Frankl's visit in 1960. At our 50th reunion in 2014, we both used the term "life-altering" to describe that fortuitous encounter.

10

Gender and Culture in Existential Therapy

We may have different religions, different languages,

different colored skin, but we all belong to one human race.

Kofi Annan

From an existential perspective, working from within requires concentrated attention to the multiple contexts in life from which clients derive meaning. Characteristics such as race, gender, religion, family, and culture-of-origin are essential building blocks in a client's self-esteem, perspective, and value systems. Each client's thoughts, feelings, and actions are embedded in a complex array of interlaced contexts. Unique representations of appropriate or inappropriate behavior are always determined culturally. From an existential perspective, there are also universal human characteristics that cross cultural boundaries.

In *Counseling Across Cultures* (2007), Pedersen, Draguns, Lonner, and Trimble distinguish between the culturally unique (*-emic*) and humanly universal (*-etic*). For existentially oriented therapists, each client is at once, a minority of one, and one of many within his or her personal ethnocultural frame.

Vontress and Epp (2015) described an ecological model of culture comprising five nested interacting rings:

(1) Universal culture: invariable facets of human existence

(2) Ecological culture: ecosystems that deeply influence day-to-day living

(3) National culture: the sum of allegiances to community heritage, customs, language, economic realities, government, territory, and so on

(4) Regional culture: focused on neighboring cultures, climate, ethnic mixtures, and blending with those in proximity[1]

(5) Racial/ethnic culture: where people of similar ethnic and racial backgrounds tend to live in enclaves that provide separateness from others (For most of the 20th century in large U.S. cities, there were identifiable "neighborhoods" [ghettos] that limited diversity and movement across, often involuntary cultural boundaries.)

Immigrants begin an evolving multigenerational process before full integration of the new culture. Initial efforts to keep alive the old ways in a new environment give way to acculturation and adjustment to aspects of the new culture and increasing assimilation. In addition, by the fourth generation in a melting pot culture, some members will feel an inclination to reclaim aspects of their original ethnic identities.

Cultural Stereotyping

Whether the approach or understanding is culturally centric or universal, there are two salient pitfalls for therapy across cultural lines: lack of respect and cultural sensitivity and the danger of reductionism.

Lack of Cultural Sensitivity

Among many others, Sue and Sue (2012) have long indicated the problems with assumptions that people who differ on cultural dimensions may not respond similarly to particular interventions or approaches. Most cross-cultural experts focus a great deal on how therapists from dominant Western backgrounds may inadvertently miss the negative impact of some of their assumptions on clients from minority cultures. Misunderstandings are common between those with different ethnic, religious, gender, cultural, regional, primary language, and generational backgrounds. Existential therapists, whose method is to develop a close working relationship, require unique sensitive understanding of clients' cultural needs.

For example, if a therapist is aware that the client is a first-generation immigrant in America from India, she must understand that his relationship with his parents and other relatives may be far different from her own fourth generation Scandinavian family background. Based on her customs and those of her family, friends, and professional associates, visits from relatives are usually short (a week or less) and at the convenience of the host, not the guests. From that perspective, a visit of indeterminate length at an inconvenient time from her client's Indian parents might indicate a serious problem: dependency or lack of individuation. Yet, from an Indian cultural perspective it is normal. Indeed, it may be customary to give the honored parental guests the master bedroom while the host sleeps on the couch.

Obviously, *normal* and *pathological* are culturally defined terms.

Reductionism

This perspective, often called *totalism* (Cannadine, 2013), is at the opposite end of the cultural understanding spectrum: stereotyping. A therapist's honest attempt to be extra sensitive to a person from a different culture may paradoxically move him or her further from understanding the client as a person.

For example, assuming that my client, named Nguyen, is Vietnamese, might lead me to inappropriate assumptions about her. In my attempt to know her from the data of her familial culture-of-origin, I may be blocked from truly understanding her subjective being-in-the-world. The reality of effective multicultural psychotherapy is far more nuanced and fluid, involving an understanding of the entire ecology of cultural influences (Vontress & Epp, 2015).

Ethnicity, Culture, and Gender Differences

Even a casual glance at the news or politics shouts the significance of ethnic similarity and differences. The ongoing struggle in the Middle East between tribal and religious factions speaks volumes about intragroup allegiances and intergroup hatred. Horrific wars have been fought to establish ascendancy of one cultural group over another. The sociologist Andrew Greeley (1969) wrote of the power of ethnicity, *"Men . . . would more or less cheerfully die for a difference rooted in ethnic origins" (p. 5).*

Therapy Across Cultures

Empathy, therapeutic alliance, and effectiveness require sensitivity to culture and ethnicity. Within some cultures, clients may truly believe that healing will be physical, spiritual, behavioral, or social. A therapist who doesn't share, or at least recognize, a particular belief will miss a most important personal connection with the client and avenue for the therapy.

C: I know there is something wrong with me. I am worried all the time and can't do my daily work.

T: Tell me about that!

C: I think my body chemistry is out of balance, and I need to get it more aligned.

T: How will we know that progress is being made in the alignment?

C: The shaking will stop, and I won't be always worrying so much.

The therapist may have a very different theory about the origin, manifestation, or relevant behavioral indications, but there are advantages to working within the client's framework.

T: What have you tried so far?

C: I go to my Sensei, acupuncture, Tai Chi. Do you know about those?

T: I know a little, and I am going to recommend that you continue with those as you see fit, while we talk about the problems in a different way. I will be particularly interested in progress from the Sensei's perspective.

By joining in the cultural notions of healing held by the client, the therapist locates the treatment within the client's life-perspective. That makes her interventions much more appealing.

Focusing primarily on cultures in Hawaii, Tseng, Maretzki, and McDermott (1980) described ethnic differences in clients' frames of reference. These included, what constituted a symptom worthy of relating, the experience of pain, beliefs about symptom causality, the treatment most desired, and what orientation they expected from the healer.

That last difference may present problems for some Western-trained therapists working with East and South Asian ethnic clients. For example, the client may desire the therapist be an expert who offers specific instructions, hardly the normal approach of psychodynamic and humanistic therapists. By contrast, there may be clients with other ethnicities who expect to do the primary work themselves with the therapist primarily as a guide and witness. Any specific suggestions from the therapist may be seen as intrusive and demeaning.

With the former, therapists are more prone to employing the kinds of directions that are ethnocentric. The therapist in the last example "recommended" that the client continue with the Sensei and added the therapy to fit in the mix. In the latter, sometimes a therapist needs to make a suggestion backward.

This client, a software engineer, was consistently describing the compelling reasons to continue in behaviors that had quite negative consequences.

C: All told, I should be able to figure out how to manipulate the situation to make it work.

T: It's like a software problem. You just need to write the correct code.

C: No, not really. I have the correct code as you say. It just doesn't work to help me out of this nasty situation with my brother.

T: Whatever you try, even when you do it correctly, somehow you end up getting hurt in the end.

C: No, not really. Something should work. I just don't know what it is yet.

T: *(It is important for him to tell me I do not understand. I need to approach this by reversing an intervention.)* What made you decide not to cut off the relationship until he seems more reasonable?

C: Oh, I didn't decide that. I guess I could.

T: I'm not sure it fits here. I wonder what that would be like as a speculation.

The therapist's embedding the suggestion in a question and reinforcing the client's need to do it himself is far more likely to work, whether it's personal resistance or just more within cultural norms.

Spiegel (1982) identified five areas on which ethnic-value orientations may offer varying assumptions: time, preferred pattern of action in interpersonal relations, preferred way to relate in groups, manner of relating to nature and the supernatural, and perspective regarding man's basic nature. A working existential diagnosis involves exploring how a client "fits" his cultural norms and how he may differ.

What does it mean if a client describes herself as "Chinese," "African-American," "Native American," "Jewish," "Methodist," "Mormon," "Irish Catholic," "a secular humanist," "Muslim," "Buddhist," "French Canadian," "Military," or "Hispanic"? What does it mean if the term is further modified as "*fourth-generation* Chinese," a "*cultural* Jew" a "*lapsed* Catholic," "an *ex*-Mormon," or "Hispanic *from Spain—not Mexico*"?

What does that indicate to the therapist? What is the likelihood that his or her assumptions about the labels and the client's are shared? From the existential perspective, ethnicity per se may be secondary to being a therapist from a similar or different culture. This is not to minimize the importance of cultural or racial identification. The essential aspect involves acknowledging and being able to discuss the cultural similarities and differences in internalized meaning attribution.

In the week following my meeting with my first client from Thailand, I spent some time in the library trying to learn about Thai culture. It was somewhat useful to learn that to have the bottom of my shoe facing him could be insulting. That was an easy adjustment that may well have avoided some discomfort for my client. However, cultural empathy extended to learning what it was like for him to talk to a Caucasian therapist, in his second language, as an immigrant in a new country.

Similarly, when I learned that saying "no"[2] was considered rude in Japan, my subsequent approach with Japanese clients has been to provide alternatives, rather than confront with disagreement. Quite a different approach than I would expect with a Silicon Valley engineer who was originally from New York.

Counseling the Culturally Diverse

It is a fact of Western cultures today that increasing ethnic diversity is more of a norm than an exception. In the United States, citizens with European ethnic backgrounds will be a minority population somewhere in the first half of this century.[3] These demographics argue persuasively for major adjustments in the provision of mental health care. Already in California, a common trendsetter for the nation as a whole, clientele for most therapists include many from cultures that have traditionally not sought or avoided psychotherapy: South and East Asians, African-Americans, and Latinos.

Among those in the forefront of multicultural counseling, Falicov (2013), Kitano (1989), McGoldrick, Giordano, and Garcia-Preto (2005), Pederson et al. (2007), Ramos-Sanchez (2009), Sue and Sue (2012), and Vontress (2003) have written extensively and persuasively about the importance of counselors recognizing the unique needs of many racial and ethnic minorities, including questioning the applicability of Euro-centric psychological theories for those from different cultures.

In a significant break from characteristic therapy settings and orientations, Sue and Sue (2012) promote the importance of what has traditionally been the purview of social workers—advocating for the client in his or her environment: teaching, intervening, and consulting. The assumption that the problem may be in the larger culture or the interaction of individual and culture is far broader than more typical intrapsychic notions. For many existential therapists, direct advocacy is unlikely as a component of treatment, but an acknowledgment of the reality in which the client lives may well help in terms of how the client deals with issues such as prejudice, injustice, and micro-aggressions (Wong, Derthick, David, Saw, & Okazaki, 2014)

Microaggressions and Therapy

According to Sue et al. (2007) therapists may inadvertently commit a variety of mostly unintended slights, insults, or discriminatory messages when dealing with race, ethnic, or cultural issues. This unintentional insensitivity can result in ruptures in the therapeutic alliance.

According to Owen, Tao, Imel, Wampold, and Rodolfa (2014) these are characteristically not addressed openly and thus not well repaired. These "micro-aggressions" are characteristically not direct slurs but are more subtle, often involving therapeutic assumptions about culture, race, or ethnicity. For example, the therapist or the therapist's theory may place underlying evaluation on the expression of affect. Another common Western assumption is the belief that talking out a problem is superior to quiet acceptance. These notions may accidentally violate those of clients from cultures where norms are quite opposite. Another area of misconnection may reflect differences in major child rearing practices.

For example, when working with Samoan clients in Hawaii, it was a significant violation of cultural ethos to recommend nonphysical punishment of children. Knowing that, seasoned therapists were able to work with the clients to avoid the head of the child and to moderate somewhat the severity of the punishment. For most of the therapists, this was suboptimal and contraindicated by their personal values and by the professional research, but they could not effectively breach the cultural norms with their own values and keep the clients in therapy.

A more subtle example involves the experience of time. In some Western cultures, respect is shown by promptness. It may be considered disrespectful or pathological when a client is consistently late for a session. Yet clients from some other cultures may not see time as a governing criterion. They deal much more in the present, and when they are together with the therapist, they are available.

C: (Knocking on the door, 20 minutes into the session time) I'm here.

T: Oh. Hello. Come on in. Were you aware we were scheduled to begin at 10:00? It's 10:20 now.

C: (Looking embarrassed) Yes.

T: Okay, well let's use the time we have. What is happening for you?

C: Oh, things are about the same. Not much really. (Looking somewhat ashamed that he let the therapist down)

T: (*He probably came late because he wants to avoid getting into something important. Now he's got the response from me that makes that even more likely. I will begin with our relationship and see what comes up.*) I think I may have sounded harsh about the late start. Did you experience it that way?

C: (Wary) Maybe a little.

T: I apologize for that tone of voice. I really look forward to our meetings and get a little frustrated when I will have less time to talk with you.

C: Maybe I can stay longer.

T: Unfortunately, I have another appointment at 11. In my world, I am culturally bound by the clock to be on time. I think we have a difference there. What might we do about that?

The therapist here is trying to be respectful and to underscore and accept the differences in cultural approaches to time. Her initial reaction was one of annoyance because the client was not conforming to her way of dealing with time.

It is not likely that any therapist will completely avoid client sensitivities or be sufficiently knowledgeable about each client's culture to avoid microaggressive slips. What is important in existential work is to constantly monitor the relationship in the room. As she observes the client's atypical nonverbal signs, it may be a valuable indicator of potential cultural violations.

It may be argued that when a client comes to a Western therapist for help, he or she is looking for Western solutions and has bought into the process. To some extent, that may be accurate, or at least a comforting delusion for the therapist, but increased sensitivity and connection to the client where he or she is, rather than where we might want him or her to be, is a hallmark of existential therapy.

The Unique Problems of Assumed Similarity

Although it is likely that we all will be unintentionally insensitive when working cross-culturally, in some ways one of the biggest pitfalls is when we believe that the client shares our own culture. When working with clients who are obviously from a different racial, cultural, or socioeconomic background, I am ready to have them educate me about relevant norms and differences. My largest blind spots may well be with someone who grew up in my old neighborhood, went to the same schools, and has a similar career. I may be drawn automatically to assume that he reacts like I do. When he doesn't, it is easy to miss or to try to correct his way of being.

This may be exacerbated in couple therapy when one partner shares my culture and the other does not. I may listen far more closely to the person who is obviously culturally different and expect automatically to share understanding, humor, or connection with the person who seems more similar.

From an existential stance, the best way to deal with such prejudices (even when they seem positive) is to treat each client as a minority of one, whose experience is sufficiently fascinating as to require full attention and wonder. In that way, I may have a unique encounter of my client and all his resources within his culture. Ideally, resolutions of concerns and growth will also be culturally coherent.

Religion as Culture

Therapy with those whose supernatural and spiritual beliefs are different also brings up a host of cultural challenges. Sometimes this may be addressed in an initial phone call. Sometimes it emerges in ongoing therapy.

C: (On phone) I'd like to come in for counseling with my boyfriend. Do you do Christian counseling?

T: If you are looking for a therapist who respects the Judeo-Christian tradition in his work, I am comfortable seeing you. If you are looking for answers in scriptures, I will be happy to refer you to a colleague who works from that perspective.

C: I am "born-again," and my boyfriend is not.

T: (*This may be pastoral counseling.*) So, you are looking for a change in his belief or . . . ?

C: I want to find out if we are as compatible as we think.

T: I am happy to offer you an appointment at . . .

There may be major differences between therapists and clients who have different religious perspectives. It is incumbent for any therapist to self-examine closely any personal deep beliefs to try to head off any unconscious micro-aggressions as much as possible.

Several years ago, I was seeing a 35-year-old devout Christian man who was frustrated and worried about the relationship with his fiancée. The evolving problem was that she wanted to begin sexual intercourse with him since they became engaged. He was demurring, and she was increasingly reporting to him that she felt unattractive and unwanted. He reported that they were both virgins and active in church life. The wedding was 6 months away.

It would have been easy to encourage him to try to meet her desires or to focus in on how long he had avoided sexual intercourse because of theorized ambivalence or hypothesized fears of performance or intimacy. Either would have represented approaching him from without: failing to comprehend the situation from his perspective. Note how my approach was to connect with him despite personal value differences.

J: That must be so frustrating for you. Here's the woman you love and find attractive, and you feel you need to hold back.

C: It's not like I don't want to have sex with her. We do (pause and with a low voice) . . . other things.

J: It sounds like it's embarrassing to talk about those.

C: Yes. I think it is for everyone. Don't you think so?

J: Right now what is important is what it's like for you. What would you like from K.?

C: I want her to know that I am ready as soon as we are married, and I don't want to be immoral.

As we talked, it was clear that his discomfort in broaching the subject was likely sending K. a mixed message. He reported that when they were alone "and kissing and getting worked up" she wanted to spend the night with him. He recommended instead that they pray for strength and patience. She was willing to do that but was also disappointed.

J: I wonder how she'd respond if, in addition to praying, you could tell her about your conflict between your own desires and attraction but need to wait regardless.

C: If we are both feeling it, won't that be worse?

J: You described that you both are feeling it, and that somehow only you are totally in charge of waiting. I wonder if both the wish and the religious issue might be shared?

An example of the danger of assumptions can be seen in Dav, who always appeared for therapy wearing a *yarmulke,* (the skull cap worn by observant, primarily Orthodox Jews). A natural assumption was that he conformed to orthodox traditions, norms, and cultural perspectives. Other natural assumptions would be that he grew up in a Jewish community in a major city, held strict dietary rules, was a regular at his synagogue, would not meet on Jewish holidays, and that his wife was also an Orthodox Jew. Approaching him on the basis of those assumptions might have created a host of micro-aggressions and significant breaks in the therapeutic alliance.

It soon became obvious that many of the stereotypical assumptions were quite inaccurate. Dav grew up in the rural south. His mother was "culturally" Jewish, but his military father was not. He was not Bar-Mitzvahed until he was in his thirties, when he decided personally to follow a more religious path. The decision was a significant problem between him and his Russian-born Jewish wife who was more atheistic than religious. He did not live in a kosher home.

Understanding these factors, it was possible to connect with his feeling of separateness from his wife, his history and, in part because of the head wear, from many coworkers. The feelings of isolation and rejection became the dominant theme in therapy. This would never have occurred had I acted on my "reasonable prejudgments" and proceeded as if I knew him because of externals.

Clients Who Choose Similarity or Difference of Religion

Cummings, Ivan, Carson, Stanley, and Pargament (2014) conclude from their review of 29 relevant studies that therapists tend to prefer clients who share their religious/spiritual beliefs and values. Despite this preference, there were no differences on process (therapeutic relationship) or treatment outcome data. Clients who want to include their religious and spiritual beliefs in counseling may wish to choose therapists who share their beliefs. Thus, many are drawn to Christian counseling centers, for example, because of the comfort they anticipate with therapists who won't be critical of their life choices.

Some therapists who share similar beliefs with clients will offer prayer as part of their work (i.e., Wade, Worthington, & Vogel, 2007). This may obviously be a disconnect for clients who hold different beliefs. Many clients prefer to keep the two separate. Joseph, a member of the Mormon Church, began the initial interview,

J: My friend Jason told me that you are not LDS but are friendly to those who are.

T: That is correct. Tell me how that may be a factor in therapy.

J: I talk to my Bishop and the elders about faith matters. I need to talk to someone about (secular) things here, and I don't want my conversations getting out into the community.

T: I can promise that what you tell me will be confidential with the exceptions of situations that may cause harm to you or others or possibilities of child or elder abuse. What kinds of things do you want to keep private?

J: Mostly about my relationship with my wife and sex in general.

Joseph wanted to keep separate those faith matters that belonged in his church and a number of feelings, fantasies, and sexual thoughts that he believed would not be acceptable in that community. One of the most important was negative feelings about his grandfather's polygamy, which he said that his family denied and refused to discuss.

Like all cultural matters, it is best discussed openly as early on in therapy as possible, unless the client's and therapist's religious values are so discrepant that they create a disconnect that might interfere with the kind of empathy and relationship that maximize effective work. When such a discrepancy exists, often the most ethical approach is making a referral.

Normally, this is most likely when one person has a fundamental belief or if the religious/spiritual beliefs are less mainstream. A client who is Methodist will have little difficulty with a therapist who goes to the Presbyterian church down the road. Christian-Jewish combinations frequently work quite well. It is probably not a great leap for an atheistic therapist to work effectively with a church-going client or vice versa.

One of my colleagues, a devout Muslim, wears a hijab (a scarf) covering her head. She reports that she always feels a need to ask new clients if that might interfere with their work. She said that approximately 10% of her new clients do not express any discomfort but fail to return for a second session. By her estimate, there is likely an equal number of clients who seek her out as a person who understands and honors religion.

A chasm in understanding may occur if the spiritual beliefs of either therapist or client is less accessible or mainstream. For example, what are the issues when a client belongs to the Church of Scientology, which holds mental health treatment to be inappropriate at best? What if a client wants to work entirely with issues from past lives? What if the client finds answers through his or her "animal spirit guide?" Can the therapist work with the shamanic animal guide system of the client to help him or her find meaning?

If the therapist can join in the client's belief system and work from within, it can be effective. If not, regardless of the nature of the divide, it cannot. During my seventh session with a 33-year-old man, the following occurred,

C: There is something I have not told you because you might think I am crazy.

J: Would you like to tell me now?

C: I believe in reincarnation, and I know I have had several past lives. They emerged during some past life regression hypnosis that I did a few years back.

J: Tell me about them.

C: In one, I was a woman of great power like Helen of Troy.

J: *(It's very unusual to have a past life as the other sex. He hasn't yet brought it up but probably worth exploring his sexual fluidity in the present.)* What does that mean to you in the present?

   In areas of great sensitivity, errors are likely to be made quite inadvertently. These errors will likely create a rupture in the alliance. Unaddressed, such a rift may diminish the impact of the therapy or end it entirely.

   For example, on Ash Wednesday, a non-Catholic therapist seeing what looks like a smudge on the forehead of a client may "helpfully alert" the client that there is "a blotch" on her forehead. A therapist may assume that appointments would meet as usual and be inflexible with scheduling with clients who celebrate Jewish high holidays, or she may attribute late afternoon tiredness during Ramadan to psychological stress instead of fasting.

   There are innumerable ways of responding that might unsettle the client or place a schism in the relationship. They are almost impossible to avoid. The existential response to these is consistent with Frankl's (1959a) position that *it is not what occurs, but how we respond to what occurs that is essential.* By monitoring the communication closely, the therapist has the opportunity to turn the client's attention to the relationship and discuss the hurt that the client is experiencing.

   The therapist here is working with a client who is Israeli. The discussion was focused on whether she would return to Israel or stay in the United States.

T: I feel like something just changed in here. Are you noticing anything different?

C: Not really. I think I am just tired. Maybe that's what you feel.

T: We were talking about your thinking about whether to return to Tel Aviv or to stay here and how you have to remake the decision frequently because of pressures from your family there and the life here. I commented that it seemed like a "Next year in Jerusalem" conflict.

C: You know, not all Israelis are religious. Many of us are Atheists.

T: So I was making an assumption about you that was inaccurate. That seems like a double misunderstanding on my part: One, to be making assumptions instead of listening more closely and two, to get it wrong.

C: Well, I am used to it. As soon as someone hears my accent or our Hebrew-sounding names, they make a lot of assumptions.

T: I would like this relationship to be different. I will try to be more focused on you as a person. . . . I wonder if you would be willing to let me know if I misstep again.

C: Maybe I will do that, but I . . . I appreciate your apology.

T: Thank you. It's sincere. I am sensing that the energy is back in the room. What's going on for you?

Socioeconomic Status

Often the most compelling cultural division is a client's socioeconomic level. In the San Francisco Bay area, Honolulu, and other cities, neighborhoods today are more likely to be segregated by socioeconomic levels than ethnic or cultural groups. Class differences may be a major cause for misunderstanding and breaks in the therapeutic alliance.

Empathy for differences in race may be more easily addressed directly than the taboo subject of finances. Most therapists live a professional, middle-class lifestyle. A therapist who does not understand the ambiance of poverty may make some very significant middle-class blunders with clients who do not share values like delay of gratification, expenditures on luxury items, or the use of lay-away plans or usurious payday loans. Many clients from low-income strata of the population may feel misunderstood, undervalued as people, or spoken to in a condescending manner. The biggest barriers to therapist understanding are the feelings of hopelessness, inaccessibility to education, and inability to improve one's lot, common to those at the lowest income levels.

Similarly, therapists may trip over values when working with far more affluent clients. In addition to envy by therapists of a client's apparent lifestyle, there may be a lack of understanding of the social pressures or the client's social circles.

C: Sorry about missing the last session. I forgot to call. I'll write you a double check today.

T: *(Wondering about resistance, perhaps irritated about the missed session)* What happened?

C: Oh, a couple of us decided at the last minute to fly over to Greece and sail the islands for a few days. Did you know it's cheaper to charter a jet for eight than to pay the airlines for eight first class tickets?

T: *(Are you kidding me, you chartered a jet at the last minute—this is way over the top.)* Was there a special occasion or . . . ?

C: No. My wife has been in Singapore for the past few weeks, and I was talking to (my friend) at the club, and he said, "hey let's have a guys' trip to the Greek Islands," and so we did. You probably know some of the guys (listing celebrities, professional athletes, and a local politician).

T: How was it?

C: I was ready to come home after a few days. I was thinking about Skyping you for our session. Do you do that?

T: I don't. How do you understand the loss of interest in a few days?

C: I don't know. Some of the guys were into the local women or call girls. That's not me.

T: You are feeling lonely with your wife gone, isolated somewhat from the other guys, and thinking about contacting me from the yacht in the Mediterranean. Let's talk about that sense of being alone.

This therapist managed to keep his cool sufficiently to bring the therapy back. Clearly, hearing about chartering a jet at the spur of the moment and spending the equivalent of twice the therapist's annual income on a week fling was troubling, and he had to struggle to get back on board with the client. His own issues with money, largesse, and nonmiddle-class values were a stumbling block.

Unless the therapist is sufficiently aware of his own values and is able to reset to the client's values and lifestyle, he will be unable to help explore the client's finding meaning in life.

When Cultures Clash

Sometimes the distance between cultural values is not bridgeable by a therapist. This can occur because of a lack of comprehension of values that are opposing to the dominant culture or to the therapist's personal values.

Every therapist has clients with whom he cannot work because of personal reasons. I was confronted one day in the late 1970s with a new client who appeared for his appointment at a college counseling center wearing a Nazi uniform. It was not likely that I could put aside my own values and feelings to work with him as a client. Indeed, it took great restraint on my part to avoid forcibly removing him from the office. I did make a referral.

Gender and Sexual Orientation

Gender is a major component of self-identification. It goes far beyond a person's biological, sexual characteristics. It involves roles, attributes, attitudes, feelings, and behaviors that are distinctive in the individual's culture. As for any other cultural form, the definition of "male" or "female," "gay" or "straight," "bisexual," "transgender," or "fluid" is an essential aspect of therapeutic understanding. However individuals self-define is the connection point for therapists.

Multiplication of Sexual Orientation/Gender Roles

For therapists, gender is not a dichotomous variable. There are significant within-group differences and even more categories of gender alliance than were previously studied. Some clients consider gender as fluid, rather than discrete.

As early as 1948, Kinsey, Pomeroy, and Martin described a seven-point continuum of sexual orientation from exclusively heterosexual to exclusively homosexual. There was an eighth point for individuals described as asexual. Gay, lesbian, bisexual, and transgender categories were acknowledged in the psychological literature and have been studied for at least 2 decades. In the past few years there has been an explosion of distinctions along the continuum. Facebook users in the United Kingdom can now choose from 71 options[4] (American Facebook users have 58 choices).[5]

The assumption of so many distinct sexual orientations is useful primarily for sociocultural reasons and potential research. For therapists, the key is accepting the client's reference and joining him or her there. Despite the explosion in categories, the centrality of the therapeutic relationship remains. A therapist who is able to appreciate the client's gender orientation is far better equipped to connect more deeply.

As for ethnicity and religion, some clients prefer therapists who have similar gender orientations, those who prefer someone who has a different orientation, and those for whom the question is less relevant. The client's perspective is more highly correlated with therapy outcome than the therapists'. If a client believes that a person who shares his or her gender orientation will enhance treatment, the placebo effect will likely be greater with that therapist.

A heterosexual therapist may not have an understanding of "being in the closet," risks of discovery, the often agonizing process of "coming out," or all the rules and ethos of an alternative life style. The therapist probably does have an understanding of the problems of romance, dating, missteps, and heartbreak.

Sex of Client; Sex of Therapist

Historically, the preponderance of case studies in all forms of therapy featured female clients and male therapists. The many cultural reasons for this divergence are beyond the scope of this book. However, because of this, there is a considerable imbalance in knowledge about male and female clients. Therapists today are far more likely to be female, and there is far more information about women as clients and an overall feminine bias toward therapy procedures.

A Feminine Bias

Clients are expected to engage in behaviors that are more characteristically female than male. These include talking about problems, vulnerability, seeking help, a focus on and verbalization of emotions, and an openness to discussing personal pain (Osherson & Krugman, 1990; Scher, 1990).

Therapists are expected to express warmth, empathy, openness to emotion, and provide a safe, nurturing environment for discussing difficult topics. Although these conditions are crucial for all effective therapists, they surely seem more on the feminine side of any sexual differentiation. The only balancing male characteristic is for therapists who present as problem solvers. However, as discussed in Chapter 8, even problem solving works best with a strong therapeutic alliance.

With the exception of addiction, domestic violence, and military concerns, women do make up a majority of clients studied. In addition, the profession is becoming increasingly female dominated. Currently, the percentage of female counselors and therapists is around 70% (Carey, 2014;

Diamond, 2014; Shapiro, 2014). In addition, according to the National Center for Educational Statistics (2013), over 80% of current students in master's level graduate programs are women. In fact, in 2014, there were more training programs geared toward treating transgender clients than treating male clients (Shapiro, 2014).

Can a Man Understand What It's Like to Be a Woman?

Over the past several years, several studies (i.e., Sue, 1993) have explored whether it was better to have therapists and clients be of the same sex or gender. The universal finding is that there is no overall difference in outcome. In the aggregate, male and female therapists are equally effective with male and female clients.

However, many researchers and clinicians will argue that the client's desire may be very significant. Sometimes a male client will feel better with a male therapist, sometimes with a female. The same is true for female clients. Although there is no clear data on this, it seems logical to assume that matching a client to a preferred therapist on any dimension (sex, culture, age) could facilitate the work.

One of my colleagues has a name that could be male or female. He has reported several awkward pauses and phone hang-ups when he identified himself. His assumption and the startled responses from a few referrals indicate that the potential new client was anticipating a female voice.

There is in the therapy world a belief held by many, particularly those in recovery and 12-step related approaches, that similarity is an essential component in improvement. The argument has some apparently compelling features. If a therapist herself is a parent, she may have greater insight into a client who is struggling with her children. If she has successfully battled addiction, she may have more compassion for the extent of that challenge. If a therapist has experienced the loss of a loved one, she may be more sensitive than a therapist who has never experienced such an event.

However, the similarity argument also has flaws, especially when carried to the extreme, when it is considered a necessary condition to be effective. A Caucasian male therapist need not have had the experience of being a Korean woman to be of service. A therapist working with a woman facing chemotherapy and probably surgery for breast cancer does not have to be a radical mastectomy survivor to help her client. Most preconditions may only work at moderate levels. At extremes, there would be questionable therapy offered to suicide survivors, clients suffering from psychoses, or those with Alzheimer's dementia. Looking outside the psychotherapy arena, consider the implication for surgeons or coroners.

Like most cultural issues, the most apt therapist is the one who can develop a strong therapeutic alliance and healing intimacy with the client.

Working With the Sexual Minority: Male Clients

It seems strange to think of a minority when it comprises 49.2% of the population. Yet any exploration of the history of psychotherapy indicates that male clients in counseling and psychotherapy are markedly understudied.[6] In a recent book review, Shapiro (2014) noted,

> although it may seem overly glib to describe our field as primarily focused on female clients and uninterested in the implications of gender roles for men, that conclusion is not necessarily inaccurate. Counseling and psychotherapy with men are far less nuanced than they are for women. (pp. 2-3)

The inattention to masculinity reflects barriers in men's use of clinical services (Englar-Carlson, Evans, & Duffey, 2014; Richards and Bedi, 2014). The oft-cited reasons given for the discrepancies between both knowledge of male concerns and men's disquiet around therapy in general are traditional male values such as the "strong, silent type" and male resistance to vulnerability. This perspective ignores how inhospitable therapy may be for men, because of a lack of understanding for the anxieties and needs of potential male clients in general, not just those mandated clients with traditional "masculine" problems.

One useful focus is to recognize that as real as male privilege may be in our culture, the unique client sitting across from the therapist may not subjectively experience any such potential privilege. Men who are poor, unemployed, uneducated, short, physically weak, and those for whom English is not a primary language are unlikely to revel in their social status.

Two relationship areas that are often neglected are a man's relationship with other men and his relationship with his father. In addition, it is common for men to enter therapy with a worry that their deficits will be the sole feature of interest. They respond particularly well to a therapist respecting their successes in the male "prime directive"—to protect and provide.

Regardless of the sex of the therapist, there are some existentially congruent approaches with men that enhance the therapy.[7] Language is one essential component of connecting with male clients (Richards & Bedi, 2014). For example, when therapy is described as a "team" effort as is common in relationally centered existential work, a male client's initial reticence may diminish significantly. Other stereotypically male-friendly terms such as *integrity, respect, trusting one's gut,* and *repair* (Todd, 2009) are more hospitable then their more feminine counterparts, such as *sensitivity, vulnerability,* and *support*. In addition, a shoulder-to-shoulder body position may enhance the notion of working together for a common goal. In general, men prefer explorations that are time limited and have clear expectations. Men frequently are more receptive to communication that preferences the bottom line before the story and single subjects discussed at a time. Self-disclosure (i.e., Westwood & Black, 2012) and humor (Shapiro, 2014a) may also be desirable. Finally, using the client's metaphors and timing are often essential.

Many years ago, I had a sports-minded client who was unable to express his fears directly. He would always begin sessions with a brief synopsis of current sports news. His particular obsession was the Boston Celtic basketball team of the 1980s. Several times, he handed me a videotape of the team's star, Larry Bird. He talked about how his own basketball career ended while he was a freshman at a college known for its basketball program.

C: I actually played a quarter against McHale when he was in college.

J: How did that go?

C: (Laughing) It was a disaster. I was the tallest guy on my team, so I had to guard him in the post. He scored at will.

J: You seem to be enjoying the memory of being taken to the cleaners by a great player.

C: It was worse. I was cut the next week.

J: What are you experiencing now as you talk about McHale and being cut?

C: I had my shot. He was just better.

J: You seemed to be thinking about something then that went unsaid.

C: You mean like I'm a better CFO than he'll ever be? No. I guess it's just that I wish my life was as exciting now as it was in college.

J: Something in particular?

C: Well, it's like there is nobody to pass the ball to anymore. It's all me going one-on-one with the CEO and the board.

J: So Larry has the ball, he gets it into McHale on the low post. Where are you?

C: I'm like DJ (Dennis Johnson, a guard on the team). I'm going to cut off the pick and get the ball in the corner.

J: So you can shoot or you can pass it to Larry or someone else going toward the hoop.

C: I don't want to shoot. I guess that I need to pass. I just don't trust anyone to follow through and score.

J: So you are stuck alone in the corner, double teamed, low probability shot . . .

C: I do this at home also. I won't let my wife help.

J: At work and at home you are trapped in the corner, 24-second clock ticking down. . . . How are you being trapped in here?

C: You won't let me get away with anything.

J: What would you like to get away with?

C: If I give up the ball, I don't know if I'll ever get it back, but if I keep it, I'm trapped.

J: That's a hard dilemma, when the only two choices are rejection or suffocation.

By joining the client in his metaphors, we were able to fairly quickly transition to the here-and-now and his freedom-security dilemma. Each advance in the relational and therapeutic depth was through metaphor about his favorite team.

Emic Redux

In looking at cultural differences, there are a number of continua on which specific cultures may differ. These dimensions may also be used to explore differences within a culture. Therapists who are more aware of the variations within these categories are likely to be more able to join with clients in their manner of being-in-the-world.

Time Orientation

Cultures are oriented differentially around past, present, and future. Customs, rituals, and attention to familial history may provide primary motivation and inspiration for thoughts, feelings, and behaviors. For those clients, a present or future orientation is less central than traditions, long patterns, and ethnic origins. Among cultures with a heritage-first orientation are British, Japanese, and Chinese (Samovar, Porter, McDaniel, and Roy (2007).

By contrast, middle-class America tends toward a future orientation. Dreams, hopes, and aspirations for something better, particularly longer range goals are primary driving forces. Delay of gratification is accepted and desired.

However, those who live in poverty and sometimes those with great wealth in America may have little reason to anticipate a better future and will often focus far more on the present experience. Many world cultures also focus first on the present. According to Spiegel (1982) and Samovar et al. (2007), present-first cultural groups include Irish and Italian immigrants, Native Americans, and many Mexican-American groups (McGoldrick, Pearce, & Giordano, 1982). For them, delay of gratification may be experienced as a lost chance, rather than a stepping stone to the future.

Helping clients involves respecting and working within the client's time orientation. This can be a challenge for therapists with a personal middle-class future orientation. Clients usually need to feel that their cultural sub-group ways are respected before they can sample aspects of the dominant orientation. When there is a time orientation clash with their therapist, it is likely to be experienced as a failure of empathy.

Learning Alternative Time Orientations

In 1974, I was in Jakarta, Indonesia and had to make a phone call to the United States. Although it may seem improbable today, there were only two available pay phones in a square in the middle of the city. Making a call involved a long line and took almost half the day. Initially, in my American middle-class way, I had to resign myself to what turned out to be a 3-hour wait. In my cultural mind, I was relieved to have a novel to read in the hot sun. When I looked up, however, I was struck by the fact that the Indonesians in line with me did not seem impatient or concerned. For them, the line was an opportunity to meet new people, chat, share food and drink, and generally treat the queue as an event in and of itself. Although it was not easy for me, once I was able to experience the line as a chance to get to know others and their culture, the time not only became irrelevant but subjectively moved far more quickly.

Cultures that have a present-first orientation are less clock-dependent and more focused on relationships, traditions, and seasonal changes. In Hawaii, the ongoing joke about time is that people are often on "Hawaiian time" rather than Greenwich Mean Time. The notion wasn't that a person was late for an event, work, or a therapy session. When the person was here, what mattered was the relationship.

In existential therapy, there is an interesting crossover. Sessions begin and end at appointed hours. Yet within sessions, the here-and-now is often the focus of attention. Middle-class clients have little difficulty adjusting to the former. The present moment often requires a learning curve.

Being and Doing

Some cultures, like the one I discovered in Indonesia, focus more on accepting, examining, and relating. Others are more oriented toward speed and productivity. Although the therapist needs to begin with the client's usual cultural orientation (more being; more doing), he or she has to recognize that the major challenge for her client is to risk the anxiety of exploring the nondominant pattern.

Ehrensaft (1987) focused on Western cultures, distinguished a gender difference between men and women on the being and doing dimension. Hollis (1993), operating from a Jungian perspective, indicated that midlife rebalancing often requires an acceptance of the lesser developed part of self. In gender terms, stereotypically for women the new challenge is the doing and for men the being aspects. For many middle-class American clients, the larger challenge in existential therapy is the "being" side.

Individualism and Collectivism

A major divergence in cultural patterns involves the manner in which the individual is considered. Is life primarily about individual growth, achievement, and success, or is it more related to being part of a larger community? Many collective cultures focus more on the group, on harmony, and on interconnectedness. An individual's identity is intimately related to others in his group. Many East and South Asian, Latin, and African cultures tend toward collectivistic ethics. In these cultures, selflessness is held in higher regard than a self-orientation. Individuals are encouraged to act in ways that are best for their family and community. In such cultures, the needs of the many outweigh the needs of the individual. Direct confrontations are best avoided.

By contrast, individualist cultures value uniqueness and self-determination. Standing out from the crowd is more valued than fitting in. Loyalty and harmony are often secondary to success. Many people from Northern European cultures are more individualistic, especially as they immigrated to new world locations such as the United States and Australia. Direct confrontation is possible and even honored. Competition is fostered, with winners and losers.

Individualist cultures may respect the rugged individual sailing away on his yacht, while collectivist ones prefer the tide raising all boats.

Guilt and Shame

As early as 1946, pioneer anthropologist Ruth Benedict distinguished between cultures that used guilt or shame in negative evaluation and moral judgment. Individualistic cultures are more guilt oriented; collectivistic cultures are more prone to shame. In the former, errors or failures of omission or commission are experienced as having let down oneself or others who are close. It primarily involves a self-evaluation, and the guilt may be expiated with an act of contrition.

Shame involves losing dignity, letting down others, often including ancestors or an entire society. The experience is of having what Tomkins, Sedgwick, and Frank (1995) have called "an inner torment, a sickness of the soul" (p. 133). In collectivist-shame cultures, exposure of errors is disgraceful and can be worse than making them. This may make openness and emotional expressiveness somewhat less appealing than control.

When shame is the controlling mechanism, *saving face* might be significant. An extreme example of this in traditional Japan, is *seppuku* (hara-kiri)—a ritual suicide to avoid shaming the family or community group. The Samurai practice was in the service of regaining honor after failure, cowardice, or defeat and designed to avoid casting shame on his community.

Therapists need to be aware of their clients' cultural dictates. Treatment for shame may involve some cleansing ritual, whereas for guilt, introspection and direct corrective action such as making amends or an apology, might serve the purpose. The therapist must be aware of options available to the client, some of which may be outside of the consulting room.

In the mid-1970s, I was treating a Hawaiian couple for both communication and structural issues. After a separation, they worked hard and effectively in therapy, making significant progress. However, she was unwilling to move back into their home because of the shame she felt about the public nature of their problems. After many sessions at a therapeutic plateau, I asked whether there was any way for them to be able to correct the community concerns. She said that the only possible answer was the ancient Hawaiian tradition of *Ho'oponopono*[8], a sacred practice led by a kahuna. They both said that they had been consulting the Kahuna and all believed that I would have to attend for it to be completely pure. After a brief conversation and invitation from the Kahuna, I agreed.

The ceremony itself was very spiritual and interpersonally powerful, especially by comparison to the encounter groups I had been leading. Not only did it have the desired effect, but I was privileged to experience something seldom possible to "outsiders."

Locus of Control

Related to the individualistic-collectivistic dimension is a well-researched variable of locus of control (Rotter, 1990). Just as individuals differ in the manner in which they see their life events, so do cultures. A culture with a more internal locus of control sees reinforcement emerging from what individuals do, say, feel, or think. The opposite end of the dimension, an external locus of control, is one in which reinforcement is viewed as a function of fate, luck, or chance.

When working with clients with an internal locus, best approaches involve active seeking. In clients from external locus cultures, change is mediated by being present, often passively, when events unfold.

Authoritarian and Democratic

Another dimension in which there can be significant cultural differences is the form and manner of power and decision making. Some cultures are far more autocratic than others. In those cultures, status and gender roles are often more circumscribed. Authority is to be trusted and obeyed. There are commonly strict child-rearing practices and limits on opportunities for mobility or choices.

Democratic cultures require that individuals balance the desires for self-advancement and gratification with a moral responsibility for the welfare of others. Because of individual differences, the democratic negotiations of individual and group needs are often less efficient, centralized, and timely.

Professional mental health organizations in the United States primarily espouse democratic rather than authoritarian principles, and most therapists believe in the equality of people regardless of culture-of-origin or gender. As much as therapists believe deeply in equality, we must also hold a pluralistic view if we are to serve our clients better. When working with people from an authoritarian subculture, encouraging their self-determination prematurely or supporting their questioning of authority could put them in jeopardy. Similarly, encouraging parents to adopt more democratic child-rearing practices is useful only if the client does it within cultural parameters and stays in therapy long enough to process the ramifications of change.

Particularly in immigrant families, adolescents, who are more acculturated to the dominant, more democratic culture than their parents, may be prone to express dissatisfaction with ongoing cultural norms at home. It is a therapeutic challenge to help them find ways to express their desire/need for increased freedom in ways that won't be counterproductive.

Sun was 17 years old when she was referred for therapy for "insolence" at home, at church meetings, and at school. Her parents, immigrants from Korea, had many rules for her behavior that seemed far too constrictive to her by comparison to her American peers. During the first session, she expressed her unhappiness with a free flowing verbal exposition that involved invectives and "blue" language, directed at her parents, school, church, and myself.

Despite that initial foray, she stayed in the session and talked with me about her anger and unhappiness about her parents' plans for her education. The key issue for her was her parents' expectation that she live at home and commute to a local college. She wanted to go away for school and wanted "out of that house."[9]

I ascertained that her college aspirations, grades, and SAT scores were in line with her desire, and that finances were not a crucial issue.

J: How have you tried to convince them that you are mature enough to go away to school?

S: I told them that they were still living in Seoul and didn't understand America, and that I would go where I wanted and they couldn't stop me. . . . I told them that I could get by without their money and that if they didn't support me, I could live with my boyfriend in his dorm.

J: *(I can see why her parents are objecting. This seems remarkably self-defeating. Perhaps it's to get me to be parental. Perhaps she is also afraid of leaving the nest. Better to try to join at first.)* This is so important for you, that you are speaking with a lot of passion about it. How is it working so far?

S: It isn't. That's why they sent me to you.

J: So if you continue to approach them in this "righteous" way, the more you are stuck with the conflict.

S: Well, I am not going to cave and just be a nice, little, quiet Asian girl.

J: I believe that! What I am wondering is how the conflict works to keep things the same. What would you have to deal with if they agreed with you and let you go with their blessings?

S: I'd like that. What do you think?

J: I think a part of you would be delighted, and another part might be anxious.

S: No. I just want to get out of that house.

J: And each time you tell them that, in that way, they send you to another professional. Between the principal, the priest, the social worker, and me, you have quite a collection.

S: (Laughing) Okay, Mr. Shrink, what method should I use?

J: I think it depends on what you want. To me, it seems like you want to go away, not too far, somewhere in California, and you want everyone to support you and miss you when you are gone.

S: Not bad. So how do I get that?

J: I don't know your parents like you do. What works with them?

S: Okay, first, I don't even have a boyfriend. I just know my dad wants to keep me a virgin until I marry.

J: We need to help you get your parents' support and also their understanding that you are also anxious about leaving and want to keep in close contact even if you go away?

As a therapist, it was essential that I recognized the two cultures in which she was operating and had to work with her currently self-defeating, democratic needs and the authoritarian culture in which she lives. Working with the needs in one culture and finding the methods within the other is a challenge, but that was Sun's reality.

Hannush (2007) offers an extensive summary of "dialectical dimensions" for therapists to consider when attempting to comprehend client culture from as close to inside as possible. These include, informality versus formality, materialism versus spiritualism, mortality-accepting versus immortality-seeking, nuclear versus extended family bonds, practicality versus idealism, logical versus intuitive orientation, self-made versus birthright, and task versus interpersonal orientation.

Is Existential Counseling and Psychotherapy Multicultural?

The multiple dimensions of differences between culture imperatives bring up an essential question for existential therapists. How may a therapy, based on 19th- and 20th-century European philosophies, serve people from many cultures that have different value systems? Does it fit, even for those of European descent in the 21st century? Does a philosophy that was dominated by male writers, fit for the female experience?[10]

On the one hand, existentialism is individually oriented, self-growth promoting, engaged in the kind of thinking that is underscored by education, open to exploring the meaning of life, and supportive of living with the anxiety that comes with ambiguity. That perspective seems quite narrow from many other cultural perspectives. On the other hand, because of its focus on human universals and a specific focus on the inexorable aspects of the human condition, it may be the ideal transcultural approach.

As much as possible, the therapist joins with the client in his or her world and works from within that unique framework to help the client reach his or her personal, culturally appropriate goals.

Human Universals Across Cultures

Regardless of culture or other aspects of personal origins, there are some givens of human life. Yalom (1980) described four basic universal concerns: mortality, freedom, isolation, and meaninglessness. He argued that confrontation with these "givens of life" produces existential anxiety which may be used to drive individuals to more fulfilling lives.

By focusing attention on a client's struggle with universals, existential therapists are well suited for work with clients from almost any ethno-religious-gender group. Anxieties about loss are not culturally unique. Fears of mortality and questioning the meaning of life on earth are not limited to philosophers. The push to determine one's place in the larger scheme of things does not belong to any subgroup.

Existential psychotherapy is inherently multicultural, because it focuses on the inevitable human struggle for survival and happiness despite hardships and awareness of mortality. From this perspective, suffering in life is unavoidable, and the primary goal is to find meaning in life's vicissitudes, rather than in a fruitless attempt to eliminate or avoid the pain.

Binswanger (1963) identified four worlds that individuals inhabit:

(1) *Eigenwelt:* the uniquely personal realm of personality

(2) *Mitwelt:* The world of interaction and relationships with others

(3) *Umwelt:* A person's natural environment and how he or she interacts with his or her natural world

(4) *Uberwelt:* The world of spirit. This is the part of individuals that reflects the love and affection of ancestors and matters larger than the self (including spirituality and morality).

Van Deurzen (2010) identifies polarities within each of these worlds of experience. In the physical dimension (*umwelt*), it is life/death. In the social dimension (*mitwelt),* the poles involve love/hate, belonging, and rejection. In the personal (*eigenwelt*), it is strength/weakness and the sense of freedom and self. Finally, in the spiritual realm (*uberwelt*), the poles are good/evil, morals, values, beliefs, and meaning.

Noting that other approaches differentially address one of these worlds, Van Deurzen distinguishes existential therapy as engaging,

> *all four dimensions of human existence equally and in this sense is an integrative approach, It will generally emphasize the dimension that requires most work at any one time for a particular person.* (2010, p. 141)

She credits the philosophical basis and stance of existential work that allows for a fuller openness to the interweaving dimensions and paradoxes within and between a person's worlds, regardless of specific cultural orientations.

Vontress and Epp (2015) take a similar viewpoint. They expand Yalom's "givens" into a multicultural realm in which they identify five transcultural spheres and the impact of the manner in which they are held in balance:

(1) Mortality. The only guarantee in all living organisms is death. Thus, although different cultures and religions examine death from unique perspectives, there is no escaping from this fact of life. There may be beliefs in a transformation or spiritual life beyond, a reincarnation in a future existence, or another form of afterlife, but corporeal finality is not in question.

(2) Isolation. Even in the most collective of cultures, individuals live their life with at least some isolation. To some extent, all humans experience life alone. Indeed, in collective societies, the greatest punishments are exile or shunning.

(3) The search for meaning. A third universal is the inherent search for life's meaning. As Frankl (1959a) noted, this is the prime driving force and essence of freedom for individuals. Many events in life are painful, disappointing, or tragic. Frankl insists that regardless of the unfolding events, a person can create meaning from them.

(4) Freedom. In his 17th-century classic, *Leviathan*, Thomas Hobbes described life as "nasty, brutish and short." Existential therapists hold to the view that there is both a freedom and responsibility to choose how to live with, and respond to, any of life's conditions.

(5) The social animal. Humans are social beings. We need others to share and enhance our experiences of life. We connect with others for safety and affiliation. We love and seek the kind of intimacy that Buber described as *I-thou* meetings.

For Vontress and Epp (2015) the "existential cross cultural counselor is a macroscopic and holistic thinker who sees beyond superficial cultural differences to find the imbalance among (Binswanger's) four worlds" (p. 477).

It is the imbalance that leads to emotional distress. The existential approach needs to be "organic" in exploring the four worlds, the interactions between them, and those places where they conflict. Like Van Deurzen-Smith (1988), they note the salience of exploring all worlds with the client, not just the presenting complaint or struggle.

Ideographic and Nomothetic

A few years ago, I noticed on an intake sheet, under the category of "ethnicity," a new client wrote, "see other side." On the blank side of the paper he wrote,

"In descending percentage order, I am Mexican, Spanish, French, Polish/ Lithuanian, Irish, African-American, Native American, and, it is rumored in my family, Incan and Filipino."

Identifying him culturally was interesting. When I read the intake sheet, I asked, "How do you identify mostly?" He replied, "I suppose I am mostly a military brat!"

What is particularly interesting is that there are stereotypical cultural characteristics for each of his identified cultures, but thinking of him along any of these lines was inappropriate without his personal description of the influence of each on his life experience. To what extent is he influenced by characteristics of each or any of those culture identifications? To what extent is he ruled by the universal experiences of all people? To what extent is he "Roberto"?

Existential approaches allow for universals, culturally specific, and individual aspects of human experience. Existential therapists work in both ideographic, deeply individual ways and at two levels of nomothetic understanding (culture-specific and universals). Within this framework there is considerable room to explore with a client a "*welt*" that is uniquely personal, another that involves his heritage (i.e., Italian), a third that includes his significant family group, the one he shares with all others, and the conflicts that interact at multiple levels.

In Chapter 12, we explore some of the clinical applications of culture with a client of mixed-racial heritage.

Notes

1. It is interesting that immigrants from an old world culture characteristically move to new lands at similar latitudes. Thus, Northern Europeans, such as Scandinavians, tend to move to the northern United States replicating climate and diurnal and seasonal fluctuations.

2. On my first trip to Japan as a consultant for the U. S. Air Force in the 1970s, I was handed an article to read on the airplane. Its title, "Sixteen Ways to Avoid Saying 'No' in Japan," conveyed a cultural "rule" that was important to know. Without such information, it would have been easy to inadvertently misunderstand, miscommunicate, or "micro-agrees."

3. By 2014, the percentage of school children from Euro-American backgrounds is already less than 50%, a dramatic shift from the 2000 census.

4. http://www.telegraph.co.uk/technology/facebook/10930654/Facebooks-71-gender-options-come-to-UK-users.html

5. http://abcnews.go.com/blogs/headlines/2014/02/heres-a-list-of-58-gender-options-for-facebook-users/

6. The exceptions are case studies involving addiction, military personnel, and domestic violence.

7. An equivalent discussion of special factors for female clients is not deemed necessary here, because the bulk of therapeutic approaches has been developed with female sensibility in mind. Of course, some male-centric theories may be inhospitable for female clients, but the characteristic work of therapy is decidedly feminine.

8. This sacred ritual, an early precursor of group therapy, included the entire community and, in true collective fashion, could end only when all were willing to forgive and experience peace.

9. It was easy for me to understand Sun's perspective, because it so closely paralleled my own at her age (Chapter 1).

10. An excellent account of women who have been influential in existential therapy can be found in Kass (2014).

11

Life Transitions and Existential Psychotherapy

Life (is a) sexually transmitted disease with a 100 percent mortality rate.

R. D. Laing

Throughout life there are periods of relative stasis interrupted by tectonic shifts that upset the status quo until a new equilibrium can be established. Transitions between these stages often require novel adaptations to both internal and external environments. Behaviors and attitudes that have previously provided a reasonable balance of both freedom and security progressively deliver less of either. The greater the gap between what is anticipated and what is experienced, the greater the increase in insecurity and existential anxiety.

Initially, individuals typically respond to new situational demands by increasing the intensity of what had customarily been successful. When these more vigorous attempts to reestablish the equilibrium fail, they experience a crisis. Existential psychotherapy is particularly attuned to life transitions as periods of both disruption and of growth. It offers clients the opportunity to create a new equilibrium by altering internal experience, adapt to the changed environment, and find meaning in the change.

My former client, Ted, aged 22, described his transition from college to work life,

I know how to do well at school. I follow the instructions, do the work, and perform on the tests and papers. Then all of a sudden, there are no instructions, no clear method to getting a job and no feedback. I really work hard on my application letters, send in my resume to lots of job sites, then . . . nothing. It's like they fall into a black hole. I don't even know why I was rejected.

The more Ted engaged in good student behavior in the new context, the longer his wait to be hired. To make his application stand out to potential employers, Ted needed to adapt to the new environment.

A few days later, I experienced a curious awakening in my own life, when I experienced an earthquake for the first time.[1] Until then, I had a "rule"—*I move, the ground stays still.* It was a comfortable fiction that allowed me to go about the regular business of my life. My new reality had to include massive uncontrollable forces that could change life without warning or my personal planning. There was a new factor in my awareness, one that occasioned a reassessment of the place of my existence in the larger scheme.

Developmental Stages

Developmental psychologists have described certain predictable transitions in life. The progression has been described by use of stage-wise (i.e., Freud, 1900; Erikson, 1963) or process sequence, such as the Piaget's (Flavell, 1968).

Characteristically, the categorizations of life transitions were focused predominantly on the first 15 years of life. Described changes involved both genetic unfolding and social-psychological upheavals. Whether they are viewed discretely as progressive stages or as a repetitious process of assimilation and accommodation, each progressive transition introduced more sophisticated functioning.

Existential thinking and therapy lend themselves well to understanding and treating the process of assimilation and accommodation to an evolving life stage. Although specific challenges and content are somewhat unique during any transition, the underlying process of rebalancing the freedom-security tension points and finding meaning are similar.

The Baby Boomer Generation: Finding Meaning, Facing Fears

The period following midlife is offered as a model of most psychological transitions in adulthood. It was chosen because this transition more directly involves existential themes of losses, mortality, and finding meaning, and because of external factors that makes the baby boomers the first generation to have to face some previously unknown issues.

The population that is currently dealing with the transition that heightens awareness of the importance of time and the impermanence of life is also the largest and most studied cohort in history. Born between 1946 and 1965, the baby boomers still number over 65 million Americans. They are frequent users of counseling and psychotherapy and have been for decades. After midlife, they are destined to adjust to a host of significant challenges.

The opposing forces of freedom and security needs have been well-depicted by two of the generation's preferred visionaries. In his song, "Me and Bobby McGee," most known in the sadly prophetic rendition by Janis Joplin, Kris Kristofferson (1970)[2] focused on the pain of abandonment. The refrain described freedom as "nothing left to lose." Robert Frost (1920) offered an apparently opposite perspective in his famous poem,

Two roads diverged in a wood, and I, I took the one less traveled by,

And that has made all the difference.

Losses Impel Transitions to New Homeostasis

In her *Necessary Losses*, Judith Viorst (1998) addressed a major stimulus to transitional adjustment. She described a variety of losses that force readjustment of the status quo or a surfeit of guilt until the changes are addressed. She stressed the psychologically difficult necessity of accepting limits that come with natural aging.

Many of the predictable, inevitable losses that propel the third quarter of life or "autumn years" transition include deaths of those close; fading physical appearance and capacities; loss of dreams, fantasies, hopes, or expectations; diminution in importance or effectiveness of characteristic roles; and disconnection from new methods, technology, or styles.

The dominant psychological loss is more abstract. It is the frequently reported disquieting sense that without warning, the rules have changed, and that continuation of prior successful adaptations yield lesser or even contradictory outcomes.

Baby-Boomers' Longevity: Good News; Bad News

For this generation at least, significant increases in longevity and social shifts have made later years and retirement far more complex: fiscally, emotionally, and relationally.

In the early 1900s life expectancy at birth was 48 for men and 51 for women. By 2003, men could expect to live to be 75 and women to be 80. Since 1980, life expectancy has risen 14% from 70 to 80. If an individual lives to be 65, life expectancy rises by 15 years or more.[3] What are the implications of this extra time? Do these figures suggest greater, more vibrant health or more chronic illness? What are the psychological challenges for people at what seems an extra stage of life? As Shapiro (2012) has indicated, 60 is truly not the "new 40!" Trying to re-do our younger selves primarily means refusing to deal with the opportunities and challenges of the current age and often emulates Freud's notion of "repetition-compulsion."

Because of new-found longevity and cultural shifts, the boomers are the first generation to have the opportunity and necessity of dealing with a new life stage. Because boomers represent between 25% and 30% of the entire U.S. population, the manner in which they deal with the transitions will likely affect trailing population cohorts as well.

Shapiro (2012) described the benefits and serious challenges associated with added longevity. On the plus side are a plethora of opportunities to grow psychologically and spiritually, to recapture those skills and avocations that were set aside to be responsible adults: earning a living, raising families, growing the community, and so on. The "autumn" years of life offer opportunities to experiment more with fantasies, new careers, avocations, and time to try something that is not part of a personal life program that was chosen before the age of 30. There now is a much longer period for generativity and mentorship (Erikson, 1963).

Yet as optimistic as that appears, there is also a darker side to longevity. The majority of this generation will have to support themselves for an additional 15 to 20 years. The extended needs for financial support, along with the decline in defined benefit (pension) plans, have caused financial experts to provide startling warnings that many boomers are likely to outlive their finances. Social Security benefits will likely be insufficient to keep up with rising living costs, and health care coverage before or after Medicare eligibility is consistently being threatened.

When Otto Von Bismark first set retirement age and state-supported benefits at age 65, very few lived long enough to avail themselves of them. Roosevelt's Social Security age of 65 was also not overly generous, because most died before using the benefits for more than a few years. Sixty-five in 1935 is roughly equivalent to an age of 80 for benefits today.

These realities are a core of concern for many. Indeed, financial issues are one of the primary matters that often arise in existential counseling. The focus is not simply on fiscal planning per se but what money means to clients and how their feelings about money and security drive their postmidlife years. This is also an area for which therapists in general are ill-trained and often uncomfortable (Shapiro, 2014c).[4]

The Times They Are A'changin'

One characteristic of the baby boomer generation has long been to question and alter traditional political, religious, and family structures. A second is their willingness to seek help from therapists, try alternative healing methods, and experiment with diverse spiritual paths. These qualities have continuing value as Baby Boomers pass midlife and begin to face mortality in a far more poignant manner. Coming to grips with the notion that death is not optional or avoidable, regardless of one's diet, exercise program, or wealth, and living with the changes that have occurred in Western cultures in family structure, government support, lifestyles and expectations, is propelling them toward an intensified search for meaning. All of this makes existential therapy uniquely desirable.

Boomers in Therapy

The content of the issues during this transition may be somewhat unique, but the process of realignment of the tension between the push for freedom and the pull of security needs is characteristic of all life transitions. The therapist's goal is to help clients become aware of their desires, the consequences of continuing the status quo, help them face their fears of the unknown, and create a new balance.

Kate (Generational Poster Girl)

For Kate (55 years old), the precipitating event to enter therapy was a recent experience with a professional organizer. "I have always been a collector," she reported, "I was the one of my four siblings that had all of the belongings from our parents' house, furniture, everything . . . The only one with enough storage space in my house . . . Anyhow, this organizer wanted me to toss it all. She kept saying, if you haven't used it for a year, dump it."

She continued, "I am the keeper of the family history. I did the genograms. I was the one who did the genetic heritage testing, but I am beginning to worry if I am just a pack rat." Later in therapy, she would describe a life-long pattern of collecting from philately and Cabbage Patch dolls "in their original packaging," to more recently, the entire set of 50 state quarters.

When I inquired what that meant to her, she continued, "My collections include, among other things, an MA, an MS, and an LLD that I don't use; a (too) big house in a good neighborhood; two ex-husbands; a partner I love and live with but won't marry; two great children out of three; a grandchild on the way; a pile of debt; a good job that is getting boring; and a general question, (she described as) is this all there is?"

As we continued, she acknowledged that her "collection" also included a host of menopausal symptoms like hot flashes; miscellaneous aches and pains; a noticeable loss of energy, hair, and memory; and a need for hearing aids and bifocal lenses.

As Kate described unfulfilled resolutions to clean out the attic, sell the "collectibles," and convert all the photo albums to electronic files, I inquired,

J: When you think of doing all that, what does it bring up for you?

K: Failure. I also have a lot of unused gym memberships and wish we could save more for retirement. Paul and I are both bad at that.

J: Failure?

K: I am not good with money, and none of the men in my life have been either. Paul and I originally planned to retire at age 55, but the dot-com crash decimated his portfolio, and my 401k was wiped out in 2008. I've recouped a lot of those losses, but last year it became clear that to cover retirement expenses, we wouldn't be retiring for 15 more years or so . . . a long time from now, probably in our seventies.

J: As you describe that to me, how does it feel?

K: Like I said, failure.

J: That's your judgment about the state of affairs. What emotions come up for you?

K: My former shrink said that I collect things to avoid dealing with my feelings

J: Such as?

K: Mostly about being left alone I guess. I always fill the house with noise when I am alone, and at work I play music on my computer. I guess I don't like the idea of being alone.

J: Are you experiencing some of that anxiety now?

K: Yes. I know that I very much want to be sure that you like me.

J: And if for some unknown reason, I did not?

K: I'd be devastated. I mean being rejected by the person you are paying to be with you. That'd be terrible.

J: I am not about to do that, but I wonder if we could explore together what is making that anxiety so high now.

K: Paul had an infection after some "minor" surgery and I thought I could lose him.

J: *(This seems like the tip of the iceberg.)* That is scary. Is there more?

K: My oldest daughter is struggling. She is bipolar and has a lot of alcohol problems. We are estranged, but I get updates from her father (Kate's first husband). I feel like she is lost forever.

J: So the losses are piling up, and you are still dealing with menopause and financial issues.

K: (Ruefully) I'm kind of a collector of problems these days.

J: Where would you like to begin to explore those with me? Is there something that is pressing or highest on the list?

K: Paul and I have lost most of our sexual relationship. Even before the surgery, our interest had diminished, and he is also dealing with his mother who has dementia and is living in one of those facilities. He visits every weekend, but she doesn't even know who he is.

J: *(It is interesting that each time she responds to a question, she adds more oblique information, particularly matters that make addressing anything specific very difficult. It's like each response brings a new collection. I could join the cognitive-internal resistance and try one time to focus her attention.)* There are so many interacting issues: bipolar disease, surgery, dementia. It's almost impossible to pull that one thread without unravelling the whole sweater.

K: I hate games like Jenga. I always worry about everything collapsing.

J: There truly are too many things to consider all at once, but I do see one commonality and that's your sense of abandonment, both physically and in time to be together.

K: Sex was always such a huge bond between us. It's hard to, you know, be more routine and comforting than exciting. Paul says he is attracted to me and has never turned me down, but I am no hard body anymore and I, this is embarrassing . . . I miss men ogling me, although I hated it when I was younger.

J: It sounds like everything is coalescing in a way that you are having trouble knowing who you are as Kate and what you'd like out of your life.

K: You know what else has been coming up a lot . . . when Paul's mother goes, we are the oldest in our families. (Voice trailing off and looking expectantly)

J: *(Another distraction. I need to stay with the theme.)* So it's natural to wonder how much time you have left. You are already almost a grandmother. That's a second replacement generation in your family. . . . I guess the big question is how you want to live the rest of your life—what do you want to do with your collected self?

K: (After a long pause) I had this dream last week. I was going somewhere exciting. At first it seemed like Boston or San Francisco, but then it was some unknown place. I was not at all scared, just looking for the next adventure. Then I saw Paul with me. He was happier than I had seen him in a while, and he reached out his hand to hold mine.

J: (*Noticing her smile and also some hesitancy—deciding that exploring the feeling tone in the dream or in session might close her off. Staying more cognitive for now.*) What meaning do you give to that dream?

K: We need to focus on the future, instead of being held down by the past.

J: Is that a new idea?

K: (Laughing) One time I didn't go on vacation because I worried about a break-in and losing some of my stuff.

J: So, instead of sheltering your shelter, your dream was saying to look toward more freedom, and it was possible with a companion.

K: How do I get there in real life?

J: That sounds like something for us to explore. We know how it is if you keep doing what you have been doing. What is the risk of doing some small things differently?

A goal of therapy with Kate was to join her in an exploration of what parts of her security are desirable and what aspects could be inhibiting her quest for a new future. She began the process with her reaction to the organizer. In therapy, she needed to explore in a safe environment, how to move forward with fewer historical burdens or less stuff. It is important to note that facing the financial issues was a major part of the therapy.

Cal and the Status Quo

Cal described himself as a very hard worker who always "tried to do my best and what was expected." He detailed this in an account of his approach to a current dilemma. He had been a client of mine 15 years earlier, in the aftermath of his ex-wife's "sudden, surprising" desertion of him and their three children. Reportedly, she had left him with a secret mountain of credit-card debt that was continuing to accrue.

He worked hard in the sessions and had stabilized his life as a single parent with limited financial resources, save his middle-class salary. Over the years, he would occasionally return for a few "check-in" sessions. In the intervening years, he had divorced his wife (in absentia), got a handle on her credit-card debt, focused on his parenting and work life, and after about 8 years, married a woman who seemed well suited to him.

When he began therapy anew, he was facing the loss of his parental role, which had been a significant part of his life for 22 years, and a great deal of rejection on the job.

According to Cal, the new younger boss had told him repeatedly that he was out of touch and "needed reeducation or to move along."

In the fifth session, I inquired about his coping strategies.

C: I am doing my best. . . . Putting in more hours now that the kids are gone and trying to meet the new standards.

J: How is that going?

C: Not so well. It's like the more I try, the more Jake criticizes and ridicules me.

J: Give me an example!

C: Well 3 weeks ago, I finished a big project early and sent it up to him. Then he sat on it, and 2 days ago, he asked for changes right at the deadline. When I told him it would take a day or two to make the changes (which incidentally were stupid, although I didn't say that to him), he started to scream that I was too old to get the job done on time and why didn't I just go into a retirement home and let someone who could do the job take over.

J: That sounds hurtful, frustrating, and abusive.

C: That's just who he is, you know. He reminds me a lot of Maureen (ex-wife) . . . demanding but offering nothing.

J: *(Deciding not to pursue the ex-wife issue for now. Holding Cal's feet to the fire regarding work).* When he said you are too old, how did that resonate with you?

C: Well, I have three opposing thoughts. One, I think maybe he's right, then I think he's just a schmuck, and then I wonder if I should file an action with HR. I'd probably have to leave the job, but the last two people he drove out got good severance packages.

J: Let's start with the first. Do you think you are too old?

C: Most of the time I don't, but when he yells at me I feel like maybe he's right.

J: And . . . ?

C: Well, then I think of all the ways that I am not as good as I used to be.

J: Would you like to enumerate them for me?

C: (Laughing) No! Bottom line, I can do the job. I may forget some names now and then, and I do have to keep my blood pressure and cholesterol in check, but I can do the job.

J: What's it like to tell me that in such an affirmative way?

C: I guess I have to figure that he is a schmuck, and I have to decide whether to go to HR.

J: That seems daunting. Does it bring up a lot of anxiety?

C: Yeah!

J: So, let's talk about the anxiety of making that kind of decision.

Cal wanted help in establishing that he wasn't "over-the-hill" and someone to reflect the difficulties with his manager. Notice that by joining him where he was questioning and asking the hard questions about meaning, he was able to come to his own decisions. The next phase of the therapy was to explore how he could gain flexibility by shifting his well-developed perseverance to a process focus, rather than intensifying his now anachronistic (trying to please with hard work) behaviors.

An interesting side event to his situation occurred when he went to his Human Relations officer to inquire about the process. She extended him some kindness by letting him know, unofficially, that Jake was about to be fired and suggested that he hold off for a few weeks. Not all oppressed workers have happy stories like Cal's, and he continued his therapy work to explore personal reactions to his changing environment.

Transition Issues

Both Kate and Cal were dealing with aging, loss, and a changing life context; common concerns for members of this generation. Therapists also need to be aware of several other problems. The presenting symptoms are often anxiety and depression, but these are often anxiety-based adaptations to larger shifts in tension on the freedom-security continuum.

Two of the most commonly described issues are relational and financial.

Relational Concerns

Significant relationships evolve throughout the course of a lifetime. Children grow, mature, and become adults. As they do, their relationships with parents commonly progress from dependence to relative independence and sometimes to caretaker. Siblings learn to adjust to changes. Friendships shift in intensity, loyalty, and amount of connected time. Romantic relationships shift in passion and caring. As individuals mature, some relationships, that were once very important, fade away or are broken, while newer relationships become more intense.

Periods of transition often parallel upheavals in relationships if, for no other reason, their differential timing in individuals' lives. Every therapist has heard a client remark, "the relationship is in trouble because I changed, and he didn't."

Primary Relationships

Transitions often put strain on the relationships with significant others. Life adjustments are mandated in transitions from couple to family, coping with infants and young children, work-related stress, parenting adolescents, caring for aging parents, and the empty nest when children leave home.

A majority of baby-boomers are in their 50s and 60s. For most, parenting is less of a day-to-day concern. Shifts in the family context precipitate adjustments in intimate relating as well. Renewal of a one-to-one primary relationship, 20 to 40 years later, can be both challenging and exciting. If a person's primary identification is as a parent, the empty-nest transition may open the door for significant adjustments.

As with most transitions, clinging to the status quo in a changed context is usually deleterious. Many describe the challenge of learning anew about a partner as an adult without the children as buffers. In an attempt to cling to the status quo, some attempt to remain in their adult children's daily lives. Others may focus on "redecorating" their partners in an attempt to push them into greater alignment with personal expectations.

Most experience the stress of facing their fears of the unknown and adjusting to the new circumstances. Some relationships do not survive the adjustment, either breaking apart or settling into an uncomfortable stasis.[5] Others transition relatively comfortably.

Relationally Based Therapy

Because existential therapy is so relationally oriented and focused on the here-and-now and future, it is well-suited for transition-related dilemmas. Having lost a primary role as a parent, clients at this stage of life are often looking for new meaning in life. They are not only looking across the breakfast table at their aging partner of many years, but they are also aware of messages from their own mirror.

Carol, at 56 years old, began therapy with a series of questions.

C: I know this seems off-the-wall, but I am thinking a lot about leaving my husband (of 33 years). He's like this lump on the couch. He doesn't want to do anything, and I am not ready to become my grandparents, waiting to see family or to die.

T: It seems that there are several things going on at once. Elaborate on the feelings and thoughts about growing old and facing the end of your life.

C: Look. It's just that I raised two great kids who are now off having their life, and I want to get back to mine. I want some freedom and I want to live. I don't want to stay around and watch TV all the time.

T: Is that what you are doing?

C: No. Well, yes. We watch the news and maybe two or three programs together. He watches more than me—some sports. It's not like the TV is on 24/7. We have our date night and we go for walks and visit friends. It's just nothing is exciting anymore.

T: What fantasies do you have about excitement?

C: I know better, because I know that dating is hard and unpleasant, but I hear my sister talking about meeting new guys online and it sounds exciting. . . . Her husband left her 2 years ago, and she's just now started to go out with men. She tells me about this one and that one and it's . . . you know like being in college again.

T: So the feeling of being in your late teens or early twenties is enticing in some ways. Kind of like if you were your daughter's age again.

C: Oh well, not like my daughter! She's stuck with her high school boyfriend and is unhappy. I've tried to encourage her to get out of a dead-end relationship, but she's too scared or something. . . . You're smiling. Yeah. You are right. I am still a mom, and if I leave, maybe she'll be able to also.

T: I was thinking that what seems more important is discovering what you want for Carol, not for Kristen. What would a return to your 20s self bring you that is desirable now?

C: I don't know. Really, I wish I did. I do love Herb, but being with him is being with an old man, and that makes me feel like an old woman.

T: Tell me what being an old woman means.

C: I think I need some new challenge to energize my life.

T: Let's explore possible challenges, but first tell me what it's like right now to be an "old woman."

Carol here is midtransition. She had not yet relinquished her mothering role and had yet to plan for her future. She does seem to have some associations with being an old woman, but she is more focused on how external factors such as how her husband's aging is holding her back. In subsequent sessions, she was able to face herself more and come to grips with some dreams and fantasies about her current life.

About 5 months into therapy, she revealed that her husband had begun talking about his own dissatisfaction with their relationship as a couple without children and his own life in general. After an initial panic that he might "jettison" her, she was able to be supportive by sharing her personal concerns and later reported that it was better to be going through the problem together. Like most couples, their encounter with a changing context and their internal reactions were not too well-coordinated. However, her lead was useful to them both.

During a session several months later, she said that she was looking forward to a number of events, and that she would be pursuing new challenges, some with Herb and some alone. In an email sent 3 months after the final session, she revealed, "I know that I am backsliding when I worry about Kristen's relationship with her ex. LOL. I wanted her to leave him and now that she has, I worry that she's alone."

Single After Midlife

Carol was dealing with the transition in a 33-year marriage. By contrast, Pablo was a single parent for many years after a divorce. Working two jobs to support himself and his three sons, he had shown little interest in having another partner. He was proud that all three of his sons were thriving and that he was able to help finance their educations "without (burdensome) debt."

He came into therapy for "depression." In an early session, he described "lumbering" around his empty home, trying to find projects to fill the time.

He claimed that keeping busy kept the sadness at bay, but "I realized that there were only so many tiles to grout and gutters to replace. Then what do I do with myself?"

During intake, I had asked him how long he had been depressed. He responded, "About 5 months, when my youngest went off to school, and my friend passed away." Although I tried to introduce the friend's passing several times, he always changed the subject rapidly, never even mentioning the friend's name. That changed in the tenth session.

P: Sorry I missed the last session. I was at a memorial mass.

J: For your friend you mentioned?

P: Yeah. Vanessa. She died a year ago, and I went to pay my respects.

J: *(First time he mentioned her name—first time I knew his friend was a woman. He may be ready to talk about her.)* What were the circumstances of her passing?

P: She had leukemia for years. It finally caught up with her. (Tearfully) We knew it was only a matter of time, but she had a longer life than expected. We were very close since school.

J: *(Trying to deepen and bring the feelings into the open indirectly)* Tell me about the relationship.

P: Well, after my wife left, she and I spent a lot of time together. She never had any children of her own, so she was close to my boys. She was a good person.

J: So losing her was a serious loss, and soon after that your youngest son left for school.

P: (Deflecting) Yeah. Hey. I was proud of my boys. They all showed for the Mass.

J: That's quite a tribute to you.

P: (Eyes very moist and sniffling) Yeah. They are great kids. I really miss Van . . . Hard to know what to do without her.

About 15 minutes later,

J: At least part of the depression is feeling all alone without the boys at home and without your best friend.

P: I know I should go out and meet someone, but there's no energy for that.

J: It's hard to do that. It's a big move. (After a long silence) What does it mean to you that you are all alone now?

P: I look at those dating websites and look at women, but I don't join any.

J: That's still not in the cards. What would it mean if you did?

P: I'd be really letting Van go. That's the final goodbye.

J: So if you went out with someone new, it'd be like losing her again?

P: Yeah. Exactly! Besides I am over 50, and people tell me that if you put your real age down on those websites, nobody is interested in someone that old.

J: This may sound funny, but I just thought that maybe you have nothing to lose, because you think you are too old for a new relationship anyhow.

P: That's what I like about you . . . always can find the negative. Aren't you supposed to tell me to try, and maybe it'll work out?

J: I could do that, but what if it won't?

P: I could deal with that. It's like now. I am just lonely.

J: It'd be nice to have someone close and lose the "skin hunger."

P: That's a strange word for it, but yeah. I need some skin connection. I just don't want to jump into anything too fast.

J: It's scary on both ends. It's sad to not have a relationship and a lot of anxiety about having one. That does seem like a very real dilemma. I guess you have to decide which demon to face.

Approximately 2 months later, Pablo reported that his sister had fixed him up with a woman from her office. He said that he felt like a kid—not knowing what to do—but she was "kind and friendly."

J: In some ways, you are a kid. You last went out on a date with your ex-wife when you were a teenager. Vanessa was a long-time friend, so it was natural. So in some ways, you're a 50-something-year-old guy with 20-year-old skills in dating, and even those skills are 30 years out of date. It's a lot to learn in a hurry.

P: (Looking pleased—perhaps to be understood) She said I was a good listener. That felt good.

J: (Therapeutic amazement) Maybe, just maybe, you know the most important skill with a new relationship—listening.

P: My sister said third date is the sex date.

J: When you hear that, what comes up for you?

P: (Blushing) I want it (this weekend), but I could wait a date or two more to see if this is going to work out.

J: What's it like to be talking about this with me?

P: It's embarrassing to talk about sex, but you don't seem to be judging me either way.

As a single man, Pablo had to address his empty nest and grief about his friend's death alone. He was also quite unprepared to face the dilemma of anxiety from either rejection or acceptance of a new relationship. He used the therapeutic relationship to explore the fears and, after a few months, begin exploring new romantic relationships. As many in this age group have described, it's no easier than dating as a young person. About 2 years after our termination, Pablo returned to let me know that he had met someone who he liked, and they were slowly pursuing a long-term relationship. He wanted to explore with me the viability of their living together without marrying.

Sexuality

Although he was over 50, Pablo was still a little embarrassed talking about sexual matters. He wasn't particularly unique in that regard. In formal studies of this generation (i.e., Shapiro, 2012) and in the ubiquitous marketing of erectile dysfunction[6] and testosterone medication[7] in popular media, it seems clear that sex is on the minds of today's boomers. As reproduction became less relevant, sex for pleasure and capability for expressing love physically was a frequent topic in responses to open-ended interviews. Despite changes in appearance and physical abilities, sex is very much a part of life after midlife.

Finances: The Last Taboo

As difficult as it is to discuss sexual matters, that reticence pales by comparison to the ability to talk openly about finances. Writing in Victorian times, Freud (1911-1915) observed,

> *Money matters are treated by civilized people in the same ways as sexual matters, with the same inconsistency, prudishness and hypocrisy.*

It is not only psychoanalytic writers who have written about money as a taboo. Whether it involves shame, cultural demands, anxiety, or other intrapsychic phenomena, clients are far more ready to disclose atypical sexual practices than they are willing to report their income.

Financial issues become exacerbated during the autumn transition for a number of reasons: denial about the financial demands for an approaching retirement, ego-attuned competitive score-keeping, embarrassment, shame or guilt about how much or how little they have achieved financially, worries about the therapist's evaluation or anxiety that he or will adjust fees accordingly and charge more.

Retirement Financials

Commonly cited figures on Americans' savings for retirement indicate that a large majority of people will have to live significantly smaller lives once they retire. Dreams of long vacations and a carefree life are simply not going to be available for most who rely on Social Security benefits and a small savings account. In a summary of studies of retirement in America, Reeves (2012) indicated that at age 50, "60% of workers report that their total household savings and investments, excluding the value of their home and any defined benefit pension, is less than $25,000." Minimal estimates by Fidelity Investments are that a couple retiring at age 65 today will need 10 times that amount. Reeves also reported that only 14% of Americans were realistically confident that they had enough money to allow them to live comfortably through their retirement.

The one generation shift from defined benefit pension plans to individually funded defined contribution plans (IRAs, 401k.s, etc.) is especially threatening to those in the baby boomer generation. Many clients look to therapy as they look into a late-life financial abyss.

Underfunded Retirement

Greg had been employed and made a decent salary his whole adult life. "I've been working since I was 14," he repeated as if it were his mantra or badge of honor. He was planning an early retirement at age 62 until he discovered that the combination of Social Security and distributions from his IRAs would force him to sell his home and downsize his living space and his lifestyle. A financial planner, arranged for by his employer, told him flatly that he'd have to work until he was 70 to have enough to live on successfully. A quick review of the numbers suggested that the planner's advice was accurate. Therapy at that point involved having him explore a new reality for his life.

Facing the discrepancy between what he expected and what was actual, was not easy. By his account, Greg had spent his whole life living by the rules, doing things right. In turn, he expected an enjoyable, easy retirement as a reward. His therapist had to be able to provide him with a relationship in which he could rail about the unfairness of the situation and how he felt cheated by assumed promises. She had to confront him on a meaning level without attributing blame and shame to his history.

T: Your meeting with the financial planner was quite a shock and very disappointing.

G: You can say that again! I just didn't figure that I'd ever have to sell my house to live.

T: It's a real blow, especially because you have worked since you were 14, always tried to be a responsible citizen, and you expected that all your hard work would be rewarded.

G: I am angry . . . mostly at myself for being naïve. I just didn't think that I'd have to work past 62 or 65 at the latest. Now it's 70. How old are you?

T: *(Best to be self-disclosing here, but don't want to get into a comparison of relative financial status)* I am going to be 70 in a few months. What does that mean for you?

G: (Tentatively) Oh. I thought you were younger. I guess you like what you do and will just keep working.

T: *(Need to refocus back on him)* I do like what I do. Is that different for you? Do you enjoy what you do for work?

G: Actually, my work is okay. I like the job and my co-workers . . .

T: But?

G: I just always had in my mind that I'd retire early.

T: So it isn't so much that the job is a problem. It's the disappointment. Does it seem like failure to you?

G: Yeah. Failure is part of it. I guess it's also the fact that I am pissed that I didn't know and walked into this trap with blinders on. It's like my whole life was wrong.

T: When you came up against this very inconvenient reality, you have retroactively begun to castigate yourself for what you did in the past. (Several minutes later she continued) Consider this alternative possibility. What you did in the past was successful, but that now with a changing world around you, there are new unexpected challenges that you have to face.

G: So don't blame myself for being stupid. Just deal with what I have to do now.

T: I am suggesting that possibly you were not stupid. You are just like many others who face a longer life and have to begin retirement later than you had anticipated. Have you talked with any friends about how they are dealing with this dilemma?

G: I'm too ashamed.

T: So you feel anger, shame, and alone all at once. And you don't feel like you can discuss this topic with your friends and co-workers.

G: Only you and the financial planner know now.

T: Would it be more shameful if others knew, even if they had similar concerns?

(At the end of this session, as Greg was leaving the door)

T: (Enhancing the fellow traveler relationship) I just thought that even when we do everything right, we don't always get the result we thought.

The Numbers Are a Symptom

Rick had the opposite problem. His inflated imagination of what he will need had him working in his mid-60s almost without reflection, despite several million in the bank. An executive in a large publically traded Silicon Valley firm, Rick's gross annual salary was in the high six figures. He and his wife owned a multimillion-dollar home in an exclusive neighborhood, and they also had considerable savings.

When he began therapy, he described being worried about finances, particularly his wife's spending. He was dressed casually without ostentatious accoutrements of wealth, except for the expensive auto in the parking lot.

The precipitating event for therapy was a very poor quarter for his company and some questions about his continuing success by the Board of Directors.

R: They really gave me the once-over about this quarter . . . down from the third quarter last year.

As is my wont with new clients who present with financial issues, I had checked in advance publically available information about his company. The news was in general very positive.

J: I thought I read recently that your stock broke out to a new high with stellar annual results.

R: Old news! Year-over-year we will be up 16%, but the new subscriber base did not grow this quarter.

J: You've been around a while. What's happened when this occurred in the past?

R: A lot of pressure from the venture capital guys on the board, but even in bad years when the stock was a third of what it is now, it always worked out.

J: So why the worries this time?

R: I'm 64, and if I lose this position, nobody else will want me—too old.

J: *(Report that I heard his concern, but also introduce some external reality to see how he responds)* Well, in your industry, a new position in your 60a might take some time. I've heard of 18 months as a minimum and then no guarantees.

R: Eighteen months is about what I am told also. (Exhales and relaxes) So you know the pressure I am under.

J: I'd like to know more from your perspective.

R: I make a lot of money now, and I have a lot of options and long term investments, but all in all, they are less than ten (million dollars). I don't think it's enough, and we might have to sell the house and move out of the area just to survive.

J: Do you have a figure in mind as to what you might need to safely retire?

R: Maybe 20 to 25 (million).

J: *(Need to do a reality check here)* I know you travel in wealthy circles, but can we just do a quick check here? (When client nods) Do you have a rough sense of your fixed expenses?

R: Maybe $400k. Our mortgage is high, and Lili's spending is also way up there.

J: So very rough figuring, worst case scenario, if you need $400k, you need to have eight mil to generate that kind of income, without touching the capital. That doesn't take into account Social Security, a severance package, or a house sale.

R: How did you do that in your head? My financial guys came up with pretty much the same number, but they took three weeks.

J: *(I am feeling proud here—danger that I could miss the angst he's feeling.)* The question is, what makes you worried when your financial experts tell you it's okay?

R: I don't know. Most of the people around me have 20 (million) or more, and they are all worried.

J: I am interested in *you*. What makes *you* worried? You are clearly out of the running for being the richest guy in the cemetery.

R: Very funny! (Chuckling) I have been thinking a lot about what comes after.

J: About dying? Say more about that.

R: Well. I am not religious. I just don't know. I'm not neurotic about it. I just wonder what my life is all about. Last summer, we were out at the cottage, and my son and one daughter were out on the lake fishing, and we got talking. They were thanking me for the blessings in their lives, and later I was lying in bed and thinking, what are my feelings of being blessed? That's when I started to think about my life ending and what it all meant.

J: When you have those thoughts, what comes up for you?

R: I mostly shut them down and think about the business and the new competition, and it just goes on until I fall asleep.

J: So one way to avoid thoughts of dying is to immerse yourself in the business. It's almost as if the more you focus on having to make more money, the less you have to think about your life ending or what it means in the bigger picture.

The session ended soon after that. Rick cancelled the next two sessions for work-related travel. When he came back in, he spent a good amount of time talking about a potential buy-out of a competitor and other business matters. With about 15 minutes remaining, I asked him,

J: I know you have been very busy and consumed by the work, but I wonder if you have given any thought to what we talked about last time.

R: You mean about the blessings? Yeah, I was thinking that my kids are all great blessings and my granddaughter is the light of my life. And before you ask me how it felt, it felt terrific . . . but then I got sad.

J: At least in part, your legacy is in the next generations. That's pretty big. Any idea about the sadness?

R: I don't see my oldest daughter and granddaughter enough. They don't live that far away. I just don't get to hang out with them. My daughter and her husband are both driven to be successful and they are doing well—very busy.

J: Their work/success is another thing to be proud of. I just wonder if the sadness is about the loss of more personal contact with the three of them.

R: There's actually four. They also have a baby boy. I don't relate as well to babies as I do children. (Smiling and pointing to a shelf containing a book I wrote on fatherhood) That's normal isn't it? (Laughing)

J: That's a good one. I am struck by how your work keeps you from thinking about your mortality and life meaning, and your daughter's work keeps you from the "light of your life." It seems a real dilemma. Work gives you some benefits and takes away others.

R: I want to talk about my wife's spending. While I was away, she hired an architect to draw up plans for a remodel of our house—mostly the kids' old bedrooms.

J: (Smiling and holding my neck) Help me out here. I almost got whip-lash from that change in direction. Tell me how that relates.

R: It could cost a half a million before she is done.

J: *(The marital issue is important, but I want to hang in a bit longer.)* That sounds really important, but I sensed that when the new topic began I experienced a lot more distance in the room.

R: I just don't like to talk about missing Alana (granddaughter).

J: I think it's worth noting that a focus on money, expenses, and finances get us away from feelings about life being short, missing time with your blessings, and even a shift in our relationship.

Rick persisted in talking about the wife's plan for spending. It was three sessions later before we came back to pursuing money as avoidance of life. For Rick, the fantasied competition with those who had far greater wealth, one which he would always lose, was his retreat from fears of the unknown. Over a 3-year course of therapy, including his wife's lengthy recuperation from surgery, he refocused on the limits on his life and worked hard to capture the parts of life away from the financial distractions. When work became "too offensive and oppressive," Rick took a severance package. When therapy ended, he was interviewing for a position as a consultant and board member of another prominent company. He opined that he liked the potential new position because it was part time and "I am still short of the 25 mil, but it's okay, isn't it?"

Relational issues and financial issue can arise during any transition. They do seem more poignant after midlife, because there is presumably less time in life to correct problems.

Time

Because time is the only truly limited commodity in life, it is the most precious. The particular amount of time in each life remains an unknown, but the task of allocating whatever time is available and making choices in the present are the essence of existential work. Regardless of expected longevity, the one guarantee in life is death. At midlife, the symbolic hourglass is turned over and, for most people, the subjective experience of passing time accelerates, making decisions at this life-stage more poignant.

Time and Therapy

Time is often an elusive issue in life and in therapy. The poet Carl Sandberg warned that "time is the only coin we have to spend in life and that there is danger in allowing others to spend" one's personal time. Clients frequently enter existential therapy with time-related concerns: how time is being spent; the extent to which the time allocations reflect what is particularly meaningful; a balance in time for needs versus wants; a sense that work or chores expand to fill any available time allotted; how much time is needed for success, happiness, or the future; a sense that life is passing by; and the question, when is it "my time?"

In a successful life, time allocation is related to life stages. The boomers today are faced with using time differently than they did when they were in their thirties. For the most part, clients in their 50s and 60s are no longer putting primary emphasis on building families and careers or trying to build for a better future for themselves and their children.

A unique challenge for this transition involves reassessing a lifelong middle-class modality of deferring gratification. Often the goal in therapy is to encourage clients to live more fully in the present. After a lifelong orientation of saving for the future, it is challenging to refocus on today. Clients need support to revise their time allocations to what is most cherished, creative, and enjoyable. That was reflected in the "richest man in the graveyard" intervention with Rick.

Bill was generally considered to be "one of the good guys." He was always available when a neighbor needed a flat tire fixed, a ride to the hospital or airport, or assistance with a home project. He was the "go-to" guy at the PTA. According to his wife, he did more than his share of housework and childcare.

The impetus for his coming into therapy was a call from his sister. She wanted him to take care of their mother, who lived near her (3,000 miles from him) for a 6-month period, while she and her husband went on an extended vacation. He said that he felt awful and guilty when he turned her down, but he had already made three trips back to the East Coast this year to be the mother's caretaker, and he had offered instead to move the mother in with him. His sister angrily broke off contact.

In the initial sessions, Bill spent a lot of time justifying his actions. I saw two interrelated issues: his excessive need to please others regardless of cost to himself and the appropriation of his time by others in his life. I suspected that there was a lot of hurt and anger underneath, but if that supposition was accurate, it wasn't evident.

In the sixth session, after a lengthy explanation of how his wife was putting pressure on him to spend some time on himself, I intervened,

J: Her support and expression of caring somehow comes across as pressure.

B: I know she loves me, but I don't have time for that. I have to deal with my mother from a distance, my sister isn't talking to me, I have three meetings at school next week, and my boss just asked if I could head up a new project.

J: I get exhausted when you describe your life.

B: Well, I have a lot of energy, and I can get through it. The project is the most important one for the company, and it's an honor to be asked.

J: Because of your energy and competence, you get asked a lot, and it sounds like you usually come through.

B: Well, that's what is expected, and if I can do it, why shouldn't I jump in?

J: On one level it does seem honorable that you take on so much. . . . I guess I am thinking, (very slowly) and this is unfair . . . if I were on a project with you, if I wanted it to be done really well, all I'd have to do is be incompetent.

B: What, (pause) what do you mean?

J: I could count on you to pick up whatever needed to be done. I could even go home early with confidence that when I came in in the morning, everything would be done.

B: Well, do people really think that way? That seems unfair.

J: Yes. I told you it would be unfair. And I can't speak for others in your life, but I thought of it in here. Maybe that's why your sister is so mad. It's the first time you didn't do everything, including leaving your family and working at a distance for her vacation.

B: (Anxiously) But if I don't do it, nobody will.

J: Well, we don't know that. They don't have to try if good old Bill is around. I even wonder if sometimes, some people might feel cheated out of a chance to be the hero, because Bill is there before they get a chance.

After a long pause, Bill remarked, "so you think my wife is right. Maybe I do need to do something for myself."

J: Let's not worry about right or wrong here. If you had free time, how would you spend it? *(Trying to take the edge off)* I know you don't, so this is only speculation. What's your fantasy?

B: I have two. I would take my wife to Hawaii to see the volcanoes, and my brother and his friend are going fishing up in Oregon next month. I like fishing a lot.

J: Doing something very nice with your wife and doing something you really enjoy. What's the best part about fishing?

B: Peace and quiet. Lots of time to think. This may sound dumb, but I don't even care what we catch.

J: Actually, it doesn't sound dumb. The focus is on the time you spend reconnecting with Bill, not the outcome.

B: Well, that's what you were saying last week about liking what I am doing instead of just jumping in to whatever anyone wants.

J: Hmm. That seems like an important connection. . . . I have another off-the-wall question. What would you have to deal with if you didn't jump in so quickly?

B: Like my sister. Nobody would like me.

J: You are only liked for what you do for others. Hmm! I just had a thought about that. You worry about being rejected if you don't do what others want, and yet, your wife, who you know loves you, wants you to spend more time for yourself. That doesn't seem to go together.

For Bill, allowing others to determine his time and priorities was a way to avoid addressing a great fear of abandonment and also a fear of a give-and-take intimacy. This combination is not unusual for many men as they traverse this transition phase of life.

I can't report that the fishing trip allowed him the kind of respite and chance to think that he had anticipated. It was instead, a comedy of errors. The motor on the boat wouldn't start, and Bill and his brother spent 2 days getting it to work. On the last day, the three men caught one fish but were cited and fined for taking a fish that was too small. He came back exhausted. We were able to use the "disaster" as a way to refocus on his using his own time in his life. Later in therapy, he told me that my idea of fishing did not work out for him. Rather than point out that I had not made that suggestion, I agreed and we both laughed that it truly did not work out as hoped. I then commented,

J: Even though I blew it with the fishing trip, you don't seem to care less for me.

B: No, of course not! Everyone makes mistakes.

J: Everyone but Bill. Sometimes it's the things we screw up that endear us to others. Maybe you don't have much experience of that.

B: You think if I screwed up people wouldn't hate me.

J: I can't say that. I just know that you saw me as screwing up, and you don't seem to hate me for it. In fact, we were laughing about it together. Perhaps your wife and others who love you might react positively.

For Bill, the issue of time pointed to other issues of intimacy. For Mindy, time was the essential concern.

When we first met, Mindy was 49 years old. She was teaching English and creative writing at a local community college. Recently divorced from a husband with addiction problems, she was eking out a living on her modest salary. Two of her three children had moved back in with her in a small two-bedroom apartment within walking distance from her job. She described the situation as "temporary" and that both sons living with her were helping out in the home. One was looking for work as a musician; the other was applying for his junior year at a state university.

She was referred by her primary care physician for anxiety and depression. She rejected his recommendations of selective serotonin reuptake inhibitor (SSRI) medication. To make ends meet, Mindy was teaching overload classes and had over 120 students in her classes. She was working on her own novel but found "precious little time for any thinking or writing." She said that she came to me because I was an author and "knew what it was like to face a blank page." When I asked what that meant for her, she provided me with a story. In fact, whenever she was confronted directly she responded with apt, erudite but indirect metaphors.

M: I came to see you because I can't get any time for myself, and I need some help planning.

J: What have you done so far? No sense going over things that don't work.

Mindy's reply to that involved stories about Hemingway, Samuel Johnson, and Ovid but no specifics on what she had tried to do to carve out some time. Then she asked me, "How do you find the time to write?"

J: (*Very aware that she will reject any specific plan of action*) What I do, probably won't work for you. I prioritize my writing time. When I set up my schedule, aside from classes I have to meet and the hours that I engage in therapy, which are set, I set aside 2 hours a day as the first item on the schedule.

M: (*As expected*) That would never work for me. I have too many student e-mails and papers. I get almost 75 e-mails a day that I have to answer, and I read and edit my student papers several times until they get them right. There aren't 2 hours left in the day.

J: That's why I didn't think it would work for you. Let's talk about the past few days and how your time was spent.

M: Okay. Today is Wednesday. This morning I awoke at 5:00 a.m. as usual, and I worked out for an hour, then I made breakfast. By seven, I was online dealing with student e-mail until 8:30, when I took my son to the doctor, and then I came here. Well, I read a few student papers when I was waiting for him. After this, I have two classes, then papers, supper, then more papers and e-mail and preparing for tomorrow's classes. Monday and Tuesday were similar except no doctor's appointment or coming here.

J: Certainly no time for your own writing or anything else for yourself.

M: That's me—Sisyphus with a rock of e-mail and student papers.

J: Who in literature would you like to be?

M: That's not easy. I don't think of characters as much as novelists—so who would I like to be—maybe Gabriel García Márquez or Charles Dickens.

J: Two writers who get our attention with great first lines. Is it for you "the best of times, the worst of times" or more like "Many years later, as he stood facing the firing squad. . . ."

M: I don't know how to start like that. When I write, I don't know where I am going.

J: It's rare to start with such an amazing sentence. For you, creativity takes an unknown path. I understand that. I write my first chapter after everything else is done, and I figure out the course my journey took.

M: They aren't buried under a mountain of e-mail.

J: *(Suddenly a very relevant song entitled, "Did Beethoven Do the Dishes?" came into my consciousness.)*[8] I wonder if you are on to something there?

M: I have to answer the students' concerns and questions. I always give them my cell number.

J: That's an interesting supposition. I wonder if it's accurate. I have a colleague who teaches college freshmen who doesn't allow either computers in his classrooms or any electronic communication.

M: I couldn't get away with that.

J: Would you like to?

She responded with a lengthy and confusing, reference-laden monologue about her philosophy of teaching and how she had many seminar classes in college, where her professors were always available.

J: Many of my classes were like that also, but my profs only had around 40 students total in a semester. You have 120 plus in a quarter.

As soon as she responded, with her philosophical beliefs about how teaching was a calling, I realized that logic of this sort was an error. It took two sessions before we got back to the issue of her being inundated.

M: I think I set a new record. I actually had my son count it up. Over the weekend, I had 38 student calls on my cell and 128 e-mails. I got 10 e-mails and two phone calls from one student alone on Sunday morning from midnight to 3:00 a.m. I'm worried about her. I can't seem to reach her by phone or e-mail.

J: You think she was in crisis?

M: No, she's done this before. She doesn't have anyone to talk to, and it gets bad on Saturday night because her roommate has a guy staying the night.

J: That's a lot of responsibility for an English teacher.

M: I know. I know. I told her to go to the counseling center, but she prefers talking to me.

J: That seems a little like a blessing and a curse.

M: So what do you do in that situation?

J: *(Go indirect. A direct self-disclosure will not go anywhere. It's hard to imagine being available by cell phone 24/7 and e-mail to students. I will join her process with a story.)* Did I ever tell you about the time I called Dr. Benjamin Spock?

M: (Leaning forward with interest) The "Child and Baby Care" guy?

J: Yeah. I wanted to ask him to do a preface for a book some years ago. Anyhow, I got his number and phoned him in Maine. I got his answering machine, the recorded message said, *"My phone hour is from 7:00 to 8:00 a.m. on weekdays. If you want to reach me, call between those hours."* I thought that was a great way to manage both conversation and intrusions. Even more so, when I set my alarm and awoke at 4:00 a.m. Pacific Time and called. To my delight, he answered, "Hello, this is Ben," and we were able to talk. I thought that was brilliant. I would like to do that myself but haven't got all the way there yet.

Mindy just looked off in the distance and stared for a minute or two. Then she asked, "didn't you feel put off by the message?" "Just the opposite," I replied. "It was a clear message of when I could reach him. No phone tag. No multiple calls. Just call at a specified time."

M: I think I am very bad at setting limits and put off time for myself till everything else is done.

J: There's an old rule in business, "Pay yourself first!" Don't just accept what is left over, because there will be nothing left over. That's about money, but time is the only commodity that is fixed. So paying yourself with time first . . .

The interventions were necessarily indirect: a story about another person and a reference to money made it somehow acceptable for her. Three weeks later, she brought in her proposed syllabus for the new term and asked for my opinion. The following words appeared: "In order for me to provide you with the best service, I have expanded my office hours, now including one hour on Friday afternoon at 1:30. I will be available for your questions at regular and expanded office hours. I will also take calls on my office phone only and will respond to e-mails at those times. If you want to contact me, please use those times."

J: How does it feel to think about giving that out?

M: Mixed. I am worried, but I checked with my department chair, and she said it was great and thanked me for the extra hour to meet students. So I'll try it. I also have to miss the next session during quarter break, my friend and I are going camping at Big Sur for 2 days, and I am going on a 2-day writer's retreat near Monterey, before school starts.

J: That sounds wonderful. I'll see you in 3 weeks. Remember, I am off the following week.

Electronic Leashes and Time

Mindy represented for me an increasing phenomenon. She was on an electronic leash. Many seem to be relinquishing freedom and quiet time to be permanently connected online, whether by call, text message, social media, or e-mail. A few years ago, I challenged my colleagues by offering to treat for lunch if they could find an undergraduate walking on campus unconnected to a cell phone. I didn't have to pay!

Electronic connection is especially important for existential therapy, because it dissipates opportunity for *I-thou* moments. Even video phone contact may serve as a buffer against, rather than facilitator, of intimacy. In addition, being constantly available and semiconnected, also forces us into creating harder boundaries for our time. Mindy was an extreme example, but many clients leave their cell phones on vibrate even during sessions: essentially an acknowledgment that their personal time is less important than that of anyone else who might want to contact them.

The issue of time for self is often a crucial issue in breaking free from the tentacles of the status quo and facing fears of being in the world alone and free. Often, it is that very issue of questioning the need for connection to the outside world during sessions that opens the in-session intimacy.

J: I notice that you are checking your cell phone for incoming messages. Is there something crucial that you are concerned about?

M: No, not really. I just like to see who's trying to contact me.

J: It's fine to continue doing that, but what do you think would occur in here if the phone was shut off like on a plane?[9]

M: I don't ever turn it off unless I am boarding a flight.

J: What do you suppose would happen if you did? Is it worth a quick 15-minute experiment, just to see what it'd be like?

This would not apply if a client said on entering that she had a family member in the hospital and was waiting to get a doctor's report. It is more the issue of disconnecting for freedom and preserving time.

Therapist Time

The issue of time is a unique concern for therapists and other professionals who basically sell their time to make a living. We provide expertise and training, but unlike manufacturers of widgets, we can only turn into remuneration those precious hours of the day.

Like our clients, therapists are choosing to allot their time to the therapy hour. This also brings up personal financial issues for therapists in private practice. How much is charged? Do I have a sliding scale? There may be a unique dilemma for therapists who are on managed-care panels. Not only are others filling the calendar, they are also determining the worth of a therapist's time.

Additional Issues for Boomers in Transition

Relationship, financial, and time worries may be exacerbated by the post-midlife transition, but they are common denominators in most transitional shifts throughout life. There are also challenges that are germane in the postmidlife period. These include concerns about health, mortality, spiritual matters, and the "shadow."

Health

Aging comes with necessary breakdowns in physical capabilities. Ling was referred to therapy for depression, pursuant to a knee replacement. He was grappling with worries about not being able to continue a number of physical activities, especially playing tennis. Guy was a former hockey player who was now suffering from severe sciatic pain. Esther had encountered multiple complications of menopause and ultimately a hysterectomy. Although she did not want to get pregnant again, the surgery caused her a great sense of loss and of aging. Many clients have had to deal with a variety of cancers or illnesses that forced considerable restrictions on their physical activities. Almost every client at this age described memory concerns, especially the elusiveness of nouns in attempts to recall. The loss of specific memory retrieval led to feelings of being less capable and a great fear that this was an early sign of dementia.

Three of my university colleagues now sport new high-end hearing aids, and almost everyone has eyeglasses or contact lenses. I can recall a personal "existential" moment on a softball field when I was in my late fifties. I had always been a decent ball player and especially was a reliable hitter. As I came up to bat, I was wearing my newly fitted progressive trifocal eyeglasses. I had quite a surprise when I swung and missed badly on a pitch that I had envisioned flying out of the park for a home run. When this happened repeatedly, I became aware that where I saw the ball as it passed through the eyeglass zones was not where the ball actually was. This was brought home vividly again, when I was in the field. A fly ball seemed to jump around in my vision, before I made a lunging catch. The clear message: My identity as a good ball player was no longer accurate. In the next game, as I tried to run out a base hit (without my glasses), I managed to pull something in my leg. The injury which had occurred previously when I was younger and healed within a week, took my almost 60-year-old body nearly 4 months to be right. My orthopedist's diagnosis: "Jerry, you are getting old!"

Another curious example I have personally shared with clients is the impact of necessary surgeries to remove body parts. The rather strange phenomenon was summed up by a woman who had a mastectomy at age 55.

W: Since puberty, my breasts have always been a part of my identity, of how I saw myself. Now, even though there is reconstruction, it's like who am I? I don't suppose a man can understand (weeping), and I knew I had to do it to save my life, but now it's like whose life?

T: It's hard to know who you are with such an important part no longer yours. Does it seem that the reconstructed breast itself is somehow alien?

W: Yes. I would not have used that word, but it's like I am damaged and unfixable.

Health in Earlier Transitions

Sometimes, health issues demand transitional adjustments for much younger people. Several former combat veteran clients expressed similar feelings about missing limbs. As one put it, "The only part of my right leg I have left is phantom pain; basically a reminder that it should be there but isn't." With each of them and with W. the question involves self-identity. Explorations of who am I now without the organ, limb, body part, or capability are usually best done directly, helping the client explore what it's like to be missing parts of how they defined themselves.

One group of people who have particular concerns are former athletes. In my career, I have worked with professional and college athletes whose careers were ended by injury or physical failure, which had a significant impact on self-identity and self-esteem. As one former professional athlete queried, "Who am I, if I am not a football player?" His query was echoed by many others, whether their athletic skills also involved their income or whether it was, as Katrina reported after a serious skiing accident, *"I am a skier, hiker, biker, mountain climber. Well, at least I was all that. Now, I'm just a high school math teacher? Don't get me wrong, I love teaching, but I always thought I was all those other things as well."*

Mortality

R.D. Laing (1960) once opined that life itself was a sexually transmitted disease with a 100 percent mortality rate. Death is the only certainty for all living beings. Awareness of that inevitability produces an existential fear that drives individuals. Yalom (1980) wrote,

> *The terror of death is ubiquitous and of such magnitude that a considerable portion of one's life energy is consumed in the denial of death.* (p. 41)

For Yalom (2009), the fear of death is the core anxiety about the human "givens" and the prime generator of avoidant neurotic anxiety. During the autumn years of life, these mortality fears may emerge through work changes, relocations, the advent of retirement, children leaving home, financial realities, and losses of others. Changes in both external and internal environments generate anxiety and often feelings of isolation. Commenting on the inevitability of both death and change, Frankl (1959) wisely observed, "When we are powerless to change the outside world, we may only find success by changing ourselves."

That is the essence of existential therapy at this life stage. Intimacy and living more fully in the present provide a healthy alternative to death anxiety. By contrast, often clients clutch to presumably life-preserving precautions to stave off the inevitable. They cling to the status quo, even as change is swirling about them and those previously effective actions are no longer as successful. Although reasonable safety precautions are wise, excessive movement toward security precludes freedom and a life well-lived. Seeking the moving balance between these two polarities is exacerbated by attention to the relative shortness of life. In the fifth session of an 18-month course of therapy, Candace (55 years old) told the therapist,

C: I had my annual check-up this week and all systems are apparently pretty good for a woman my age. That's the good news of the week.

T: And . . . ?

C: My dreams of being marooned and of Joe leaving me keep coming up. I've also been worrying needlessly about my daughter getting Ebola or some other horrible virus in Kenya.

T: How do you understand these worries?

C: I don't know. There have been a lot of deaths announced at my church lately. Three women my age died in the past few months. It's shaken me.

T: What were the causes of their deaths?

C: Well, one had a terminal illness and—nobody is supposed to know this—had an assisted suicide. Another one died in a car crash. I don't know the third. I think it might have been a heart attack.

T: (Looking for death anxiety) Those deaths make you feel more vulnerable. Like maybe your time is coming up?

C: (Staring at the therapist with a "deer-in-the-headlights" look)

T: You look startled. What went through your mind when I brought up your mortality?

C: I guess it happens to us all, right? I didn't think anything, just had a feeling in the pit of my stomach, like fear. I have been occasionally thinking that I'd like to do something new and different while I still have time, but it's all fantasies.

T: I like fantasies. What are some of yours?

Candace began to ponder her legacy on her job and at home. She reported that Joe was very cautious, loved routine, and would not be interested in some of her "wild ideas." In this way, she had Joe to keep the status quo and could have flights of fantasy, but the internal conflict was causing some frightening thoughts and dreams.

About 4 months later, she reported,

C: Joe didn't want to go, but I forced him to see *The Bucket List*. I love Morgan Freeman. You know it's Hollywood, so unrealistic, but it was good to think about.

T: To think about your own bucket list?

C: Yeah. Mine is much more modest. My daughter has a midsemester break in Greece next month. She asked me to meet her there. I am thinking about going.

T: That seems like quite a tribute to you to have your daughter want to spend her break with you and to share Greece together. What are the hesitations?

C: Joe won't go for sure. He doesn't travel to any place where they don't speak English. What if something happens? I thought the plane could get hijacked or crash.

T: Well, let's talk about that. You could die in such an event.

C: (Smiling) Aren't you supposed to reassure me, that it's safe?

T: (Also smiling) What if I did?

C: I wouldn't believe you. So you think I should go?

T: The big questions here are (1.) do you want to go, and (2.) What if you didn't? Would you be giving up something on your "bucket list"?

Note that the therapist held up for Candace the death anxiety and provided both risks of security and of freedom. An interesting sidelight to this discussion was that Candace did go, had a good time with her daughter, and had some trying adventures as well, including spending 40 hours in the Athens airport with flight problems.

When she returned, she claimed to be "done travelling for a while" followed by, "I am taking Joe to Ireland for his 60th next year. He has a mess of relatives there, and he has always wondered what would have happened to him if his grandparents hadn't emigrated. . . . That's the one place I can probably get him to go." Toward the end of the session, Candace opined, "I guess I could die on a trip like that, but I could get hit by a cable car in San Francisco also, and I want to see some places before I am too old—I suppose I found my bucket list."

Poignant Worries About Mortality

I had been seeing Andy intermittently over a 5-year period. When he came in for a session following his 61st birthday, he looked atypically depressed.

He reported that he had an onset of weakness in his arm and neck and that he had fallen when he got out of bed. During the session, his left hand was shaking. When he said that he had not seen a doctor, I recommended that he see a neurologist as soon as possible. He seemed very worried when he left, but when he returned in 2 weeks, his anxiety was higher than I had ever seen.

A: They think I have "Lou Gehrig's." I'll know in a week when they do some more tests to rule out other possibilities.

J: Oh my goodness! How are you dealing with that?

A: Well, you know me. I'm an internet junkie. I've been reading about everything. It's not good. It will kill me in probably 3 to 4 years. Nobody knows how much time, but it's a degenerative disease. Did you know when you saw my hand shaking last time?

J: No! I was just concerned. As you read all this stuff online, what is coming up for you?

A: I will deteriorate and die and there's not much that can be done. Do you know much about ALS? There are some new experimental treatments, but they really don't know much about the success rates.

J: *(Feeling very sad. I was also thinking about a classmate who died from ALS and two friends who have advanced stages of Parkinson's disease.)* This is a real blow. I can only imagine how hard it is to take in.

A: I'm still denying that it's ALS. I have to wait for the next tests.

In the remainder of the session, his attention turned to work problems. I was unable to keep the focus on the "elephant in the room." When he returned 2 weeks later, he began the session saying that he had a tentative diagnosis.

A: Well, I probably don't have ALS, but the news is still not good. It's some kind of progressive muscular deterioration that will, in fact, have me in a wheelchair and needing help just to feed myself. It's a lot slower than ALS, but I will probably not make another 10 years.

J: So the good news is that you have more than a few years, but still not as long as you had imagined, and that you'll be increasingly incapacitated.

A: Yeah. I can still work for a while, and they say it won't affect my brain or my breathing until the very end.

J: It's your breathing that will give out?

A: That's the prediction, but who knows? I could have a heart attack and die next week. Actually, the doc said my heart is good. (Said in a cavalier manner, but then his lips began to quiver.)

J: *(I am aware of my own desire to avoid this conversation. It's hard to know how to address it. My own avoidance is leading to thoughts of a referral to an expert who specializes with terminal illnesses. When I focus back on Andy, I want to help him normalize mortality and also help him understand the unique challenge he's facing.)* You are in a very unusual situation. Unlike most of us, you know most likely how you will die. What's it like for you to have that knowledge?

A: What do you mean?

J: *(Clearly, I am not connecting with him at the feeling level.)* (Tearing up) Well, it is so sad for me right now. I am wondering what it is like for you?

A: I am kind of numb. How do you mean about knowing about dying?

J: Before this happened, we both knew that we'd both die at some unknown time and manner. Now you have a likely manner. Did the neurologist indicate whether your illness is fast or slow moving? *(I am aware of my continuing semi-avoidance of his death notice.)*

A: I'm not sure. The next tests will tell more, but she thought it was the slower developing type.

J: So, knowing that your life limits are more present, what would you like to experience in here and also in your life?

My hope was that by sharing my sadness, we could set in motion the seeds of our upcoming work on how he might live out the time he had. I also tried to normalize that dying was not unique. What we needed to focus on subsequently was the timeline and how he would choose to live. This was meant as just laying out my willingness to hang in with him, but I was concerned that I was moving prematurely to assuage my personal discomfort.

We stayed in a present focus for most of the session. Before leaving, Andy said, "I am glad that I know I can count on you to keep me on track while I am alive." Then after shifting his weight from foot to foot as he stood by the door, he asked, "Can I have a hug before I go?" I was comfortable accommodating him.

Therapy continued for approximately 2 years. He joined a therapy group of members who had terminal diagnoses. I did keep track of him afterward. Five years later, he was wheelchair bound. I did not have any further sessions with him, at least in part, because my office was not wheelchair accessible.

At one point he phoned me to "remind" me, "Hey, you probably don't realize it, but today is the tenth anniversary since my diagnosis. I am lucky that it has progressed very slowly, and I am still alive and doing as well as can be expected . . . just not kicking."

Spirituality

Questions about larger meaning of life also re-emerge during this period. For many, those answers lie in the spiritual realm. Many reconnect with spiritual beliefs from their own childhoods or embrace new ways of seeing the larger picture. Specific connections to personal mortality and losses of parents and friends often accelerate less-secular exploration.

"Sex, drugs, and rock and roll" may have been the public motto of the generation, but the baby boomers have also had a long tradition of spiritual quests, not limited to The Beatles' India travels and celebrities embracing Kabbalah, Scientology, Buddhism, Islam, and Christianity. Existential therapy is ideally suited to these concerns. The philosophical base of the approach is uniquely relevant to help clients' spiritual searches.

At age 60, Fred's wife of many years was diagnosed with a terminal illness. He cared for her in her final months of life and after her passing was referred for grief counseling. Although I normally referred grief clients to experts in my community, Fred was insistent on working with me. He said that he had sufficient support from a survivors' group to deal with his grief but wanted therapy to focus on some larger questions. In the fourth session, he made this clear.

F: When Belle passed, I was struck with my own vulnerability and my need to understand what my life really meant. That's what I want to work on in here. I had an inkling when my parents died, but when Belle died it really brought it home, that I don't know why I am here.

J: That sounds very important. Would you fill me in on your current speculations?

F: I grew up Catholic but pretty much strayed over the years. Recently, I went back to a local church, but it was strange: The Mass had really changed, and the church was more modern than the old cathedral I went to growing up. I didn't get any feeling except a reminder of why I stopped going in college.

J: So, feeling alienated and alone.

F: Yes. That's the word, *alienated*. It just didn't speak to me. I went to the priest later and talked with him. He was very kind but mostly tried to get me to have faith that it would come back to me. That's not going to work for me.

J: I wonder if instead of looking backward to find something lost, we might explore what meaning you'd like to create in the future.

F: I don't know if I should tell you this, but sometimes at night I still have talks with Belle. I hope you don't think I am crazy.

J: Tell me about the talks.

F: Mostly they are reassuring. I get the feeling that we are still connected in some noncorporeal way, and I can relax some with the idea that . . . I don't know.

J: I guess that speaks to the great emotional and spiritual bond the two of you shared for so long. Even after she's passed, she is part of you.

F: Exactly. It's like our connection is forever, and she has left a lot of herself in me. Sometimes I look at a few of her belongings like her watch, and I can feel like we are still communicating. It feels good, but I don't think I can talk about it even in my group. You know, people will think that I am weird and not moving toward letting go.

J: Let's take a moment to consider taking-in instead of letting go. The relationship with Belle means so much to you that you continue to feel connected even after she is physically gone.

F: Doesn't it seem wrong to hang onto her as if she were still alive?

J: What about it seems wrong for you? What you describe is a movement toward a spiritual connection, which is what you wanted to find. This may sound a little strange, but being on your spiritual quest may be more important than any end goal.

Finding the Spiritual: A Process

Moody and Carroll (1997), described a sequence of spirituality that begins with a focus on an inner voice, followed by finding fellow seekers, some kind of trial and struggle, an inner awakening, and finally an integration of the new experiences into an enhanced everyday life.

One of the potential outcomes of a spiritual search at this age may be a movement toward new experiences, friends, introspection, and distancing from the prior status quo. Frankl (1959a) wrote that the search for meaning involves making choices. Choices toward more freedom may well be transpersonal, metaphysical, or spiritual.

Shadow

A classic premise for Jung (1955) was that at midlife and beyond, psychological growth involves increasing awareness and acceptance of one's "shadow" side. For present purposes, the shadow is viewed broadly as encompassing those parts of self that have been underdeveloped, while individuals have been surmounting prior transitions. During this transition, individuals may have opportunities to reflect on and recapture skills, traits, desires, and aptitudes that were relatively submerged in the process.

Jung often worked with dialectic opposites, and, for him, the shadow was integrated with gender. Thus, the shadow side of masculine functioning was the feminine and vice versa. For men, or those oriented around the "doing" aspects of life (masculine), the challenge of this transition requires embracing those characteristics that involve (the feminine) "being." Whether Jungian archetypes are relevant constructs for individual therapists or clients, a characteristic of clients at this transition is the desirability of revisiting and integrating those qualities that were *correctly* set aside to build a successful work and family life. Assisting clients recapture some of their youthful talents and enthusiasms may be most beneficial in addressing some of those "bucket list" mortality issues.

One of the most crucial therapeutic aspects is to honor choices the client has made and look at the need for different choices moving forward. Often, when clients in this transition begin therapy, they present their past as errors.

Lenora was a retired military nurse when she came in for therapy. After 30 years in the service and 6 years as an administrator at a local civilian hospital, she reported,

"My life has not worked out the way I hoped." She described a vague sense of ennui and "no real direction anymore."

When I asked about her lack of direction, she said that everything seemed okay until recently when she began to realize that she was unhappy at work and that her marriage of 30 years seemed "stale," since her husband "retired and was now taking art classes."

J: So the job is not interesting. Your connection with your husband seems like it's not growing, and you don't really know what the best path is for you.

L: We don't need the money from my job. I am just doing it because it's what I do.

J: Let's focus on who you are, more than what you do.

L: I have made lots of mistakes to end up here. Maybe I shouldn't have gone into nursing. Maybe being a military nurse was wrong. Maybe I chose the wrong husband. Maybe it's just me.

As we spoke further, Lenora described a very good life in her career, a loving marriage, three grown children, and two grandchildren "so far."

J: So help me understand the mistakes. It sounds like you have made a lot of choices that worked at the time and only now are those choices not working as well for you.

L: Yeah. So I am wondering whether it was as good as I thought at the time.

J: What if you made the right decisions then, and your situation has changed sufficiently that new good decisions need to be made?

L: (Smiling) So my whole life may not have been a disaster?

J: What do you have to face if that is true?

L: When I tell Ron I want to retire, he just says, "Great, come to my art classes with me."

J: From the look on your face, that doesn't seem appealing.

L: Doing things with him is nice. I just don't want to paint.

J: Perhaps you haven't yet found what you'd like to do, and with the job stress, you don't have time or energy to find out you best path for now.

L: What if I don't find it?

J: What is your pattern, when you don't find the right answer?

L: Keep looking. Something will turn up.

For some clients, like Lenora, feelings while dealing with a new transition and life stage may instigate some significant life transitions. For others, it's a matter of integrating more aspects of being into awareness and daily life. When both members of a couple are doing this simultaneously, there is often a need for enhanced communication and patience.

Men Decline; Women Soar?

There are both literature and politically correct observational evidence that after menopause, some women lead richer, fuller lives. Examples in popular literature abound of women starting new careers, opening or expanding businesses, or rising to higher levels of an organization as they age. By contrast, there are corresponding examples of men who spend several years of their employed life in "retirement jobs," holding on in noncreative and often nonproductive ways or those who don't know what to do with themselves after retirement. They can be seen in slow decline without the prop and excitement of work.

For therapists, these generalizations are to be treated with caution. Regardless of the sex of the client, the issue often involves his or her capacity to explore the less-traveled personal path. For many male clients, this takes a form of replacing competition with socialization. One of the dominant issues to emerge in men's therapy groups is the deep need to establish, develop, and maintain friendships.

I have found that for most men, the difficult adjustment from full-time work life represents more than the loss of something to do or somewhere to go, it pushes them to revisit old friendships and to create new ones. Intimacy and creativity are often linked for these clients.

After a successful career as a professional athlete, Howard was a coach at college and professional levels. When management changed, he was forced out and at age 59, did not get a lot of other offers.

H: I have been in the final two for two head coaching jobs, but my heart wasn't really in either. Oh, I know I could do the job, but, I just feel like it was more of the same.

J: Been there done that, got the t-shirt. It doesn't seem to grab you like before.

H: It doesn't. Actually, the last few years of coaching seemed like that also. The teams did well, but it was them, and I was more in the background.

J: You know, I did not have the level of athletic career you had by any means, but when I had to let it go, the thing I missed was the guys and the locker room and deep friendships that came from working hard together as a team.

H: (Showing emotion) I met (Hall-of-Fame football player) Jerry Rice once, and I asked him, what was the hardest part of retiring from football? He said he missed the guys. As the head coach, I had to be more distant. It wasn't the same. I became the old guy. Most of my assistants were closer in age to the players.

J: So where is *your* group?

H: (Showing a lot of nonverbal sadness) Do I have one?

J: Up to now, when we have talked about what's next, you always focused on a new job or volunteer work. This seems much more important; friends and people who will understand you without having to educate them.

H: You get me. You don't need much educating—maybe that's the kind of work I should do.

J: I do feel connected to you, but let's talk about who else you are close or could be closer to.

I felt that I had to keep Howard from retreating into what he could do as a vocation or avocation. It seemed much more important that he find a way to feel more intimately connected with others, particularly other men. Howard was fortunate to have a good, solid, supportive 35-year marriage. He could count on his wife and their relationship, but his connection to other men was diminished, and that's the goal we pursued.

Transitions

Transitions do not represent life failures. Transitions are a time to take stock, shift priorities, and discover new ways to successfully meet normal life exigencies. Whether these involve career, finances, relationships, new possibilities, or losses of any kind, life has a way of indicating that it is time to adapt or adjust or to suffer the stagnation of failing when circumstances change.

Clients are most likely to enter therapy during the throes of a transition to a new life stage. They may come in because a relationship is no longer working, a job has become a dead end, they notice a loss of energy, or they have to face some other unknowns such as life in retirement or losses.

Existential therapy is ideally suited to such crises. Life changes are needed, not symptom alteration. The issues in transition are the big issues in life, and a here-and-now intimate therapeutic relationship can help clients negotiate a path to meaning, while facing frightening questions. It offers a caring tuned-in companion as they rebalance the tension between freedom and security needs in life.

Notes

1. At least the first earthquake in my awareness, I discovered later two major quakes occurred in New England on the day of my birth in a Boston-area hospital.

2. The Kristofferson–Rita Coolidge version can be heard at http://www.youtube.com/watch?v=PQQPgECUORs.

3. According to the World Health Organization (2015), the United States ranked 34th, the United Kingdom 28th, and most of continental Europe higher in longevity.

4. Additional information on relevant financial issues is available at http://jerroldleeshapiro.com/uploads/BONUS_CHAPTER_of_FMFF_-_Money_and_retirement.pdf.

5. One couple I saw in therapy had divided their home into two sections, each with a separate bedroom, bathroom, land-line telephone, and specified kitchen times.

6. Estimated in 2006 as over $3 billion in pharmaceutical sales.

7. AndroGel reached over $2 billion in sales in 2012.

8. Reilly, G. & Maloney, D. (2000). *Did Beethoven do the dishes?* Best of Reilly & Maloney: A Collection. Pelican Records.

9. In October, 2014, the BBC reported that many European airlines would soon allow complete access to cell conversations during flights. It may be a problem to have no personal respite from others, but sitting next to a fellow passenger who is sharing their life on the phone through a lengthy trip may be extremely intrusive and cause major confrontations during flights.

12

An Existential Case Study

M any of the elements of existential therapy discussed in this book appear in this case study:

(1) Focus on meaning and the centrality of the relationship

(2) Joining resistance

(3) Attention to the phase of therapy

(4) Therapist self-disclosure

(5) Addressing cultural issues within client and between client and therapist

(6) Addressing aging and loss during the post midlife transition

(7) Culture and gender

(8) Development of intimacy within and out of sessions

(9) Therapist use of observation and internal processing

(10) Process focus

Dana

When she first came in for therapy, Dana was 46 years old. On her intake form, which I read after our first meeting, she described herself as a divorced mother of two daughters, both attending high-tier private colleges out of the area. She is of "mixed race," "no longer" drank, smoked, or used any nonprescription medication. She was currently using ibuprofen for "aches and pains." She held a responsible position in the hospitality industry.

Preparation

The initial phone conversation was brief and professional. Dana reported that she wanted help dealing with her recent divorce from her second husband, after a 6-year marriage. She had divorced her first husband, the girls' father, after about 12 years together. When she arrived on time for the first meeting, she was professionally dressed. She is a slender woman, apparently in good health. Her hair was short, peppered with gray. She had procured the clipboard with relevant forms and completed all the documents, including releases from two former therapists and her primary-care physician.

Transition

During the first session, she began by establishing the sense that she was shopping for the right therapist and that this session would be a job interview.

D: My old marriage counselor gave me the names of three therapists. I made an appointment with all three. You are the second—the only male. The first one did not work out.

J: (*Creating a lot of initial distance. I wonder what might be the threat here.*) You know that is unusual. Most people don't take the time to shop for just the right therapist. It's probably a very wise thing to do. Tell me about what didn't work out with the first therapist.

D: She had all these rules and spent a good 15 minutes going over charges, missed sessions, and a lecture on how she worked.

J: (*Sounds like Dana wants to set the agenda.*) What about that didn't work for you?

D: It's like she was selling herself. She didn't seem to notice me or what I wanted.

J: So let us approach this differently. Please tell me what you want here.

D: (Looking wary) I . . . I . . . I want help getting over this divorce. I have been really depressed, lonely, and angry (voice rising). I can't deal with men cheating, and this is my second husband to do so.

J: That seems like it's hurtful and it makes you angry.

D: Wouldn't that be normal for any woman?

J: (*Curious that she identified it as a female experience, especially when talking to a man. I will try to empathize and include myself.*) I know I'd have a similar reaction to disloyalty and betrayal, especially if that was such a hot button because it happened before.

D: (Sniffling back a tear) I told him before we were married that cheating was the one thing I couldn't handle. Then he went ahead and had this thing with a younger woman.

J: (*I wonder if aging is a part of this also.*) Is the younger part an issue or is it the cheating under any circumstances?

D: It's both! Men just discard you when you are getting gray and start losing your appearance.

J: You are feeling less attractive now that you are in your mid-forties and think that your ex and other men see you as . . .

D: Look. I'm sure you know. When a woman gets perimenopausal, her body changes. I am obviously suffering from gravity and losing my hips.

J: (*That may have been a request for telling her that she is attractive. Best to go with her experience and empathize than to try to refute it.*) That's a major loss to be in a situation where you see yourself as less attractive than before, less attractive than younger women to your ex, and maybe other men.

D: (Looking like she is mulling something over but not verbalizing it) Why do you think two husbands have cheated on me?

J: (*I am guessing that she was pondering whether to confront me regarding attractiveness and then pulled back to a more intellectual level.*) For me, the important thing is what it means to you.

D: I don't know. Maybe my looks. Maybe I'm too headstrong. Maybe it's just how all men are.

J: Let's look at each of those and even the combination of all three.

D: I am very headstrong. I have had to be in my business. I figure out what's best and I go for it.

J: Do you feel that you are being headstrong now?

From the look on her face, as soon as I queried about the here-and-now, I knew that the here-and-now intervention was premature. The opportunity would be subterranean for a few more sessions.

A Brief History

The remainder of the session went to a more distant description of her history with relationships. She said, "I am lucky at work, unlucky in love." Her first marriage dissolved when she discovered that her husband had a sexual encounter with an ex-girlfriend. Despite attempting couple therapy at the time, she was not able to "forgive and forget and move on." After 6 months of therapy, she decided to file for divorce. She claims that the two of them continued to parent their daughters together, and that he was a good father, "just not a good husband."

Dana's early relational history was problematic. Her parents divorced when she was two and she saw her father infrequently after that. She had no current contact with him. She reported that he was from somewhere in South America, maybe Argentina, and her mom and dad met when her mom was in college on a junior year abroad. Dana was conceived just before her mother returned stateside, and her father followed. They got married before Dana was born and, shortly thereafter, he returned to his native land.

Racial-Cultural Background

She claimed that she had problems as a child because she was one of the few dark-skinned children in a White neighborhood. Her mother was the first African-American woman to hold increasingly powerful positions in education in their rural Oregon home. In her twenties, Dana "became obsessed with finding my roots in Africa and Chinook tribes on my mom's side and on my father's Austrian, Spanish, and maybe Incan heritage." Now living in the Bay Area, she reported that she feels less different, and that her "first husband was Black and the second, lily-White."

Commitment to the Therapy

At the end of the session I asked,

J: Do you want to meet again, or do you want to check out the other therapist first?

D: I'd like to meet next week. I think you may be able to help . . . (looking a bit undecided)

J: *(Picking up on her mixed feelings)* Well, from what you have told me, I'd be happy to work with you, but maybe you can keep the other option open if we don't have the right chemistry for you, after a few more sessions.

Testing Trust: The Floor

The second through fourth sessions were taken up entirely by a crisis of her older daughter (Tiffany) at school. Dana had flown back East twice and was monitoring the situation carefully. Her daughter had fainted while playing basketball and had spent the night in the emergency room. She continued to have dizziness for several days. Apparently, the combination of too much alcohol at a weekend party, some prescribed medication, and exertion had all contributed to the problem. The girl's father had also flown back and was working from there until she was cleared after a series of tests.

Most of our sessions involved empathy for her anxiety about her daughter and feelings of helplessness. Once the crisis was resolved, Dana also expressed anger at her daughter's stupidity with alcohol use, "when she knows we have some family history with alcohol problems." Explorations of that family history were not particularly fruitful. There was one family of second cousins who had serious addiction problems and a likely grandfather who was a very heavy drinker. In the fourth session,

J: I noticed that you do not drink at all. Is that related?

D: Well, I did when I was Tiff's age. I was a big partier in college. . . . Had to learn my lesson the hard way (long pause). . . . I never got to experiment in high school. My mom would have killed me. So when I got to college, I went into a wild sorority and drank a lot. . . . I hope Tiff isn't doing what I did. I made some poor choices about sex with guys, and even once with another girl in the house. Mostly if I drank, I'd do almost anything. That's why I stopped.

J: Tiff's experience brings up some of your past and also makes you feel vulnerable.

D: I do. It's like if anything ever happened to either of the girls (getting teary, voice breaking), I don't think I could survive.

J: (Empathizing and normalizing) I can feel how scary that is (holding my hand over my chest). There's no vulnerability like that through our children.

D: You have kids?

J: I do. Tell me what it's like for you to know that.

D: Well, I guess you know what it's like. Did yours go away to school? My younger one wants to go to Senegal for her junior year.

J: Both of mine did. It seems like more to worry about when she's away on another continent and harder to reach. Even less control.

In sessions five, six, and seven, Dana wanted to talk in depth about how she still loved her first husband and couldn't figure out why he had the affair. When she asked him, he could only report that it was a huge mistake, and that he still loved her. Despite the fact that he was in a long-term relationship, he "hit on" Dana during the time they were both back East dealing with the recent crisis.

D: I was tempted. He's still attracted to me. In the end I decided that it would be a bad idea to do that to his live-in lady friend.

J: *(The reference to the other woman seems important. She is not focused on herself. I want to see if we can get there yet.)* What about for you?

D: Oh. I knew it'd be good sex. It always was, and I have been alone for a while now since Sven (second husband), but I figured I'd get all entangled and suffer more if I did. Besides, and I don't know if you can understand this, I wouldn't have liked myself afterward.

J: *(It would be interesting to probe into history here to learn how she knows that, but this is also an opening to connect here. Also, I noticed that she was pushing me away, by suggesting that I would not understand, only then was she more vulnerable.)* That seems very important. . . . Taking care of yourself. Is that unusual in your life?

D: (Blushing a bit) I think so. I usually do what others want. I don't usually think of me much.

J: What's it like to tell me that? You seem more open.

D: (Blushing more, then abruptly pulling back) I'm supposed to tell you things like that, right?

Treatment

There was an evolution from transition to treatment in the eighth session. Dana came in red-eyed and very tearful. She was apparently distraught and grabbed the box of tissues from the table and put it in her lap when she sat down.

J: You seem very upset, what's happening?

D: (Long pauses, punctuated by quiet weeping) I just found out from my friend that my Sven is marrying that other woman.

J: *(Trying to connect further)* The younger one?

D: Yeah. The twenty-something whore.

J: This is hitting you really hard.

D: *(Looking as if she was deciding whether to respond to the caring or to let the anger out)* It's been a stressful week, and this is just the topper.

J: *(Let's attempt to get inside the angst, but start cognitively)* For a moment it seemed as if you were deciding whether to scream or cry.

D: No. I was just thinking of the ridiculousness of the situation. Why do I even care if my discard ends up with what he deserves? It's his funeral! Hah. I meant wedding. Maybe it's both.

J: *(She's pulling back from the emotion and from the relationship. Try to join her cognitively and see if we can get reconnected.)* So on one level, he gets the wedding or funeral he deserves. You put out the trash, but it's surprising that you care if someone goes through it.

D: Yeah. It's like that. Why do I care?

J: *(I could reply cognitively here, prefer to support her finding her own meaning)* That's really a good question. How might we address it?

D: Is it just like my daughter says, "You don't want him, but you don't want anyone else to have him either."

J: *(Struggling to connect)* What do *you* think of that? (When she shrugs, J continues.) Perhaps it means that your marriage is really over, or maybe it underscores your feeling of being too old.

D: I've been thinking of that a lot. Like, what if my time has passed? What if I am just one of those invisible middle-aged women?

J: What would that be like to lose your younger self and become invisible?

A Brief Reversion to Transition

D: (Crying heavily now, as the tears dry, she turns toward J and expresses with some force.) It's the damn patriarchy. It's the glass ceiling. It's 70 cents for women and a dollar for men to do the same job. And on top of that, being a minority woman makes it even worse. You can't know what it's like to be a woman and to be put down for your sex and as soon as your reproductive days are over, you are in the trash, not your ex, who caused all the trouble following his penis around in the first place.

Joining the Resistance

J: *(Wondering where that content came from and wanting to refute some of the factual errors. Clearly a method destined to put out the fire with Sterno—what am I feeling now? Hurt, attacked, pushed away, alone— I'll join her in the resistance by confirming and see what happens.)* Dana, I don't know what it's like to be in your shoes as a mixed race 46-year-old woman. What I am hearing is how isolated you feel, and that even your therapist may not be able to understand you. When I try to put myself in your place, it feels very painful.

D: Well, you are a man. You don't know about being rejected because you are 46.

J: *(More pushback. How may I join? Feelings of empathy may be premature—join cognitive external)* Even in here, you are alone, and you need to keep up the vigilance, because I am not a woman and may not understand the full implications of what you are experiencing.

D: (Calming) Thank you! I think you may be trying to understand what my life is like. Do you know what it's like to be a minority that has to find a new identity?

J: *(Offer empathy but keep up response to resistance)* I do know what it's like to feel different and alone, and I know this may seem unfair, that you will have to be wary of where I don't understand your feelings of isolation and devastation, especially thinking about Sven's marrying that young woman. Does that seem unfair of me to ask you to fill me in?

D: (Making eye contact) No. I think that's okay, just don't get upset if I tell you so.

J: What's it like to feel partially understood here if only for a moment?

D: Good, of course.

J: How scary is it?

D: I'm surprised you asked. I am feeling a little anxious.

J: Say more about the anxiety about being understood as well as the anxiety at being misunderstood.

Return to Treatment

The last 10 minutes of the session involved her talking about her frequent worry about being rejected, abandoned, and lonely. When the session ended, she extended her hand to shake mine for the first time and said "thank you."

At the beginning of the next session, Dana talked about some work-related issues for about 10 minutes and then reported that she had a meeting with Sven. "He actually came on to me. He is already cheating on his new wife. I was feeling strong when I told him he had a problem and needed help, but we were divorced and it wasn't coming from me!"

After looking at me and smiling, she said quietly,

D: That last meeting was very powerful for me. I've been thinking about it all week.

J: *(I think she means our last session, but it could be her meeting with Sven.)* What stood out as particularly important?

D: Feeling good about being understood and feeling scared about it also.

J: Closeness brings both what we want and also the fear of losing it or maybe even having it?

D: My whole life I've wanted to have someone take care of me and protect me and keep me safe, like my mom did . . .

J: But?

D: I get so worried about losing it, I don't even enjoy it. This is embarrassing. . . . I really love to be out on the water . . . but I noticed the last few times I went sailing, instead of enjoying it, I was thinking about how much work it'd be hosing down the boat and cleaning up the gear afterward, that I wasn't enjoying the feeling of the wind and gliding over the water. It was like, "This is fun. When will it be over and I can go back to my life?"

J: So the anxiety about what's coming next interferes with what's happening now.

D: Exactly. And what's happening now is missed altogether.

J: *(Chance to return to the here-and-now)* So, what are you experiencing right now?

D: I was thinking about what I have to do after lunch today.

Dana's distancing was following a repeated pattern of deeper connection followed immediately by pulling back and distancing. It seemed an opportune moment to help her stay a bit longer and to be aware of her anxiety, rather than pre-emptively break it off. There wasn't much on the surface that was offering an opening. In order to approach her more effectively, I tapped into the auditory track of music in my mind. Lyrics to the Dan Hill tune, "Sometimes when we touch, the honesty's too much"[1] indicated to me that a focus on the fear of intimacy was a viable approach, if offered carefully. The risk of an *I-thou* connection with me was obvious, but I guessed that treating herself as a "thou" instead of an "it," might be even more important.

J: That's good. It's the perfect example of how the after-lunch stress is overwhelming what is occurring with you. Could we try a short little experiment for a few moments? (with her nod) Imagine that you are just focused on what's occurring now. What comes up for you?

D: I want to run away.

J: *(Music continuing—and I have to close my eyes and hide)* From?

D: I was about to say you, but I know it's probably me.

J: That seems really important that part of you wants to run away from Dana.

D: I'm feeling close to something important and soon our time will be up, and I'll have to leave for a week.

J: *(Again coming up to her fear of intimacy and finding a way to pull back. Rather than push it again at the feeling level, I can reach it cognitively.)* That seems a powerful a metaphor for life. If we worry about what comes next, we may lose out on what is happening now.

D: (Laughing) Getting a little philosophical are we?

J: Stay with that playful side. What's that like?

Trust-Testing Revisited in Anticipation of Greater Depth

Dana cancelled the next appointment because of a work-related assignment out of town. I wondered if it was related to my holding her to the here-and-now intimacy of the last session but did not know if I wanted to confront it in the next session. She came to her next appointment, dressed very casually.

D: So this is the other me!

J: The casual Dana?

D: Yeah. I took 2 days off this week, after the weekend of work, and I just didn't feel like getting dressed up for our meeting.

J: *(A change in client appearance may be an important message. Is this a test of how I might reject her if she were not professional and proper? Is this a way to cement a perceived change in the level of our deeper communication last session? Have to let her unwrap it.)* What's it like for you to come in on a day off—dressed differently?

D: It feels good.

J: Good. Where would you like to begin?

D: I have a confession to make. I almost didn't make it at all. They scheduled a meeting at this time for several weeks, and I didn't speak up and say "I can't make a 10:00 a.m. Tuesday meeting." I didn't want to answer any questions about being in therapy. So I took the day off and then asked my admin to reschedule the meeting for the next several weeks.

J: *(Once again, right after a closer connection, there is a rebounding distance. This time, she caught it. Do I acknowledge that and how deeply? Perhaps I could reframe and focus on her courage.)* So, what's it like for you to take care of yourself, even in the face of work demands?

D: It's okay. I don't need to tell my admin why, and she can't tell them.

J: I am struck by your courage at prioritizing yourself. That seems new.

D: It was scary doing it, but I am glad I did. Do you think I look younger in my sweats?

J: *(Again, close then distant—at least it wasn't "Do these pants make me look fat?" Wonder whether the comment about appearance might have been provocative or seductive—will respond with asocial therapeutic questions.)* What if I said they do make you look younger?

D: Well do they? If you said that, I'd probably think you were not a very good observer.

J: And what if I said that they make you look the same or older?

D: I'd challenge you and say I think it makes me younger.

J: So either way, I'd be wrong. I guess for me the important thing is how they make you feel about your appearance and the concern with aging.

D: I don't want you to think I am being disrespectful.

J: I don't, but could we look for a moment at the desire to please others, even in therapy. What if I didn't like certain clothing, or what if I expressed my male prerogative and didn't notice?

D: I would think that maybe you didn't care about how I looked.

J: And what if that were true?

D: I just felt that upsurge in anxiety again. Why does this matter so much for me?

J: Let's not worry about the why right now. Let's just focus on the anxiety.

Process Focus

For the next several sessions, the relationship built as she explored how she pushed me away and drew me closer. Each time she became slightly more authentic and empowered in her abilities. I wanted to encourage her to do it consciously and to take control, instead of having to rely on others' preferences. At one point I asked her,

J: We've noticed several times how you have effectively drawn me closer and held me further back. What do you think would occur if you let go of the burden of getting me to figure it out, and you just put out your preference.

D: Like I want you to be more understanding of my perspective or I need some space.

J: Try that, only add the word *now* to the end of the sentences.

D: I want you to understand me better now. . . . Whoa, that felt powerful, and then I worried about how you'd react.

J: Try it again with the other statement.

D: I'd like some space now. (Said in a girlish tone of voice with an upward inflection as if it were a question)

J: Say it like you mean it, and I'll respond honestly.

D: I'd like some space now.

J: *(Still less firm than I would prefer, but closer)* Sure, but I have a favor to ask in return. Will you let me know when you want to reconnect?

D: I like that.

J: *(Self-disclosure in the moment)* It feels good to me also. I don't have to guess.

J: (Opening the subject of transfer of training) So who in your life might you want to interact with that way?

D: (Smiling) You want a list?

J: (Smiling) Just the top two names.

D: This guy at work and Leon, a friend who asked me out a few times. I don't know if I'm ready.

J: What's it like to be asked out? You pretty much thought that was a thing of the past.

D: I was going to say, "It's just Leon." (Making quotation marks with her fingers) I've known him forever, and his son knows my daughters, so it's no big deal, but if I am honest with you, I am a little excited and a little anxious. I don't want to ruin a good friendship.

J: All your concerns seem like something to keep in mind, but what if we just focused for a moment on the excitement–anxious part?

D: Leon is a good man. He's older than I by a few years, but he's attractive, honest, has a good job with the airlines, and he's a widower. He's been single and I think not dating for at least a couple of years.

J: I'm aware that you focused on what Leon is like there. That seems important, and I'm very interested in what's going on inside you.

D: I'm scared. I am not ready to be hurt again. I need to go slow.

J: So taking care of Dana means testing the waters before plunging in. That seems wise.

D: It's not my history with men. I usually end up sleeping with guys and then figuring out what's happening later.

J: You do what you think they want first to hold on to them, before you decide if you want them at all.

D: Yeah! I don't know why I don't learn that lesson.

J: What does it mean to you that you keep doing the same thing?

D: I am so scared of being rejected, I turn myself inside out to be attractive and do what they want.

J: (Focus on consequences) So, you've done it that way several times now and the result is that you keep them around, but then they are unfaithful. That seems a high price for the initial security. Your approach with Leon seems more cautious and about what you might want.

D: You have a way of making everything seem like it's so meaningful. What if I want to have sex, just for the fun of it?

J: What if you do? Do you have experience with that?

D: (Laughing) No! If I am sexual, it means more.

J: Your heart and head are in it, and it involves opening yourself to another person and being deeply connected, even if only for a time.

D: (Tearful) You know me too well. Then I get worried and pull back and want something more from them, but they don't offer it, and I never ask.

J: *(The situation seems very close but not sexually charged.)* What might you want in our relationship that you are not asking for?

D: I can't tell you . . . (silence) Well, I want to know if you care about me, or if you are like this with everyone. How is that for a big question?

J: (Here and now self-disclosure) Right now, I am feeling very connected to you and care a lot about what you are experiencing. I am also aware of my own vulnerability as I say that. (pause of several seconds) What's it like to hear that?

D: (Smiling) I feel like you are the father I never had, and you are looking out for me. . . . It feels good . . . and at least for now, I am trying to avoid thinking about you not being there, someday.

Talk about the transitory nature of intimate moments and of life itself continued for the next two sessions. At one point she asked, "Is it wrong for me to think that I could take some of you with me, because I know you care and don't expect anything from me except to show up?"

J: *(The learning is important, and I don't want to go to a more distant connection at a time of vulnerability. I'll try to stay with the "I-thou" as much as possible.)* As you say that, I feel very touched and honored that you would be able to take something from this relationship with you as part of your life going forward.

Dana just nodded at that and later said that it meant a lot to her that I wasn't critical of how she thought or felt. She also reported that she had been practicing what we discussed with her daughters and with Leon.

Early Termination

Late in the therapy, during the termination process, there was a reversion back to testing trust and treatment. Initially it occurred with only 10 minutes left in a session.

Previously Unknown Siblings and Family History

D: I heard from my sister last week. Actually, she's my half-sister. It didn't go well. It almost never does. We were trying to plan for Christmas with mom, and she just had all these demands on me.

J: (*I don't recall any prior mention of a sister. Have to check my notes. This is occurring at a time when any deep exploration is impossible. Is this a termination issue, or is it finally safe to bring it up? I will stay generic and check it out next week.*) That sounds important. Could we begin next session with it?

D: Well, I don't know if it's important. It's fine to put it on hold till next week. I don't plan to talk with her again until the week after. She and her husband are traveling.

As promised, I instituted the discussion after checking in with her.

J: Where are you today?

D: I'm okay . . . feeling pretty good actually. Had a good week at work, and Leon and I spent the weekend together. It was really nice . . . stress-free. Chloe had some women's problems, but it was just a simple urinary tract infection and she's doing better.

J: Last week, you mentioned an interaction with your sister. Would you like to pursue that a bit?

D: Yeah. I didn't think you'd forget. But it's good we talk, because I have to get the Christmas plans worked out with her.

J: I was surprised when you brought it up. I don't think you mentioned having a sister before.

D: I have a half-sister and a half-brother. We all three have different fathers. She is 2 years younger than me, and my brother is 5 years younger—he's had a hard time. They think he has bipolar disease or maybe severe ADHD. His father committed suicide around 10 years ago. He was very depressed. They both live up north, not far from Mom. I don't see them too often, and they don't play too big a part in my life. But they now want me and the girls to come up to Oregon for Christmas, and Keisha wants to control every last detail.

J: How does that affect you?

D: It probably doesn't. If I do what she wants, I can just skate, and she'll do most of the dinner and hard work.

J: *(This seems far more distant and intellectual. Not much connection between us here. That's a real change. I will try again to connect the dots here. If that fails, try to connect the current emotional dots with some history.)* As you present this, it almost seems like a nonissue, but it also feels distant. Can you help me with that?

D: Keisha and I have a long, mostly not good, history. She is also a bit of a pain for Joey (half-brother).

J: Take a few minutes and tell me how she came into your life and what the issues have been.

Dana began describing her mother's frantic dating after her father left. She said that her mom got pregnant with Keisha but was unsure about the father, because she was with two men at the time. Both men are African-American, and one wanted to stay and be an involved father. Subsequent tests showed that he was the biological father. Keisha's parents divorced after 2 years, and then Dana, Keisha, and their mother moved in with another man, who was "wealthy but very sad." Like Keisha's father, he is African-American.

Keisha's father remains very involved in her life. She lived with him and his current wife in Seattle during her "turbulent" high school years, during which Dana and Keisha had limited contact. When Dana asked if he was coming to Christmas, Keisha retorted indignantly, "Of course!"

D: (Looking very sad) So there you have it; my family's long weird history. Three kids, one mom, and three dads. We are cordial but not close. I am closer to my mom and my daughters.

Racial Isolation in Family of Origin

J: *(One of the pieces of the story that stood out was that she was racially different from everyone else in the family. That may relate to her sense of isolation.)* I am aware of two things. One is of your sadness. The other is that everyone else in your family of origin is mostly African-American. You are more mixed (Making the implicit explicit).

D: (Staring—could be angry or sad) Yeah. That is something I was made aware of my entire childhood. I never felt like I was completely okay in the Black community and certainly not in the White community. For mixed-race people, there is a lot of pressure to choose one and disidentify with the others.

J: So in the household, you were the oldest, but you also felt like somewhat of an outcast.

D: Keisha's dad was in the "Black power movement" down in Oakland when he was young, and he has been involved in Black political movements ever since. He is very identified with being "Black and proud." He always welcomed me, but he also wanted the whole family to be Black, and I am only half or less.

J: That seems lonely even as you say it now.

D: I haven't felt like I could talk about this before. You don't know what it's like to be mixed race. I don't think you could ever understand.

Cultural Test of Trust

J: *(We are back in transition—testing trust—I will join with her as before and see if we can bring it into our current relationship as it has grown. Probably best to stay away from my experiences as a minority and just stay with her feelings.)* That's true. I don't know. I am going to have to rely on you to let me know where I misunderstand what it's like.

D: (Smiling) I like that you know that you don't get it. Usually, people tell me that I am special, or that they talk about liking Obama or something . . . like they know.

J: Help me where I miss the main point here. To me, it sounds like you are isolated and lonely and, to some extent, a minority of one here, at work, and even growing up in your home; not even sharing the racial heritage of your siblings and stepfathers.

D: (Smiling some more) That's pretty good. . . . The other piece is that I keep trying to make sense of what I truly am.

J: *(Back in treatment here)* It's hard to know what all that means in who you are and what your life is about.

D: (Big tear going down her cheek) Yeah. I really don't know. What we have been talking about is how I can make my own meaning and it feels good when I do, but it's hard when it's constant.

J: That seems a big challenge to do on your own. Maybe we could address parts of it here, instead of your facing it alone all the time. Of course, it is ultimately you discovering or creating who Dana is and will be.

D: I do think about this stuff at home, too. My little girl is going through it now as a college freshman. She's trying to figure out who she is and where she belongs. She says that at her school, everyone seems to mix pretty well, but she is aware that she is of color.

J: I'm having two reactions to what you just said, first I am feeling how vulnerable it makes you to have Chloe going through this, and second, I am thinking how fortunate she is to have one of the few people who truly understands, you, to help her.

D: (Crying freely) That makes me so happy to hear. I can help her, and I do understand. I worry about her going to West Africa, though. That may stir up a lot.

J: Maybe that's why she is planning to go. She has the level of support to be able to face those difficult questions.

Later Termination

The session ended shortly thereafter, and termination continued. The primary focus during termination was how Dana could keep facing her anxiety about isolation and rejection, especially in the face of a developing relationship with Leon. She spent an entire session trying to find a guarantee that he'd be faithful, "because I do not want to go through that again." Together we connected that fear to the isolation of her identity, especially about being a minority of one.

The other termination issue revolved around losing our sessions.

D: I know this is all professional work, but I am really going to miss you after next month.

J: I will miss you and our meetings as well. How would you like to deal with the end of our weekly meetings?

D: I want to be the one to say goodbye. I do not want to think that you are pushing me out the door.

J: *(Is this a way to re-open the abandonment/isolation issues, or is it her taking care of herself? I will go with the latter and see what happens.)* That seems wise. What is your sense of when we should complete our work?

D: Well, we originally planned four more sessions, but how do you feel about three?

J: The question is, what is your preference?

D: (Chuckling) I'd feel best with three.

J: Three it is. That means our last meeting will be Dec. 4th. . . . You are smiling.

D: I like feeling like I have a say, and I trust that you'd tell me if you thought it was a mistake.

J: I would.

Follow-Up

About 2 years after the termination, I got a hand-written card in the mail. Dana wrote,

> *I have mixed feelings about what I have to tell you in this note. I did not want it to be impersonal like an e-mail. So here goes. First of all, I am doing very well and remembering a lot of how we talked. It made a real difference in my life. Chloe is back from Senegal—we skyped weekly and you were right about her choosing to challenge her identity questions. Tiffany is in graduate school, in psychology of all things. The big news is that Leon and I have been living together and we are getting married in two months. Here is the difficult part. I want you to know about the wedding, because I know you'd be happy for me. The hard part is that I am not going to invite you. Please don't be hurt by that. If I ever need to come in again, I want you to be there for me. If you met my family in person, I am not sure that I could do that. I hope that it is okay with you and that you understand. Leon's therapist is not coming either. We are committed to making a strong start on our own feet. I will write again in time.*

I sent back a note wishing her well and expressing my pleasure about the upcoming nuptials, that I was not hurt by her taking care of herself, and that I would be available if she wanted to return to therapy. I did not tell her that it might have been a potential ethical dilemma for me to consider coming to her wedding.

Dana did write again about a year later and informed me that her life was "better than ever." I have not seen or heard from her since: a testament to the temporary, powerful, here-and-now intimacy (*I-thou* moments) that, like life, must inevitably end, but has the potential of enriching the lives of all those who partake. This is the essential goal of existential psychotherapy.

Note

1. Dan Hill and Barry Mann, "Sometimes When We Touch" can be heard at http://www.youtube.com/watch?v=IATz8ZVTAL.

References

American Psychological Association Presidential Task Force on Evidence-Based Practice. (2006). Evidence-based practice in psychology. *American Psychologist, 61*(4), 271–285.

Argyle, M. (1988). *Bodily communication* (2nd ed.). Madison, WI: International Universities Press.

Bandler, R., & Grinder, J. (1975). *The structure of magic: A book about language and therapy.* Palo Alto, CA: Science and Behavior Books.

Barlow, S. (2010). Evidence bases for group practice. In R. K. Conyne, *The Oxford handbook of group counseling* pp. 207–230. New York, NY: Oxford University Press.

Barrett-Lennard, G. T. (1962). Dimensions of therapist response as causal factors in therapeutic change. *Psychological Monographs, 76*(43, Whole No. 562), 1–33.

Bateson, G. (1972). *Steps to an ecology of mind: Collected essays in anthropology, psychiatry, evolution, and epistemology.* San Francisco, CA: Chandler.

Battegay, R. (1989). Apparent and hidden changes in group members according to the different phases of group psychotherapy. *International Journal of Group Psychotherapy, 39*(3), 337–353.

Beck, A., Rush, A. J., Shaw, B., & Emery, G. (1979). *Cognitive therapy of depression.* New York, NY: Guilford Press.

Beck, J. S. (2011). *Cognitive behavior therapy,* (2nd ed.): *Basics and beyond.* New York, NY: Guilford Press.

Becker, E. (1973). *Denial of death.* New York, NY: Free Press.

Beier, E. G., & Young, D. M. (1984). *The silent language of psychotherapy,* (2nd ed.). New York, NY: Aldine.

Benedict, R. (1946). *The chrysanthemum and the sword: Patterns of Japanese culture.* Boston, MA: Houghton Mifflin.

Bernadett-Shapiro, S. T., Peltz, L. S., Bischoff, R. J., Shapiro, J. L., & Kovachy, E. M. (1999, May). Increasing therapeutic effectiveness with interactive computer-assisted homework: Presentation, demonstration & ethics. Presented at the annual meeting of the California Association of Marital and Family Therapists, San Francisco, California.

Berne, E. (1969). *Games people play.* New York, NY: Vintage.

Beutler, L. E., Harwood, T. M., Michelson, A., Song, X., & Holman, J. (2011). Resistance level. In J. C. Norcross (Ed.), *Relationships that work: Therapist contributions and responsiveness to patient needs* (2nd ed.) pp. 261–278. New York, NY: Oxford University Press.

Binswanger, L. (1958). The existential analysis school of thought. In R. May, E. Angel, & H. F. Ellenberger, (Eds.), *Existence* pp. 214–236. New York, NY: Basic Books.

Binswanger, L. (1963). *Being-in-the-world: Selected papers of Ludwig Binswanger* (Needleman, Trans.). New York, NY: Basic Books.

Bion, W. R. (1962). *Learning from Experience*. London, UK: Heinemann.

Boeree, C. George (1998). Otto Rank. Retrieved from http://webspace.ship.edu/cgboer/rank.html

Bohart, A. C., & Greenberg, L. S. (1997). *Empathy reconsidered: New directions in psychotherapy*. Washington, DC: American Psychological Association.

Bohart, A. C., & Tallman, K. (2010). Clients, the neglected common factor in psychotherapy. In B. L. Duncan, S. D. Miller, B. E. Wampold, & M. A. Hubble (Eds.)., *The heart and soul of change: Delivering what works in therapy* (2nd ed., pp. 83–111). Washington, DC: American Psychological Association.

Boss, M. (1963). *Psychoanalysis and daseinanalysis* (L. Lefebre, Trans.). New York, NY: Basic Books.

Boss, M. (1979). *Existential foundations of medicine and psychology*. New York, NY: Jason Aronson.

Boszormenyi-Nagy, I. & Spark, G. (1973). *Invisible loyalties: Reciprocity in intergenerational family therapy*. New York, NY: Harper & Row.

Bowen, M. (1985). *Family therapy in clinical practice*. Oxford, UK: Jason Aronson.

Breitbart, W., Rosenfeld, B., Gibson, C., Pessin, H., Poppito, S., Nelson, C., & Olden, M. (2010). Meaning-centered group psychotherapy for patients with advanced cancer: A pilot randomized controlled trial. *Psycho-Oncology, 19,* 21–28. doi:10.1002/pon.1556

Brown, M. W. (1942). *The runaway bunny*. New York, NY: Harper and Row.

Buber, M. (1957). Distance and relation. *Psychiatry,* 20, 97–104.

Buber, M. (1966). *I and thou* (W. Kaufman, Trans.). New York, NY: Touchstone.

Buber, M. (1970). *I and thou* (W. Kaufmann, Trans.). New York, NY: Scribner. (Original work published 1937).

Buchanan, R. (2007). Retrieval of emotional memories. *Psychological Bulletin* 133(5), 761–779.

Bugental, J. F. T. (1965). *The search for authenticity*. New York, NY: Holt, Rinehart & Winston.

Bugental, J. F. T. (1987). *The art of the psychotherapist*. New York, NY: W. W. Norton.

Bugental, J. F. T. (1999). *Psychotherapy isn't what you think*. Phoenix, AZ: Zeig, Tucker & Co.

Bugental, J. F. T., & Bugental, E. K. (1984). A fate worse than death: The fear of changing. *Psychotherapy,* 21(4), 543–549.

Burlingame, G., Fuhriman, A., & Johnson, J. (2004). Process and outcome in group counseling and psychotherapy: A perspective. In J. DeLucia-Waack, D. Gerrity, C. Kalodner, & M. Rive (Eds.), *Handbook of group counseling and psychotherapy* (pp. 49–61). Thousand Oaks, CA: Sage.

Busteed, B. (2012, September 8). GPA, SAT, ACT...RIP. *The Huffington Post.* Retrieved from http://www.huffingtonpost.com/brandon-busteed/gpa-sat-actrip_b_3566672.html

Cameron, W. B. (1963). *Informal sociology, a casual introduction to sociological thinking.* New York, NY: Random House.

Cannadine, D. (2013). *The undivided past.* New York, NY: Knopf.

Carey, B. (2014, May 21). Need therapy? A good man is hard to find. *New York Times.* Health Section, p. A1.

Carkhuff, R. R., & Berenson, B. (1967). *Beyond counseling and therapy.* New York, NY: Holt, Rinehart & Winston.

Carlson, C. I., Ross, S. G., & Stark, K. H. (2012). Bridging systemic research and practice: Evidenced-based case study methods in couple and family therapy. *Couple and Family Psychology: Research and Practice, 1*(1), 48–60.

Chambless, D. L., & Crits-Christoph, P. (2006). The treatment method. In J. C. Norcross, L. E. Beutler, & R. F. Levant (Eds.), *Evidence-based practices in mental health* (pp. 191–200). Washington, DC: American Psychological Association.

Cissna, K. N., & Anderson, R. (1994). The 1957 Martin Buber-Carl Rogers dialogue, as dialogue. *Journal of humanistic psychology, 34*(1), 11–45.

Classen, C., Butler, L. D., Koopman, C., Miller, E., DiMiceli, S....Spiegel, D. (2001). Supportive-expressive group therapy and distress in patients with metastatic breast cancer—A randomized clinical intervention trial. *Archives of General Psychiatry, 58*(5), 494–501.

Coche, J. M. (1990). Resistance in existential-strategic marital therapy: A four-stage conceptual framework. *Journal of Family Psychology, 3*(3), 236–250.

Coche, J. M., & Coche, E. (1990). *Couples group psychotherapy: A clinical practice model.* New York, NY: Brunner/Mazel.

Connell, G., Mitten, T., & Bumberry, W. (1998). *Reshaping family relationships: The symbolic therapy of Carl Whitaker.* Philadelphia, PA: Brunner/Mazel.

Cooper, M. (2003). *Existential therapies.* London, UK: Sage.

Cooper, M. (2013). Experiencing relational depth in therapy: What we know so far. In R. Knox, D. Murphy, S. Wiggins & M. Cooper (Eds.), *Relational depth: New perspectives and developments* (pp. 62–76). Basingstoke: Palgrave.

Cooper, M., & Reeves, A. (2012). The role of randomised controlled trials in developing an evidence-base for counselling and psychotherapy. *Counselling and Psychotherapy Research,12*(4),303–307. doi:10.1080/14733145.2012.687388

Corey, G., & Corey, M. S. (1987). *Groups process and practice* (3rd ed.). Pacific Grove, CA: Brooks/Cole.

Corey, M. S., Corey, G., & Corey, C. (2013.). *Groups process and practice* (9th ed.). Pacific Grove, CA: Brooks/Cole.

Correia, E., Cooper, M., & Berdondini, L. (2014). Existential psychotherapy: An international survey of the key authors and texts influencing practice. *Journal of Contemporary Psychotherapy.* doi:10.1007/s10879-014-9275-y

Cuijpers, P., van Straten, A., Hollon, S. D., & Andersson, G. (2010). The contribution of active medication to combined treatments of psychotherapy and pharmacotherapy for adult depression: A meta-analysis. *Acta Psychiatrica Scandinavica, 121,* 415–423. doi:10.1111/j.1600-0447.2009.01513.x

Cummings, J. P., Ivan, M. C., Carson, C. S., Stanley, M. A., & Pargament, K. I. (2014). A systematic review of relations between psychotherapist religiousness/ spirituality and therapy-related variables. *Spirituality in Clinical Practice, 1*(2), 116–132.

Cummings, N. A., O'Donahue, W. T., & Ferguson K. E., (Eds.). (2003). Behavioral health in primary care: Beyond efficacy to effectiveness. *Cummings Foundation for Behavioral Health: Health utilization and cost series* (Vol. 6). Reno, NV: Context Press.

Davanloo, H. (1999). Intensive short-term dynamic psychotherapy—Central dynamic sequence: Head-on collision with resistance. *International Journal of Intensive Short Term Dynamic Psychotherapy, 13*(4), 264–282.

Decety, J., & Ickes, W. (Eds.). (2009). *The social neuroscience of empathy.* Cambridge, MA: MIT Press.

Decety, J., & Lamm, C. (2009). Empathy versus personal distress: Recent evidence from social neuroscience. In J. Decety & W. Ickes (Eds.), *The social neuroscience of empathy* (pp. 199–213). Cambridge, MA: MIT Press.

de Shazer, S. (1980). *The death of resistance.* Unpublished manuscript.

Diamond, M. J. (2010). The impact of the mind of the analyst: From unconscious process to intrapsychic change. In M. J. Diamond & C. Christian, *The second century of psychoanalysis: Evolving perspectives on therapeutic action* pp. 205–236. London, UK: Karnac.

Diamond, M. J., & Shapiro, J. L. (1973). Changes in locus of control as a function of encounter group experiences: A study and replication. *Journal of Abnormal Psychology, 83*(3), 514–518.

Diamond, M. J., & Shapiro, J. L. (1975). Method and paradigm in encounter group research. *Journal of Humanistic Psychology, 15,* 59–70.

Diamond, S. (2014). End of men: The "feminization" of psychotherapy. *Psychology Today.* Retrieved from http://www.psychologytoday.com/blog/evil-deeds/ 201210/end-men-the-feminization-psychotherapy

Dies, R. R. (1985). Research foundations for the future of group work. *Journal of Specialists in Group Work, 10*(2), 68–73.

Dostoevski, F. (1917). *Crime and punishment.* Cambridge, MA: Harvard Classics.

Dreikurs, R. (1951). The unique social climate experienced in group psychotherapy. *Group Psychotherapy, 3,* 292–299.

duPlock, S. (1997). *Case studies in existential psychotherapy and counseling.* New York, NY: Wiley.

Ehrenreich, B. (2009). *Bright-sided: How positive thinking is undermining America.* New York, NY: Metropolitan Books.

Ehrensaft, D. (1987). *Bringing in fathers: The reconstruction of mothering.* New York, NY: The Free Press.

Elliott, R., Bohart, A. C., Watson, J. C., & Greenberg, L. S. (2011). Empathy. *Psychotherapy 48*(1), 43–49.

Elliott, R., Watson, J., Goldman, R., & Greenberg, L. S. (2003). *Learning emotion-focused therapy: The process-experiential approach to change.* Washington, DC: American Psychological Association.

Elliott, R., Watson, J., Greenberg, L. S., Timulak, L., & Freire, E. (2013). Research on humanistic-experiential psychotherapies. In M. J. Lambert (Ed.), *Bergin & Garfield's handbook of psychotherapy and behavior change* (6th ed., pp. 495–538). New York, NY: Wiley.

Englar-Carlson, M., Evans, M. P., & Duffey, T. (Eds.). (2014). *A counselor's guide to working with men.* Alexandria, VA: American Counseling Association.

Erickson, B. A., & Keener, B. (2006). *Milton H. Erickson, M.D.: An American healer.* Sedona, AZ: Ringing Rocks Books.

Erikson, E. (1963). *Childhood and society* (2nd ed.). New York. NY: W. W. Norton.

Erickson, M. (1978). *Non-verbal hypnotherapeutic techniques.* Personal communication, Phoenix, AZ.

Falicov, C. J. (2014). *Latino families in therapy* (2nd ed.). New York, NY: Guilford.

Feldman, D. B., & Kravetz, L. D. (2014). *Supersurvivors: The surprising link between suffering and success.* New York, NY: HarperWave.

Fidelity Investments Retirement Planning. Retrieved from https://www.fidelity.com/retirement-planning/overview

Fiebert, M. S. (1963). Sensitivity training: An analysis of trainer interventions and group process. *Psychological Reports 22*(8), 829–838.

Flavell, J. H. (1968). *The developmental psychology of Jean Piaget.* New York, NY: Van Nostrand.

Foulds, M. L., & Hannigan, P. S. (1974). Effects of psychomotor group therapy on ratings of self and others. *Psychotherapy: Theory, Research & Practice, 11*(4), 351–353.

Foulds, M. L., & Hannigan, P. S. (1976). Effects of Gestalt marathon workshops on measured self-actualization: A replication and follow-up. *Journal of Counseling Psychology, 23*(1), 60–65. doi:10.1037/0022-0167.23.1.60

Framo, J. L. (1976). Family of origin as a therapeutic resource for adults in marital and family therapy: You can and should go home again. *Family Process, 3*, 193–210.

Frank, J. D. (1961/1993). *Persuasion and healing: A comparative study of psychotherapy.* Baltimore, MD: Johns Hopkins University Press.

Frankl, V. E. (1959). *From death camp to existentialism.* Boston, MA: Beacon Press.

Frankl, V. E. (1959a). *Man's search for meaning: An introduction to logotherapy.* New York, NY: Washington Square Press.

Frankl, V. E. (1991). On the occasion of the presentation of a special honorary degree for life work. Santa Clara University.

Frankl, V. E. (2006). *Man's search for meaning* (Kushner, Trans.). Boston, MA: Beacon Press.

Frazier, J. G. (1890). *The golden bough: A study in comparative religion.* London, UK: Oxford University Press.

Freud, S. (1900/1952). *A general introduction to psychoanalysis.* New York, NY: Washington Square Press.

Freud, S. (1911–1915). Papers on technique. *Standard Edition,* 12, 85–346.

Friedman, T. L. (2014, September 10). It takes a mentor. *New York Times,* p. A12.

Frost, R. (1920). The road not taken. *Mountain Interval.* New York, NY: Harry Holt.

Gebler, F. A., & Maercker, A. (2014). Effects of including an existential perspective in a cognitive-behavioral group program for chronic pain: A clinical trial with 6 months follow-up. *The Humanistic Psychologist 42,* 155–171.

Gelso, C. J. (2011). *The real relationship in psychotherapy: The hidden foundation of change.* Washington, DC: American Psychological Association. doi:10.1037/12349-000

Goldenberg, H., & Goldenberg, I. (2012). *Family therapy: An overview* (8th ed.). Belmont, CA: Brooks/Cole.

Goldfried, M. R. (2007). What has psychotherapy inherited from Carl Rogers? *Psychotherapy: Theory, Research, Practice, Training,* 44(3), 249–252.

Goldman, R. N., Greenberg, L. S., & Angus, L. (2006). The effects of adding emotion-focused interventions to the therapeutic relationship in the treatment of depression. *Psychotherapy Research,* 16, 537–549.

Goleman, D. (1995). *Emotional intelligence: Why it can matter more than IQ.* New York, NY: Bantam.

Gottman, J. M. (1999). *The marriage clinic: A scientifically based marital therapy.* New York, NY: W. W. Norton.

Gould, W. B. (1993). *Viktor E. Frankl: Life with meaning.* Belmont, CA: Brooks/Cole.

Greeley, A. M. (1969). *Why can't they be like us?* New York, NY: Institute of Human Relations Press.

Greenberg, L.S. (2015). *Emotion-focused therapy: Coaching clients to work through their feelings* (2nd ed.). Washington, D.C.: American Psychological Association.

Gurman, A. S. (Ed.). (2008). *Clinical handbook of couple therapy* (4th ed.). New York, NY: Guilford.

Gurman, A. S. (Ed.). (2010). *Clinical casebook of couple therapy.* New York, NY: Guilford.

Habibi, A., & Damasio, A. (2014). Music, feelings and the human brain. *Psychomusicology: Music, Mind, and Brain,* 24(1), 92–102.

Hackney, H. L., & Cormier, L. S. (2001). *The professional counselor: A process guide to helping* (4th ed.). Boston, MA: Allyn & Bacon.

Haldane, D., & McClusky, U. (1982). Existentialism and family therapy: A neglected perspective. *Journal of Family Therapy,* 4, 117–132.

Haley, J. (1963). *Strategies of psychotherapy*. New York, NY: Grune and Stratton.

Haley, J. (1976). *Problem solving therapy*. San Francisco, CA: Jossey-Bass.

Haley, J. (1986, December 6). *Zen and the art of therapy*. Unpublished, spontaneous reaction to question. The Second Evolution of Psychotherapy Conference, Phoenix, AZ.

Hannush, M. J. (2007). An existential-dialectical-phenomenological approach to understanding cultural tilts: Implications for multicultural research and practice. *Journal of Phenomenological Psychology, 38*(1), 7–23.

Heatherington, L., Messer, S. B., Angus, L., Strauman, T. J., Friedlander, M. L., & Kolden, G. G. (2012). The narrowing of theoretical orientations in clinical psychology doctoral training. *Clinical Psychology: Science and Practice, 19*(4), 364–374. doi:10.1111/cpsp.12012

Heidegger, M. (1962). *Being and time*. New York, NY: Harper and Row.

Henry, S. (1981). *Group skills in social work: A four dimensional approach*. Itasca, IL: Peacock.

Hofmann, S. G., & Weinberger. J. (2007). *The art and science of psychotherapy*. New York, NY: Routledge.

Hollis, J. (1993). *The middle passage (Studies in Jungian psychology by Jungian analysts)*. Toronto, CA: Inner City Books.

Hora, T. (1959). Existential group psychotherapy. *American Journal of Psychotherapy, 13,* 83–92.

Horney, Karen. (1945). *Our inner conflicts*. New York, NY: W. W. Norton & Co.

Hubble, M. A., Duncan, B. L., & Miller, S. D. (1999). Directing attention to what works. In M. A. Hubble, B. L. Duncan, & S. D. Miller (Eds.), *The heart and soul of change: What works in therapy* (pp. 1–19). Washington, DC: American Psychological Association.

Husserl, E. (1931). *Ideas: General introduction to pure phenomenology* (W. Gibson, Trans.). New York, NY: Macmillan.

Husserl, E. (2008). On the phenomenology of the consciousness of internal time (1893–1917). *Edmund Husserl Collected Works*. New York, NY: Springer.

Husserl, E. (2014). *Ideas for a pure phenomenology and phenomenological philosophy* (Dahlstrom, Trans.). Indianapolis, IN: Hackett.

Jaspers, K. (1964). *The nature of psychotherapy*. Chicago, IL: University of Chicago Press.

Johnson, S., Hunsley, J., Greenberg, L., & Schindler, D. (1999). Emotionally focused couples therapy: Status & challenges (A meta-analysis). *Journal of Clinical Psychology: Science and Practice, 6,* 67–79.

Johnson, S. M. (2008). Emotionally focused couple therapy. In A. S. Gurman (Ed.), *Clinical handbook of couple therapy*. New York, NY: Guilford.

Jordan, J. V. (2010). *Relational-cultural therapy*. Washington, DC: American Psychological Association.

Jung, C. G. (1955). *Modern man in search of a soul*. New York, NY: Harcourt, Brace, Jovavovich.

Jung, C. G. (1959). *The archetypes and the collective unconscious.* Princeton, NJ: Princeton University Press.

Kaiser, D. (2014, November 14). Is quantum entanglement real? *New York Times Sunday Review,* p. 10.

Kaplan, A. (1964). *The conduct of inquiry: Methodology for behavioral science.* San Francisco, CA: Chandler.

Kass, S. A. (2014). Don't fall into those stereotype traps: Women and the feminine in existential therapy. *Journal of Humanistic Psychology, 54*(2), 131–157.

Kelly, G. (1955). *Principles of personal construct psychology.* New York: Norton.

Kierkegaard, S. (1841). *The world historic split in Western philosophy: The expurgation of hegelism.* Retrieved from https://www.marxists.org/reference/archive/hegel/help/1841.htm

Kierkegaard, S. (1980). *The concept of anxiety: A simple psychologically orienting deliberation on the dogmatic issue of hereditary sin* (R. Thomte, Ed. & Trans.). Princeton, NJ: Princeton University Press. (Original work published 1844)

Kinsey, A. C., Pomeroy, W. B., & Martin, C.E. (1948). *Sexual behavior in the human male.* Bloomington, IN: Indiana University Press.

Kissane, D. W., Bloch, S., Miach, P., Smith, G. C., Seddon, A., & Keks, N. (1997). Cognitive-existential group therapy for patients with primary breast cancer—Techniques and themes. *Psychooncology, 6,* 25–33. doi:10.1002/(SICI)1099-1611 (199703)6:1<25::AID-PON240>3.0.CO;2-N

Kissane, D. W., Bloch, S., Smith, G. C., Miach, P., Clarke, D. M., Ikin, J., & McKenzie, D. (2003). Cognitive-existential group psychotherapy for women with primary breast cancer: A randomised controlled trial. *Psychooncology, 12,* 532–546. doi:10.1002/pon.683

Kissane, D. W., Grabsch, B., Clarke, D. M., Smith, G. C., Love, A. W., Bloch, S., & Li, Y. (2007). Supportive-expressive group therapy for women with metastatic breast cancer: Survival and psychosocial outcome from a randomized controlled trial. *Psychooncology, 16,* 227–286.

Kitano, H. (1989). A model for counseling Asian Americans. In P. B. Pederson, J. Draguns, W. J. Lonner, & J. J. Trimble (Eds.), *Counseling across cultures* (3rd ed., pp. 139–151). Honolulu: University of Hawaii Press.

Knox, R. (2013). Relational depth from the client's perspective. In R. Knox, S. Wiggins, D. Murphy, & M. Cooper (Eds.), *Relational depth: New perspectives and developments* (pp. 21–35). Basingstoke, UK: Palgrave.

Knox, R., & Cooper, M. (2010). Relationship qualities that are associated with moments of relational depth: The client's perspective. *Person-Centered and Experiential Psychotherapies, 9*(3), 236–256.

Kohler, W. (1947). *Gestalt psychology: The definitive statement of the Gestalt theory.* New York, NY: Liveright (W. W. Norton).

Krause, M. S., & Lutz, W. (2009). Process transforms inputs to determine outcomes: Therapists are responsible for managing process. *Clinical Psychology: Science and Practice, 16,* 73–81.

Kristofferson, K., & Foster, F. (1970). Me and Bobby McGee. On *Kristofferson* album, Washington, DC: Monument Records.

Krug, O.T. (2009). James Bugental and Irvin Yalom: Two masters of existential therapy cultivate presence in the therapeutic encounter. *Journal of Humanistic Psychology, 49*(3), 329–354.

Kuhn, T. S. (1970). *The structure of scientific revolutions.* Chicago, IL: University of Chicago Press.

Laing, R. D. (1960). *The divided self.* London, UK: Tavistock.

Lambert, M. J. (1992). Psychotherapy outcome research: Implications for integrative and eclectic therapists. In J. C. Norcross & M. R. Goldfried (Eds.), *Handbook of psychotherapy integration* pp. 94–129. New York, NY: Basic Books.

Längle, A. (2001). Old age from an existential-analytical perspective. *Psychological Reports, 89,* 211–215.

Lantz, J. (1993). *Existential family therapy.* Northvale, NJ: Jason Aronson.

Lantz, J., & Walsh, J. (2007). *Short-term existential intervention in clinical practice.* Chicago, IL: Lyceum Books.

Lebow, J. (2000). What does the research tell us about couple and family therapies? *Journal of Clinical Psychology, 56*(8), 1083–1094.

Levy, K. N., & Anderson, T. (2013). Is clinical psychology becoming less diverse? And if so, what can be done? *Clinical Psychology: Science and Practice, 20,* 211–220.

Lewin, K. I. (1951). *The field theory in social science.* New York, NY: Harper & Bros.

Lorig, K. R., Sobel, D. S., Steward, A. L., Brown, B. W., Bandura, A., Ritter, P., . . . Holman, H. R. (1999). Evidence suggesting that a chronic disease self-management program can improve health status while reducing hospitalization: A randomized trial. *Medical Care, 37,* 5–14. doi:10.1097/ 00005650-199901000-00003

Luborsky, L., Singer, B., & Luborsky, L. (1975). Comparative studies of psychotherapies: Is it true that "everyone has won and all must have prizes"? *Archives of General Psychiatry, 32,* 995–1008.

MacKenzie, K. R. (1990). *Introduction to time limited group psychotherapy.* Washington, DC: American Psychiatric Press.

Markin, R. D., Kivlighan, D. W., Gelso, C. J., Hummel, A. M., & Siegel, E. B. (2014). Clients' and therapists' real relationship and session quality in brief therapy: An actor partner interdependence analysis. *Psychotherapy, 51*(3), 413–423.

Maslow, A. H. (1968). *Toward a psychology of being* (2nd ed.). New York, NY: Van Nostrand Reinhold.

May, R. (1969). *Love and will.* New York, NY: W. W. Norton.

May, R. (1977). *The meaning of anxiety.* New York, NY: W. W. Norton.

May, R. (1983). *The discovery of being.* New York, NY: Norton.

May, R., Angel, E., & Ellenberger, H. F. (Eds.). (1958). *Existence: A new dimension in psychiatry and psychology.* New York, NY: Basic Books.

McGoldrick, M., Giordano, J., & Garcia-Preto, N. (2005). *Ethnicity and family therapy* (3rd ed.). New York, NY: Guilford.

McGoldrick, M., Pearce, J. K., & Giordano, J. (1982). *Ethnicity & family therapy.* New York, NY: Guilford.

McHugh, R. K., Ott, M. W., Barlow, D. H., Gorman, J. M., Shear, M. K., & Woods, S. W. (2007). Cost-efficacy of individual and combined treatments for panic disorders. *Journal of Clinical Psychiatry, 68,* 103–104.

Medina, M. (2010). All for one and one for all? An existential perspective on family and systems work as a form of therapeutic intervention. *Existential Analysis 21*(2), 263–271.

Mehrabian, A., & Ferris, S. R. (1967). Inference of attitudes from nonverbal communication in two channels. *Journal of Consulting Psychology 31*(3): 248–252.

Mehrabian, A., & Wiener, M. (1967). Decoding of inconsistent communications. *Journal of Personality and Social Psychology 6*(1): 109–114.

Miklowitz, D. J., & Scott, J. (2009). Psychosocial treatments for bipolar disorder: Cost-effectiveness, mediating mechanisms, and future directions. *Bipolar Disorder, 11(Supplement 2),* 110–122.

Miller, R. (2008). *Buddhist existentialism: From anxiety to authenticity and freedom.* Victoria, GB: Shogam.

Miller, W. R., & Rollnick, S. (2012). *Motivational interviewing: Helping people change (applications of motivational interviewing)* (3rd ed.). New York, NY: Guilford Press.

Minuchin, S. (1974). *Families and family therapy.* Cambridge, MA: Harvard University Press.

Minuchin, S., & Fishman, H.C. (1981). *Family therapy techniques.* Cambridge, MA: Harvard University Press.

Moody, H. R., & Carroll, D. (1997). *The five stages of the soul: Charting the spiritual passages that shape our lives.* New York, NY: Anchor Books.

Moyers, T. B., & Rollnick, S. (2002). A motivational interviewing perspective on resistance in psychotherapy. *Journal of Clinical Psychology, 58*(2), 185–193.

Mullen, H. (1955). The group analyst's creative function. *American Journal of Psychotherapy, 9,* 320–334.

Mullen, H. (1992). Existential therapists and their group therapy practices. *International Journal of Group Psychotherapy, 42,* 453–468.

Mullen, H., & Rosenbaum, M. (1967). *Group therapy: Theory and practice.* New York, NY: New York Free Press.

National Center for Educational Statistics. (2013). *Table 318.30. Bachelor's, master's, and doctor's degrees conferred by postsecondary institutions, by sex of student and discipline division: 2011–12.* Retrieved from https://nces.ed.gov/programs/digest/d13/tables/dt13_318.30.asp

Nathan, P. E., Stuart, S. P., & Dolan, S. L. (2000). Research on psychotherapy efficacy and effectiveness: Between Scylla and Charybdis? *Psychological Bulletin 126*(6), 964–981.

Neill, J. R., & Kniskern, D. P. (1982). *From psyche to system: The evolving therapy of Carl Whitaker.* New York, NY: Guilford.

Nickerson, R. S. (1998). Confirmation bias: A ubiquitous phenomenon in many guises. *Review of General Psychology 2*(2), 175–220.

Nietzsche, F. (1974). *The gay science* (W. Kaufman, Trans.). New York, NY: Vintage Books.

Norcross, J. C. (1987). A rational and empirical analysis of existential psychotherapy. *Journal of Humanistic Psychology, 27*, 41-68.

Norcross, J. C. (2011). *Psychotherapy relationships that work: Evidence-based responsiveness.* New York, NY: Oxford University Press.

Norcross, J. C. (2014, May 1). Psychotherapy relationships and responsiveness that work: A look at evidence-based practice. Presentation at Santa Clara University.

Norcross, J. C., Beutler, L. E., & Levant, R. F. (Eds.). (2006). *Evidence-based practices in mental health: Debate and dialogue on the fundamental questions.* Washington, DC: American Psychological Association.

Norcross, J. C., & Lambert, M.L. (2014). Relationship science and practice in psychotherapy: Closing commentary. *Psychotherapy, 51*(3), 398–403.

Ogden, T. H. (1997). *Reverie and interpretation: Sensing something human.* London, UK: Jason Aronson.

O'Hara, M. M. (1986). Heuristic inquiry as psychotherapy: The client centered approach. *Person Centered Review, 1*(2), 172–184.

Osherson, S., Krugman, S. (1990). Men shame and psychotherapy. *Psychotherapy: Theory, Research, Practice, Training, 27*(3), 327–339.

Owen, J., Tao, K. W., Imel, Z. E., Wampold, B. E., & Rodolfa, E. (2014). Addressing racial and ethnic microaggressions in therapy. *Professional Psychology: Research and Practice, 45*(4), 283–290.

Panksepp, J., & Biven, L. (2012). *The archaeology of mind: Neuroevolutionary origins of human emotion.* New York, NY: W. W. Norton.

Panskepp, J., & Panskepp, J. B. (2013). Toward a cross-species understanding of empathy. *Trends in Neurosciences, 36*(8), 489–496.

Pascal, B. (1941). *The works of Blaise Pascal: Pensees.* New York, NY: Black's Reader Services.

Pedersen, P. B., Lonner, W. J., Draguns, J. G., & Trimble, J. E. (2007). *Counseling across cultures* (6th ed.). Thousand Oaks, CA: Sage.

Perls, F. (1968). *Gestalt therapy verbatim.* New York, NY: Bantam.

Piaget, J. (1967). *Six psychological studies by Jean Piaget.* New York, NY: Random House.

Piper, W. (1930). *The little engine that could.* New York, NY: Platt & Munk.

Popper, K. (2002). *The logic of scientific discovery.* New York, NY: Routledge.

Portuges, S. H., & Hollander, N. C. (2011). The therapeutic action of resistance analysis: Interpersonalizing and socializing Paul Gray's close process attention technique. In M. J. Diamond & C. Christian (Eds.), *The second century of psychoanalysis: Evolving perspectives on therapeutic action.* London, UK: Karnac Books.

Prochaska, J. O., & DiClemente, C. C. (2005). The transtheoretical approach. In J. C. Norcross & M. R. Goldfried (Eds.), *Handbook of psychotherapy integration* (2nd ed., pp. 141–171.). New York, NY: Oxford University Press.

Prochaska, J. O., & Norcross, J. C. (2001). Stages of change. *Psychotherapy: Theory, Research, Practice, Training, 38*(4), Special Issue: Empirically Supported Therapy Relationships: Summary Report of the Division 29 Task Force (pp. 443–448). Washington, DC: American Psychological Association.

Qiu Y. H., Wu X. Y., Xu H., Sackett, D. (2009, October). Neuroimaging study of placebo analgesia in humans. *Neuroscience Bulletin 25*(5): 277–82. doi:10.1007/s12264-009-0907-2, PMID 19784082

Quatman, T. (2015). *Essential psychodynamic psychotherapy: An acquired art.* London, UK: Routledge.

Ramos-Sanchez, L. (2009). Counselor bilingual ability, counselor ethnicity, acculturation, and Mexican Americans' perceived counselor credibility. *Journal of Counseling & Development 87*(3), 311–318.

Rank, O. (1936). *Willing therapy.* New York, NY: Alfred Knopf.

Rank, O. (2004). *The myth of the birth of the hero.* Baltimore, MD: John Hopkins University Press.

Reeves, J. (2012). 17 frightening facts about retirement savings in America. *The Motley Fool.* Retrieved from http://www.fool.com/retirement/general/2012/10/15/17-frightening-facts-about-retirement-savings-in-.aspx

Richards, M., & Bedi, R. (2014). Gaining perspective: How men describe incidents damaging the therapeutic alliance. *Psychology of Men and Masculinity,* Online First Publication, http://dx.doi.org/10.1037/a0036924

Rogers, C. R. (1951). *Client-centered therapy: Its current practice, implications, and theory.* Boston, MA: Houghton Mifflin.

Rogers, C. R. (1957). The necessary and sufficient conditions of therapeutic personality change. *Journal of Consulting Psychology, 21,* 95–103.

Rogers, C. R. (1961). *On becoming a person.* New York, NY: Houghton Mifflin.

Rogers, C. R., Gendlin, E. T., Kiesler, D. J., & Truax, C. (1967). *The therapeutic relationship and its impact: A study of psychotherapy with schizophrenics.* Madison: University of Wisconsin Press.

Rogers, W. R. (1985). Tillich and depth psychology. In J. L. Adams, W. Paulk, & R. L. Shinn (Eds.), *The thought of Paul Tillich* pp. 102–118. San Francisco, CA: Harper and Row.

Rosen, S. (1982). *My voice will go with you: The teaching tales of Milton H. Erickson.* New York, NY: W. W. Norton.

Rotter, J. B. (1990). Internal versus external control of reinforcement: A case history of a variable. *American Psychologist, 45*(4), 489–493.

Rutan, S. J., Stone, W. N., & Shay, J. J. (2007). *Psychodynamic group psychotherapy.* New York, NY: Guilford.

Safran, J. D., & Muran, J. C. (2000). *Negotiating the therapeutic alliance.* New York, NY: Guilford.

Samovar, L. A., Porter, R. E., McDaniel, E. R., & Roy, C. S. (2007). *Communication between cultures* (8th ed.). Boston, MA: Wadsworth.

Sartre, J. P. (1943; 1956). *Being and nothingness: A phenomenological essay on ontology.* New York, NY: Washington Square Press.

Sartre, J. P. (1964). *Nausea*. New York, NY: New Directions.

Satir, V. (1967). A family of angels: An interview with Virginia Satir. In J. Haley & L. Hoffman, *Techniques of family therapy* (pp. 97–117). New York/London: Basic Books.

Schachter, S., & Singer, J. E. (1962). Cognitive, social, and physiological determinants of emotional state. *Psychological Review, 65*(5), 379–399.

Scharf, R. S. (2004). *Theories of psychotherapy and counseling: Concepts and cases.* Belmont, CA: Brooks/Cole.

Scheflin, A. W., & Shapiro, J. L. (1989). *Trance on trial.* New York, NY: Guilford.

Scher, M. (1990). Effect of gender role incongruities on men's experience as clients in psychotherapy. *Psychotherapy: Theory, Research, Practice, Training, 27*(3), 322–326.

Schimmack, U. (2008). The structure of subjective well-being. In M. Eid & R. Larsen (Eds.), *The science of subjective well-being* (pp. 97–123). New York, NY: Guilford.

Schneider, K. J. (Ed.). (2008). *Existential-Integrative psychotherapy: Guideposts to the core of practice.* New York, NY: Routledge.

Schneider, K. J., & Krug, O. T. (2010). *Existential-humanistic therapy.* Washington, DC: American Psychological Association.

Schneider, K. J., & May, R. (Eds.). (1995). *The psychology of existence: An integrative clinical perspective.* New York, NY: McGraw Hill.

Schutz, W. C. (1967). *Joy: Expanding human awareness.* New York, NY: Harper and Row.

Schutz, W. C. (1973). *Elements of encounter: A bodymind approach.* New York, NY: Joy Press.

Seligman, M. E. P. (1995). The effectiveness of psychotherapy: The Consumer Reports study. *American Psychologist, 50*(12), 965–974.

Seligman, M. E. P. (2002). Positive psychology, positive prevention, and positive therapy. In C. R. Snyder & S. J. Lopez (Eds.), *Handbook of positive psychology* (pp. 3–9). New York, NY: Oxford University Press.

Seligman, M. E. P., & Csikszentmihalyi, M. (2000). Positive psychology: An introduction. *American Psychologist, 55*(1), 5–14.

Sexton, T. L., Gordon, K., Gurman, A. S., Lebow, J., Holtzworth-Munroe, A., & Johnson, A. (2011). Guidelines for classifying evidence-based treatments in couple and family psychology. *Family Process, 50,* 337–392.

Shadish, W. R., & Baldwin, S. A. (2003). Meta analyses of MFT interventions. *Journal of Marital and Family Therapy, 29,* 547–570.

Shapiro, J. L. (1970). An investigation into the effects of sensitivity training procedures. (Doctoral dissertation, University of Waterloo, 1970). *Dissertation Abstracts International,* 1971, Vol. 32(2–A), p. 799.

Shapiro, J. L. (1978). *Methods of group psychotherapy and encounter.* Itasca, IL: Peacock.

Shapiro, J. L. (1978a). Positive implication of treatment at on-base, Family Resource Centers: personnel and fiscal considerations. Unpublished report to CINC,

USAF-Pacific, CINCPACFLT (Pearl Harbor) and USAHAW (Tripler Army Medical Center).

Shapiro, J. L. (1984). A brief outline of a chronological divorce sequence. *Family Therapy, XI*(3), 269–278.

Shapiro, J. L. (1987). Message from the masters or breaking old ground? The evolution of psychotherapy conference. *Psychotherapy in Private Practice 5*(3), 65–72.

Shapiro, J. L. (2010). At the risk of losing our misery: Existential couple therapy. In A. S. Gurman, *Clinical Casebook of Couple Therapy* (pp. 399–426). New York, NY: Guilford.

Shapiro, J. L. (2010a). Brief group therapy. In R. K. Conyne (Ed.), *Oxford handbook of group counseling*. New York, NY: Oxford.

Shapiro, J. L. (2012). *Finding meaning, facing fears in the autumn of your years (45–65)*. Atascadero, CA: Impact.

Shapiro, J. L. (2013). Multi-person therapies. In T. G. Plante (Ed.), *Abnormal psychology across the Ages* (Vol. II, pp. 25–258). New York, NY: Praeger.

Shapiro, J. L. (2014a, August 8). Existential psychotherapy: Best evidence. Symposium presentation, American Psychological Convention, Washington, DC.

Shapiro, J. L. (2014b). *When she's pregnant: The essential guide for expectant fathers*. Bloomington, IN: Xlibris.

Shapiro, J. L. (2014c). The psychology of money in professional relationships. Unpublished keynote address. Available at http://jerroldleeshapiro.com/uploads/BONUS_CHAPTER_of_FMFF_-_Money_and_retirement.pdf.

Shapiro, J. L., & Diamond, M. J. (1972). Increases in hypnotizability as a function of encounter group training. *Journal of Abnormal Psychology, 79*(1), 112–115.

Shapiro, J. L., & Gust, T. (1974). Counselor training for facilitative human relationships: Study and replication. *Counselor Education and Supervision, 13*(3), 198–207.

Shapiro, J. L., Peltz, L. S., & Bernadett-Shapiro, S. T. (1997). *Brief group treatment: Practical training for therapists and counselors*. Monterey, CA: Brooks/Cole.

Shapiro, J. L., & Ross, R. R. (1971). Sensitivity training in an institution for adolescents. *Journal of Applied Behavioral Science, 7*(6), 710–723.

Shapiro, J. L., & Ross, R. R. (1973). Sensitivity training for staff in an institution for adolescent offenders. In J. G. Cull, J. G., & R. E. Hardy (Eds.), *Law enforcement and correctional rehabilitation* (pp. 237–245). Springfield, IL: Thomas.

Shedler, J. (2010). The efficacy of psychodynamic psychotherapy. *American Psychologist, 65*(2), 98–109.

Shedler, J. (2011). Science or ideology? *American Psychologist, 66*(2), 152–154.

Siegel, D. J. (1999). *The developing mind: Toward a neurobiology of interpersonal experience*. New York, NY: Guilford.

Sifneos, P. E. (1973). *Short term psychotherapy and emotional crisis*. Cambridge, MA: Harvard University Press.

Solms, M., & Panskepp, J. (2012). The 'ID' knows more than the 'Ego' admits: Neuropsychoanalytic and primal consciousness perspectives on the interface between affective and cognitive neuroscience. *Brain Sciences, 2*(2), 147–175.

Spence, D. P. (1982). *Narrative truth and historical truth: Meaning and interpretation in psychoanalysis.* New York, NY: W. W. Norton.

Spiegel, D., Butler, L. D., Giese-Davis, J., Koopman, C., Miller, E., DiMiceli, S., . . . Kraemer, H.C. (2007). Effects of supportive-expressive group therapy on survival of patients with metastatic breast cancer: A randomized prospective trial. *Cancer, 110,* 1130–1138.

Spiegel, J. (1982). An ecological model of ethnic families. In M. McGoldrick, J. K Pierce, & J. Giordano, *Ethnicity and family therapy.* New York, NY: Guilford.

Spinelli, E. (1997). *Tales of un-knowing: Eight stories of existential therapy.* New York: New York University Press.

Spinelli, E. (2005). *The interpreted world: An introduction to phenomenological psychology* (2nd ed.). London, UK: Sage.

Spinelli, E. (2007). *Practicing existential psychotherapy: The relational world.* London, UK: Sage.

Stanislavski, C. (1989). *An actor prepares.* New York, NY: Routledge.

Stiles, W. S. (2009). Responsiveness as an obstacle for psychotherapy outcome research: It's worse than you think. *Clinical Psychology: Science and Practice, 16,* 86–91.

Sue, D. W. (1993). Confronting ourselves: The white and racial/ethnic-minority researcher. *The Counseling Psychologist, 21*(2), 244–249.

Sue, D. W., Capodilupo, C. M., Torino, G. C., Bucceri, J. M., Holder, A. M. B., Nadal, K.L., & Esquilin, M. (2007). Racial microaggressions in everyday life: Implications for clinical practice. *American Psychologist, 62*(4), 271–286.

Sue, D. W., & Sue, D. (2012). *Counseling the culturally diverse: Theory and practice* (6th ed.). New York, NY: Wiley

Szentagotai, A., & David, D. (2010). The efficacy of cognitive-behavioral therapy in bipolar disorder: A quantitative meta-analysis. *Journal of Clinical Psychiatry, 71,* 66–72.

Tillich, P. (1952). *The courage to be.* New Haven, CT: Yale University Press.

Tillich, P. (1960, February 27). *Existentialism and psychotherapy.* Paper presented to Conference on Existential Psychotherapy in New York City.

Tillich, S. R. (1972). The nature of group therapy: A debate. King Kalakaua Center, Honolulu, HI

Todd, D. (2009, November 14). A new vocabulary for men. Retrieved from http://blogs.vancouversun.com/2009/11/14/a-new-vocabulary-for-men/11/14/09

Tomkins, S. S., Sedgwick, E. K., & Frank, A. (Eds.). (1995). *Shame and its sisters: A Silvan Tomkins reader.* Durham NC: Duke University Press.

Toseland, R. W., & Rivas, R. F. (1984). *An introduction to group work practice.* New York, NY: Macmillan.

Truax, C. B., & Carkhuff, R. R. (1965). Experimental manipulation of therapeutic conditions. *Journal of Consulting Psychology 29*(2), 119–124.

Truax, C. B., & Carkhuff, R. R. (1967). *Toward effective counseling and psychotherapy, training and practice.* Chicago, IL: Aldine.

Truax, C. B., & Mitchell, K. M. (1971). Research on certain therapist interpersonal skills in relation to process and outcome. In A. E. Bergin & S. L. Garfield (Eds.),

Handbook of psychotherapy and behavior change (pp. 299–344). New York, NY: Wiley.

Tseng, W. S., Maretzki, T. W., & McDermott, J. F. (1980). *People and cultures of Hawaii, a psychocultural profile.* Honolulu: University of Hawaii School of Medicine.

Tuckman, B. W. (1965). Developmental sequences in small groups. *Psychological Bulletin, 63,* 384–399.

Van Deurzen, E. (2010). *Everyday mysteries: A handbook of existential psycho-therapy.* East Sussex, UK: Routledge.

Van Deurzen, E. (2012). *Existential counselling and psychotherapy in practice* (3rd ed.) [electronic edition]. London, UK: Sage.

Van Deurzen, E., & Adams, A. (2010). *Skills in existential counseling and psycho-therapy.* London, UK: Sage.

Van Deurzen-Smith. (1988). *Paradox and passion in psychotherapy: An existen-tial approach to therapy and counseling.* West Sussex, UK: John Wiley and Sons.

Viorst, J. (1998). *Necessary losses.* New York, NY: Fireside.

Vontress, C. E. (2003). On becoming an existential cross-cultural counselor. In F. D. Harper & J. McFadden, (Eds.). *Culture and counseling: New approaches* Needham Heights, MA: Allyn & Bacon.

Vontress, C. E., & Epp, L. R. (2015). Existential cross-cultural counseling: The courage to be an existential counselor. In K. J. Schneider, J. F. Pierson, & J. F. T. Bugental, *The handbook of humanistic psychology: Theory, Research and Practice* (2nd ed.). Thousand Oaks, CA: Sage.

Vos, J., Craig, M., & Cooper, M. (2014). Existential therapies: A meta-analysis of their effects on psychological outcomes. *Journal of Consulting and Clinical Psy-chology,* Online First Publication, July 21, 2014, http://dx.doi.org/10.1037/a0037167

Wade, N. G., Worthington E. L., Jr., & Vogel, D. L. (2007). Effectiveness of reli-giously tailored interventions in Christian therapy. *Psychotherapy Research, 17,* 91–105. doi:10.1080/10503300 500497388

Wampold, B. E. (2001). *The great psychotherapy debate: Models, methods, and findings.* Mahwah, NJ: Erlbaum.

Wampold, B. E., Imel, Z. E., & Minami, T. (2007). The placebo effect: "relatively large" and "robust" enough to survive another assault. *Journal of Clinical Psy-chology* 63(4): 401–403. doi:10.1002/jclp.20350, PMID 17279522

Wampold, B. E., Mondin, G. W., Moody, M., Stich, F., Benson, K., & Ahn, H. (1997). A meta-analysis of outcome studies comparing bona fide psychothera-pies: Empirically, "all must have prizes." *Psychological Bulletin 122*(3), 203–215.

Watson, J. C. (2001). Re-visioning empathy. In D. Cain & J. Seeman (Eds.), *Human-istic psychotherapies: Handbook of research and practice* (pp. 445–471). Washington, DC: APA.

Watzlawick, P., Bavelas, J. B., & Jackson, D. (1967). *Pragmatics of human commu-nication.* New York, NY: W. W. Norton.

Wertheimer, M., & Spillman, L. (2012). *On perceived motion and figural organization*. Cambridge, MA: MIT Press.

Westra, H. A., Aviram, A., Connors, L., Kertes, A., & Ahmed, M. (2012). Therapist emotional reactions and client resistance in cognitive behavioral therapy. *Psychotherapy, 49*(2), 163–172.

Westwood, M. J., & Black, T. G. (2012). Introduction to the special issue. *Canadian Journal of Counselling and Psychotherapy, 46*, 285–291.

Whitaker, C. (1988, April 5). *Meeting with the couple*. Invited Address. Santa Clara University, Santa Clara, CA.

White, M., & Epston, D. (1990). *Narrative means to therapeutic ends*. New York, NY: WW Norton.

Whorf, B. (1956). Language, thought, and reality: Selected writings of Benjamin Lee Whorf. In J. B. Carroll (Ed.), Cambridge, MA: MIT Press.

Wong, G., Derthick, A. O., David, E. J. R., Saw, A., & Okazaki, S. (2014). The what, the why, and the how: A review of racial microaggressions research in psychology. *Race and Social Problems 62*(2), 181–200.

World Health Organization (WHO). (2015). *World health statistics: Part II global health indicators*. Retrieved from http://www.who.int/gho/publications/world_health_statistics/EN_WHS2015_Part2.pdf?ua=1

Yalom, I. D. (1970/2005 with M. Leszcz). *The theory and practice of group psychotherapy* (5th ed.). New York, NY: Basic Books.

Yalom, I. D. (1980). *Existential psychotherapy*. New York, NY: Basic Books.

Yalom, I. D. (1990). *Understanding group therapy*. Video. Pacific Grove, CA: Brooks/Cole.

Yalom, I. D. (2001). *The gift of therapy*. New York, NY: Harper Collins.

Yalom, I. D. (2009). *Staring at the sun: Overcoming the terror of death*. San Francisco, CA: Jossey-Bass.

Young, D. M. & Beier, E. G. (1998). The silent language of psychotherapy: Social reinforcements of unconscious processes (3rd. Ed.) Chicago: Aldine Publishing.

Zimmerman, J. L., & Dickerson, V. C. (1996). *If problems talked: Narrative Therapy in Action*. New York, NY: Guilford.

Index

Note: n in page locator refers to endnote number.

Philosophy
  Christian-based, 20–21
  existential/phenomenological,
    19–26, 25–26 (table)
  as foundation of psychological
    theories, 19
Piaget, J., 274
Placebo impact, 88–89
Pluralism, 8–9
Pomeroy, W. B., 257
Popper, Karl, 198
Poppito, S., 211
Porter, R. E., 263
Positive psychology, 77–79
Post-Traumatic Stress Disorder
  (PTSD), 83n2, 136–137
*A Pragmatic Existential Approach to
  Counseling and Psychotherapy*
  (Buber), xiii
Prejudices. *See* Culture
Prochaska, J. O., 154
Psychoanalysis and existentialism, 26
Psychodynamic therapy
  efficacy of, 209–210
  and resistance, 89
Psychotherapy, phases of
  follow-up and evaluation,
    186–187, 335
  initial call, 159–160
  initial session, 160–161, 318–319
  intrasession progression,
    152–153
  in multiperson therapy,
    155, 156 (table)
  preparation stage, 158–162, 318
  regression, 179–180
  seven-stage process model, 153–154,
    153–154 (table)
  six-stage trans-theoretical change
    model, 154–155, 154 (table)
  stage of group therapy model,
    156–158, 157 (table)
  termination phase, 181–184,
    330–335
  transition phase, 162–176,
    323–330
  treatment stage, 176–181,
    322–323

  See also Existential psychotherapy,
    overview; Termination stage;
    Transition stage
Psychotherapy Isn't What You Think
  (Bugental), 33
Purpose and meaning, importance
  of, 25, 34–35, 58–63, 80,
  269–271

Quatman, T., 133

Ramos-Sanchez, L., 247
Rank, Otto, 26
Reality
  and awareness, 32
  consensual, 5
  shared, 58
  subjective, 2, 14, 40–42
Reductionism, 244
Reeves, A., 212
Reeves, J., 289
Reilly, G., 316n8
Relationships
  extramarital affairs, 225–228
  freedom-security tension,
    219, 238–239
  I-it, 16–17, 23–24
  I-thou, 16–17, 23–24, 43, 229,
    235–236, 240, 270
Religious perspectives
  Jewish Mystical tradition, 22, 23
  spirituality, 310–311
  therapist-client relationship and,
    250–255
Representational systems, 146
Resistance
  affective away style, 97 (table),
    110–112, 110 (table)
  affective external style, 97 (table),
    100–102, 100 (table)
  affective internal style, 97 (table),
    105–107, 105 (table)
  anxiety of change, 84–85, 93
  as client strength, 85–86
  cognitive away style, 97 (table),
    107–110, 108 (table)
  cognitive behavioral therapy
    and, 90–93